Mission on the Way

Other books by Charles Van Engen:

The Growth of the True Church, 1981
God's Missionary People, 1991
You Are My Witnesses, 1992
The Good News of the Kingdom (co-editor), 1993
God So Loves the City (co-editor), 1994

Charles Van Engen is Arthur F. Glasser Professor of Biblical Theology of Mission at Fuller Theological Seminary's School of World Mission. The son of missionaries, he himself worked for twelve years as a missionary in the state of Chiapas, Mexico, and served as a consultant to the pastors of Presbyterian churches in southern Mexico. In addition to degrees from Hope College and Fuller, Van Engen earned a Th.D. from the Free University of Amsterdam.

Mission on the Way

Issues in Mission Theology

Charles Van Engen

Baker Books
A Division of Baker Book House Co
Grand Rapids, Michigan 49516

Published by Baker Books
a division of Baker Book House Compnay
P.O. Box 6287
Grand Rapids, MI 49516-6287

Second printing, Octoebr, 2000

Printed in the Unites States of America

Library of Congress Cataloging-in-Publication Data

Van Engen, Charles Edward.
    Mission on the way : issues in mission theology / Charles Van Engen.
      p. cm.
    Includes bibliographical references and index.
    ISBN 0-8010-2090-5 (pbk.)
    1. Missions—Theory. I. Title.
BV2063.E54   1996
266′.001—dc20   96-41593

For information about academic books, resources for Christian leaders, and all new releases available from Baker Book House, visit our web site:
http://www.bakerbooks.com/

Contents

Foreword

Mission outreach has always disturbed the peace of the church. This was true of the early church as it encountered and finally incorporated Gentile converts into Christian fellowship (Acts 13, 15). It was true when missionaries evangelized the tribes of Europe and Inner Asia. It is true today as Western churches encounter non-Western cultures and religions on a global scale.

So long as the church turns in on itself, its task remains relatively easy—building a community of worship and faith. It focuses its attention on developing the social organization that holds the church together—on defining and allocating roles, making the best use of economic resources, assigning power and legitimacy. It can give itself to defining the orthodox beliefs and practices of the community. Once these social and cultural systems are operational, they normally need only minor adjustments to keep the church functioning over time.

Mission to the outside world challenges this comfortable order. It raises profound questions of cultural and historical differences. Who are these strangers we now encounter? What is the nature of these others and their religious beliefs? How can we communicate the gospel to them faithfully and accurately without imposing our own cultural beliefs? What is the gospel in their context? And what, in retrospect, is the gospel in our context? These are critical questions that we are forced to ask when we enter into mission.

The questions multiply when we gain converts in these new cultures. How do we help give birth to living churches in these societies, and how should we relate to them after they are born? These others are now part of us, but they are so different from us, not only in their languages, customs, and beliefs, but also in their interpretations of the Bible and their theological reflections. Should they adopt our theological teachings? If so, how do we keep theology from being forever foreign in their lives? If not, how do we avoid theological

9

confusion and the fragmentation of the church into a thousand islands of beliefs in a sea of relativism?

Charles Van Engen addresses these central missiological issues in this volume. He examines the question of constructing theologies in specific contexts, such as in the city, and shows us both the benefits and the concerns we experience when we encourage all believers to theologize in their own settings—when we take seriously the priesthood of all believers. He traces the current debates on issues raised by religious pluralism and wrestles with how we can proclaim the uniqueness of Christ without being arrogant and triumphalistic. He looks at the impact modernity and postmodernity are having on the mission movement in the West, and calls for a renewal of our own commitment as followers of Jesus Christ in the harsh cultural environments of our day. He explores the changing roles of missionaries and ministers in young churches, and he raises difficult questions related to the unity of the church in the midst of its global proliferation, diversity, and fragmentation. Of exceptional value are the way Van Engen traces the history of recent discussion on each of these issues and the wealth of bibliographic sources he gives us for further study. Equally important are new answers he offers to these questions—answers that help us move beyond the impasses that characterize so much of our current thinking. In this, he has contributed greatly to the cause of Christian mission in our day. Not all will agree with every one of Van Engen's suggestions, nor does he expect them to. What he challenges us to do is to face these questions honestly, to hear what others have to say about them, and to submit our understandings to the authority of Scripture.

Van Engen does much more, however, than review the debates on the key issues raised by the modern mission movement and suggest new, biblical solutions. More significantly, he provides us with a metatheology—a theology of how we should do theology—that helps us deal with all such problems that emerge in our mission outreach to a lost and broken world. It is this model that provides the underlying coherence of the book. Van Engen begins with the principle of an unquestioned faith in the Bible as fully inspired, divine revelation—the authority by which we must test all theological truth. But how are we to interpret Scripture in our day, given our own cultural and historical contexts and biases? Whose interpretation should we follow? Here Van Engen turns to his second metatheological principle, namely, that the church is a hermeneutical community: we are to read the Scriptures together and discern what God's Spirit is saying to us through them. Too often we have made theologizing the task of a few. Consequently, ordinary Christians are not taught to think biblically about what it means to be Christian in their own daily settings. Moreover, our theologies are often divorced from real life. The author calls us to let the Bible address people in their own contexts. This theology-on-the-way will transform each of us as individuals and the church as a whole. The result will be a living, relevant theology rooted in Scripture and issuing in mission and transformation.

What keeps the church from becoming an ingrown community cut off from the world around it? Van Engen's third hermeneutical principle is that the church in its study of Scripture must be a community that is always in mission. Mission is at the very heart of the gospel and the life of the church. Mission is not one of the many tasks the church is called upon to do. It is of the very essence of the church itself. And, of course, in order to communicate the gospel meaningfully and to serve effectively as God's prophetic agent calling for the conversion and transformation of people, societies, and cultures, the church must know the sociocultural and historical contexts in which it lives and ministers.

If we are to apply this metatheological model to our mission outreach today, we will be forced to redefine the concept of mission itself. Van Engen does not back away from facing this central issue. His greatest contribution in this volume may be to challenge us to rethink our understandings of our calling, and to bring us back to the biblical meaning and methods of doing mission-on-the-way.

Paul G. Hiebert

Preface

Some months ago I met with a friend who teaches missiology at a nearby seminary. With furrowed brow and concerned demeanor my friend said, "Chuck, I have a question for you that may have implications for the whole of my ministry—and maybe yours as well. It is a matter of deep concern to me."

My friend proceeded to explain that he had recently attended a conference of missiologists where a person who enjoyed significant prestige had stated something to this effect: "There is no such thing as theology of mission or mission theology. There are only biblical exegesis, systematic theology, and mission practice. 'Mission theology' is a meaningless term, an oxymoron, for it does not refer to anything."

Needless to say, my friend was disconcerted. "I teach a course we call 'mission theology.' I consider myself a theologian of mission! But what if there is no such thing? Chuck, you have as part of your academic title the phrase 'theology of mission.' Can you tell me what theology of mission is?"

This volume seeks in a small way to offer the beginning of a response to my friend's question. Over the last ten years I have written a number of articles that appear in a variety of books. In each I do mission theology with reference to a particular missiological issue or set of issues. A significant number of highly gifted students at Fuller's School of World Mission have encouraged me to bring all of these pieces together into one accessible format. This I have sought to do in the present volume. Taken together, its chapters do not intend in any way to be exhaustive of the issues that face us today in mission theology. Rather, they seek to illustrate the kind of reflection involved in the task of doing mission theology.

It is my prayer that this volume may help my friend understand more fully the profound significance of his work of doing, teaching, and facilitating others in mission theology. And it is my hope that this volume will stimulate Christian leaders to think theologically about the mission of the church and reflect missiologically about the theology they espouse. May we all together as the church of Jesus Christ continually seek greater proximity to our Lord and Savior, in whose mission we participate.

Pasadena, California
Spring 1995

Acknowledgments

The author and publisher gratefully acknowledge permission to reprint modified versions of the following material:

Chapter 1 originally appeared under the title "The Relation of Bible and Mission in Mission Theology," in *The Good News of the Kingdom*, edited by Charles Van Engen, Dean S. Gilliland, and Paul Pierson, 27–36 (Maryknoll, N.Y.: Orbis, 1993).

The material in chapter 2 has been greatly enhanced by the questions, research, and creative reflection of Les Henson, Nancy Thomas, Christine Accornero, Juanita Leonard, and Kathy Mowry, doctoral students who have helped me (and pushed me) to gain a clearer understanding of, and deeper appreciation for, the potential contributions that narrative theology can make to missiology. Jude Tiersma, colleague, friend, and student, has been a great help in demonstrating to me the role of narrative in reflection on mission in the city. (See Van Engen and Tiersma 1994.)

Chapter 3 originally appeared as "The New Covenant: Knowing God in Context," in *The Word among Us*, edited by Dean S. Gilliland, 74–100 (Waco: Word, 1989).

Chapter 4 originally appeared as "Constructing a Theology of Mission for the City," in *God So Loves the City*, edited by Charles Van Engen and Jude Tiersma, 241–69 (published in 1994 by MARC, 800 West Chestnut Avenue, Monrovia, Calif., 91016-3198).

Chapter 5 was originally published as "The Holy Catholic Church: On the Road through Ephesians," in the *Reformed Review* 37.3 (1984): 187–201.

Chapter 6 originally appeared as chapter 4, "The Essence of the Local Church in Historical Perspective," in Charles Van Engen, *God's Missionary People*, 59–71 (Grand Rapids: Baker, 1991).

Chapter 7 originally appeared under the title "A Broadening Vision: Forty Years of Evangelical Theology of Mission," in *Earthen Vessels: American*

Evangelicals and Foreign Mission, 1880–1980, edited by Joel A. Carpenter and Wilbert R. Shenk, 203–34 (Grand Rapids: Eerdmans, 1990).

Chapter 9 was originally published as "The Effect of Universalism on Mission Effort," in *Through No Fault of Their Own? The Fate of Those Who Have Never Heard*, edited by William V. Crockett and James G. Sigountos, 183–94 (Grand Rapids: Baker, 1991).

Chapter 10 was originally published as "The Uniqueness of Christ in Mission Theology," in *Christianity and the Religions: A Biblical Theology of World Religions*, edited by Edward Rommen and Harold Netland, 183–216 (Pasadena: William Carey Library, 1995).

Chapter 11 originally appeared as "Evangelism in the North American Context," in *Reformed Review* 41.1 (1987): 9–20.

Chapter 13 was published as "Pastors as Missionary Leaders in the Church," in Fuller Theological Seminary's *Theology, News and Notes* 36.2 (1989): 15–18.

The conclusion, "Faith, Love, and Hope: A Theology of Mission-on-the Way," was originally published in *The Good News of the Kingdom*, edited by Charles Van Engen, Dean S. Gilliland, and Paul Pierson, 253–64 (Maryknoll, N.Y.: Orbis, 1993).

Finally, let me also express my deepest admiration, gratitude, and respect to Nancy Thomas, whose loving, joyful, precise, and conscientious work has been a tremendous asset to me in compiling, typing, redesigning, and shepherding this volume toward completion. Thank you is also well deserved by Michael Kennedy, Anne White, and Fuller's Word Processing Office for the care and thoroughness they have shown in typesetting the manuscript—especially considering the difficult task of bringing together the Works Cited.

Introduction

What Is Mission Theology?

The introduction will briefly define what mission theology is and then proceed to examine five of its essential characteristics: mission theology seeks to be multidisciplinary, integrative, definitional, analytical, and truthful. But first a note regarding the rise of mission theology as a separate discipline.

For the past thirty years mission theology has taken a backseat to mission practice, which, after the two world wars and particularly in the 1960s, began to borrow heavily from the social sciences: sociology, anthropology, linguistics, economics, politics, statistics, sociology of religion, and so forth. Whether Roman Catholic, Orthodox, conciliar, evangelical, or Pentecostal/ charismatic, the major missiological agendas that dominated the scene after the early 1960s dealt primarily with the strategy and practice of mission. Regardless of the theological tradition, missiology concerned itself with a host of activist issues and agendas like the role of the church (its clergy, structures, and members) in the mission enterprise, relevant economic and sociopolitical action, liberation, evangelism, church growth, relief and development, Bible translation, theological education, mission-church partnerships, church-to-church sharing of resources, dialogue with people of other faiths, and the relation of faith and culture. Unfortunately, in the midst of such busy global activism, the deeper questions of mission theology were too seldom asked. During the last ten years this has begun to change, and people of all theological stripes in mission today are reexamining theological presuppositions that underlie the mission enterprise.

The discipline that reflects on these presuppositions is theology of mission or mission theology.[1] Prior to the 1960s, a number of prominent thinkers like

---

1. I see the two terms "theology of mission" and "mission theology" as interchangeable. However, I am beginning to find "mission theology" more appropriate than "theology of mission." In the introduction I will use "theology of mission," particularly in the section on the integrative function of the discipline. But "mission theology" will increasingly become the dominant term in this volume.

17

Figure 1
Missiology as a Discipline

Gisbert Voetius, Josef Schmidlin, Gustav Warneck, Karl Barth, Karl Harten-stein, Martin Kähler, Walter Freytag, Roland Allen, Hendrik Kraemer, J. H. Bavinck, W. A. Visser 't Hooft, Max Warren, Olav Myklebust, Bengt Sund-kler, Carl Henry, and Harold Lindsell reflected on the theological issues of mission. However, if we seek to find theology of mission as a separate disci-pline with its own elements, methodology, scholars, and focuses, we find that theology of mission as such really began only in the early 1960s through the work of Gerald Anderson. In 1961 Anderson edited *The Theology of the Christian Mission*, a collection of essays which I consider to be the first text of the discipline.

Ten years later, in the *Concise Dictionary of the Christian World Mission*, Anderson defined the main concerns of theology of mission as "the basic pre-suppositions and underlying principles which determine, from the stand-point of Christian faith, the motives, message, methods, strategy and goals of the Christian world mission. . . . The source of mission is the triune God who is himself a missionary. . . . In this 'post-Constantinian' age of church history, mission is no longer understood as outreach beyond Christendom, but rather as 'the common witness of the whole church, bringing the whole gospel to the whole world'" (Neill et al. 1971, 594).[2]

Mission Theology as Multidisciplinary

Mission theology is a difficult enterprise because its object of reflection is the entire field of missiology, which itself is a multi- and interdisciplinary enter-prise. For the sake of brevity, this section will graphically represent and sim-ply state a series of short propositions that describe the multidisciplinary en-terprise that is missiology and the way mission theology interfaces with it.

2. Anderson attributes this phrase to the 1963 Mexico City gathering of the Commission on World Mission and Evangelism/World Council of Churches. See Orchard 1964, 175.

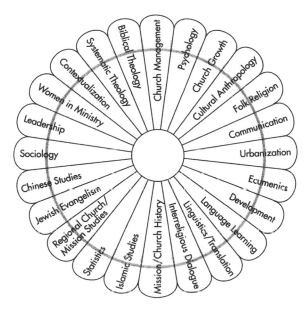

Figure 2
Missiology as a Multidisciplinary Discipline

1. In the first place, missiology is a unified whole; it is a discipline in its own right, centered in Jesus Christ and his mission (see figure 1). As the church participates in the mission of Jesus Christ, it participates in God's mission in God's world through the power of the Holy Spirit.

2. While missiology is known to be a unified discipline, it is also a multidisciplinary discipline (see figure 2). As a multidisciplinary discipline, missiology draws from many areas of skill, cognate disciplines, and bodies of literature.[3]

3. The list of cognate disciplines from which missiology draws to describe, understand, analyze, and prescribe the complex nature of mission is long. Those represented in the diagram are only illustrative. A more complete list might include biblical studies, church history, mission history, systematic theology, contextualization, cultural anthropology, linguistics and translation, sociology, the study of other faiths, dialogue with other faiths, studies of women in mission, sociology of religion, social psychology, urban studies/anthropology and sociocultural analysis of the city, socioeconomic and political analysis, ecumenics and studies of the world church, statistics and futurology, evangelism, the history of evangelism, church growth, studies of missionary congregations, dynamics of cross-cultural communication, relief and development, discipleship, spirituality and spiritual formation, leadership formation, structures for mission, mission administration, theological education, congregational renewal, history of revivals, cross-cultural counseling, preaching, the missionary family, psychological issues of many types, ecclesiastics and the relationship of churches, mission organization, mission funding, mission promotion/recruitment/personnel, the relation of church and state, nominalism and secularization, and others.

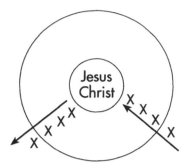

Figure 3
Proximity to or Distance from Jesus Christ

Figure 4
The Integrative Center

3. Mission theology helps us clarify our proximity to or distance from the center, Jesus Christ (see figure 3), and asks whether there is a point beyond which the cognate disciplines may no longer be helpful or biblical.

4. Mission theology helps us reflect on the central idea (the *habitus*) which integrates and motivates our missiology (see figure 4).[4]

4. Missiologists have differed in the integrating idea or phrase they have chosen to use as the center of their missiology. Examples of integrating ideas would include the conversion of the heathen, the planting of the church, and the glory of God (Gisbert Voetius), the Great Commission (William Carey), the lostness of humanity (Pietism), the praise of God (Orthodox missiology), the people of God (Vatican II), making disciples of *panta ta ethnē* (Donald McGavran), the God of history, God of compassion, God of transformation (David Bosch), the kingdom of God (Arthur Glasser), and humanization (the World Council of Churches). Among other integrating concepts are the pain of God, the cross, bearing witness in six continents, ecumenical unity, the covenant, and liberation.

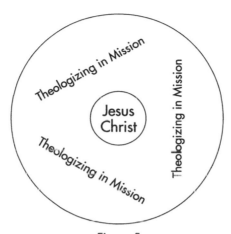

Figure 5
Theologizing in Mission

5. Mission theology helps us integrate who we are, what we know, and what we do in mission. It helps us bring together and relate to the cognate disciplines of missiology our faith relationship with Jesus Christ, our spirituality, our consciousness of God's presence, the church's theological reflection throughout the centuries, a constantly new rereading of Scripture, our hermeneutic of God's world, our sense of participation in God's mission, and the ultimate purpose and meaning of the church (see figure 5).

6. Mission theology helps us move continually between the center and the outer limits of the multiple cognate disciplines of missiology as we constantly

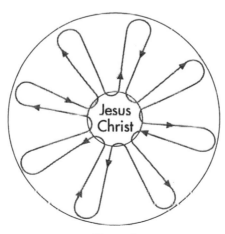

Figure 6
Mission Theology

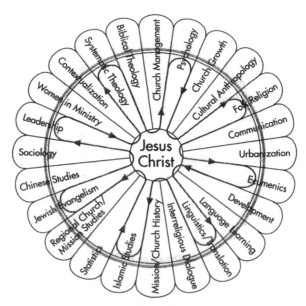

Figure 7
Mission Theology in Missiology

seek integration, deepened understanding, and mutual enrichment of the various disciplines as *one* discipline—missiology (see figure 6).

7. Mission theology serves to question, clarify, integrate, and expand the presuppositions of the various cognate disciplines of missiology. In doing so, mission theology is a discipline in its own right, yet it is not merely one of the petals alongside the others, so to speak, for it fulfils its function only as it interacts with all of them (see figure 7).

Mission Theology as Integrative

When mission happens, all the various cognate disciplines are occurring simultaneously. So missiology must study mission not from the point of view of abstracted and separated parts, but from an integrative perspective that attempts to see the whole all at once. One of the most fruitful ways to do this involves perceiving missiology as the interlocking of three circles that bring together all the various cognate disciplines we mentioned above (see figure 8). Theology of mission encompasses three arenas: biblical and theological presuppositions and values (A) are applied to the enterprise of the ministry and mission of the church (B), and are set in the context of specific activities carried out in particular times and places (C).[5]

5. The three-arena nature of missiology is not original with me. A number of others, particularly those who deal with contextualization from a missiological perspective, have highlighted

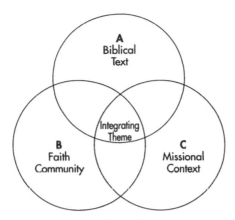

Figure 8
The Tripartite Nature of Theology of Mission

The reader will see that the three circles are brought together by means of an integrating theme that constitutes the central idea interfacing all three circles. The integrating theme might be the people of God, reconciliation, the cross, compassion, church growth, or the glory of God (for other examples see figure 4). It is selected on the basis of being contextually appropriate and significant, biblically relevant and fruitful, and missionally active and transformational. It will help hold our various ideas together—particularly when we are moving from circle A to circle B, that is, from a rereading of Scripture to praxeological action-reflection in order to discover the missiological implications of our rereading of Scripture.

To explicate the three-arena nature of the discipline, it will be helpful to speak of theology of mission rather than mission theology. First, note that theology of mission is *theology* (circle A) because fundamentally it involves reflection about God. It seeks to understand God's mission, God's intentions and purposes, God's use of human instruments in God's mission, and God's working through God's people in God's world.[6] Thus theology of mission deals with all the traditional theological themes of systematic theology—but it does so in a way that differs from how systematic theologians have worked down through the centuries. The difference arises from the multidisciplinary missiological orientation of its theologizing.

something similar. See, e.g., Nida 1960; Míguez-Bonino 1975; Coe 1976; Conn 1978; 1984; 1993a; 1993b; Hiebert 1978; 1987; 1993; Glasser 1979b; Kraft 1979; 1983; Kraft and Wisley 1979; Fleming 1980; Coote and Stott 1980; Schreiter 1985; Branson and Padilla 1986; Tippett 1987; Luzbetak 1988; Shaw 1988; Gilliland, ed., 1989; Hesselgrave and Rommen 1989; Sanneh 1989; William A. Dyrness 1990; Bevans 1992; and Jacobs 1993.

6. See, e.g., Niles 1962; Vicedom 1965; Taylor 1973; Verkuyl 1978, 163–204; and Stott 1979.

In addition, because of its commitment to remain faithful to God's intentions, perspectives, and purposes, theology of mission shows a fundamental concern over the relation of the Bible to mission. It attempts to allow Scripture not only to provide the foundational motivations for mission, but also to question, shape, guide, and evaluate the missionary enterprise.[7]

Second, theology of mission is "theology *of*" a specific missional context (circle C). In contrast to much systematic theology, here we are dealing with an applied theology. Because of its applicational nature theology of mission at times looks like what some would call pastoral or practical theology. This type of theological reflection focuses specifically on a set of particular issues—those having to do with the mission of the church in its *context*.

Theology of mission draws its incarnational nature from the ministry of Jesus, and always happens in a specific time and place. Thus circle C involves the missiological use of all the social-science disciplines that help us understand the context in which God's mission takes place. We begin by borrowing from sociology, anthropology, economics, urbanology, the study of the relation of Christian churches to other religions, psychology, the study of the relation of church and state, and a host of other cognate disciplines to understand the specific context in which we are doing our theology-of-mission reflection. Such contextual analysis moves us, secondly, to a more particular understanding of the context in terms of a hermeneutic of the setting in which we are ministering. This in turn, thirdly, calls us to hear the cries, see the faces, understand the stories, and respond to the vital needs and hopes of the persons who are an integral part of that context.

A part of this analysis today includes the history of the way the church in its mission has interfaced with a particular context down through history. The attitudes, actions, and events of the church's mission that occurred in that context prior to our particular reflection will color in profound and surprising ways the present and the future of our own missional endeavors. Thus we will find some scholars dealing with the history of theology of mission.[8] While not especially interested in the theological issues as such, they are concerned about the effects of mission theology upon mission activity in a particular context. They will often examine the various pronouncements made by church and mission gatherings (Roman Catholic, Orthodox, ecu-

---

7. See, e.g., Glover 1946; G. Ernest Wright 1952; Gerald H. Anderson 1961; Boer 1961; Blauw 1962; Allen 1962a; George Peters 1972; Costas 1974a; 1982; 1989; De Ridder 1975; Stott 1975b; J. H. Bavinck 1977; Newbigin 1978; Verkuyl 1978, ch. 4; Bosch 1978; 1991; 1993; Gilliland 1983; Van Rheenen 1983; William A. Dyrness 1983; Senior and Stuhlmueller 1983; Hedlund 1985; Spindler 1988; Gnanakan 1989; Glasser 1992; and Van Engen 1992b; 1993. A combined bibliography drawn from these works would offer an excellent resource for examining the relation of the Bible and mission.

8. See, e.g., Bassham 1979; Bosch 1980; Scherer 1987; 1993a; 1993b; Glasser and McGavran 1983; Glasser 1985; Utuk 1986; Stamoolis 1987; and Van Engen 1990.

menical, evangelical, Pentecostal, and charismatic) and ask questions, sometimes polemically, about the results for missional action.[9] The documents resulting from these gatherings become part of the discipline of theology of mission.

Third, theology of mission is specially oriented toward and for *mission* by the faith community (circle B). The most basic reflection in this arena is found in the many books, journals, and other publications dealing with the theory of missiology itself.[10] However, neither missiology nor theology of mission can be allowed to restrict itself to reflection only. As Johannes Verkuyl (1978, 6, 18) has stated, "Missiology may never become a substitute for action and participation. God calls for participants and volunteers in his mission. In part, missiology's goal is to become a 'service station' along the way. If study does not lead to participation, whether at home or abroad, missiology has lost her humble calling. . . . Any good missiology is also a *missiologia viatorum*—'pilgrim missiology.'"

Theology of mission, then, must eventually emanate in biblically informed and contextually appropriate missional action. If our theology of mission does not emanate in informed action, we are merely a "resounding gong or a clanging cymbal" (1 Cor. 13:1). Intimate connection of reflection with action is absolutely essential for missiology. At the same time, if our missiological action does not itself transform our reflection, our great ideas may prove irrelevant or useless, and sometimes even destructive or counterproductive.

So the missional orientation that comes forth as a fruit of our theology of mission must translate into action. And missional action always occurs in a context. This brings us back to circle C—and our pilgrimage of mission-on-the-way begins again to reflect on a hermeneutic of the context, which in turn calls for a rereading of Scripture that flows forth into new missional insights and action.

One of the most helpful ways to interface reflection and action is by way of the process known as "praxis." Among the different understandings of this process,[11] Orlando Costas's formulation (1976, 8) is one of the most constructive:

---

9. See, e.g., McGavran 1972a; 1972b; 1984; Johnston 1974; Hoekstra 1979; Hedlund 1981; and Hesselgrave 1988. One of the most helpful recent compilations of such documents is Scherer and Bevans 1992.

10. Examples of some readily accessible works include Sundkler 1965; J. H. Bavinck 1977; Verkuyl 1978; Bosch 1980; 1991; Padilla 1985; Scherer 1987; Verstraelen 1988; Phillips and Coote 1993; and Van Engen et al. 1993. Clearly the most comprehensive work, which will be considered foundational for missiology for the next decade, is Bosch 1991.

11. See, e.g., Robert McAfee Brown 1978, 50–51; Vidales 1979, 34–57; Spykman et al. 1988, xiv, 226–31; Schreiter 1985, 17, 91–93; Costas 1976, 8–9; Boff and Boff 1987, 8–9; Scott 1980, xv; Leonardo Boff 1979, 3; Ferm 1986, 15; Padilla 1985, 83; Chopp 1986, 36–37, 115–17, 120–21; Gutiérrez 1984a, 19–32; 1984b, vii–viii, 50–60; and Clodovis Boff 1987, xxi–xxx.

Missiology is fundamentally a praxeological phenomenon. It is a critical reflection that takes place in the praxis of mission. . . . [It occurs] in the concrete missionary situation, as part of the church's missionary obedience to and participation in God's mission, and is itself actualized in that situation. . . . Its object
is always the world, . . . men and women in their multiple life situations. . . . In
reference to this witnessing action saturated and led by the sovereign, redemptive action of the Holy Spirit, . . . the concept of missionary praxis is used. Missiology arises as part of a witnessing engagement to the gospel in the multiple
situations of life.

The concept of praxis helps us understand that not only the reflection, but
profoundly the action as well, is part of a theology-on-the-way that seeks to
discover how the church may participate in God's mission in God's world.
The action is itself theological, and serves to inform the reflection, which in
turn interprets, evaluates, critiques, and projects new understanding in transformed action. Thus the interweaving of reflection and action in a constantly
spiraling pilgrimage offers a transformation of all aspects of our missiological engagement with our various contexts.

The mission theologian takes the biblical text (circle A) utterly seriously.
It is equally true, as Johannes Verkuyl (1978, 6) has said, that "if study does
not lead to participation, . . . missiology has lost her humble calling." Thus
we find that theology of mission is a process of reflection and action involving a movement from the *biblical text* to the *faith community* in its *context*.
By focusing our attention on an integrating theme, we encounter new insights as we reread Scripture from the point of view of a contextual hermeneutic. These new insights can then be restated and lived out as biblically informed, contextually appropriate missional actions of the faith community
in the particularity of time, worldview, and space of each context in which
God's mission takes place.

Mission Theology as Definitional

One of the most crucial yet frustrating tasks of mission theology is to assist
missiology in defining the terms it uses. And within this enterprise the most
central question has to do with how one may define "mission" itself. What
is mission? and what is not mission? The reader will notice that nearly every
chapter in this book will deal in some way or other with this question and its
implications.

For the sake of brevity, and in the hope of helping the reader more fully
understand subsequent chapters, let me offer my own preliminary definition
of mission:

> Mission is the people of God intentionally crossing barriers
> from church to nonchurch, faith to nonfaith,

to proclaim by word and deed
the coming of the kingdom of God
in Jesus Christ;
this task is achieved by means of the church's participation
in God's mission of reconciling people
to God, to themselves, to each other, and to the world,
and gathering them into the church
through repentance and faith in Jesus Christ
by the work of the Holy Spirit
with a view to the transformation of the world
as a sign of the coming of the kingdom
in Jesus Christ.

Mission Theology as Analytical

The mission enterprise is complex enough just in terms of its practice. It becomes more complex when we begin to examine the host of theological assumptions, meanings, and relations that permeate that practice. For this reason, mission theologians have found it helpful to partition their task into smaller segments. We noticed that Gerald Anderson's definition of mission uses the terms "faith, motives, message, methods, strategy, and goals." Similarly, in analyzing *Eastern Orthodox Mission Theology Today* (1987) James Stamoolis organizes his work around "the historical background, the aim, the method, the motives, and the liturgy" of mission as it takes place among and through the Eastern Orthodox.

However, there is another way in which mission theologians have classified the various aspects of their task. This method stresses the fact that mission is *missio Dei*—it is God's mission. So one finds mission theologians asking about God's mission (*missio Dei*),[12] mission as it occurs among humans and utilizes human instrumentality (*missio hominum*), missions as they take many forms through the endeavors of the churches (*missiones ecclesiarum*),[13] and mission as it draws from and impacts global human civilization (*missio politica oecumenica*).[14]

The *missio Dei*, which is singular, is pure in its motivation, means, and goals, for it derives from the nature of God. The *missio hominum* is simulta-

12. Georg Vicedom brought the term *missio Dei* to the attention of the world church before and during the 1963 Mexico City meeting of the Commission on World Mission and Evangelism/World Council of Churches. See his *Mission of God* (1965).

13. The discussion in conciliar circles over whether to use "mission" or "missions," and the subsequent change in the name of the *International Review of Missions* to *International Review of Mission*, were the fruit of confusion between God's mission, which is one, and the enterprises of the churches ("missions"), which are many.

14. See, e.g., Verkuyl 1978, 394–402.

neously just and sinful, related to fallen humanity, and always mixed as to its motivations, means, and goals. The *missiones ecclesiarum* are plural because of the multiplicity of the activities of the churches, the lack of unity among them, and the mixture of centripetal (gathering) activities with centrifugal (sending) activities; another factor is that their shape is heavily influenced by what is going on within the churches and the Christians who form them. Finally, the *missio politica oecumenica* pertains to God's concern for the nations, God's interaction through God's people with the civilizations, cultures, politics, and human structures of this world, and the way Christ's kingdom mission always calls into question the kingdoms of this world.

These are important distinctions. And a final one needs to be made. Mission is also both *missio futurorum* and *missio adventus*. *Missio futurorum* has to do with the predictable results of God's mission as it takes place in human history. Thus *missio futurorum* extrapolates into the future the natural human results of the missions of the churches in the midst of world history. But the story of mission is incomplete if it stops there. We must also include *missio adventus*. *Adventus* is the inbreaking of God, of Jesus Christ in the incarnation, of the Holy Spirit at Pentecost, of the Holy Spirit in and through the church. *Missio adventus* is, then, God's mission as it brings unexpected surprises, radical changes, new directions, almost unbelievable transformation in the midst of human life: personal, social, and structural. God works in the world through both *missio futurorum* and *adventus*. And in sorting out the theological issues of mission theology the mission theologian needs constantly to be asking about their difference and their interrelation.

Once we have seen the two ways of classifying the aspects of mission theology, we will want to bring the two systems together. I have attempted to do this in a "Working Grid of Mission Theology" (see Figure 9). Notice that at each horizontal level of the grid there are at least five different types of questions to be asked; for example, in regard to the motives of mission, there are God's motivation, human motivation, the motivations of the churches, motivations in relation to global civilization, and motivation in terms of *missio futurorum* as distinguished from *adventus*. Notice also that one can work vertically, asking, for example, how *missio Dei*, in contrast with the other vertical columns, informs the motives, means, methods, and goals of mission.

Clearly no one missiologist can do all that is represented by this grid. That is not necessary. Only one or two of the many boxes may represent the area to investigate in a particular context at a particular moment and in relation to specific actions of mission. However, I have been discovering that the grid can both offer us simplicity of analysis by differentiating the topics to explore and point to the complexity of the whole enterprise. My students and I have begun to see that almost every master's thesis or doctoral dissertation in missiology naturally falls primarily into one of the squares. Yet when the researcher begins to reflect in terms of mission theology as related to that one

	Missio Dei	Missio Hominum	Missiones Ecclesiarum	Missio Politica Oecumenica	Missio Futurorum/ Adventus
Mission Context					
Agents of Mission					
Motives of Mission					
Means of Mission					
Methods of Mission					
Goals of Mission					
Results of Mission					
Centripetal/ Centrifugal Activities					
Utopia/Future Hope					
Presence					
Proclamation					
Persuasion					
Incorporation					
Structures					
Partnerships					
Power					
Prayer					
Praise					
Other?					

Figure 9
Working Grid of Mission Theology

narrow area, the investigation leads naturally to questions about many of the other areas represented by the grid.

Mission Theology as Truthful

In the social sciences, and in fact in all scholarly enterprises, one of the most important questions has to do with the basis on which one can determine the validity and reliability of one's investigation. In the social sciences that have heavily impacted missiology, normally the concept of validity has to do with the question, "How can we be sure that we are collecting the right data in the right way?" The concept of reliability, on the other hand, is understood to address the question, "How can we be sure that if the same approach were taken again, the same data would be discovered?"

However, in evangelical mission theology these questions are not the right ones. For the mission theologian is not particularly concerned about the quality of the empirical data nor the repeatability of the process so as to yield identical results. In fact, the opposite is true. Given that the mission theologian studies God's mission, the data should always be new (and will sometimes call into question earlier data), and the results should often be surprising.

Evangelical mission theology, therefore, offers a particular way of recognizing acceptable research. The question of validity must be transformed into one of *trust*, and the matter of reliability must be seen as one of *truth*. Thus these are the two major groups of methodological questions facing the mission theologian:

Trust

Did the researcher read the right authors, the accepted sources?

Did the researcher read widely enough to gain a breadth of perspectives on the issue?

Did the researcher read other viewpoints correctly?

Did the researcher understand what was read?

Are there internal contradictions either in the use (and understanding) of the authors or in their application of the issue at hand?

Truth

Is there adequate biblical foundation for the statements being affirmed?

Is there an appropriate continuity of the researcher's statements with theological affirmations made by other thinkers down through the history of the church?

Where contradictions or qualifications of thought arise, does the mission theologian's work adequately support the particular theological directions being advocated in the study?

Are the dialectical tensions and seeming contradictions allowed to stand, as they should, given what we know and do not know of the mystery of God's revealed hiddenness as it impacts our understanding of *missio Dei*?

These methodological questions lead to specific criteria to evaluate whether the result of mission theology's work as it interfaces with missiology is acceptable:

Revelatory—Acceptable mission theology is grounded in Scripture.

Coherent—It holds together, is built around an integrating idea.

Consistent—It has no insurmountable glaring contradictions, and is consistent with other truths known about God, God's mission, and God's revealed will.

Simple—It has been reduced to the most basic components of God's mission in terms of the specific issue at hand.

Supportable—It is logically, historically, experimentally, praxeologically affirmed and supported.

Externally confirmable—Other significant thinkers, theological communities, or traditions lend support to the thesis being offered.

Contextual—It interfaces appropriately with the context.

Doable—Its concepts can be translated into missional action that in turn is consistent with the motivations and goals of the mission theology being developed.

Transformational—The carrying out of the proposed missional action would issue in appropriate changes in the status quo that reflect biblical elements of the *missio Dei*.

Productive of appropriate consequences—The results of translating the concepts into missional action would be consistent with the thrust of the concepts themselves, and with the nature and mission of God as revealed in Scripture.

Theology of mission is prescriptive as well as descriptive. It is synthetic (bringing about synthesis) and integrational. It searches for trustworthy and true perceptions concerning the church's mission that are based on biblical and theological reflection, seeks to interface with the appropriate missional action, and creates a new set of values and priorities that reflect as clearly as possible the ways in which the church may participate in God's mission in a specific context at a particular time.

When mission theology is abstracted from mission practice, it seems strange and too far removed from the concrete places and specific people that are at the heart of God's mission. Mission theology is at its best when it is intimately involved in the heart, head, and hand (being, knowing, and doing) of the church's mission. It is a personal, corporate, committed, profoundly transformational search for always new and more profound understanding of the ways in which the people of God may participate more faithfully in God's mission in God's world.

Part 1

Mission Theology
and the Bible

1

The Relation of Bible and Mission

One of the most basic aspects of mission theology has to do with the relation of the Bible to mission theory and practice. Initially, one would think that this would be obvious. Such is not the case. In each generation there is a need to reflect again on the way the church uses or abuses the scriptural understanding of mission.

The Need to Approach the Bible as a Whole

Determining the scriptural understanding of mission is not as simple as we might think. According to David Bosch (1978, 33), "we usually assume far too easily that we can employ the Bible as a kind of objective arbitrator in the case of theological differences, not realizing that [all] of us approach the Bible with [our] own set of preconceived ideas about what it says. . . . This means that it is of little avail to embark upon a discussion of the biblical foundations of mission unless we have first clarified some of the hermeneutical principles involved." In a similar vein, Donald Senior and Carroll Stuhlmueller end their magnificent work on *The Biblical Foundations for Mission* (1983, 332) with the statement that they have not meant to "imply that the biblical style of mission is absolutely normative for mission today. There is no definite biblical recipe for proclaiming the Word of God. . . . Nevertheless there is a value in reflecting on the biblical patterns of evangelization."

Biblical scholars and mission practitioners have contributed to the confusion by ignoring each other for too long. Lesslie Newbigin (1986; 1989a) has observed that Western culture's preoccupation with the origin of the created order and human civilization brought with it a degree of blindness to questions of purpose, design, and intention. To a large extent biblical scholars

35

have followed this same path in their examination of the biblical text. With notable exceptions, their analysis of Scripture has seldom asked the missiological questions regarding God's intentions and purpose.

On the other hand, the activist practitioners of mission have too readily superimposed their particular agendas on Scripture, or ignored the Bible altogether. Thus Arthur Glasser (1992, 26–27) calls for a deeper missiological reflection on the biblical message: "All Scripture makes its contribution in one way or another to our understanding of mission. . . . In our day evangelicals are finding that the biblical base for mission is far broader and more complex than any previous generation of missiologists appears to have envisioned. . . . In our day there is a growing impatience with all individualistic and pragmatic approaches to the missionary task that arise out of a proof-text use of Scripture, despite their popularity among the present generation of activistic evangelicals."[1] Johannes Verkuyl (1978, 90) advocates a similar change in hermeneutical approach: "In the past the usual method was to pull a series of proof-texts out of the Old and New Testaments and then to consider the task accomplished. But more recently biblical scholars have taught us the importance of reading these texts in context and paying due regard to the various nuances. . . . One must consider the very structure of the whole biblical message."[2]

The basic contours of a broader hermeneutic were explored thirty years ago in part 1 of *The Theology of the Christian Mission*, edited by Gerald Anderson (1961, 17–94). Here G. Ernest Wright, Johannes Blauw, Oscar Cullmann, Karl Barth, Donald Miller, and F. N. Davey surveyed a wide range of biblical material, deriving from the Bible what the church's mission ought to be.[3] At about the same time the missiological reflection of the Second Vatican Council on the role of Scripture (e.g., in *Lumen gentium* and *Ad gentes divinitus*) closely followed this model (Flannery 1975, 350–440, 813–62). Subsequent papal encyclicals like *Evangelii nuntiandi* and *Redemptoris missio* have appealed to Scripture, though this appeal has at times appeared like elaborate proof-texting to buttress predetermined ecclesiastical agendas (Bevans 1993). So over the last several decades a significant global consensus has emerged with regard to the Bible and mission. David Bosch (1978, 44–45) explains this phenomenon: "Our conclusion is that both Old and New Testaments are permeated with the idea of mission. . . . [But] not everything we call mission is indeed mission. . . . It is the perennial temptation of the Church to become [a

---

1. See also Bosch 1980, 42–49; Verkuyl 1978, 89–100; and Scherer 1987, 243.

2. Verkuyl points to two works as exemplifying this approach: Blauw 1962 and De Groot 1966. We could add Boer 1961; Berkhof and Potter 1964; Vicedom 1965; Sundkler 1965; De Ridder 1975; Stott 1975b; Bosch 1980, 42–49; Senior and Stuhlmueller 1983; Conn 1984; Gilliland 1983; Padilla 1980; 1985; Glasser 1992; and Ray Anderson 1991.

3. Their approach to the Bible represents a step forward from older attempts to give a "Bible basis" for mission, like those of Robert Glover (1946) and H. H. Rowley (1955).

club of religious folklore]. . . . The only remedy for this mortal danger lies in challenging herself unceasingly with the true biblical foundation of mission."

Ways to Approach the Bible as a Whole

Clearly missiologists are in need of a hermeneutical method that will enable them to deal with the whole of Scripture as a diverse unity. We cannot have mission without the Bible, nor can we understand the Bible apart from God's mission. The *missio Dei* is *God's* mission. Yet the *missio Dei* happens in specific places and times in our contexts. Its content, validity, and meaning are derived from Scripture, yet its action, significance, and transforming power happen in our midst. Even when we affirm that we will take the whole of Scripture seriously, we still need a way to link the numerous contexts of the Bible with the here and now of our missionary endeavor today. The remainder of this chapter will review four familiar suggestions as to how the connection can be made, and then will introduce a fifth for the reader's consideration.

From Above

One of the most common linkages between the Bible and mission involves a "theology from above." In Roman Catholic and mainline Protestant denominational mission alike, this has involved using church tradition as the link. The church interprets the Scriptures, and through its teaching authority or its denominational mission structures it derives missional action from what it sees in Scripture. The extension of the institutional church and its agendas becomes the heart of mission.

But there is a second method that falls in the "from above" category. This involves seeing the Bible as a source of commands for mission. William Carey was a champion of this method, viewing the Great Commission of Matthew 28:18–20 as the basic link. This imperative type of biblical support is common in evangelical Protestant missiology, and especially in Church Growth theory, as popularized by Donald McGavran's unending appeal to Matthew 28:18–20.

The basic problem with both these approaches is that the Scriptures themselves are not allowed to interact with the present contexts of our mission. They are mediated, reduced, and filtered either by the agendas of the institutional church or by the guilt-based appeal of those who expound on the commands. Curiously, this approach causes Protestants who would avidly defend a gospel of grace to fall into a pit of legalism when it comes to mission. When we place church tradition or missional command between the Bible and our mission context, we reduce the impact that Scripture can have in transforming the way we understand, exercise, and evaluate our missional action.

From Below

After World War II many Protestant churches and missions, especially those associated with the World Council of Churches, became concerned with relevance. Although commendable in many ways, the hermeneutic of relevance pushed much mission reflection to an almost purely "from below" perspective. This hermeneutic, which has dominated the World Council of Churches, was exemplified in the heavy emphasis on "acts of faithfulness" at the 1989 San Antonio meeting of the Commission on World Mission and Evangelism. The starting point is not the Bible, but rather particular contextual agendas.[4] Once these agendas have been determined, exemplary cases and useful proof-texts are sought in the Bible to illustrate and validate the predetermined course of action.

But evangelicals should not judge the ecumenical approach too harshly. When evangelicals need to find justification for mission activities involving development, health, church planting, education, or urban ministries, they invariably scramble around the pages of the Bible to find illustrative cases (sometimes oddly chosen minute texts read in a literal and biblicist fashion) to legitimize their already determined agendas.

While the positive side of this approach is its contextual commitment, the downside is its loss of the normativity of Scripture. The Bible is not allowed to critique the assumptions, motivations, or rightness of the action itself—it is used only as a justification for what has already been predetermined. This mission is not God's. It belongs to the practitioners. The text is used primarily as a justification of the activity.

The Hermeneutical Circle of Liberation Theology

The idea of "the hermeneutical circle" has been around since the early 1800s, and is often associated with Friedrich Schleiermacher as well as Wilhelm Dilthey, Edmund Husserl, Martin Heidegger, Rudolf Bultmann, and Hans-Georg Gadamer.[5] But Latin American liberation theologians have transformed the concept into an intentional, creative, and revolutionary methodology.

Perhaps the best liberationist articulation of the hermeneutical circle in an effort to link Bible and mission is that of Juan Luís Segundo (1976).[6] Segundo outlined four specific steps in the process of the hermeneutical circle.

---

4. This perspective was also dominant at the 1992 Hawaii meeting of the International Association of Mission Studies. The reason was, in part, the strong influence exerted at that gathering by conciliar missiologists from the older mainline Protestant churches of Europe and North America.

5. See Mueller-Vollmer 1989; Muller 1991, 186–214; and Branson and Padilla 1986.

6. See also Gutiérrez 1974; Cook 1985; Clodovis Boff 1987; Boff and Boff 1987; Padilla 1985; Branson and Padilla 1986; Escobar 1987; Míguez-Bonino 1975; and Haight 1985.

First, we experience reality, which leads us to ideological suspicion. Second, we apply this ideological suspicion to our understanding of reality in general, and to Scripture and theology in particular. Third, we experience a new way of perceiving reality that leads us to the exegetical suspicion that the prevailing interpretation of the Bible has not taken important pieces of data into account. This calls for rereading the biblical text. Fourth, we develop a new hermeneutic, that is, we find a new way of interpreting Scripture with the new perceptions of our reality at our disposal. This leads us to look once more at our reality, which begins the process all over again.

Through their intentional and positive formulation of the hermeneutical circle, and by adding particular contextual data to the equation, Latin American liberation theologians offer missiology a very creative way of linking Bible and mission. (See Cook 1985.) But in part because of the heavy borrowing from European and Marxist sociopolitical theory, Latin American liberation theology tends to reduce this new hermeneutical method to narrow socioeconomic and political agendas. (See Chopp 1986.) This in turn shrinks the basis on which the Bible is being read. The method would look different if the analysis of reality were itself governed by biblical perspectives.

Critical Hermeneutics through Mission Paradigms

Before his untimely death David Bosch was able to finish what will be considered his magnum opus—*Transforming Mission*. One of the most helpful parts of Bosch's monumental work is the hermeneutical methodology he illustrates.

Bosch (1991, 22–23) begins by affirming:

> We cannot, with integrity, reflect on what mission might mean today unless we turn to the Jesus of the New Testament, since our mission is "moored to Jesus' person and ministry.". . . To affirm this is not to say that all we have to do is to establish what mission meant for Jesus and the early church and then define our missionary practice in the same terms, as though the whole problem can be solved by way of a direct application of Scripture. . . . [Because of both historical and sociocultural gaps between then and now,] a historico-critical study may help us to comprehend what mission was for Paul and Mark and John but it will not immediately tell us what we must think about mission in our own concrete situation.

Bosch then offers a new approach to the problem by drawing from the theory of paradigm construction that Hans Kung and David Tracy (1989) adapted from the philosophy of science.[7] Bosch's suggestion is to recognize

---

7. See Barbour 1974; Kuhn 1962; 1977; Lakatos 1978; Toulmin 1972; and Murphy 1990.

that self-definitions are offered in the biblical text as well as in our modern contexts. Thus "the approach called for requires an interaction between the self-definition of early Christian authors and actors and the self-definition of today's believers who wish to be inspired and guided by those early witnesses" (1991, 23). This in turn would move us to reread the biblical text, incorporating the newer sociological analysis of the Bible in its various contexts, then going beyond to a series of self-definitions of mission for today's contexts. Bosch calls this "critical hermeneutics":

> The critical hermeneutic approach goes beyond the (historically-interesting) quest of making explicit the early Christian self-definitions. . . . It desires to encourage dialogue between those self-definitions and all subsequent ones, including those of ourselves and our contemporaries. . . . The challenge to the study of mission may be described . . . as relating the always-relevant Jesus event of twenty centuries ago to the future of God's promised reign by means of meaningful initiatives for the here and now. . . .
>
> The point is that there are no simplistic or obvious moves from the New Testament to our contemporary missionary practice. The Bible does not function in such a direct way. There may be, rather, a range of alternative moves which remain in deep tension with each other but may nevertheless all be valid. [1991, 23–24][8]

Following this method, Bosch examines what he calls the "missionary paradigms" of Matthew, Luke, and Paul. Bosch does not try to reconcile the distinct paradigms of mission he finds in the New Testament. Although he demonstrates the internal coherence and consistency of each paradigm, he shows no compulsion to demonstrate coherence or consistency between paradigms. In fact, he seems to feel that the breadth of their differences may offer new linkages between the New Testament paradigms and the five other paradigms of mission that Bosch traces throughout the mission history of the church.[9]

In the end, Bosch tantalizes us by suggesting a host of "elements of an emerging ecumenical missionary paradigm," but he does not help us construct it. Thus we need to find a way to build on Bosch's work and go a step further.

The Bible as a Tapestry of God's Action in the World

One way to build on Bosch's hermeneutical method is to approach Scripture from the perspective of a number of themes and subthemes (or motifs) of

8. Bosch's thought in terms of theology of mission seems to echo what Paul Hiebert from an anthropological perspective calls "critical contextualization." See, e.g., Hiebert 1978; 1987; and 1989.

9. For a friendly critique of Bosch's approach, see Du Plessis 1990.

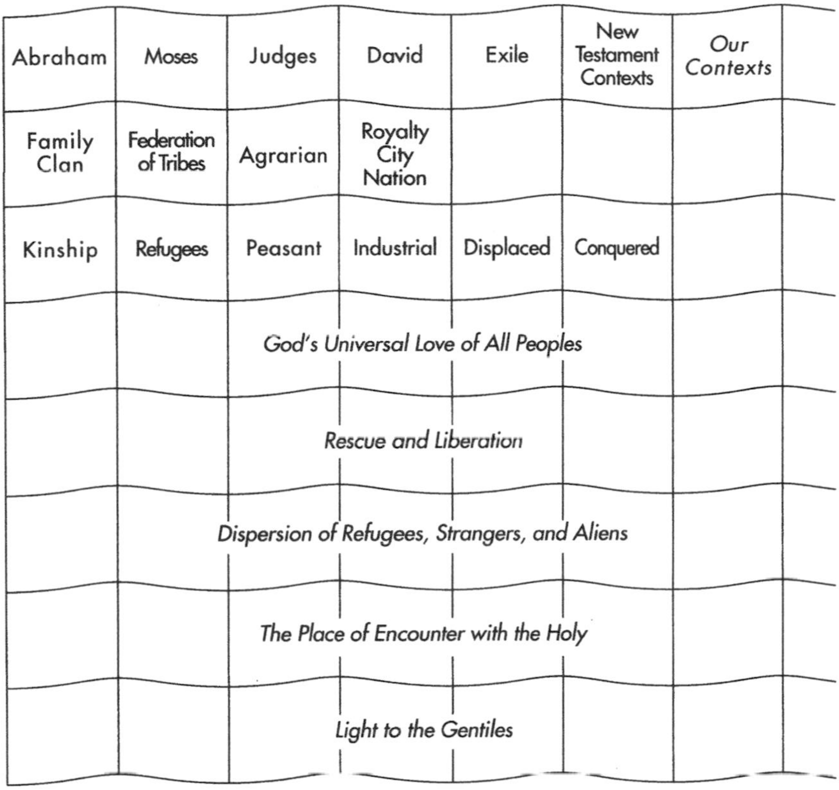

Abraham	Moses	Judges	David	Exile	New Testament Contexts	Our Contexts	
Family Clan	Federation of Tribes	Agrarian	Royalty City Nation				
Kinship	Refugees	Peasant	Industrial	Displaced	Conquered		
God's Universal Love of All Peoples							
Rescue and Liberation							
Dispersion of Refugees, Strangers, and Aliens							
The Place of Encounter with the Holy							
Light to the Gentiles							

Figure 10
The Bible as a Tapestry of Missional Motifs in Context

God's action in the world. Figure 10 views the Bible as a tapestry, with the woof (horizontal threads) of various themes and motifs interwoven in the warp (vertical) of each historical context. This yields a perspective simultaneously involving a view "from above" and "from below." The themes may be approached from above because they are the action of God in history. They are from below because they occur in the midst of human history in the context of the lives of men and women. Maybe Johannes Verkuyl (1978, 91–96) had a similar approach in mind when he suggested the Universal Motif, the Motif of Rescue and Liberation, the Missionary Motif, and the Motif of Antagonism as the places to begin formulating a biblical foundation for mission.

By viewing the Scriptures as an interwoven tapestry, we can affirm the Bible as a unified whole and also deal intentionally with the diversity of the history and cultures of the Bible (Glasser 1992, 9; Van Engen 1981, 160–66).

This is not an allegorical approach, nor is it purely literalist. We are not advocating a simple one-to-one correspondence of biblical response to our perceived needs, nor is it strictly a matter of discovering dynamic equivalence (Kraft 1979). Rather, we are seeking an intimate interrelationship of text and new contexts through the vehicle of particular themes or motifs that bridge the text's initial context with today's contexts of mission. This, then, provides a creative interaction of word and deed throughout the history of God's missionary activity. Such a critical hermeneutic helps us get away from finding a few proof-texts or isolated nuggets in the Bible to buttress our missional agendas. It goes beyond the search for a few key words of the gospel that might lend themselves for missiological reflection (Berkhof and Potter 1964). And it is broader and deeper than a set of commands that may be external to the people of God and to their context, both old and new.

Approaching the Bible as a tapestry calls us to take seriously the uniqueness of each biblical context in terms of its history, sociology, anthropology, and grammatical peculiarities. We must be able, therefore, to use all that we have learned so far from source, form, redaction, historical, rhetorical, and canon criticism (Muller 1991, 194–96). But we must go beyond them to ask the missiological question of God's intention in terms of the *missio Dei* as it occurs in word and deed in each particular context (Bosch 1991, 21). This method involves a critical hermeneutic that attempts to discover the particular self-definition (Bosch 1991, 23) of God's people in a particular time and place—and then challenges all subsequent self-definitions, including our own.

Daniel Shaw (1988, 31–33) has demonstrated from anthropology that the various contexts in biblical history fall into a "three cultures model": kinship, peasant, and industrial societies. Yet interwoven in a word-deed conjunction throughout these radically different contexts are clearly identifiable themes and motifs of God's self-definition of missional revelation throughout human history. To discover them, we must break down the biblical data to focus on specific themes and motifs that course their way through the tapestry of God's mission. As will be seen in chapter 3, the concept of God's covenantal relationship with his chosen people ("I will be your God, and you will be my people") is a theme that, though always the same, is radically different in each context.

But this is only half the story. The themes and motifs from the biblical narrative are chosen precisely because they interface with specific deepstructure themes or motifs of the worldview of the people in a specific missional context (Shaw 1988, 193–94). As we delve more profoundly into the deep-level meanings of a culture, we will encounter certain themes and motifs that are central to that culture's worldview. These worldview themes provide the connecting links whereby the self-definition of the people of God at a particular time in biblical history can be associated with the self-definition of the mission of God's people in that new context. The variety of biblical contexts where the theme or motif may appear provides a number of comparisons (some close, some remote) with the ways in which the theme may work itself out in the modern context. Such new manifestations of ancient motifs seem to be what Lamin Sanneh (1989, 215) means by the "translatability of Christianity."

By way of illustration, we could mention the following themes: the mission of the remnant; mission through dispersion of refugees; God's mission as a tree of life whose leaves are for the healing of the nations; human encounter with the divine; mission and washing, forgiveness, refreshment, water; mission and wholistic healing; mission and true (or false) prophets; mission and God's rule over all nations; mission and monotheism (versus poly- and henotheism); mission and wealth and poverty; mission and the stranger in our midst; mission as light in darkness, "a light to the Gentiles"; mission and food, eating, table fellowship; mission as reconciliation, return, re-creation.[10]

In selecting only certain themes as threads out of both the biblical tapestry and the contextual worldview, we may narrow the gospel too much. On the other hand, if we end up with too large a list of seemingly unrelated themes, we cannot achieve a cohesive and consistent missiology. But neither of these problems need arise. Rather, if we are able to discover an integrating idea that holds together a number of themes and motifs, we may be able to construct a truly biblical basis of mission for a particular context (Van Engen 1987, 523–25). Bosch's concept of the missionary God of history and of compassion who radically transforms humanity was for him just such an integrating central idea that allowed biblical missiology to impact the South African context (1978, 44). For Verkuyl and Glasser, along with many others, the kingdom of God provides the necessary unifying idea. The concept of covenant or the glory of God might also serve as a viable integrating idea. The point is that the themes selected, their interaction, and the particular integrating idea that presents itself to hold them together—all these must arise from self-definitions both in the biblical contexts and in the new missionary context. As Glasser (1992, 23) has said, "We have rather deliberately chosen the Kingdom of God as the particular diachronic theme most seminal to understanding the variegated mission of the people of God touching the nations."

Bible and mission! May all of us involved in missiological reflection continue to explore new methods whereby we may preserve the unique authority of Scripture as our only rule of faith and practice, and allow it to question, shape, direct, and deepen our understanding of, and commitment to, our ongoing participation in God's mission.

---

10. For a recent exploration of this theme in the South African context see Wielenga 1992.

2

The Importance
of Narrative Theology

We turn now to a hermeneutical approach to the Bible and its implications for allowing the Bible to shape our mission theology. Our thesis is that narrative theology as viewed from an evangelical perspective offers a creative and fruitful way to integrate the Bible's affirmations about the mission of God with our understanding of mission theology and its multiple, dynamically interacting horizons of text, community, and context.[1]

1. Drawing from Friedrich Nietzsche and Edmund Husserl before him, Hans-Georg Gadamer, professor of philosophy at Heidelberg from 1949 to 1968, suggested the notion of "horizons" as a way of describing and relating a person's perspective within a particular context of history and a historical context in the past which that person may be studying. This was a way of getting beyond the historicism of European (especially German) thought of the nineteenth century. Gadamer proceeded to make a case that historical studies involve a "fusion of horizons," not the least of these being the person's present horizon and the horizon from which the person studies the past historical context (see Mueller-Vollmer 1989, 269–73). Jürgen Habermas critiques Gadamer from the point of view of what he calls "the ontological construction of hermeneutical consciousness" (cf. Mueller-Vollmer 1989, 294–319). For a careful summary and critique of Gadamer's emphasis and its implications for an evangelical perspective that preserves the "original intended meaning of the text," see Osborne 1991, 369–71.

One of the most helpful works in the area of philosophical hermeneutics is Anthony Thiselton's *Two Horizons* (1980). Thiselton critiqued and adapted the "two-horizon" perspective in relation to history, theology, and linguistics and semantic meanings. "The goal of biblical hermeneutics," Thiselton writes, "is to bring about an active and meaningful engagement between the interpreter and text, in such a way that the interpreter's own horizon is reshaped and enlarged" (1980, xix). Thiselton sought to find ways both to affirm the horizon of the author's intended meaning, which interacts with the text's original community and context, and to recognize the contention of the philosophers of language (spearheaded by Ludwig Wittgenstein, among others) that the interpreter's horizon influences meaning.

The view of Scripture as a tapestry of God's action (see pp. 40–43) takes seriously both the vertical multiplicity of historical contexts and cultures in which biblical revelation occurs, and the horizontal continuity of God's self-disclosure in history, with particular emphasis on God's mission (*missio Dei*). Also to be taken seriously is the narrative structure of a large part of the Bible, a fact that has been recognized throughout the church's history. Recently there has been an increasing awareness that "the biblical narratives contain both history and theology, and . . . are brought together via a 'story' format. The historical basis for the stories is crucial, but the representation of that story in the text is the actual object of interpretation."[2] So the question is: How do the themes (as parts) and the biblical narrative (as a whole), which arise out of the faith communities in their contexts, reveal to us God's mission as it occurred "at many times and in various ways" (Heb. 1:1)? Further, how do these themes in the narrative interact with the motifs and themes of the narrative faith-pilgrimage of our faith communities in mission in diverse contexts today? Narrative theology is an attempt to build bridges both between the various horizons in Scripture and from Scripture to our day. Mission theology can learn from this movement. According to Alister McGrath, narrative theology is "one of the most important theological

---

Grant Osborne (1991, 386) summarizes Thiselton's viewpoint: "Thiselton finds four levels at which the 'illusion of textual objectivism' becomes apparent. (1) Hermeneutically, the phenomenon of preunderstanding exerts great influence in the interpretive act. This subjective element cannot be denied. (2) Linguistically, communication demands a point of contact between the sender and the recipient of a message, and this distanciation provides a major barrier to recovering a text's meaning. The differing situations of the hearers remove any possibility of a purely objective interpretation. (3) These problems are magnified at the level of literary communication, where other factors such as narrative-time, plot development, characterization and dialogue enter the picture. . . . (4) Philosophically, meaning is never context-free but is based on a large list of unconscious assumptions between sender and receiver. When these connecting links are not present, 'literal meaning' becomes extremely difficult if not impossible, for meaning can never be context-free." Osborne himself draws heavily from Thiselton in developing what Osborne has called *The Hermeneutical Spiral* of biblical interpretation—a spiral that goes beyond the "two-horizon" perspective, and recognizes that there is a dynamic, constant interaction of text, community, and context through time in relation to meaning. Osborne (1991, 366–415) gives an outstanding, clear, concise, and helpful overview of the issues of meaning as they relate to the problem of author-text-reader. I have depended on Osborne's work at a number of points in the preparation of this chapter.

Borrowing from Thiselton, D. A. Carson points out that "any Christian who witnesses cross-culturally must concern himself not only with *two* horizons, but with *three*. He must attempt to fuse his own horizon of understanding with the horizon of understanding of the text; and having done that, he must attempt to bridge the gap between his own horizon of understanding, as it has been informed and instructed by the text, and the horizon of understanding of the person or people to whom he ministers" (1984, 17).

2. Osborne 1991, 153, points to Marshall 1970, Martin 1972, and Stephen Smalley 1978 as biblical commentators who recognize this. We could add Knight 1976; Tannehill 1986; 1990; and Witherington 1994 as also recognizing the interaction of history and theology in the narrative nature of biblical story.

movements to develop in the last twenty years" (1991, 22; 1994, 170–71).[3] An evangelically reshaped narrative theology may offer us a way to draw most richly from both the warp of the contextual particularity of God's revelation at specific times and places, and the woof of the temporal universality of the mission of God, the "I am" who was and is and is to come.

A Description of Narrative Theology

This chapter will first describe narrative theology and take a close look at its basic elements. Second, it will evaluate narrative theology from the evangelical viewpoint and in the process summarize how an evangelical adaptation thereof would seek to preserve the historicity of God's acts, the authority of Scripture, matters of truth and revelation, and the author's intended meaning. Third, it will suggest several ways in which missiological reflection could be enriched by using this adapted form of narrative theology.

The Rise of Narrative Theology

Grant Osborne (1991, 153) points out that "the current interest in literary criticism in biblical studies was spawned in large part by the failure of form and redaction criticism to interpret the text. The tendency to break the text into isolated units is widely perceived as counterproductive, and so scholars turned to the much more literarily aware field of narrative criticism to bridge the gap." John Hayes and Frederick Prussner (1985, 263–64) have also described the rise of narrative theology:

> In light of the stalemate in the discussion over confessional and critical history, two developments in recent discussion are noteworthy. (1) First of all, much attention has shifted to focus on tradition and the way in which traditions and streams of tradition have been shaped in the Old Testament. . . . (2) A second development is the treatment of the narrative material as a story rather than as history although it may be history-like in many places. . . .
>
> Exactly how such an approach to the Old Testament as story will work itself out has yet to be demonstrated in Old Testament theology. . . . Is the resort to story as a description merely a means to avoid the issues over which the debates about history, salvation-history and God's acts in history, and other matters have so long ranged?[4]

3. Although he apparently defines narrative theology a little differently than do some, Gary Comstock echoes McGrath's sentiment when he says, "Narrative theology, reflection on the religious claims embedded in stories, is one of the most significant currents of late twentieth century thought" (1987, 687).

4. Hayes and Prussner 1985, 241–44, mention seven different arguments against close linkage of historical events and revelation, criticism brought by John Priest, Langdon Gilkey, James Barr, David Kelsey, J. J. Finkelstein, Franz Hesse, and Hartmut Gese. (For the relevant bibliographic data see Hayes and Prussner 1985, 239–40.)

Michael Goldberg traces the beginnings of narrative theology to the work of H. Richard Niebuhr and G. Ernest Wright:

> Although many religious thinkers had noticed that much of what the Bible has to say is cast in story form, Niebuhr was among the first explicitly to address the significance of that feature for theology. . . . [In Niebuhr] history becomes not just any story, but *our* story. In Niebuhr's view, a justifiable theology ultimately does not merely *read* biblical narrative: it *confesses* it. . . .[5]
>
> Most certainly, that theme resonates through the work of G. E. Wright, who saw a biblically based theology as "first and foremost a theology of recital, in which Biblical man confesses his faith by reciting the formative events of history as the redemptive handiwork of God."[6]
>
> For Wright, as it had been for Niebuhr, that story is an essentially historical account whose meaning extends to all of history. . . . Wright believes that in the last analysis, the justifiability of both faith and theology depends on the justifiability of the interpretative context displayed by historical biblical narratives. . . .
>
> However, as attractive and powerful as the views of Wright and Niebuhr seemed to be, . . . [they] never really made it clear whether that message resided in the biblical text itself, in a phenomenon "behind" the text, or in some combination of text plus event. Due to their lack of clarity on this point, Wright and Niebuhr are thus left open to the even more damning criticism of James Barr [1966], who claims that "while they may have succeeded in taking history seriously, they nevertheless have failed to take *the biblical text* seriously."[7]

Hayes and Prussner (pp. 263–64) also suggest five significant contributions of narrative theology: "The consequences of reading the narrative as story or as a literary form are several. (a) It allows one to dispense with or hold in abeyance the issue of whether events happened as they were told. (b) The locus or dynamics of revelation, if one chooses to use this word, can be seen as associated primarily with the people and the process which produced the story and secondarily with the story rather than with the events it tells about. (c) The story can be seen as one of the ways in which Israel chose to give order and cohesion to its life by producing a symbolic context for its present and a basis for its future. (d) The story, not the actual history of Israel, can be viewed as what Israel wished to express about its own self-understanding. (e) The Old Testament story may be read by the contemporary person as paradigmatic and as informing just as any other meaningful story in world literature."

For an excellent overview of earlier trends in Old Testament hermeneutics (e.g., Julius Wellhausen's source theory, Gerhard von Rad's and Martin Noth's history-of-tradition approach, Hans Walter Wolff's and Walter Brueggemann's development of Pentateuchal traditions and sources), see Hayes 1979, 159–97. For a superb discussion from the time of those trends see Wolff 1963.

5. Goldberg is quoting from Niebuhr 1941, 47–61.

6. Goldberg is quoting here from G. Ernest Wright 1952, 38.

7. Goldberg refers to Brevard Childs's (1970, 52) tracing the development of the biblical theology movement. Childs follows it from its rise in the early 1940s to its decline in the mid-1960s. At its height the movement embraced such diverse figures as Niebuhr, Wright, Floyd V. Filson, Otto Piper, John A. Mackay, H. H. Rowley, and James D. Smart; at its center was the shared conviction that the biblical narratives provide the proper locus for significant theological reflection. According to Goldberg (1981, 267), Childs (1970, 65) apparently believed that Barr's critique "was the final blow to the biblical theology movement."

By uncritically allowing the category of biblical narrative to collapse into a vague notion of "revelation-in-history," Niebuhr and Wright had set the stage for the collapse of much of the theoretical foundation used to support their claims. While a good deal of biblical narrative does display certain historical elements and features, a truly narrative theology must not forget that what has primacy is *the narrative* and *not* the various component parts which the narrative contains. [Goldberg 1981, 147–54]

These difficulties led to a number of options being offered. Source criticism, form criticism, redaction criticism, rhetorical criticism, structuralist hermeneutics, deconstructionism, canon criticism, reader-response hermeneutics—each approach tried to wrestle with the nature of the text, the intention (or lack thereof) of the author, the issue of the historicity of the events, and the implications (if any) for Old Testament theology. All this has deepened the crisis of Old Testament theology. As Robert Hubbard (1992, 31) has said, "Though it is centuries old, OT theology is now uncertain of its true identity. At the heart of the crisis lies an uncertainty about the proper way to do OT theology. . . . Nevertheless, the church desires—indeed, needs—to hear the OT's theological voice afresh today."

Definitions of Narrative Theology

Narrative theology is difficult to define.[8] As Gabriel Fackre has pointed out:

The variety and imprecision of terminology in the discussion of narrative are striking. The theological conversation about "story" is influenced by fields as diverse as literary criticism, psychology, linguistics, social ethics and communications theory, with formulations showing the marks of these pursuits and the partisans within them. The interdisciplinary character of narrative study is one of its strengths, but the too simple transfer of categories or ideology from a favorite sector as key to the theological subject matter can exclude the insights of other disciplines, and, more importantly, obscure the unique features of narrative *theology*. [1983, 340–41]

Fackre defines narrative theology in terms of story:

As a literary form, story or narrative refers in the broadest sense to the account by a narrator of events and participants moving in some pattern over time and space. In this inclusive sense a history book and an accident report in a newspaper are manifestations of narrative. But the word "story" as it is used in theological inquiry is related to the narrower literary meaning: an account of char-

---

8. Ironically, although noted evangelical theologian Donald Bloesch begins his *Theology of Word and Spirit* (1992, 16–18) with an insightful, concise, and significant discussion of the pitfalls of narrative theology, he does not offer a definition of it.

acters and events in a plot moving over time and space through conflict toward resolution. {1984, 5]

Narrative theology is discourse about God in the setting of story. Narrative (in its narrow sense) becomes the decisive image for understanding and interpreting faith. Depiction of reality, ultimate and penultimate, in terms of plot, coherence, movement, and climax is at the center of all forms of this kind of talk about God. [1983, 343]

In contrast, James Gustafson (1988, 19–20) defines narrative theology in relation to its role in the life of a community: "Narrative functions to sustain the particular moral identity of a religious (or secular) community by rehearsing its history and traditional meanings, as these are portrayed in Scripture and other sources. Narratives shape and sustain the ethos of the community. . . . Narratives function to sustain and confirm the religious and moral identity of the Christian community, and evoke and sustain the faithfulness of its members to Jesus Christ."[9]

George Stroup (1981, 72) defines "narrative" in terms of religious expression: " 'Narrative' is used to describe and explain the location of religion in human experience and the meaning of 'faith' in relation to a person's encounter with other people and the world. The 'religious dimension' of human experience is interpreted as having something to do with the narratives people recite about themselves or the narrative they use in order to structure and make sense out of the world."

David Tracy (1988, 207) notes that "human beings need story, symbol, image, myth, and fiction to disclose to their imaginations some genuinely new possibilities for existence: possibilities which conceptual analysis, committed as it is to understanding present actualities, cannot adequately provide."[10]

Typologies of Narrative Theology

There have been a number of attempts to categorize the various authors and thinkers who use narrative theology. Michael Goldberg (1981, 156–83) sees the field as comprising three activities: (1) "Structuring the Story" (e.g., Hans Frei, Sallie McFague), where the structure itself provides part of the theological content and meaning of the narrative; (2) "Following the

---

9. Robert Schreiter 1985, 82, places "narrative" within the framework of "theology as variations on a sacred text: commentary, narrative, and anthology. . . . Narrative differs from commentary," Schreiter says, "in that signs within a text are extended through a series of transformations which not only extend the meaning of the original text, but engage the hearer by getting him or her to identify with some of the agents in the narrative. . . . Retelling of the biblical stories subtly weaves together biblical and commentary narrative to open the semantic possibilities of the biblical text."

10. Alister McGrath 1991, 22, emphasizes the contribution narrative theology can make "in reforging the often neglected link between systematic theology and the study of Scripture."

Story" (e.g., Paul Van Buren and Irving Greenberg), where the narrative's connection to life is emphasized; and (3) "Enacting the Story" (e.g., Stanley Hauerwas and John Howard Yoder), where the ethical dimensions are stressed.[11]

Ronald Grimes (1986) offers a six-point typology: (1) a sacred biography group; (2) a faith-development group (e.g., James Fowler); (3) a psycho-biography group; (4) a character and community group—theological ethi-cists (e.g., Stanley Hauerwas, James McClendon, Jr., and Michael Novak); (5) a biblical narrative group (e.g., Hans Frei, John Dominic Crossan); and (6) a myth and ritual group. Grimes's typology is helpful in its inclusive scope, yet it also serves to point to the confusing variety within narrative theology.

Gary Comstock reduces his typology to two categories. Rejecting other possible dual categorizations,[12] Comstock suggests one group be termed the "pure narrative theologians: antifoundationalist, cultural-linguistic" think-ers tied to or inspired by the Yale Wittgensteinian descriptivists. In this group Comstock includes Hans Frei, George Lindbeck, Stanley Hauerwas, and David Kelsey. "They believe narrative is an autonomous literary form partic-ularly suited for the work of theology. They oppose the excessive use of dis-cursive prose and abstract reason, insisting that Christian faith is best under-stood by grasping the grammatical rules and concepts of its texts and practices. Narrative is a privileged mode for doing this" (1987, 688).

Comstock has termed the second group the "impure narrative theolo-gians: revisionist, hermeneutical, Gadamerian-inspired correlationists." Here he includes Paul Ricoeur, David Tracy, Julian Hartt, and Sallie Mc-Fague. A better name for the second group might have been "applied narra-tive theologians." According to Comstock (1987, 688), the members of this group "deny narrative unique theological status. Believing that Christian sa-cred narratives are irreducibly infected with historical, philosophical, and psychological concerns, they seek to apply the methods of these disciplines to their interpretation. For them, narrative is neither pure nor autono-mous."[13] Comstock makes a strong case that these two camps are quite dis-tinct in their view of narrative theology and in their methodology. There is, in fact, a "nasty tension in the ranks" (1987, 687).

11. Paul Lauritzen 1987 offers a helpful comparison of J. B. Metz and Stanley Hauerwas that echoes some aspects of Goldberg's typology.

12. Comstock offers and then rejects the following categorizations: "Chicagoans-Yaleys" (the problem is where to put the Berkeley folks); "Foundationalists-Antifoundationalists" (this classification is too narrow to encompass the variety of issues involved); "Experiential-expressivist/Cultural-linguistic" (there is more at stake than this describes). Comstock com-ments, "Current labels are misleading, at best" (1987, 688).

13. See, e.g., Mitchell 1981. Avery Dulles 1992, 82–83, places Frei, Lindbeck, and Ronald Thiemann within the Yale group.

Comstock's two-camp approach seems forced, and leaves a number of significant people out of the picture. A more helpful typology for our purposes was developed by Gabriel Fackre. Fackre (1983, 343; 1984, 6–7) speaks of three categories: (1) "canonical story" (literary analysis of biblical material); (2) "life story" (psychosocial resources used in the explanation of personal experience); and (3) "community story" (communal lore and the sedimentation of tradition). Fackre considers his own work as falling into the third group—community story. Unfortunately, as Fackre develops his theology in *The Christian Story* (1984), the narrative qualities (in terms of narrative sources, narrative forms of thought, and narrative articulation of the community's faith) seem to dissipate.

Studying the typologies above, one begins to realize that it is practically a misnomer to speak of a narrative theology "movement." The presuppositions, methodologies, agendas, and styles of the players in narrative theology are too diverse to be lumped into a single cohesive movement. However, there are some emphases they all have in common, as we will soon see.

A final observation on typology is necessary. In attempting to understand narrative theology, we need to be careful not to confuse it with canon criticism.[14] Although the two approaches have influenced each other and both stress dealing with the entire text as text, they are quite distinct methods. James Barr, Brevard Childs, and James Sanders, to name some of the principal figures in canon criticism, have emphasized the way particular contextual and community factors gave rise to the text as canonically received—and, vice versa, how the canonical shaping of the text influenced the community. However, canon criticism does not restrict itself to studying the dynamics of narrative. Neither does it see the narrative process as necessarily influencing the way canonical hermeneutics operates.

14. Without getting embroiled in all the complexities of contemporary discussion of Old Testament theology and Old Testament hermeneutics, we can characterize the general idea behind canon criticism as treating the Old Testament as a whole document, following the form in which the canon has been received, neither breaking it apart into small pieces according to origins or sources, nor superimposing one idea into which we would try to squeeze the whole of the Old Testament revelation. See, e.g., James Sanders 1984; 1987; Childs 1985; Brueggemann 1992, 1–44, 95–117; Clements 1978; Hubbard 1992, 31–46; and Bush 1992. See also Glasser 1992, 13–14, where he discusses the work of Childs 1970.

Although there does not seem to be a direct relationship between narrative theology and canon criticism, yet the two parallel developments have influenced each other, particularly in affirming the wholeness and unity of the text in its received canonical form. This form includes much that is narrative. And the way canonicity occurred in the ongoing life of the faith community is itself a narrative development. Thus, recent emphasis on a narrative approach to the Old Testament has found it necessary to deal with the text in its present discourse-level canonical form. See, e.g., Fackre 1983, 340–53; Goldberg 1981; Gunn 1987; Gustafson 1988; Hauerwas and Jones 1989; Long 1987; Osborne 1991. Brueggemann 1991 speaks of "canonical recital."

The Basic Elements of Narrative Theology: Story and Dogmatics and More

Narrative Theology as More than Story

Narrative theology is story. As we saw from the definitions given above, "narrative theology is discourse about God in the setting of story," (and by "story" we mean) "an account of characters and events in a plot moving over time and space through conflict toward resolution" (Fackre 1983, 343; 1984, 5). So, for example, to understand God's covenantal relationship with Abraham, we must allow our theology to emerge from the entire narrative of Abraham's life (Gen. 11:27–25:11). So also the "story" of Jonah is not merely a recital of events in the life of one man—but rather, profoundly, a revelation of what God is like (merciful and gracious, full of compassion), a depiction of God's mission (the salvation of Nineveh), and a call to repentance and transformation on the part of all the Jonahs in Israel who would encapsulate God's grace within the narrow confines of their own selfishness.

The narrative of Scripture, then, is more than story; it is more than fiction, more than mythical (in the common usage of the word) moralisms like Aesop's fables with no connection to the real world except by way of the moralism being advocated. Biblical narrative is so powerful precisely because it is grounded in history, occurs in the midst of the human story, and has to do with the tangible acts of God. But narrative is not merely the recital of events in historical sequence. Rather, in the midst of the recital, biblical narrative seeks to convey a deeper meaning, a deep-level revelation of the nature and purposes of God who breaks into human history. "The Bible is God's story to us. . . . The Bible itself is a grand and cosmic story" (Robert Paul Roth 1985, 174).

Further, the historical groundedness of biblical narrative is essential because the narrative is born in the midst of a faith community. The narrative shapes the community, is shaped by the experiences in history of the faith community (Israel and the church), and intends to teach those inside and outside the community the nature, acts, and purposes of Israel's God. "Systematic theology engages the intellect; storytelling engages the heart and indeed the whole person" (Bausch 1984, 16, 27). In other words, biblical narrative is both descriptive of events and prescriptive of faith in Israel's (and the church's) God, who is portrayed as intimately associated with those events. Thus, for example, Paul's sermons in Acts, although autobiographical recitals, are most profoundly an articulation of Paul's faith. So also the story of Esther is not merely a recital of the events that led to an Israelite young woman's role as queen of Persia. It is also a profound revelatory confession of faith about a God who works mysteriously and quietly—but carefully and intentionally—in the seeming coincidences of life through chosen instruments like Esther to preserve and save God's people, even in the midst of exile.

David Duke stresses that biblical narrative has dimensions beyond story: "Theology needs life stories not just for illustrative purposes and not just to give personal examples of doctrine and morals. Rather, one's theology 'must be adequate to the intensity and spiritual seriousness' of these life stories" (1986, 140).[15] He then gives nine "criteria for (theologically) valuable biography" (ibid., 141–45) and concludes, "One of the most significant functions of narrative, especially biography, is the true-to-life capability of portraying meaning *through* the narrative process" (ibid., 147). Once the biblical narrative is read in this light, it becomes a powerful influence on our theology. For "generally speaking, a recognition of the value of story can be a valuable corrective to the dominant tendency in western theology to abstract and analyze" (Moberly 1986, 77).[16]

Having recognized the theological significance of biblical narrative (it is more than story), we must hasten to add some important cautions. When the biblical narrative is taken at face value as canonical text, it clearly intends to reveal truth about God.[17] Too many of the "pure narrative theologians" (especially the Yale group) tend to reduce biblical narrative to individual and historical relativism (*a* story, not *the* story), to mere horizontalism (the story of Israel's self-perception and sociocultural religious thought from which an ontologically separate God is absent), to pure description (what happened and how the story functioned in the community rather than what Israel's

15. Duke quotes here from McClendon 1974. "I agree with McClendon," states Duke, "that biography as theology cannot and should not replace propositional theology, but complement, challenge, and enhance it" (1986, 139).

16. Moberly 1986, 78–79, suggests seven ways in which narrative helps our theologizing: "First, an interest in story will alert the reader to elements in a text that are characteristic of a story—plot, foreshadowing, irony, echo, repetition, contrast, tension, resolution, etc.; elements which are clearly present in many of the most famous and memorable Old Testament stories. . . . Secondly, there is the fact that some truths can best, or perhaps only, be conveyed in story form because of the importance of symbol and image in human understanding. . . . Thirdly, a story may communicate through what it does not say as well as through what it does say. . . . [Fourthly], a story can communicate through assumption and suggestion. . . . Fifthly, a story may deliberately leave something vital to its understanding unsaid. This means the readers [are] obligated to use [their] understanding and intelligence if [they are] to understand the story properly. . . . Sixthly, a story can provide a pattern or framework for understanding life and experience. . . . Finally, a story can act as a mirror to help people see themselves more clearly." See also Crites 1971.

Bausch 1984, 195–99, offers ten propositions regarding the importance of story in theology and in the church: "(1) Stories introduce us to sacramental presences. . . . (2) Stories are always more important than facts. . . . (3) Stories remain normative. . . . (4) Traditions evolve from stories. . . . (5) Stories precede and produce the church. . . . (6) Stories imply censure. . . . (7) Stories produce theology. . . . (8) Stories produce many theologies. . . . (9) Stories produce ritual and sacrament. . . . (10) Stories are history."

17. Gabriel Fackre 1983, 351, emphasizes this issue.

covenantal response to God should have been), and to mostly ethereal image, symbol, metaphor, and fiction (like any other human story, not the story of God's inbreaking into human history). This reduces biblical narrative to inspiring life-stories rather than the revelatory faith-pilgrimage of God's people. Ultimately, however, narrative theology must face the issue of truth (Moberly 1986, 80–81).[18]

When the meaning of the narrative is deconstructed too far, all that may be left is the reader's response, which ascribes meaning to the text on the basis of the reader's particular horizon and the reader's personal agendas. This violates the most basic intent of the biblical narrative itself as that shaped, and was shaped by, the faith community in the text's original horizon. With reader-response hermeneutics we no longer have biblical narrative, we have merely the imposition of the reader's horizon. The narrative quality of the text, and the deeper meaning intended by the text, become eclipsed by the reader's response. We come to know something about the reader, but we lose sight of the narrative itself.

Narrative Theology as More than Dogmatics

Just as narrative theology is story but more than story, so narrative *theology* is theology but more than propositional dogmatics. Contra the Yale "pure narrative" horizontalists, the text of Scripture, when taken at face value and read in its most obvious forms, clearly intends to speak about God—to articulate theology. In discussing "the theological aspect of narrative," J. B. Metz has affirmed that narrative, as a "medium of salvation and history," involves an "inseparable connection between narrative and [theological] argument" (1989, 256). In fact, Metz makes a case that to explain issues like salvation history and human suffering, theology in fact needs narrative (ibid., 258–59).

The narrative of Scripture intends to be theology—it intends to point to and signify the reality of God, whose existence and nature are ontologically distinct from, and not determined by, the language used to refer to God. And to the extent that it refers realistically and accurately to the reality of God, narrative is theological. Wentzel Van Huyssteen (1989, 147) speaks of the "reality depiction of theological statements. . . . The relational nature of religious language is ultimately founded on the fact that it is never a mere ex-

18. "We are saying," says Robert Paul Roth (1985, 178, 182), "that we cannot have truth without meaning, nor meaning without truth. . . . The criteria by which to evaluate this truth of the Spirit are the gracious gifts of faith, hope and love as they function in the community of believers. . . . The sequence, as Paul tells the story, involves a succession of sin, wrath, law, and death, which are met, again in sequence, with Christ's suffering on the cross, the grace of mercy, the Spirit giving life, and the resurrection." Roth cites Paul Ricoeur at this point with reference to his "hermeneutics of testimony."

pression of religious feelings but is in fact referential." He goes on to speak of the "critical-realist" approach to doing theology, a methodology that offers theology a way to deal with its referential nature, a characteristic that it shares with scientific investigation: "The strength of the critical-realist position certainly lies in its insistence that both the objects of science and the objects of religious belief lie beyond the range of literal description" (1989, 156).[19]

We are faced here with the difficult problem of how human language can speak about God.[20] Ultimately we confront the question of the referential nature of theological language—an issue that very much influences the way we understand narrative as being *theological*. Paul K. Jewett (1991, 34–35, 39) suggests that language about God is analogical in the sense of *analogia fidei*, analogy of faith,

> for all the truths of revelation come to us by faith in him who is the source of revelation. . . . For this reason, the statements that the theologian makes are faith statements, for theology's task . . . is to mirror faith in thought. . . .
>
> God is not reached by our analogies based as they are on the experience of the finite created world. Though we necessarily speak of God in analogies, metaphors, symbols, and parables taken from the world, we do not find him out *by* these. Rather, we find him *in* these because he stoops to reveal himself to us in them.

True, *all* language about God is *analogia fidei*, and speaks as much about what we do *not* know about God as what we do. Even so, because of God's acts in history, because of God's ultimate and final revelation in Jesus Christ, and because of God's illumination by and in the power of the Holy Spirit, we believe (we trust in faith and respond in obedience) that the Scriptures are in fact doing what they intend to do: they *refer* to and show us the nature of the God of the Bible. And one of the most profound ways this referential activity occurs in Scripture is through narrative.

But narrative theology is more than propositional dogmatics. Let us briefly look at four important ways in which narrative theology, while theological, is broader and deeper than dogmatic propositions. In the first place, narrative theology is based in the community of faith. Although it is not acceptable to reduce narrative to a horizontalist extrapolation of the self-consciousness of the community, yet the Bible's narrative is inescapably communal. From the story of Abraham onward, articulation of the revelation of who God is happens in and through the life of Israel and the church. As canon criticism has

---

19. For an excellent discussion of the use of models in doing theology, see Dulles 1992, 46–52.

20. In a number of places in the *Church Dogmatics*, Karl Barth offers some insights into the mystery of divine Word in human words—the heart of the difficulty to which we are referring here.

shown so well, the text cannot be separated from the faith community in which it was born, shaped, transmitted, and explained. Narrative theology appropriately emphasizes the place and role of the community in shaping the meaning of the text (Hauerwas 1981, 15).

Secondly, narrative theology is more than dogmatics in that it is intertwined with human history. Narrative theology places God's self-revelation in the midst of human history. This is not to imprison theology within Enlightenment historicist categories as was done in the nineteenth century, nor to reduce all theology to discussion of salvation history, nor is it to squeeze theology into a historical process as was done in the process theology of Alfred North Whitehead and those who followed him. Rather, this involves a recognition that our understanding of who God is must be historically grounded, happens in history, transforms our history, and re-forms the way we participate in history.

This means that theology cannot and must not be an ethereal, theoretical, removed speculation—but must always interact with and be shaped in human history. It also means that we must recognize the historical development of theology. When God does new things in human history, we must rethink the way we understand God. Thus in Acts 15 the leaders of the early church in Jerusalem had to rethink their theology, given what God had done in sending the Holy Spirit into the midst of the Gentiles in Cornelius's house (Acts 10). Similarly, the apostle Paul devoted years to reshaping and rearticulating his theology on the basis of his encounter (in human history) with Jesus the Christ on the road to Damascus. And in this century this matter has been at the foreground of Roman Catholic theological discussion since the Second Vatican Council.[21] Thus Karl-Otto Apel speaks of theology as "a new narration of a history" (1989, 329), and Paul Ricoeur has stressed that "narrativity and temporality are closely related" (1981, 165). Narrative helps us understand that God's self-disclosure is intimately connected with the historicality of God's people. (See Hendrikus Berkhof 1985, 57–73).[22]

Thirdly, narrative theology is more than dogmatics in that it involves faith-pilgrimage over time. Whether narrative theology is approached from the point of view of ethics (Stanley Hauerwas), canon criticism (James Sanders and Brevard Childs), education (Thomas Groome 1991), stages of faith (James Fowler 1981), or women's issues (Phyllis Trible 1984)—a more fundamental matter involves the narrative of the faith-pilgrimage of God's peo-

21. For an excellent discussion of this issue from a Protestant point of view, see Berkouwer 1965. Berkouwer was one of only a few Protestant theologians invited as official guests to the Second Vatican Council.

22. Robert Hubbard, Jr., says, "In actual fact, read straightforwardly, the Bible does present God as very much involved in the day-to-day world. Only a method that reckons with the OT's 'faith' dimensions can be truly 'historical exegesis'—that is, one that does full justice to all the levels of meaning present in the text" (1992, 35).

ple over time. This prevents a reduction of the revelatory nature of Scripture to a purely confessional element of Israel's idea of God, as if God existed only in relation to what Israel said or thought about God. Rather, narrative theology recognizes that there is development in the way Scripture portrays Israel's and the church's deepening understanding of God's self-revelation. Thus God's self-disclosure is seen as taking place in the midst of a faith-journey, that is, through the walk of God's people with God. Of course, we must be careful here not to extrapolate our own spiritual experience (or that of Israel or the church) to define the nature, purpose, and mission of God. And yet narrative theology helps us realize that most fundamentally theology flows from the experiences of the faith community in their encounter with God. Here is where theology relates closely to both individual and corporate confession, to creed, and to the church's tradition (Hendrikus Berkhof 1985, 28–56, 74–89). Narrative theology gives us a means of integrating spirituality and dogmatics in a very fruitful way.

Finally, narrative theology is more than dogmatics in that it integrates word and deed. When taken at face value, the narrative of Scripture does not split the person from the work of God, as has too often been done in traditional theology, for example, with Christology. Rather, God's deeds serve to provide a platform for the words, and the words give meaning, significance, and normativity to the encounter between God and humanity that occurs in God's deeds. As Carl Henry (1987, 8) says, "The Bible conveys the meaning of God's redemptive acts; since it is the divine salvific acts it interprets, the acts are indispensable presuppositions of that meaning." Thus, for example, in Exodus the deliverance from Egypt (deeds) is the backdrop for the Decalogue (words), and together they provide the stage for the tabernacle, where the structure of this "tent of meeting," the priestly ritual, and the words of God's revelation all come together in God's covenantal tabernacling in the midst of his people.[23]

So we see that narrative theology is highly integrative, allowing community, context, history, culture, relationships, faith-pilgrimage, and word-deed conjunctions to be acceptable data for theology. Not only do these contribute to the theological task, but they are themselves transformed by their inclusion in the narrative. In the final analysis, however, they all are secondary to the issue of articulating God's self-revelation in the covenantal relationship established between God and God's people. This bottom-line issue

---

23. The same kind of deed-word integration can be seen in John 6, where Jesus' feeding of the five thousand provides the stage for the words, "I am the bread of life." It is clearly a violation of the text of John 6 to split the deed from the words. Narrative theology provides an important tool for the integration of these two aspects of God's self-disclosure—two sides of the same coin that have for too long been separated from each other in both the method and content of theology.

is the primary concern of evangelical theologians with regard to narrative theology.

Evangelical Assessments of Narrative Theology

The issues we have just explored lie at the heart of the assessment that evangelical scholars (biblical, dogmatic, and missiological) have made of narrative theology.[24] Carl Henry (1987, 7) comments: "A lively debate is under way in some evangelical circles over whether narrative hermeneutics should be welcomed as an ally that is essentially orthodox. Some conservative scholars see a kinship between the emphasis of narrative proponents that the entire Book is important to the meaning and the orthodox emphasis on the authority and plenary inspiration of the whole scriptural text." Mark Wallace (1989, 169) has said, "I find the Yale postliberal alternative [of narrative theology] to be a welcome development as it seeks to redirect the Christian community's vision back to its scriptural sources and to the Bible's distinctive, even unique, vision of reality." In the interest of space, we will briefly list five reasons for evangelical appreciation of narrative theology and five concerns that evangelicals have expressed.

Positive Elements

In the first place, evangelicals have shown their deep appreciation for narrative theology's concern to deal with the whole text.[25] After such a long time during which biblical studies broke the text up into little pieces (the standard practice of source criticism, historical criticism, demythologizing types of criticism, form criticism, redaction criticism, and some of the newer hermeneutical approaches), evangelicals have welcomed an approach that, recognizing that much of the Bible is offered in story form, takes the whole text seriously. Indeed, "narrative is the main literary type found in Scripture. . . . To affirm faith in Jesus is to affirm faith in the narrative of his birth, crucifixion, death, resurrection, and ascension—a continuous story" (McGrath 1991, 23).

Second, evangelicals affirm narrative theology's interest in the interaction of the text with the community.[26] Given the penchant in modernity to reduce faith to a purely individual matter—and to reduce questions of source and

24. See, e.g., Bloesch 1992, 17–23; Brueggemann 1992; Carson 1984a; Duke 1986; Fackre 1983; Finger 1987; Gottwald 1987; Grenz 1993; 1994; Groome 1991; Gunn 1987; Henry 1987; Herion 1988; Long 1987; Longman 1988; Mann 1991; McGrath 1991; Moberly 1986; Morgan 1988; Osborne 1991, 153–73; Stroup 1981; and Wallace 1989.

25. See Bloesch 1992, 17; Finger 1987, 213–17; Gottwald 1987, 61; Gunn 1987, 67; Henry 1987, 7, 15; Longman 1988, 31–32, 42; and Wallace 1989, 169.

26. See, e.g., Henry 1987, 15; Fackre 1983; 1984; Morgan 1988, 72, 79–80.

author to purely individual issues—evangelicals have long stressed the Protestant Reformation's emphasis on the priesthood of all believers, particularly in terms of the communal nature of Israel and the church, the role of Scripture in the church, and the specific place of the Bible within the life of the faith community. Narrative theology's stress on the significance of the faith community in the shaping of the text is seen as positive. In addition, narrative theology is viewed positively to the extent that it helps us see the faith community's confessional understanding of God's self-revelation in their midst. Thus Alister McGrath (1991, 24) comments, "Recognition of the narrative character of Scripture effectively conveys the tension between the limited knowledge on the part of the human characters in the story and the omniscience of God."

Third, evangelicals have been concerned with the relationship of what Anthony Thiselton calls the two horizons (those of the text and of the interpreter) of their hermeneutical approach to Scripture.[27] Evangelical pursuit of a grammatico-historical approach to the text is a recognition that the text emerged in particular contexts. Here evangelicals have borrowed with seeming appreciation from narrative theology and also from the canon criticism of Brevard Childs and James Sanders. Donn Morgan (1988, 77–79) comments: "The importance of canon for OT theology is that it establishes a perspective from which the literature was understood by historic Israel. . . . The appeal to the canonical form of the Scriptures at least seeks to establish a common text as the grounds for theological reflection."[28]

Fourth, evangelicals have appreciated the way narrative theology helps us read Scripture from a wholistic perspective that recognizes that all of life is encountered in God's revelation and needs to be taken into consideration in our reading of the text. Biblical storytelling "appeals to the whole man, it involves our whole being—intellect, will, emotions—to a greater extent than, say, the Westminster Confession. . . . Which communicates more vividly: the statement 'Love your neighbor as yourself' or the story of the Good Samaritan?" (Longman 1988, 42).

The wholistic reading of Scripture harmonizes with the evangelical affirmation that faith in Jesus Christ should interact with and transform *all* aspects of a person's life. Narrative theology "avoids the dulling sense of abstraction that is a feature of much academic theological writing. . . . Part of the attraction of narrative theology is its ability to bring the Christian faith into close contact with the everyday life of those outside its bounds, just as Jesus was able to make such connection through his use of parables"

27. See, e.g., Osborne 1991; Longman 1988, 35; Morgan 1988, 79.
28. The reader needs to keep in mind what was said before: canon criticism is not to be confused with narrative theology, yet there are intimate connections between them, as in this case. (See Henry 1987, 4.)

(McGrath 1991, 23). A narrative reading of Scripture also has transformational power: "The gospel is not primarily about a set of ethical principles; it is about the effect of an encounter with God in the lives of individuals and the histories of nations. By relating such stories, the biblical writers are able to declare: 'Look! that is what happens when someone is transformed by the grace of God!' That is what Christian behavior is meant to be like!" (McGrath 1991, 24).[29]

Fifth, evangelicals appreciate narrative theology for the methodological contribution it offers in approaching biblical theology. "Narrative theology shows real promise as a technique. It reminds us that Scripture recounts the story of God's dealings with his people, and invites us to relate our own story to this greater narrative. . . . Narrative theology reminds us of the power of the biblical stories to convey the gospel—and challenges us to be more faithful communicators of the thrilling news that God has entered into the story of his creation and his creatures, in order to change it: history becomes 'his story'" (McGrath 1991, 24; see also Longman 1988, 41). This matter of methodological technique ties in with evangelical approaches to inductive Bible study, evangelism and preaching, contextualization and conversion.[30] Further, in cross-cultural missions narrative theology has proven very helpful in doing semantic structural analysis of the discourse-level meanings of a text, an approach to Scripture used extensively today by Bible translators.

Deep Concerns

Although evangelicals display a significant support for narrative theology, yet at some points they are profoundly uneasy about it. First, evangelicals show broad consensus in their concern about preserving the authorial intent of the text.[31] Tremper Longman (1988, 36) says, "If there is anything that unites secular theory since the advent of New Criticism in the middle of this century it is the denial of the author. Traditional criticism invested a lot of stock in the author." Carl Henry (1987, 10) comments, "Evangelicals insist that authorial intention and grammatico-historical interpretation do not exclude a single divine Author and a single sense that permeates the diverse genres and constitutes an undergirding and overarching unity. They do so, however, on the premise that the Bible is a singularly inspired book."

The present alternative to recognizing the author's intent in Scripture is to move to a "reader-response" approach in which modern readers essentially ascribe meaning to the text in terms of the meaning they discover while en-

---

29. See also, e.g., Osborne 1991, 172; Longman 1988, 41.
30. See, e.g., Osborne 1991, 171–73; Morgan 1988, 72–73.
31. See, e.g., Henry 1987, 8–9; Long 1987, 105; Longman 1988, 36; Gunn 1987, 69. Grant Osborne makes this a pivotal issue in his treatment of "Narrative," ch. 6 of *The Hermeneutical Spiral* (1991).

countering the text. For evangelicals this is unacceptable. Grant Osborne (1991, 165) says it this way: "Reader-response criticism is the final stage of a lengthy movement away from the author in the author-text-reader schema, which is at the heart of the hermeneutical debate. Most proponents of this school accept some form of the autonomy theory, that a text becomes autonomous from its author as soon as it is written down. . . . Yet this dichotomy is unnecessary. . . . There is no need to banish the biblical author from his work."[32] David Gunn (1987, 69) concludes, "Reader-oriented theory legitimizes the relativity of different readings and thus threatens to unnerve conventional understandings of biblical authority [in terms of the author's intended meaning]."

Second, evangelicals "are concerned about narrative theology's tendency to deny or severely limit any referential function to literature" (Longman 1988, 37).[33] Although we recognize the difficulty of understanding how human language can speak about God, yet all through Scripture there is an articulated assumption that what is being said about God in fact refers appropriately to who God really is. But, Carl Henry (1987, 13) points out, "narrative hermeneutics removes from the interpretative process any text-transcendent referent and clouds the narrative's relationship to a divine reality not exhausted by literary presence. For Calvin the distinctive of Scripture lay not in a certain literary form or style but above all else in the fact that the transcendent God himself is speaking to us in His Word." Accordingly, an evangelical adaptation of narrative theology will need to carefully preserve the Bible's clear affirmation that the narrative of Scripture is not fiction, nor an extrapolation of a community's particular ideas of God. Rather, it intends to refer realistically to the nature, purpose, and mission of God as disclosed in human history in the midst of God's people. The referential quality of Scripture is not negotiable.

Third, evangelicals are uneasy about the way narrative theology tends to downplay the contextual grounding of the text.[34] Despite its emphasis on the way the text and the faith community have interplayed over time, narrative theology has, unfortunately, tended to ignore the impact of the context of particular communities on the formation and meaning of the text. Yet the text itself clearly arises out of a wide variety of cultural contexts. From a no-

---

32. Osborne, who has done evangelicals a real service in wrestling with this issue thoroughly and carefully, notes with approval that Thiselton offers a way both to preserve the place of the author and to recognize the impact of the reader's viewpoint.

33. See, e.g., Henry 1987; Osborne 1991, 75–81, 366–415. Donald Bloesch and Paul K. Jewett (1991, 25–39) are among those who have wrestled with this matter from an evangelical standpoint. Of course the whole question of the referential nature of language itself is part of the issue here, and has as many implications for areas like the philosophy of science and postmodern epistemology as for theology. See, e.g., MacIntyre 1989a.

34. See, e.g., Finger 1987, 214–19; Gottwald 1987, 64–67; and Henry 1987, 7, 11.

madic, sheepherding family-clan environment in the Pentateuch, the biblical narrative moves progressively to a community of slaves in Egypt, a loose federation of tribes migrating through the desert, an agrarian culture in early Palestine, a city-state culture in David's time, and a culture of refugees and displaced people during the exile. The context of Palestine in Jesus' day is different from anything that had come before, and differs markedly from the church's multiple cultures later as it spread over the face of the Roman Empire. Clearly, the contextual situation of the faith community affects the meaning of the narrative as much as does the nature of the community itself. Yet this element is severely limited in the hermeneutical endeavor of canon criticism and narrative theology.

Admittedly, the evangelical movement has also tended to ignore the unique features of the cultural, sociopolitical, economic, and worldview dynamics of the setting of the text.[35] Evangelicals could probably strengthen their insistence on the grammatico-historical integrity of the hermeneutical task if they took these other elements of the contexts of the biblical narrative more seriously.

Fourth, probably the most common objection that evangelicals have voiced about narrative theology has to do with the issue of the historicity of the text:

> Narrative theology focuses its attention on the literary structure of Scripture. It thus tends to ignore more historical figures. In concentrating on the literary structure of narratives, the simple historical questions—Is this true? Did it really happen?—tend to be ignored. How can we tell the difference between fiction and history? Both possess narrative structures, yet they have a very different historical and theological status. For example, the narrative of the resurrection of Jesus will have one meaning if it is treated as fiction and a quite different meaning if it is treated as history! [McGrath 1991, 24][36]

We saw earlier that one of the strengths of narrative theology is that it offered a way out of the historicism of the nineteenth century. But this can go too far, at least as evangelicals view the situation:

> Representations of biblical history by many narrative theologians leave one with the uneasy sense that their commendable reservations about the historical method are correlated with a view that important aspects of biblical history

---

35. Stanley Grenz 1993, 70–71, mentions this failure. He quotes John Jefferson Davis with apparent approval as reflecting "the opinion of many when he faults the older evangelical approach for not taking 'adequate account of the social context of the theological task and the historicity of all theological reflection.' Davis claims that this approach 'tends to promote a repetition of traditional formulations of biblical doctrine, rather than appropriate recontextualizations of the doctrines in response to changing cultural and historical conditions.'"

36. See also Longman 1988, 35; Henry 1987, 10; Osborne 1991; and Jewett 1991, 145.

belong to a different historical category than the history that contemporary historians investigate. . . . But if reading the biblical accounts narratively requires setting aside narrated occurrences as historical revelation the sense of the accounts is strikingly diluted. . . . Evangelical theism insists that God reveals himself in external history and nature, and supremely in redemptive history. [Henry 1987, 11–12]

Evangelical adaptation of narrative theology will call for traveling the hard road of the historical distance between the horizons of Scripture and of the modern reader—and not take the easy way of eliminating the tension between the horizons by simply ignoring the "historical actuality" of the text itself (Henry 1987, 12).

Fifth, evangelicals are concerned about the concept of truth in narrative theology.[37] Donald Bloesch (1992, 17, 23) centers his critique of narrative theology on this point:

The strength of narrative theology is its focus on Scripture rather than on abstract philosophical concepts. Its weakness lies in its tendency to obscure or downplay the metaphysical implications of the faith. The Bible is accorded a mainly functional rather than ontological significance. . . . The essence of the theological work is not the recital of narrative or the elucidation of religious or generally human experience but the promulgation of a gospel that is both the truth and the power of salvation.

Evangelicals insist that narrative theology be tested against the touchstone of biblical notions of truth—what precisely is its proximity to or distance from Jesus Christ, who is "the way and the truth and the life" (John 14:6)?[38] This is crucial for evangelical mission theology. No matter how

37. See, e.g., Henry 1987, 8, 19; Finger 1987, 217–33; Bloesch 1992, 16; Herion 1988; Wallace 1989, 169–81; Gunn 1987, 69; McGrath 1991, 24; and Osborne 1991.

38. We have here what Paul Hiebert (1994, 122–31) describes as a centered-set approach to doing theology. In this approach categories such as "Christians" and "church" are formed not on the basis of the essential nature of the members, but on the basis of relationship. Hiebert lists four characteristics of centered sets:

First, a centered set is created by defining a center or reference point and the relationship of things to that center. Things related to the center belong to the set, and those not related to the center do not. . . . Second, while centered sets are not created by drawing boundaries, *they do have sharp boundaries* that separate things inside the set from those outside it—between things related to or moving towards the center and those that are not. Centered sets are . . . formed by defining the center and any relationships to it. The boundary then emerges automatically. Things related to the center naturally separate themselves from things that are not. . . . Third, there are two variables intrinsic to centered sets. The first is membership. All members of a set are full members and share fully in its functions. There are no second-class members. The second variable is distance from the center. Some things are far from the center and others near to it, but all are moving toward it. . . . Fourth, centered sets have two types of change inherent in their structure. The first has to do with entry into or exit from the set. Things headed away from the center can turn and move toward it. . . . The second type of change has to do with movement toward or away from the center. Distant members can move toward the center, and those near it can slide back while still headed toward it.

much we work with the narrative, with the nature of the community, with a careful study of the context, and with the flow of the characters, plot, and structure of the narrative—the bottom line for evangelical mission theology is whether the narrative of Scripture has brought us to deeper faith in and allegiance to Jesus Christ our Lord. We are to "test the spirits," in John's words (1 John 2:20–23; 4:1–3). An evangelical adaptation of narrative theology will continually test itself to see if it is centered in Paul's narratively articulated view of truth: "If you confess with your mouth, 'Jesus is Lord,' and believe in your heart that God raised him from the dead, you will be saved" (Rom. 10:9). Evangelical mission theology, then, must be careful in its adaptation of narrative theology—careful to be faithful to the authorial intent of the text as it seeks to refer accurately to God's nature, purpose, and mission through the story of God's interaction with humanity in the midst of God's people in specific contexts in human history, and to communicate truthfully (referentially and realistically) God's will in Jesus Christ for God's people in God's world.

This approach to Scripture involves what David Bosch called "critical hermeneutics" (1991, 22; 1978; 1993).[39] Bosch's critical hermeneutics, as he developed it in *Transforming Mission* (1991), provides a helpful bridge between, on the one hand, the hermeneutical and theological issues we have been facing and, on the other, biblically faithful and culturally appropriate ways in which mission theology may adapt narrative theology for missiological reflection.

Hiebert demonstrates that Hebrew culture was structured as a centered set: it was based on relationship, especially the covenantal relationship of the people of Israel to the God of Abraham, Isaac, and Jacob. He then explains how the concept of "Christian" would be defined in centered-set terms:

> First, Christians would be defined as followers of the Jesus Christ of the Bible, as those who make him the center or Lord of their lives. . . . Second, there would be a clear separation between Christians and non-Christians, between those who are followers of Jesus and those who are not. The emphasis, however, would be on exhorting people to follow Christ, rather than on excluding others to preserve the purity of the set. . . . Third, there would be a recognition of variation among Christians. . . . Fourth, two important types of change would be recognized in centered-set thought. First there is conversion, entering or leaving the set. . . . The second change is movement towards the center, or growth in a relationship. A Christian is not a finished product the moment he or she is converted. Conversion, therefore, is a definite event followed by an ongoing process. Sanctification is not a separate activity, but the process of justification continued throughout life.

Hiebert then proceeds to look at the church and missions as centered sets.

Hiebert's centered-set approach is especially useful as a hermeneutical guide to the reading of Scripture in evangelical mission theology. It provides a means by which we can be firmly and tightly anchored in truth in Jesus Christ, yet simultaneously open to differing worldviews, differing cultural glasses with which to read the Scripture, all within the same world church comprising the disciples of the one center, Jesus Christ.

39. Notice the similarity between Bosch's approach to hermeneutics and what from an anthropological perspective Paul Hiebert has called "critical contextualization."

Areas in Which Narrative Theology
May Contribute to Mission Theology

God's Trinitarian Mission

In what follows we will explore five ways in which narrative theology may be helpful for doing biblical theology of mission. First, it helps us understand that the narrative of Scripture is the story of God's trinitarian mission. When we take seriously the narrative of Scripture, we are impressed with the fact that mission in the Bible is profoundly *God's* mission. As we saw earlier, God's mission happens simultaneously through word and deed. It occurs in multiple horizons because, although God is always the same, his self-disclosure breaks into multiple contexts at different times. The more we immerse ourselves, therefore, in the word-deed narrative of God's mission as articulated in Scripture, the more clearly we will understand the way we can participate in God's mission.

Further, the narrative of Scripture demonstrates the way God the Father, God the Son, and God the Holy Spirit works through human instruments for the redemption of humanity. In fact, the narrative unity itself profoundly integrates the way in which the threeness of our trinitarian perception of God operates in oneness in God's self-disclosure in the midst of humanity. Thus Jesus Christ's mission is always in the power of the Spirit, and has to do with the announcing of the coming of the kingdom of God in Jesus (Luke 4). When we have seen Jesus Christ, we have seen the Father (John 14). And this same Jesus promised to send the Holy Spirit (John 16:5–15). By the work of the Holy Spirit the disciples learned *agapē* love; when they demonstrated this self-giving love for one another, Jesus and the Father came to be in their midst (John 14:23) in such a way that others knew that they were Jesus' disciples (John 13:35). The purpose was "that the world may believe" that the Father had sent Jesus (John 17:21). Thus, in John's words, "these [words about the deeds of Jesus] are written that you may believe that Jesus is the Christ, the Son of God, and that by believing you may have life in his name" (John 20:31). The trinitarian nature of God's mission bridges the multiple horizons of the biblical narrative—and, further, spans the gulf between the horizon of Scripture and our own.

God's Wholistic Mission

Second, narrative theology gives us a way to speak about God that bridges and integrates both propositional, left-brain (so-called objective) language about God and experiential, right-brain (so-called subjective) language about God so that being, knowing, and doing come together in real life. God's mission involves the radical transformation of all aspects of one's life and being. And, by the same token, participation in God's mission involves all aspects of the life of God's people, the human instruments of that mission.

Here narrative theology helps us integrate a number of arenas of human existence and thought that have traditionally been separated. Diverse writers have demonstrated the wholistic potential of narrative in terms of, for example, constructing local theologies (Schreiter 1985), fostering religious education (Groome 1991), and transmitting values (Higgins 1992). What is striking despite these disparate emphases is the agreement with regard to the way narrative can bring a wholeness to our understanding of the nature of the human person—and with regard to the way faith involves a narrative process that transforms all aspects of human life.

If narrative theology can help us see God's mission as oriented to whole persons in their humanness, then it may be that narrative theology can offer us a tool to bridge the evangelism–social action dichotomy that has plagued evangelical missiology for most of the twentieth century. The narrative approach to integrating word and deed that we noted earlier may help us develop a mission theology that does not split evangelism and social action. That word-deed conjunction can be brought to bear upon our missiology only if we discover ways by which narrative can emphasize that the totality of the human person is impacted by God's mission and then in turn participates in the narrative of God's mission.

God's Universal Mission

A third contribution that narrative theology may make to evangelical mission theology involves the matter of temporal and cultural universality. Narrative helps us bridge the issues in the text with the matters of life in today's contexts. Chapter 1 ended with the suggestion that viewing Scripture as a tapestry may offer us a way to link the deep-level themes of Scripture with similar themes in the worldview of the new missionary contexts in which we find ourselves. Les Henson (1992a, 1992b) explains how narrative theology can link Scripture's themes to specific contextual themes. As we become participants in the narrative of Scripture and are encountered by God in and through that biblical narrative, we begin to discover that this same God discloses himself in our time and in our contexts today. This is not to suggest an open canon, since in our case it is not a matter of revelation but of illumination. "History" becomes "his story," and, being the same yesterday, today, and forever, he therefore may impact my life in such a way that "his story" becomes "my story in him." I come to find that my own narrative is located "in Christ," to use Paul's well-known phrase.

Thus narrative theology may offer us a way to preserve a close connection between the particularity of God's covenantal relation (always specific to particular times, peoples, cultures) and the universality of Christ's lordship over all times, peoples, and cultures. Such narrative is both culturally particular and cross-culturally universal. This is the gospel that is infinitely "translatable," to use Lamin Sanneh's phrase (1989). In narrative theology we do not stress so much the cultural distance as affirm that despite cultural distance and multiple horizons there is a profound proximity of all cultures in Jesus Christ, in whom "we live and move and have our being" (Acts 17:28).

God's Corporate Mission

Fourth, narrative theology may help us discover a way to bring together text, context, and faith community. It has been common for theology to stress one of these three elements to the detriment of the other two. Yet when God discloses himself, a simultaneous interaction of the three is invariably involved. Narrative theology may be able to help us think in the highly integrative and multidisciplinary ways that are essential to good missiology. And one of the most profound integrations that we need to comprehend is the intertwining realities of text, faith community, and context.

God's Contextual Mission

Finally, narrative theology may provide us the images, pictures, metaphors, and stories that are necessary for rounding out the propositional, textual, and historical aspects of today's global theological conversations in missiology. Now that the church circles the globe, and the center of gravity of Christianity has shifted to Africa, Asia, Latin America, and Oceania, we need new tools for doing mission theology in the midst of multiple contexts around the globe. We are in danger of atomizing the gospel into plural theologies, forgetting that "there is one body and one Spirit . . . one Lord, one faith, one baptism; one God and Father of all, who is over all and through all and in all" (Eph. 4:4–6). Multiple contexts do not necessarily entail multiple narratives or multiple theologies. Rather, narrative theology may offer us a means of affirming that while diverse cultures may express their understanding of God in a variety of ways, at the same time they participate in one narrative: the story that "God so loved the world, that he gave his only begotten Son" (John 3:16 KJV).

In the ancient cultures of Africa, Asia, and Latin America, wisdom about the divine has often been couched in proverbs, sayings, fables, and stories. These forms convey ancient corporate understanding on the part of a particular culture with regard to some of its most profound values. A narrative approach to Scripture may provide us with cultural bridges of both form and content that can connect the ancient wisdom of Scripture with the wisdom found in the proverbs, sayings, and stories of those ancient cultures. In order to do so, narrative theology must contribute a range of possibilities in terms of theological method. Narrative theology is especially helpful in bringing together—in the context of life—the various images, pictures, metaphors, and stories that could offer us a new global conversation in the midst of multiple contexts. In his work on *Images of the Church in the New Testament* (1960) Paul Minear spoke of the role of images in bringing about not only a descriptive but a normative, visionary, motivational self-consciousness on the part of the faith community. Such images become amazingly powerful motivators for mission when they form a part of the narrative story of the faith community as it participates in God's mission in God's world.

The story of God's dealings with humankind is not finished. And the narrative of the participation of God's people in God's mission in God's world is also incomplete. In a profound sense, the acts of the Holy Spirit in mission to the world through the church are still going on—until Jesus Christ comes again. Narrative theology may provide us an ongoing tool whereby we may explore more deeply the wonderful mystery "that through the gospel the Gentiles are heirs together with Israel, members together of one body, and sharers together in the promise in Christ Jesus" (Eph. 3:6). The ancient story becomes our story, and that of those who come after us. The story of God's mission involves all "those who will believe in [Jesus Christ] through [the disciples'] message" (John 17:20). So the narrative continues in this interim time between Christ's ascension and his return. It is the story of *God's* mission. And we are a part of the story!

Part 2

Mission Theology
in Context

3

The New Covenant: Mission Theology in Context

The thesis of this chapter is that the covenant of grace in the Old and New Testaments provides clues for our understanding how God's revealed hiddenness may be expressed in new (*kainos*) ways that are different from, yet in continuity with, all past moments of God's self-disclosure throughout human history. This in turn offers us a new epistemological paradigm of contextualization that can inform both the content and the method of contextualizing the gospel in today's world.

The misfit of the gospel with human cultures has been a perennial problem faced by the church in its mission. The apostle Paul referred to God's hidden self-disclosure both in terms of the created order and in relation to God's special revelation in Jesus Christ (Rom. 1:20; 11:33–34). Revealed hiddenness— this is the paradox of divine self-disclosure in human consciousness and the most difficult part of contextualization theory.[1] The very fact that we know God through *faith* should tell us that we do not know all there is to know about God. In fact, we see only as through a mirror, darkly (1 Cor. 13:12). Texts like Job 36:26; Psalm 139:6; Acts 14:16–17; Romans 11:25, 33–36; 1 Corinthians 2:7; Ephesians 3:3; Colossians 1:15, 26; 1 Timothy 1:17; 3:16; and Revelation 10:7 emphasize the mystery and unknowability of God.

---

1. See Karl Barth, *Church Dogmatics* (1936–69), 2.1:184. Barth devotes an entire section (27; pp. 179–254) of this volume to discussion of the knowledge of God, which he divides into two parts: the *terminus a quo* (the point from which our knowledge proceeds by the grace of God's self-revelation to us) and the *terminus ad quem* (the point to which our knowledge conduces—faith in the hidden God). It is important to compare this section of Barth's *Dogmatics* with 1.2, section 17 (pp. 280–361); 4.1:478–501; and 4.3:135–65.

Many theologians have affirmed this basic characteristic of God's revelation.[2] So the first contextualization of the gospel involves the mystery of God's self-revelation in human cultures.

A second and more complex sense of the misfit of the gospel with human culture is the mismatch that came as a result of the Christian missionary movement.[3] As the gospel crossed cultural barriers over several centuries, the faith assertions of Christendom did not seem to fit the new cultures encountered with the gospel. So a progression of attempted solutions were suggested, with an accompanying succession of words like "persuasion," "Christianization," "compellere," "accommodation," "adaptation," "fulfilment," "syncretism," "indigenization," "transformation," "enculturation," and "dialogue."[4] A recent word, "contextualization," involves some difficult theological issues like incarnation, revelation, truth, divine-human interaction, and the shape of corporate religious experience. Contextualization takes seriously the difference between gospel and culture, and accepts the fact that "the gospel always stands in divine judgement on human culture" (Hiebert 1979a, 63).

Models of Contextualization

Contextualization theory has generated a number of models for explaining how the gospel may take shape in various cultural contexts. Krikor Haleblian (1983), for example, points out the difference between the "translation model" of contextualization exemplified by Charles Kraft's work, and the "semiotic model" developed by Robert Schreiter.[5] Stephen Bevans (1985) describes six distinct models of contextual theology: the anthropological, translation, praxis, synthetic, semiotic, and transcendental. David Hesselgrave (1984, 694) speaks of the impact of contextualization on "the translation of the Scriptures, the interpretation of the Scriptures, the communication of the gospel, the instruction of believers, the incarnation of truth in the individual and corporate lives of the believers, and the systematization of the Christian faith (theologizing)."[6] For our purposes we will distinguish four

2. See, e.g., Louis Berkhof 1932, 1:17–19; Berkouwer 1955, 285–332; Brunner 1949, 117–36; and Hendrikus Berkhof 1979, 41–56, 61–65.

3. Richard Niebuhr highlighted this matter in his famous book *Christ and Culture* (1951). Charles Kraft took a major step forward beyond Niebuhr in *Christianity in Culture* (1979).

4. Each of these words represents a particular approach to relating the gospel to a new culture. Each also entails a particular understanding of God's self-disclosure in the midst of human cultures and the ability or inability of those cultures to "know" God in the context of their own cultural forms.

5. Haleblian is referring primarily to Kraft 1979 and Schreiter 1985. See also Haleblian 1982; Gilliland and Huffard, n.d.

6. Hesselgrave goes on to discuss at length four epistemic preunderstandings or models of revelational epistemology: the demythologization of Rudolf Bultmann and Paul Tillich, the

major models of contextualization on the basis of their primary purposes: communication, cultural relevance, liberation, and interfaith dialogue.[7] We will then suggest a fifth.

Contextualization as Communication

The first approach to incarnational contextualization arose with the advent of the journal *Practical Anthropology* and involved a combination of linguistics, translation, and communication theory (names to mention here would include William Wonderly, William Smalley, Louis Luzbetak, Marvin Mayers, Eugene Nida, Jacob Loewen, and Charles Kraft).[8] The view of contextualization as a process of communication assumes that the communicators know and understand the message, but may not know nor fully understand either the receptors or the means by which the receptors might comprehend that message and gain a "dynamically equivalent" understanding.[9] Luzbetak (1981) points out that the communicational model is particularly important when the gospel is first taking root in a new culture. Communicational contextualization demonstrates a serious and careful cultural sensitivity in relation to the receptors, while also seeking to be true to the sender's understanding of the gospel.

Contextualization as Cultural Relevance

A second model of incarnational contextualization has to do with the cultural relevance of the church once the gospel has taken root in foreign soil. This was a primary concern of Shoki Coe and others involved in the Theological Education Fund. The matter of cultural relevance is also central to Robert Schreiter's (1985) triple dialectic of "constructing local theologies,"

---

dynamic equivalence of Charles Kraft, the providential preservation of Edward Hills, and the relational centers of Bruce Nicholls. See also Hesselgrave and Rommen 1989, 128–43.

7. For an excellent review of the literature on the various models within the incarnational approach see Conn 1977.

8. A handy compilation of some of these early writings may be found in William Smalley 1978.

9. In a discussion concerning contextualization, David Hesselgrave (1988, 161) bases his own perspective on the communication model, but feels that Charles Kraft has gone too far. Hesselgrave suggests an "apostolic contextualization" which goes further than Bruce Nicholl's strictly verbal forms, but leaves the basic biblical message intact. See also Hesselgrave and Rommen 1989, 144–96. Note the predominance of communication theory, communicational language, and linguistics/translation issues in the Willowbank Report and the accompanying papers in Coote and Stott 1980. Further background may be found in Nida 1960, 33–61; McCurry 1976; and Nicholls 1975. The Lausanne movement also defines contextualization in strongly communicational terms. (See Douglas 1975, 1226–27.) Bruce Fleming (1980, 13) distinguishes between the supracultural, transcultural, and cultural aspects of gospel contextualization; cf. Buswell 1978.

which involves a movement between gospel, church, and local culture. The broad range of theological positions possible within the cultural-relevance model is brought out by Bong Rin Ro (1984), who speaks of four types of contextualization in Asia: "syncretism, accommodation, situation theology, and biblically-oriented Asian theology." Dean Gilliland (1989, 52) suggests four basic questions: What is the general (culture-specific, contextual) background? What are the presenting problems? What theological questions arise? What appropriate directions should the theology take?

Contextualization as Liberation

Liberation theology in Latin America is a third type of incarnational contextualization, but in this case the relevance of the gospel is spelled out primarily in terms of sociopolitical and economic categories.[10] The hermeneutical questions are different from those found in the first two models, but even here the basic gospel is assumed to be understood. The economic, social, and political realities of the context, however, call for new texts to be examined, new affirmations made, and new kingdom ethics lived out.[11]

Contextualization as Interfaith Dialogue

A fourth model arises out of the phenomenology of experiential faith and the common search for the holy. Basing its theology primarily on the concepts of creation and humanity, this model developed in relation to interfaith dialogue as it spilled over into contextualization. Here the Christian faith was viewed as one of the world's religions standing beside other world religions. In the context of cultures where Islam, Hinduism, Buddhism, and other religions were accepted, Christians were to compare their experiences of faith with those of people of other faiths. In an increasingly pluralistic world many sought, rightly, to demonstrate their acceptance of radically diverse cultural forms. But the growing awareness of cultural diversity sometimes contributed to the acceptance of religious relativity as well.[12]

The relativizing of faith as a product of the diversity of cultures is an idea with a long history. In our century this perspective received its major impetus from William Hocking (1932) and the Laymen's Foreign Missions Inquiry

10. The imposition of the Spanish, Portuguese, and (to a lesser extent) French cultures upon a myriad of local cultures has created a multitude of cultural layers in the warp and woof of Latin American society, resulting in a context where issues like power sharing, economic equity, and social justice become crucial for bringing about change in Latin America.

11. For a recent example of a socioeconomic contextualization of the gospel in the North American context see Lowell Noble 1987. See also Luzbetak 1981, 53.

12. See Visser 't Hooft 1963, 85–86. The subsequent discussion of "Christian Universalism" (96–103) is very helpful. See also Neill 1964, 455–56; Bosch 1980, 161–64; and Gerald H. Anderson 1988, 106–8.

entitled *Re-Thinking Missions*. More recently Wilfred Cantwell Smith, Paul Knitter, John Cobb, John Hick, and Raimundo Panikkar are among those following a similar path, although seeking major refinements and redefinitions of the thinking of the 1930s.[13]

Contextualization as Knowing God in Context

Is it time for the contextualization debate to move further in the process of understanding the gospel in culture? Might there not be another major model from which to understand the task of contextualization? The remainder of this chapter will examine the biblical theology of covenant as a model for knowing God in multiple cultural contexts.[14]

The New Covenant:
A Biblical Model for Knowing God in Context

Nowhere is the mystery of God's revealed hiddenness more poignantly expressed than in the conceptual framework of a biblical theology of the covenant. We will not deal here with the extensive and complicated aspects of biblical theology of the covenant. Nor are we looking at covenantal theology as it developed in the Reformed tradition during the two centuries after the Protestant Reformation. Rather, we are interested in using the newer methods of exegesis which examine the text as it has been received, viewing it as a narrative articulation of the theological perspectives of the people of God throughout the centuries. Our major concern is the covenantal perspective as a possible paradigm for knowing God's hidden revelation in diverse contexts.

Harvie Conn is among those who have called for a covenantal perspective as a new theological center for a contextual hermeneutic:[15]

> Emerging from the debate [surrounding evangelical hermeneutics] is an evangelical call to see theology as the discipled (not simply disciplined) reflection/action of "knowing God." This process may be called contextual hermeneutic, the covenant conscientization of the whole people of God to the hermeneutical obligations of the gospel in their culture. . . . The core of this contextual herme-

---

13. See, e.g., Knitter 1985; and Hick and Knitter 1988. In a review of the latter work Carl Braaten (1988, 136) states, "The essence of this pluralistic theology is not as new as these authors imagine. None of the leading ideas—relativism, mystery, justice—as the core of the religious enterprise is new." An enlightening discussion of this matter can be found in the *Journal of Ecumenical Studies* 24.1 (Winter 1987). Cf. Verkuyl 1986. The efforts of people like Phil Parshall, Johannes Verkuyl, Kenneth Cragg, and J. Dudley Woodberry in relation to Islam, for example, represent approaches which differ markedly from those of Smith, Knitter, and Hick.

14. Harvie Conn's first allusions to this concept (1978) are further refined in 1984, 211–60.

15. See, e.g., Conn 1978; Glasser 1979b, 403–9; Archer 1979; and Lind 1982.

neutic is the recovery of the covenant dimension of doing theology—a dimension modeled most beautifully by John Calvin's expository method, of *theologia pietatis*.[16]

The Historical Development of the Covenant

Covenant refers to the actions of God in history in relationship with his people through time and space, actions which reveal the eternal God's hiddenness. But this presents a real problem, as Martin Noth (1963, 77) has explained: "In the biblical witness we deal with a revelation of God which has occurred within history while, after all, God cannot be limited to history and time." To soften the dialectic between God's eternality and humanity's temporalness, Noth speaks of Israel's continual "re-presentation" and constant reenactment, that is, the reparticipation of the people of God in both past and future events where God breaks into history in relationship with his people. "As in all history, so this history is especially involved in the tension between the course of time and the presence of God which is not bound by time, between the 'mediateness' and the 'immediateness' of God, of which Karl Barth speaks in discussing God's unending creations. 'Re-presentation' is founded on this—that God and his action are always present, while man in his inevitable temporality cannot grasp this present-ness except by 're-presenting' the action of God over and over again in his worship" (Noth 1963, 85).

The Covenant: Same Meaning, Many Forms

In the covenant we find a historically conditioned (or better, a historically contextualized) relationship between an eternally present God and a temporally specific humanity. The historicity of the covenantal forms also means a tremendous variety of cultural, political, and social contexts in which the covenant may be found. Thus in the covenant we have essentially the same relationship at all times and in all places, and yet one which takes on radically different forms in each time and place. Referring to this relationship as "the covenant of grace," Herman Bavinck (1956, 274–76) emphasized its eternal sameness:

> The covenant of grace is everywhere and at all times one in essence, but always manifests itself in new forms and goes through differing dispensations. . . . God remains the first and the last in all the dispensations of the covenant of grace, whether of Noah, Abraham, Israel, or the New Testament church. Promise, gift, grace are and remain the content of it. . . . The one great, all-inclusive promise of the covenant of grace is: "I will be thy God, and the God of thy people." A single straight line runs from the mother-promise of Gen. 3:15 to the apostolic blessing of 2 Cor. 13:13. . . . It is always the same Gospel (Rom. 1:1–

16. Conn 1978, 43; see also Conn 1984, 229–34; Hohensee 1980, 131–45.

2 and Gal. 3:8), the same Christ (John 14:6 and Acts 4:12), the same faith (Acts 15:11 and Rom. 4:11), and always confers the same benefits of forgiveness and eternal life (Acts 10:43 and Rom. 4:3).[17]

Bible scholars like Norman Gottwald (1979, 95),[18] Lucien Cerfaux (1959, 31–32),[19] and Gerhard von Rad (1962, 1:129–33)[20] have emphasized the continuity of the covenant concept throughout Israel's history. Although we may not subsume the great diversity of scriptural perspectives as tightly within the covenant concept as Walther Eichrodt (1961; 1967) did, it is impossible to understand the continuity and meaning of God's revelation to humanity apart from the concept of the covenant. The most fundamental and essential meaning of the covenant could be stated, "I will be your God, and you shall be my people."[21] The expressions of this timeless relationship in various epochs had strikingly similar structural elements:

1. There is a recitation of God's mighty acts.
2. The Word of God spells out the covenantal relationship.
3. Promises are associated with the covenantal relationship.
4. Worship and sacrifice are carried out by the people.
5. YHWH gives a physical sign or symbol of the covenant. [22]

Grace, revelation, law, cultic practice, communal self-identity, corporate response, and the meaning and goal of YHWH's acts in history are all incorporated and given expression in this covenantal relationship. Quoting W. van der Merwe, John Kromminga summarizes, "The covenant is to be understood as that relationship between God and creature, ordained in eternity, instituted in history and directed to consummation" (Dekker 85, 1).

17. For a recent similar perspective see Klooster 1988, 150.

18. Gottwald points to Exod. 19:3–8; 24:1–11; 34:2–28; Deut. 26:16–19; and Josh. 24 as examples of "theophanic and covenant texts [which were] included as sources for premonarchic Israel because they contain reflections of how the relations between Yahweh and Israel were conceived in early times" (1979, 57). See also Gottwald 1959, 102–44; and Newsome 1984, 40–43, 57, 120–23, 210.

19. See also Jocz 1968, 283. Fred Klooster 1988, 149, calls the covenant "basically an oath-bound promissory relation." See also Watson 1986.

20. Von Rad points to Deut. 26:5–10 as an example of the historical summaries which articulate this unified-covenant perspective. See also Patrick 1987.

21. Compare, e.g., Gen. 17; Exod. 19, 24, 29, 34; Lev. 26; Josh. 24; 1 Sam. 12; 2 Sam. 23:5; Ps. 89; Jer. 31; 2 Cor. 6; and Rev. 21. See Roth and Ruether 1978, 2–3; Jocz 1968, 23–31; and Cerfaux 1959, 31–32. On the universal significance of Israel's covenantal theology see Van Engen 1981, 116–60 (the accompanying footnotes give bibliographical support). See also *diathēkē* in Kittel and Friedrich 1964–76, 2:106–34; Bright 1959, 128–60, 356–59, 440–42; and Hendrikus Berkhof 1979, 229–30, 339–40, 423–26.

22. For the details concerning the structural forms of the covenant see Van Engen 1981, 123–24; Hayes 1979, 195–97, 303–4.

And yet we are all aware of the radically distinct contexts in which this timeless relationship has been expressed. This incredible diversity can be illustrated by summarizing the covenant in at least six contextual manifestations:

1. *Adam:* The covenant and the ultimate victory over evil (Gen. 3:9–21).
2. *Noah:* The covenant and the preservation of all living things (Gen. 6:17–22; 9:1–17).
3. *Abraham:* The covenant and the election of Abraham's seed for the sake of the nations (Gen. 12, 15, 17—we must also include here the re-presentation of that covenantal relationship in both an inherited and a personal way with Isaac [Gen. 26:3–5] and with Jacob [Gen. 28:13–15]).
4. *Moses:* The covenant and the law—a nation formed (Exod. 2:24; 19:4–6; 20:1–17; 24:1–10; 25:10–22; 31:16–17; 32; 34:1–10; 40:18–38; Lev. 26:6–12; Num. 14; Deut. 9:15). In Exodus 32 and Numbers 14 God offers to make from Moses "a great nation," each time specifically in reference to promises made earlier to Abraham. (With Joshua, the covenant is related to possession of the Promised Land, but intimately connected with Moses and the exodus [Deut. 29–30; Josh. 5, 24].)
5. *David:* The covenant and the Davidic reign—a kingdom (1 Chron. 16:15–17; 17 [parallels in 2 Sam. 7; 23:5]; Ps. 89:34–37; 105:8; 106:45; 111:5; Isa. 42:6; 55:3; 59:21).
6. *Jesus Christ:* The covenant and the Holy Spirit, redemption wrought once-for-all, the church, the kingdom come and coming (Isa. 54:10; 55:3; Jer. 4:3–4; 31:31; 32:36–41; Ezek. 34:24; Matt. 3:11, 16; 26:28; Mark 14:24; Luke 22:20; Acts 3:25–26; Rom. 11:27; 1 Cor. 11:25; 2 Cor. 3:6; Heb. 7:22; 8:6, 8; 9:15, 19–20; 10:12, 29; 13:20–21).[23]

The Covenant: Same Meaning, Fuller Knowledge

Thus we see the continuity of the covenantal relationship of God with God's children at all times and in all contexts. But there is also something wonderfully progressive about this history which forces us to accept the fact that what Adam, Noah, Abraham, Moses, and David knew of God's nature and revealed will was incomplete. Precisely because we see the continuity of progressive revelation, we also see the deeper, fuller, and more complete self-revelation of God down through history. This seems to be the intention of the writer of Hebrews when he says, "In the past God spoke to our fore-fathers through the prophets at many times and in various ways, but in these

23. See Van Engen 1985, 41–51; *NIV Study Bible* (Grand Rapids: Zondervan, 1985), 19; G. Ernest Wright 1950, 54–59; and Rowley 1955, chs. 2–4.

last days he has spoken to us by his Son, whom he appointed heir of all things, and through whom he made the universe" (1:1–2).

Whether it was an understanding of God's nature, God's redemptive activity, God's providential care of the world, God's love for all the nations, or God's ultimate plan for the whole of creation—in each manifestation of the covenant there was something more deeply revealed, something more fully understood. Here is the crux of the matter. Within a fundamental sameness of the relationship, each subsequent historical-cultural-political context revealed something more concerning God's nature and relationship with his people.

The Covenant: A Series of Hermeneutical Circles

One way we may comprehend the progressive nature of covenantal revelation is to view it as a series of hermeneutical circles which together form a hermeneutical spiral through time. (Cf. Osborne 1991.) The concept of the hermeneutical circle is not new, but has received a renewed emphasis in the praxeological methodology of Latin American theologians of liberation (e.g., Segundo 1976, 8; Míguez-Bonino 1975). The methodology is also proving helpful to many who are not Latin American theologians (Bosch 1983, 493, 496).

With regard to our knowledge of God, the covenant gives us an opportunity to understand how each hermeneutical circle served in each context to reveal something deeper and fuller about God's nature. Paul referred to this as "the mystery made known to me by revelation" (Eph. 3:3). What could have been more discontinuous, more mysterious for Paul than the salvation of the Gentiles? Yet precisely in radically new historical contexts (through Jesus Christ, after Pentecost, in the church, and by the spread of the gospel throughout the Gentile world) Paul saw God's revelatory purposes taking on deeper and fuller meaning. God's "intent was that now, through the church, the manifold wisdom of God should be made known to the rulers and authorities in the heavenly realms, according to his eternal purpose which he accomplished in Christ Jesus our Lord" (Eph. 3:10–11).

The various historically contextualized manifestations of the covenant can be represented as a hermeneutical spiral through which over time the eternal God becomes progressively more completely known to God's people (see figure 11). Of course, God's self-revelation never really gets beyond the most basic issues of God's triumph over evil (Adam), and God's election of a people for service as a blessing to all the nations (Abraham) (see 1 Pet. 2). God's law is never abrogated, nor are the promises of David's eternal reign ever annulled. And yet in each new context something deeper and fuller is revealed. Paul's statement that as in Adam all died, so in Christ all will be made alive (Rom. 5:12–21), exemplifies this discontinuous continuity.

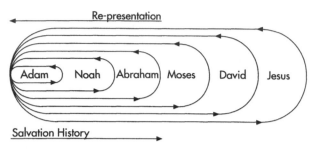

Figure 11
Re-presentation in Salvation History

The Revelational Contextualization of the Covenant

Once we have seen God's covenantal revelation as a continuous progression through time, we need to go back and look at it contextually. Not only are there an expansion and a deepening across time, but in each context where the covenant is manifested, it is shaped precisely for that particular context.

The Covenant as Historical Contextualization

Consider the first humans, created in God's image, living in perfection in Eden yet with the possibility of disobeying their creator. The crucial question in that particular context is whether they will continue to obey or, on the other hand, allow evil to enter the world. With their fall comes an even more urgent question—will evil triumph over God's good? The covenantal formula in Genesis 3:15 clearly speaks to this issue, though the promise is darkened by the dire consequences of Adam and Eve's sin for themselves and their children.

In the case of Noah the context is the increasing sinfulness of humanity chronicled in Genesis 4–6. Such was the distance of the created ones from their creator that God "was grieved that he had made man on the earth, and his heart was filled with pain" (Gen. 6:6). Here the crucial question has to do with the continued existence of all living things, including humanity whose sin has tainted all creation. God's revelation in this context contains all the basic elements of the covenantal formula (recitation of God's acts, command, promises, worship/sacrifice, and a sign), and conveys a specific knowledge of God for the particular situation.

The contextualization of God's covenantal revelation followed a similar pattern in relation to Moses, David, and Jesus Christ. The particularity of each context led to revelation of a deeper and fuller knowledge about God's hiddenness; each context called forth a degree and content of revelation hitherto unknown.

Development from Covenant to New Covenant

The combination of the particularity of revelational contexts and the action of God over time seems to be the background of the biblical theology of the "new covenant," articulated in the prophets and later in the New Testament. This development of the covenant idea is linked to the terminology in the Septuagint (Kittel and Friedrich 1964–76, 2:126–27).

As we move from the perspectives of Isaiah and Jeremiah through the intertestamental period into the age of the New Testament, we see an intricate interweaving of two terms that are applied to the concept of covenant: *kainos* and *neos*. And precisely in the difference between these two terms we may find an approach to epistemological contextualization which both preserves the continuity of God's revelation and deepens the knowledge of God's hiddenness as revealed in each new context.

The Neos Covenant and Discontinuity

"Of the two most common words for 'new' since the classical period, namely, *neos* and *kainos*, the former signifies 'what was not there before,' 'what has only just arisen or appeared,' the latter 'what is new and distinctive' as compared with other things. *Neos* is new in time and origin, i.e., young, with a suggestion of immaturity or of lack of respect for the old. *Kainos* is what is new in nature, different from the usual, impressive, better than the old, superior in value or attraction" (Kittel and Friedrich 1964–76, 3:447).

Neos represents the idea of radical discontinuity which we normally associate with the English concept of "new." But it is quite rare in the New Testament (Matt. 9:17; Luke 5:39; 1 Cor. 5:7; Eph. 4:23; Col. 3:10; and Heb. 12:24).[24] In each case the emphasis is on a complete break with the past, something totally disjunctive in kind from that which went before. Only in Hebrews 12:24 is the term used specifically concerning the covenant.

With the New Testament comes a radical break between the "law and the prophets" and the complete, unique revelation of God in Jesus Christ. Paul emphasizes this radical discontinuity when he speaks of the covenant in legal terms as being like a marriage pact which is canceled upon the death of one of the parties (Rom. 6:1–7:6). The same disjunction is emphasized by Paul in 2 Corinthians 3:6–18, contrasting the former (written) covenant with the new covenant (of the Spirit) (Kittel and Friedrich 1964–76, 4:896–901). Earl Ellis (1978, 166–67) speaks of this discontinuity in terms of the "typological" use which the New Testament writers made of the Old Testament, marking the consummation of the old covenant in Jesus Christ.[25]

The uniqueness of the Christ event has a two-pronged significance for contextualization. In terms of the past it affirms the radically different nature

---

24. Other texts where the term means "young, younger," do not relate to this discussion.
25. See also Gottwald 1959, 370–71; Geerhardus Vos 1979, 23–26; Van Ruler 1971, 75–79.

| Adam | Noah | Abraham | Moses | David | Jesus |

Figure 12
A Series of Biblical Contexts

of the new age inaugurated in Jesus Christ, the age of the Spirit, the church, grace through faith, and circumcision of the heart. But this discontinuity also impacts the future. The sequence of Adam, Noah, Abraham, Moses, David, Jesus Christ in fact stops with Jesus Christ, for there is nothing more to be fulfilled, or added, or completed. In terms of the contextualization of the gospel we may never go beyond the Christ event; we may never add to it another gospel (in Paul's terminology) or take away from it the completeness found in Jesus Christ. To do so is anathema (Rev. 22:18–19). This forces us to look again at the covenant.

The Kainos Covenant and Continuity

The predominant idea of "new" in the New Testament is represented by *kainos*, and speaks of continuity in the midst of change (see Mark 16:17; Luke 22:20; John 13:34; Rom. 6:4; 1 Cor. 11:25; 2 Cor. 3:6; 5:17; Gal. 6:15; Eph. 4:24; Heb. 8:8; 9:15; 2 Pet. 3:13; 1 John 2:8; Rev. 2:17; 3:12; 21:1) (Kittel and Friedrich 1964–76, 2:130–32, 3:447–54).

Jesus used this concept in the context of his farewell speech (Hendrikus Berkhof 1979, 302–3). In reference to the coming of a radically different age, Jesus issued a "new" *(kainos)* commandment: to love (John 13:34). But this was not really new. The disciples of Jesus understood *agapē* as simply an enrichment of that love which had been enjoined upon the people of God from very early times. Love for neighbor "is found already in the Old Testament (Lev. 19:18; Prov. 20:22; 24:29). In fact, love for God and for neighbor is the summary of the law (Mk. 12:29–31)" (Hendriksen 1954, 2:253).[26] C. H. Dodd (1953, 405) pointed to the matter of continuity in John's teaching on love. But Jesus called it a *kainos* commandment. C. K. Barrett (1955, 452) explains, "The commandment is new in that it corresponds to the command that regulates the relation between Jesus and the Father (Jn. 10:18; 12:49f.; 15:10); the love of the disciples for one another is not merely edifying, it reveals the Father and the Son." This is the revolutionary factor being injected by Jesus. "His followers are to reproduce, in their mutual love, the love which the Father showed in sending the Son, the love which the Son showed in laying down his life" (Dodd 1953, 405). This ancient command to love is now given to those followers who will live "between the times," after Jesus' going and before Jesus' coming again. The concept is the same as that found in Deuteronomy, but now fuller, deeper, and more significantly revelatory of

26. See also C. K. Barrett 1955, 451.

Adam	Noah	Abraham	Moses	David	Jesus
1ᶜ	2ᶜ	3ᶜ	4ᶜ	5ᶜ	6ᶜ

Figure 13
A Series of Covenantal Revelations in Context

God's nature and will than ever before. It is a *kainos* commandment giving living expression to the *kainos* covenant, sealed in Jesus' shed blood, and signified in the cup of communion (Luke 22:20; 1 Cor. 11:25).

The covenant is always the same, but it faces ever-new contexts. This perspective has been referred to as "the pilgrim principle" (Bosch 1983, 501, quoting Walls 1981, 45)—in each context something deeper and fuller is revealed, yet only in relation to and in continuity with what has gone before. Donald Senior and Carroll Stuhlmueller (1983, 20–21) emphasized this with regard to the "new" covenant in Hebrews. Richard De Ridder (1975, 176–79) pointed to the impact of this concept on our understanding of the Great Commission (Matt. 28:18–20).

This constantly deepening perspective of the new covenant in pilgrim continuity with the old might be represented as a series of contexts labeled Adam, Noah, Abraham, Moses, David, and Jesus (see figure 12). To this representation we could add the covenantal revelation of God in each context (1^C, 2^C, 3^C, 4^C, 5^C, and 6^C in figure 13). We might then understand the *kainos* covenant in Jesus Christ to be related to the earlier contexts by a quasi-mathematical formula depicting a relationship that is not additive or cumulative, but that entails a deepening understanding and a greater fulfilment of that which was always there previously (see figure 14). What appears below the line qualifies and gives meaning to what is above the line. That which is above the line is (1) revelation given at a particular time in a specific context and (2) a function, extension, deepening, and fulfilment of what appears below the line. Taken together, they represent the totality of God's revealed hiddenness in the fullness of time; they have, as Hebrews 1:2 says, been completed in Jesus Christ "in these last days."

The New Covenant: A Model of Contextualization Today

Now we can return to our original problem. The square peg of God's revelation does not fit well within the round holes of today's cultures. Clearly if

$$\frac{6^c}{1^c/2^c/3^c/4^c/5^c} = (\text{God's revealed hiddenness})$$

Figure 14
Revelation in Jesus Christ

in each culture we force the gospel to take on radically different content (in the sense of *neos*), we are being unfaithful to the continuity of God's revelation in Jesus Christ.[27] On the other hand, to force the round holes of our world cultures to configure themselves to a specific understanding of the gospel will violate the uniqueness and richness of the contexts in which God wishes to be known.[28] For God can be known only in the here and now of our historically and culturally conditioned existence. As Roger Haight (1985, 8–9, 56) reminds us, "Revelation has always been considered by Christians as the word of God. But that word of God must 'appear' in human consciousness to be heard."[29] In the midst of such a complex dialectic, it seems that the *kainos* concept of the covenant holds the most promise for a gospel that is both revelationally continual and contextually relevant.

New Suggestions for Old Problems

Understanding covenantal revelation as *kainos* may help us avoid some of the common pitfalls faced by contextualization. It may get us beyond what Paul Hiebert (1987, 108) has called "uncritical contextualization." It may spur us to begin recognizing that questions of truth are important and legitimate rebuttals to unacceptable religious relativity (Conn 1984, 210).

The *kainos* understanding of the covenant will provide a continuity with the history of revelation, which protects the church in all contexts from syncretism. As Saphir Athyal (1976), Gleason Archer (1979, 202), and Bruce Nicholls (1980) have rightly pointed out, syncretistic mixing of God's truth with human falsehood has been one of the major dangers of contextualization. The *kainos* understanding of the covenant can provide a major touchstone whereby God's revelation in each culture, though contextually relevant, can be revelationally consistent with that which has previously been known about God.

Such a touchstone will result in healthy contextualization: "As converts together study and obey the Scriptures, and as their testimony begins to penetrate the broader context, it is indeed the aim of contextualization to promote the transformation of human beings and their societies, cultures, and structures, not into the image of a western church or society, but into a locally appropriate, locally revolutionary representation of the Kingdom of God in embryo, as a sign of the Kingdom yet to come" (Taber 1979a, 150). Moreover, Stephen Knapp seems to have the *kainos* understanding of covenantal revelation in mind when he says, "Every command of Christ through the Scripture is also de facto a command to contextualize" (1976, 15). This

---

27. For a warning against such "aberrant contextualization" see Hesselgrave 1988, 153–58.
28. See Loewen 1986; Netland 1988.
29. Taylor 1963, 75–84, has highlighted the effects in Africa of missionary teaching about a transcendent God who is not in the here and now of African experience.

understanding is also in view when Conn (1978, 43) speaks of "covenant witness" and "covenant life": "In terms of hermeneutic, this divine pattern of covenant speaking forbids us from isolating covenant witness from covenant life. It does not permit a split between thought and action, truth and practice. Covenant witness affirms the divine word given and calls the creature to covenant life before the Creator in the world of history and its cultures. Unconditional submission to covenant remains the responsibility of covenant man in context."

New Contributions in Changing Contexts

We have seen that the *kainos* understanding of the covenant involves a continuity with a basic core of biblical revelation which is dynamically relevant to the multiple contexts of today's world. In the midst of cultural diversity, the people of God are guided by the never-changing covenant of God, "I will be your God, and you shall be my people"—now, in a totally new context. However, in the *kainos* perception the covenant also takes on deeper and fuller, and sometimes quite unexpected meaning which had not been understood before. This calls for theologians in each culture to accept a most difficult task, as Daniel von Allmen (1979, 335) has outlined: "It will be seen that the prime quality required of a theologian is careful attention to the living expression of the Church's faith, coupled with a sharp eye for detecting in that expression of the faith both where the promising efforts are to be found and where its fatal tendencies and heretical inclinations might be." Charles Taber (1979b) suggests that the criteria for theology in this endeavor would include being biblical, transcendent, christological, prophetic, dialogical (with the community and the world), open-ended, and subject to the Holy Spirit.

There is a sense, therefore, in which *kainos* covenantal contextualization would not allow us to speak of "theologies." Further, if by "theology" we mean the knowledge of God in *context*, we would do better to speak of God's self-revelation in the culturally conditioned here and now through a covenantal relationship with God's people. However, if by "theology" we mean the knowledge of *God* in context, we must also allow God's self-disclosure in each new context to influence all other understandings, all other theology arising in other times and cultures. Clearly we are dependent on the Holy Spirit here. During his farewell discourse, Jesus emphasized the didactic role of the "Spirit of truth. . . . The Counselor, the Holy Spirit, whom the Father will send in my name, will teach you all things, and will remind you of everything I have said to you" (John 14:17, 26). Again, there is a clear unity of the truth, the truth of Jesus Christ, which will not be a *neos* truth. It will be a *kainos* truth which is both continuous with previous revelation and discontinuous in its radical contextualization.

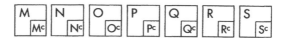

Figure 15
A Series of Historical Contexts

New Methodology for an Unchanging Gospel

So down through the history of the church, beginning in Acts, we find a development of the knowledge of God, resembling what we saw earlier. We can see throughout the church's history the work of the Holy Spirit developing a deeper understanding of all previous knowledge of God. We could, for example, represent the early Jewish-Christian community as "M," and subsequent contexts (Greek, Roman, Eastern Orthodox, medieval European synthesis, the Protestant Reformation, the Industrial Revolution) as "N," "O," "P," "Q," "R," and "S" respectively. The covenantal self-disclosure of God in each of these contexts could then be represented by M^c, N^c, O^c, P^c, Q^c, R^c, and S^c (see figure 15). These various contexts are not independent of

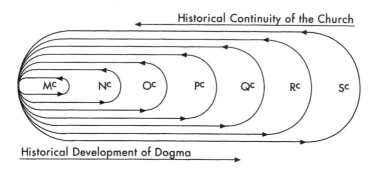

Figure 16
The Historical Development of Dogma

each other. Over time, each is related to the others in a hermeneutical spiral, as can be seen in figure 16.[30]

But it is also important to see the relationship of this spiral to the covenant formula by which we depicted the *kainos* perspective (see figures 13 and 14). The knowledge of God in ever-changing contexts throughout the history of the church must at once incorporate the closure of the canon of Scripture, and the ever-new inspiration, guidance, and teaching of the Holy

30. The concept of the hermeneutical circle as it works out to a hermeneutical spiral of deepening understanding has been explored in Padilla 1980, 76; 1985, 83–94; Schillebeeckx 1987, 103–4; and Osborne 1991.

$$\frac{\text{Jesus Christ}^c}{\text{Adam}^c/\text{Noah}^c/\text{Abraham}^c/\text{Moses}^c/\text{David}^c} = \frac{M^c/N^c/O^c/P^c/Q^c/R^c/S^c}{\text{(God's revealed hiddenness)}}$$

Figure 17
A Deepening Understanding of Revelation

Spirit. This relationship is depicted in figure 17. What appears above the right-hand line is an extension, a deepening and fulfilment, a greater understanding of God's revealed hiddenness, which in turn is the completed but not fully comprehended revelation of God from Adam to Jesus Christ. Notice that this understanding of *kainos* contextualization down through history does not involve a cumulative process. New opinions are not stacked up in an endless addition of theological thought. Nor are we dealing with knowledge of God that essentially differs from, contradicts, or substitutes for that which has gone before (that would be subtraction). What we have here is more like a picture taken by a Polaroid camera, which needs time and light to be developed. The picture is already recorded, but to see it takes time and study. Each context is understood with reference to (divided by) all other revelation which has gone before. Here we are able to preserve the uniqueness of God's self-disclosure in a particular context and affirm its *kainos* relationship to God's self-disclosure of the same covenantal relationship in earlier contexts.

Now we are entering the twenty-first century, a new situation in relation to the world church, and we deal with a multitude of contexts that struggle to know God. We could represent the covenantal knowledge of God in the contexts of Asia, Africa, Latin America, North America, Western Europe, and Eastern Europe by I^c, II^c, III^c, IV^c, V^c, and VI^c (see figure 18). And the

Figure 18
A Series of Cultural Contexts

kainos knowledge of God in these contexts can be related to all that has gone before by supplementing the formula we introduced earlier (see figure 19). It is clear that we need to avoid reinventing the wheel theologically. Our present contextual theology is neither an addition to nor a subtraction from historical theology. Rather, it is divided by that which has gone before; it is a function of what has preceded. And that historical theology has itself de-

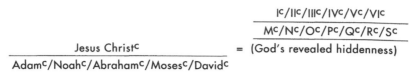

Figure 19
A Developing Contextual Theology

veloped as a reflection upon, a deepened understanding of, and an extension of God's unique covenantal self-revelation in Scripture as fulfilled in Jesus Christ.

Yet we must also affirm the special nature of God's self-disclosure in each new context. There is something unique and in that sense discontinuous about the radically different cultures, languages, and peoples which form the new contexts of God's covenantal self-revelation. This allows us to ask new questions, develop deeper understanding, and gather surprising new insights which are especially and uniquely relevant to those new contexts. Notice that the entire world church in figure 19 is at the same level, and that each context is related to the others not by a "+" sign, but by a "/," meaning that we are accountable to learn from each other God's nature and will for all of God's people. A good example of this methodology is P. J. Robinson's missiological treatment of the Belhar Confession (1984, 42–52), according to which "knowing God" in the South African context entails calling the entire world church to ask *kainos* questions about themselves, their faith, their Scriptures, and their obedience to God.[31]

Maybe by working all together as one church we can come to know God in context through the model of covenantal revelation. On the basis of a *kainos* perspective of the covenant, we may be able to enter a new era of contextualization. In this new age of the world church the *kainos* perspective may open the way for us to know God's revealed hiddenness. As Morris Inch (1982, 16) has stated: "God's revelation lies at the heart of our theological endeavor. There are not, strictly speaking, many truths, but one truth viewed from differing perspectives. Christianity is not capable of radical reinterpretation; rather, it is one faith communicated to all [humanity]. Ignoring the common heritage in the Christian fellowship is as grievous an error as failing to appreciate its rich diversity."

As the gospel continues to take root in new cultures, and God's people grow in their covenantal relationship to God in those contexts, a

---

31. The growing number of church confessions being elaborated by churches around the world constitutes a very positive sign that the *kainos* type of contextualization is beginning to find a place.

broader, fuller, and deeper understanding of God's revelation will be given to the world church. In the end we may come to appreciate what Augustine of Hippo (354–430), in his conflict with the Donatists, affirmed: the truth is that which everyone everywhere has always believed about the gospel.[32]

32. See Pelikan 1971, 1:292–307; Bettenson 1970, 240; and Schaff 1974, 1:391.

4

Constructing Mission Theology in the City

O Jerusalem! Jerusalem! you who kill the prophets and stone those sent to you, how often I have longed to gather your children together, as a hen gathers her chicks under her wings, but you were not willing! Look, your house is left to you desolate. I tell you, you will not see me again until you say, "Blessed is he who comes in the name of the Lord." [Luke 13:34–35]

Were these words of Jesus a sigh of deep pathos, a cry of excruciating agony, or an exasperated pronouncement of judgment? Matthew (23:37–39) places them after the triumphal entry. Closely joined to the seven woes pronounced on the leaders of the Jews,[1] they are an integral part of Matthew's long discourse on eschatological issues related to the end of the age. In Luke, Jesus utters these words when on his way to Jerusalem prior to his triumphal entry (19:28–44); he is responding to warnings that Herod is plotting to kill him.

Whether viewed through the Matthean paradigm or the Lukan,[2] Jesus' cry, "Jerusalem! Jerusalem!" could be taken as a profound statement (a hermeneutic?) by Jesus concerning God's mission in the city.[3] Among the obvious elements here are the loving commitment of God to be involved with,

---

1. Note that these woes can in no way be construed as anti-Semitic. To the contrary, they denounce the leaders of the people for having misled the Jewish nation for whom God cares deeply.
2. See Bosch 1991, 56–122.
3. Comparing Babylon and Jerusalem, Greenway 1992 offers a provocative analysis of Jerusalem as an image of urban missiology. Oddly enough, he omits reference to this passage. See also Olley 1990.

and related to, the city; God's initiative in sending (mission) messengers to the city; and Jerusalem's mixed (mostly negative) response to God's love. But the dominant image is one of pained, loving, salvific tenderness: a hen clucking furiously to gather her wayward chicks under her wings.

Though Jerusalem kills the prophets, God does not flee from or give up on Jerusalem. Rather, God sends his Son, who comes as a descendant of King David and "in the name of the Lord." He comes riding on a donkey on his way to the cross and the empty tomb—events that occur in the midst and for the sake of Jerusalem.

In fact, Jesus' entire ministry might be viewed from the perspective of his encounter with Jerusalem. We do not know from his cry over the city whether he is aware of the coming destruction of the temple in A.D. 70. Yet we are assured from the structure of the text in both Matthew and Luke that ultimately, through his death and resurrection, Jesus offers redemption and transformation of the old Jerusalem into the new city of God, referred to later by John in Revelation 21. True to God's form of response throughout the history of Israel, there is always grace in the midst of judgment; in the end, there is a rewriting of the story of Jerusalem. "The last chapter in the Jerusalem story awaits the future. . . . She is called the Holy City and her Bridegroom is the Lamb. Life in the new Jerusalem is peaceful. There are no tears, nor causes for them. Death and mourning are gone, and so are pain and suffering. Best of all, in this city God in Christ dwells forever with his people in perfect relationship. Grace has triumphed and *shalom* is established" (Greenway 1992, 10–11).

When I hear those words of Jesus about Jerusalem, I hear the deep pain of an urban missionary. And it seems to me Jesus is offering some profound theological truths that are simultaneously historical, contextual, relational, and missiological. Is it not possible that these words also constitute a challenge and a call to search anew for a theology of mission for the city? We need to search for what Ian Bunting, a missionary for more than thirty years in the urban areas of northern England, called for: "an integrated method of training [urban missionaries] which can truly be described as global in scope, mission-oriented, and thoroughly contextual." Especially important here is the search for a correlation of reflection with action, of values with programs, of theology with practice:

> While there is general agreement on a method of learning theology which involves seeing, judging and acting, there is no such agreement about the way to correlate theology and practice. There is, in fact, a sharp disagreement between those who look for more theoretical or systematic correlations (often the trainers in universities, colleges, and courses) and those who pursue more practical theological correlations (normally to be found in urban training centers and institutes). The issue is as much about where we learn our theology as

how we go about it. There is not much evidence that this divide between the academic and the practical has been bridged by more than a few. [Bunting 1992, 25]

Why Construct a Theology of Mission for the City?

Many urban missiologists are looking for ways to better build on, and interact with, the literature and programs that deal with urban missiology. Although an impressive quantity of reflective thinking about urban mission has appeared over the last twenty years,[4] many of us are restless to find new ways to integrate those insights with our theology and missiology.

It seems that in urban missiology it has been difficult to deal with the whole system of the city. On the one hand, those involved in microministry deal with individual persons and their needs in the city—but they are often burning out in the process, in part because they are not dealing with the entire system. On the other hand, those who spend much energy doing macrostudies in sociology, anthropology, economics, ethnicity, politics, and religion in the city seldom seem to get down to the level of the streets and the people of the city. Their recommendations for concrete action seem weak, and their activism mostly dulled by the largeness of their scope of investigation. The staggering complexity of an urban metroplex like Los Angeles makes it nearly impossible for the students of the macrostructures to convert their findings into specific, timely, compassionate, personal ministry.

Then, too, many seem to be caught up in one agenda or another. Community organization is an area that needs further reflection and action by the church in the city, an emphasis that Robert Linthicum has called for.[5] William Pannell (1992, 6–22) points out that mass evangelism has too often been blind to the systemic issues of the city and has seldom sought the more radical, wholistic transformation of the cities in which its evangelistic enterprises occur. John McKnight (1989, 38, 40) highlights this tension:

4. E.g., Cone 1991; Felder 1989; Steele 1990; Linthicum 1991a; 1991b; Bakke 1987; Tonna 1985; Rose and Hadaway 1984; Frenchak and Keyes 1979; Frenchak and Stockwell 1984; Grigg 1984; 1992; Conn 1987; Greenway and Monsma 1989; Greenway 1973; 1976; 1978; 1979; 1992; Claerbaut 1983; Gmelch and Zenner 1988; Garreau 1991; Michael Peter Smith 1988; Recinos 1989; Elijah Anderson 1990; Whyte 1989; Gulick 1989; Pannell 1992; Sample 1984; 1990; Meyers 1992; among related works are Cox 1965; 1984; Ellul 1970a; DuBose 1978; Sheppard 1974; Schaller 1987; and Elliston 1992.

5. Linthicum 1991b, 109, says, "Participation in community organization provides the church with the most biblically directed and most effective means for bringing about the transformation of a community—through the assumption of responsibility by the community's residents to solve corporately their own problems." For a number of years Alfred Krass (1978) has voiced this concern as well, apparently wanting to keep evangelism, mission, community organization, and urban missiology together in a more integrated fashion. See also Messer 1992.

When I'm around church people, I always check whether they are misled by the modern secular vision. Have they substituted the vision of service for the only thing that will make people whole—community? Are they service peddlers or community builders? Peddling services is unchristian—even if you're hell-bent on helping people. Peddling services instead of building communities is the one way you can be sure not to help. . . . Service systems teach people that their value lies in their deficiencies. They are built on "inadequacies" called illiteracy, visual deficit, and teenage pregnancy. But communities are built on the *capacities* of drop-out, illiterate, bad-scene, teenage-pregnant, battered women. . . . If the church is about community—not service—it's about capacity not deficiency.

In addition, while there is increasing interest in planting and growing house churches in the city,[6] too few of them seem to have a strong missional intention to be God's agents of the transformation of the city itself.

Although generalizations like these are dangerous, the overall impression is that deficiencies are pervasive. At one end of the spectrum, many social service agencies give assistance to individuals but have little regard to the systems of the city (much less to gathering people into worshiping congregations). At the other end, many evangelistic, church-planting efforts do not deal with the entire scope of evil in the city. We see activists who seldom stop to do the broader reflection, and reflective investigators who do not often get around to doing anything to change the reality of the city they are studying.

Meanwhile, urban churches continue to struggle to find how to be viable missional communities of faith in the city. For the church of Jesus Christ, life and ministry in the city involve profound tensions. The church is not a social agency—but is of social significance in the city. The church is not city government—but is called to announce and live out the kingdom of God in all its political significance. The church is not a bank—but is an economic force in the city and is to seek the economic welfare of the city. The church is not a school—but is called to educate the people of the city concerning the gospel of love, justice, and social transformation. The church is not a family—but is the family of God, called to be a neighbor to all of those whom God loves. The church is not a building—but needs buildings and owns buildings to carry out its ministry. The church is not exclusive, not unique—but is spe-

6. See, e.g., Sheppard 1974; Neighbour 1990; Birkey 1988; Hadaway et al. 1987; Lois Barrett 1986; Lee and Cowan 1986; Banks and Banks 1989; and John Noble 1988. It would be interesting to study the base ecclesial community movements in Latin America as possibly a new form of the church in an urban setting—but that is outside the scope of this book. The astounding multiplicity of small Pentecostal storefront churches found in cities all over the world is another well-known phenomenon that has received too little attention from those who study the ministry of the church in the city. The megachurches that arose all over the world during the 1980s might have offered themselves as another new model for the church in the city—except for the fact that few of them have shown any intention to contribute to the wholistic transformation of the cities in which they are found.

cially called by God to be different in the way it serves the city. The church is not an institution—but needs institutional structures to effect changes in the lives of people and society. The church is not a community-development organization—but the development of community is essential to the church's nature.

We need to search for a theology of mission that will give us new eyes for perceiving our city, inform our activism, guide our networking, and energize our hope for the transformation of our city.

How May We Construct a Theology of Mission for the City?

The remainder of this chapter presents a brief summary of steps found to be helpful in constructing a theology of mission for the city. The reader will notice a dependence on the three-arena approach to missiology, the use of narrative, and a missiological approach to Scripture—topics developed earlier in this book. Clearly, the methodology followed here is not the only way to proceed. Neither do its steps represent the last word on this matter. This section will merely highlight the broad outline, leaving it for readers to envision the way the process might take shape in their context. A most significant discovery has been that the manner in which the process applies to each given urban context is *itself contextual*. In other words, not only the content, but also the method itself must be transformed to fit critically and appropriately the particular issues, style, agendas, and themes arising in each context.

Approaching the City

As can be seen from figure 20, our method for constructing a theology of mission for the city involves walking through the three multi- and interdisciplinary circles we saw earlier—and adapting for a particular urban context what we have learned from and about each of them. Thus the first step in our process is to be self-conscious and self-critical in approaching the city.

We begin by setting the stage, asking about the perceptions, images, and lenses that we use to exegete the city. Some (primarily in the United States) would view the city as a series of concentric circles, a perspective that gave rise to terms like "inner city" and "suburb." Others (primarily Europeans) might see the city in terms of "old town" and "new town." Persons from the Third World see the city as a central business district with surrounding *barrios*, or *favelas*, "districts," "cantonments," or "slums." The city might also be viewed as a network of extended-family relationships, or as a compilation of ethnic subsystems. City planners see streets and buildings, politicians see voters, the police see violence, the educators see schools, bankers and economists see businesses, and commuters see traffic. The media see through

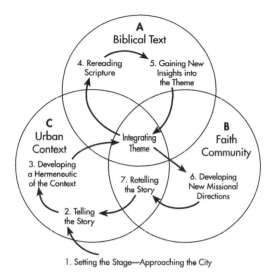

Figure 20
Methodological Components of a Biblical Theology of Mission in the City

a narrow, selective, and restricted lens, looking for sensational stories that will sell.[7]

Still others look at the city through the grid of spiritual warfare and see good and evil forces battling for the allegiance of the people and the structures of the city. All of us "see through a glass, darkly" (1 Cor. 13:12 KJV). All of us are insightful in what we see, and blind in what we miss. Yet a full-fledged theology of mission for the city will call us to look past the limits of our peripheral vision to gain some understanding of the complexity of systems and subsystems (interlocking and independent) that make up the urban metroplex.

A useful image here is a rose. Each petal (subsystem) is different from the others, yet interconnected with them. A petal alone does not make a rose. Yet the rose cannot exist except as the sum total of its petals. At the same time, the rose draws from a whole system of supports involving the rose bush, just as a city draws from a host of supporting cultural, geographic, national, global, and historical elements that help sustain it. Like the rose, the city also has intangible elements of beauty and smell that cannot be specifically identified with any given petal—it is the interweaving of the various petals that gives each city its unique flavor. Also like the rose, the city is full of thorns

---

7. It is a generally held opinion that the media significantly contributed to making the Los Angeles riots of 1992 worse than they would otherwise have been. The irresponsible television coverage almost invited additional looting and rioting.

and must be handled carefully and gingerly. Finally, the city is similar to the rose in its fragility. Cut the rose and it wilts quickly. Likewise the city. Life in the city is fragile, death is often too near.[8]

Thus the first step in our method involves a commitment to view the city systemically, wholistically, and critically while we search for biblical values and insights that may inform our life and ministry there. This in turn forces us to be willing to maintain touch with the complexity of the whole, while at the same time we keep our feet grounded in the specificity of the here and now of persons living in the city. A good way to do this is to begin on the sidewalks of our cities by telling a story.

The Story

The second step involves standing in circle C (the urban context) and relating not just any anecdote or historical moment, but a specific kind of story. This method draws somewhat from the anthropological technique of participant observation, as well as from the case study approach of sociology and counseling. However, since ours is a specifically theological task, our stories will most fruitfully borrow from the insights of narrative theology. Although narrative theology has typically been associated with a rather recent hermeneutical development in the way scholars approach the Bible, the method itself contributes powerfully to seeing the macroissues of the city through the microconcerns of persons.[9]

Narrative theology is a method that goes beyond the purely historical, sequential retelling of an episode. At the same time it is necessary, at the other end of the spectrum, to stop short of a totally subjective approach that would ascribe to the event whatever meaning one feels led to give it. Rather, we are searching for particularly appropriate stories that will serve as specific time-and-place windows to larger macrostructural issues. As the stories are seen within the social, cultural, religious, relational, and personal context of the original urban setting, their meanings will illuminate our understanding of missiological praxis in the city.

The selection of the stories is a critical step in the reflective process, for we want to focus on narratives that are in some way representative of our ministries, central to our contexts, and rich in hermeneutical meaning for a deeper understanding of the cities in which they happen. When the story is

8. At Lausanne II in Manila in 1989, Fletcher Tink offered a "jungle-profile" view of the city that many found helpful. Among the many aspects of a primeval jungle that are analogous to modern cities are its subterranean life, surface life, its small plants, lower canopy, middle canopy, and upper canopy, its diurnal and nocturnal variations, and its ecological symbiotic systems.

9. For a discussion of this hermeneutical approach from a number of differing perspectives, see, e.g., Comstock 1987; Duke 1986; Fackre 1983; Goldberg 1981; Grimes 1986; Gunn 1987; Tracy 1988; Hauerwas and Jones 1989; Lauritzen 1987; Long 1987; MacIntyre 1989b; Moberly 1986; Mueller-Vollmer 1989; Muller 1991; and Osborne 1991.

appropriate, it naturally leads us to broaden our perspectives, to see through it like a window that looks out beyond the particularity of the event and helps us better understand the third step in the process: developing a hermeneutic of the context.

A Hermeneutic of the Context

The third step of the process involves listening with new ears, seeing with new eyes, allowing the imagination to be impacted by the city in ways it may not have been previously—thus yielding a new hermeneutic of the city. This use of the word *hermeneutic* does not refer to deriving the meaning from a text of Scripture.[10] Neither does it refer to reading the signs of the times,[11] as was common in the missiology of the World Council of Churches of the 1960s and early 1970s, when there was talk of letting the world set the agenda. Rather, this type of hermeneutic involves rereading the urban context in terms of the symbols, meanings, and perspectives that have been there but to which we may have previously been blind.[12] Probably the best methodological treatment of this type of hermeneutic is found in Juan Luís Segundo's *Liberation of Theology* (1976). Although I would not espouse the way Latin American liberation theologians have reduced their hermeneutical method to narrow socioeconomic and political agendas, yet the process which Segundo describes seems to help us reflect on the new reality facing us in today's cities (see pp. 38–39).

Rereading Scripture

The third step leads naturally into the fourth. Having looked at the urban context with new suspicions, new questions, and new eyes, we raise our sight and find that we now have new questions to bring to Scripture as well. The reader will see in figure 20 that the movement from step 3 to step 4 is by way of an integrating theme that constitutes the central idea interfacing all three circles. Because of the complexity of the inter- and multidisciplinary task, the mission theologian in the city must focus on a specific integrating idea that can serve as the hub through which to approach a rereading of Scripture. Clearly we try to avoid bringing our own agendas to Scripture and superimposing them on it. This was the mistake made by liberation theologians,

10. See, e.g., Luke 4:14–30; 24:27, 45; Acts 2:14–39; 8:30–31; and 15 as New Testament illustrations of this type of hermeneutic with regard to the Old Testament. Paul's writings, Hebrews, and 1 Peter are also excellent places to investigate.

11. See, e.g., Matt. 16:1–4.

12. Examples of this can be found in Num. 13 and Deut. 1 (the differing reports of the spies regarding Canaan), Ps. 137:1 and Dan. 1:19–21 (the differing attitudes to being exiles in Babylon), and John 1:36 and 4:35 (the differing perceptions that John and Jesus had as compared to those around them).

from which they have not recovered. Rather, we must find a way to bring a new set of questions to the text, questions that might help us see in the Scriptures what we have missed before. This new approach to Scripture is what David Bosch (1991, 20–24) called "critical hermeneutics."

New Insights into the Theme

As we reread Scripture, we are faced with new insights, new values, and new priorities that call us to reexamine the motivations, means, agents, and goals of our urban missiology. This in turn will call for rethinking each one of the traditional theological loci. Thus we will be involved in a contextual rereading of Scripture to discover anew what it means to know God in the city. The issues of creation and chaos, revelation, Christology, soteriology, pneumatology, ecclesiology, and eschatology, for example, take on quite significantly unique hues when colored by the reality that faces us in the urban context. Robert McAfee Brown calls this type of reflection *Theology in a New Key* (1978) and *Unexpected News* (1984). In Latin American theology, this theological process has focused especially on issues of Christology and ecclesiology. In the city we need to allow our rereading to offer us new insights into the scope and content of our missiology, insights derived from a profound rethinking of all the traditional theological loci.[13]

New Missiological Directions

The next step, developing new missional directions, involves a movement from circle A to circle B. Because of the complex nature of the enterprise, it seems best in this step to focus again on the integrating theme, which can help hold the various ideas together.

How do we go about coming up with new directions? Relevant here is a lengthy 1987 discussion by the Association of Professors of Mission as to what missiology is and how it does its reflection:

> The mission theologian does biblical and systematic theology differently from the biblical scholar or dogmatician in that the mission theologian is in search of the "habitus," the way of perceiving, the intellectual understanding coupled with spiritual insight and wisdom, which leads to seeing the signs of the presence and movement of God in history, and through his church in such a way as to be affected spiritually and motivationally and thus be committed to personal participation in that movement. . . .
>
> Such a search for the "why" of mission forces the mission theologian to seek to articulate the vital integrative center of mission today. . . . Each formulation of the "center" has radical implications for each of the cognate disciplines of the social sciences, the study of religions, and church history in the way they

13. Conn 1993a, 102–3, gives a summary form of this process.

are corrected and shaped theologically. Each formulation supports or calls into question different aspects of all the other disciplines. . . . The center, therefore, serves as both theological content and theological process as a disciplined reflection on God's mission in human contexts. The role of the theologian of mission is therefore to articulate and "guard" the center, while at the same time to spell out integratively the implications of the center for all the other cognate disciplines. [Van Engen 1987, 524–25]

Conceptually we are involved here in something that philosophy of science has called paradigm construction or paradigm shift.[14] We know that paradigm shift is normally understood (especially in philosophy of science) as a corporate phenomenon that occurs over a rather long period of time and involves the reflective community's interacting with a particular issue. However, David Bosch has initiated many of us into seeing paradigm formation as a powerful way of helping us reconceptualize our mission with reference to specific communities in specific contexts. In these terms a paradigm becomes "a conceptual tool used to perceive reality and order that perception in an understandable, explainable, and somewhat predictable pattern" (Van Engen 1992b, 53). It is "an entire constellation of beliefs, values and techniques . . . shared by the members of a given community" (Küng and Tracy 1989, 441–42). Thus a paradigm consists of "the total composite set of values, worldview, priorities, and knowledge which makes a person, a group of persons, or a culture look at reality in a certain way. A paradigm is a tool of observation, understanding and explanation" (Van Engen 1992b, 53). In formulating our paradigm for urban mission we take the new insights gained from rereading Scripture and through the focusing mediation of the integrating theme restate them as contextually appropriate missional orientations of the church in the city.

A number of people have sought to describe the various possible missional orientations of the church. David Moberg (1962), for example, analyzed the impact of the church as a social institution. Lesslie Newbigin, on the other hand, has spoken of the congregation as "a hermeneutic of the gospel," meaning that persons and institutions in the surrounding contextual environment read the gospel through the mediation of the local church: "I confess that I have come to feel that the primary reality of which we have to take account in seeking for a Christian impact on public life is the Christian congregation" (Newbigin 1989a, 227).[15]

14. See, e.g., Hempel 1965; 1966; Toulmin 1961; 1972; Barbour 1974; 1990; Kuhn 1962; 1977; Fetzer 1992a, 147–78; 1992b; Küng and Tracy 1989, 3–33; and Bosch 1991, 349–62.

15. The last chapter of Newbigin's *Gospel in a Pluralist Society* contains some fascinating beginning points for a new reflection on what it could mean for the church to be intentional about its missiological orientation to the city. Newbigin highlights the local congregation as (1) a community of praise, (2) a community of truth, (3) deeply involved in the concerns of its neighborhood, (4) prepared for and sustained in the exercise of priesthood for the world, (5) a community of mutual responsibility, and (6) a community of hope.

One of the most creative ways to approach this matter was developed by David Roozen, William McKinney, and Jackson Carroll in their study of the *Varieties of Religious Presence* (1984). Their case studies of ten different congregations in Hartford, Connecticut, revealed four different types of mission orientation: (1) the congregation as activist; (2) the congregation as citizen; (3) the congregation as sanctuary; and (4) the congregation as evangelist. Clearly these four characterizations do not exhaust the various missional dimensions, intentions, and relations of the communities of faith (the church) with the city. However, it might be interesting for readers to examine their own faith communities to discover how many congregations and missional situations can in fact be encapsulated within each one of these four missional orientations.

Retelling the Story

The final, but at the same time initial, step in the process involves suggestions for contextually appropriate, biblically informed missional action. This step is called "Retelling the Story," because it brings us back to the here and now of the person on the sidewalks of our cities and asks very specifically about the actions that need to be taken within and without the faith community to respond to the initial situation faced.

Here we find ourselves on the middle ground between biblically informed missiological theory and contextually appropriate missiological action. As we saw in the introduction (p. 26), one of the most helpful ways to interface reflection and action is through the process known as praxis. In *The Praxis of Pentecost* (1991), Ray Anderson presents the concept of praxis through a reflection on Jesus' ministry and specifically the story of the woman caught in adultery (John 8:1–11). On the basis of this story, Anderson offers a hermeneutic of Jesus' ministry as "a paradigm of Christopraxis" (1991, 48). Anderson then goes on to speak of Christ's "praxis of liberation," "praxis of sanctification," and "praxis of empowerment" (1991, 49–62).

In praxis, not only the reflection, but profoundly the action becomes part of a theology-on-the-way that seeks to discover how the church may participate in God's mission in the city. To reiterate what was said in the introduction: The action is itself theological, and serves to inform the reflection, which in turn interprets, evaluates, critiques, and projects new understanding in transformed action. Thus the interweaving of reflection and action in a constantly spiraling pilgrimage offers a transformation of all aspects of our missiological engagement with the city. This leads us back to a faith commitment, a loving engagement, and a hopeful visioning of ways in which we pray the story might be retold. Thus we return to where we began, and we boldly proclaim the retelling of the story.

Jerusalem! Jerusalem!

"I saw the Holy City, the new Jerusalem, coming down out of heaven from God, prepared as a bride beautifully dressed for her husband. And I heard a loud voice from the throne saying, 'Now the dwelling of God is with [people], and he will live with them. They will be his people, and God himself will be with them and be their God" (Rev. 21:2–4).

Part 3

Mission Theology and the Church

5

The Missionary Church
in Ephesians

To construct a new image of the missionary nature of the church and the local congregation, we will begin by examining the essence of the church. One of the most important biblical sources for this is Paul's Letter to the Ephesians. A careful study of Ephesians from the perspective of a dynamic ecclesiology will reveal Paul's view of the missionary nature of the local congregation. What follows is not meant to be a detailed exegesis or a complete hermeneutic of Ephesians. Rather, we want to look at Ephesians as a window to Paul's missionary ecclesiology. Paul saw the local church as an organism which should continually grow in the missional expression of its essential nature in the world. The phrase "one, holy, and catholic" as applied to the essential nature of the church can be traced back to the Apostles' Creed, where the term *one* is implied by the singular noun *church*. The Apostles' Creed is itself based on the earliest Christian confessions. So it should not surprise us that Paul was already working with these basic ideas in his images of the church in Ephesians.

In dealing with the missionary ecclesiology of Ephesians we could spend an inordinate amount of time examining the various words which refer to the church. Martin Luther detested the old German word *Kirche* because of its institutional and hierarchical associations, preferring such words as crowd (*Haufe*), convocation (*Versammlung*), assembly (*Sammlung*), and congregation (*Gemeinde*). In fact the actual words are not as important as is the Reformation emphasis on the nature of the church as expressed in the Apostles' Creed—the communion of saints. This emphasis on the church as congregation, communion, or fellowship was central to Paul's definition of the church, which was based on the Old Testament concept of the people of God

(Hanson 1986). The New Testament uses the word *ekklēsia* more than a hundred times, and invariably the meaning involves the idea of an assembly—either the gathering or the individuals gathered (Kittel and Friedrich 1964–76, 3:501–13).

But overall, a semantic study does little to enrich our understanding of the nature of the church. Linguistic anthropologists have suggested that in order to understand a given concept in its cultural milieu, it is helpful to search for dynamic equivalents of thought, image, and feeling. One aspect of this method involves word-pictures which graphically convey meaning. Paul Minear (1960) found ninety-six different images of the church in the New Testament. A careful analysis of the images of the church in Ephesians can be particularly helpful for understanding Paul's view of the church's mission.

In Ephesians we find that the word *ekklēsia* appears only nine times. This is surprising in view of the fact that many scholars recognize Ephesians as being the high point of Paul's thought regarding the church. The absence of the word *ekklēsia* from Ephesians should make us aware that in this epistle Paul develops his thought not so much with Greek logical propositions as with Hebrew-style pictorial representation or images. A closer look at the epistle reveals at least fifteen different word-pictures concerning the nature of the church. The most important of these are saints, the body, soldiers wearing the armor of God, and the wife of Christ. Then there is a series of lesser images used to embellish the major ones: the chosen people of God, the sons or family of God, the workmanship of God, the building or temple of God, a song of praise or an offering, and a new humanity or new self. And finally a whole range of images which flash only once in the epistle: the breadth, length, height, and depth of Christ's love; imitators of God; the kingdom of Christ; children of light; wise men; and ambassadors. These lucid photographs help us understand the nature of the church as Paul saw it. In the following exposition we will interweave these images with the ancient words of the creed, "one, holy, and catholic." This means we must begin at the very heart of the epistle—with the concept of the unity of the body of Christ.

The Church's Mission as Unity (Eph. 4:1–16)

The apostle Paul states categorically, "There is one body and one Spirit—just as you were called to one hope when you were called—one Lord, one faith, one baptism; one God and Father of all, who is over all and through all and in all" (4:4–6). We do not confess "holy catholic churches," or "families of God," or "peoples of God," or "bodies of Christ," or "new Israels." In the biblical view of the church the plural refers only to geographical location, not existential being. In its essence there is only one, and there never can be more than one church. In Ephesians the word *ekklēsia* appears only in the singular.

We accept on faith the fact of the oneness of the church. This oneness is something given by God, not fabricated by humans. It is a oneness bonded by the Spirit of God who gathers the church. The church remains the mysterious *creatio Dei*, created by the presence of the Comforter in the midst of elected, justified sinners. Paul speaks of the fact that the church comes into being just as a building is put together—and God through Son and Holy Spirit is the divine builder (Eph. 2:10, 21–22). The means of God's building activity is mission; the fruit of God's building activity we receive as a gift from God in the unity of the body of Christ. As Karl Barth has put it, "The Church is His Body, created and continually renewed by the awakening power of the Holy Spirit. There is no justification, theological, spiritual or biblical, for the existence of a plurality of churches genuinely separated in this way and mutually excluding one another internally and therefore externally. A plurality of churches in this sense means a plurality of lords, a plurality of spirits, a plurality of gods."[1]

As an article of the creed, the church's oneness is an affirmation of faith. But amidst our brokenness and dividedness the church's oneness is not obvious. We are Gentiles, strangers, aliens held apart by the dividing wall (Eph. 2:11–14). Yet we accept by faith the fact of one body because we believe in one God, in one Jesus Christ, in one Spirit.

This confession has practical significance. Because we accept on faith the oneness of the church, we therefore strive to achieve that oneness (Eph. 4:1–3). Paul exhorts us that we walk worthy of our calling (to oneness), that we be humble, gentle, patient, forbearing—precisely because we are to "spare no effort to make fast with bonds of peace the unity which the Spirit gives" (v. 3 NEB). This oneness of the body is not only external, institutional, organizational unity, but involves more profoundly an internal unanimity. Paul speaks of this unified spirit in Philippians 2:1–11 and 1 Corinthians 1:12–13. This is a matter of being members one of another (1 Cor. 12)—the joys and the honors, the griefs and the pains of each member have repercussions among all members, for all are *one* body. In Ephesians Paul does not speak of denomination or council or association. Paul speaks of body. He wants us to accept on faith the oneness of the church and strive to achieve it *in the exercise of our gifts in service to the world.*[2] Paul's admonition in Ephesians 4:1–6 that we be one is explained more fully in 4:7–16, which presents the idea of one body with members who exercise their gifts as part of that body. Each member has been given a gift (4:7). The giver is the cosmic Christ who has filled the universe (4:8–10).

---

1. Barth 1936–69, 4.1:661, 675. In this section Barth goes to great lengths to affirm the work of Christ and the Holy Spirit in creating the church as his body.

2. Barth 1936–69, 4.2:614–41, stresses this point. His phrase in this regard is "being for the world."

The gifts themselves include the capabilities to be apostles, prophets, evangelists, pastors, and teachers (4:11–12). The purpose of the gifts is to equip the saints for diaconal service and for the upbuilding of the body of Christ (4:12).

So the idea of oneness does not involve putting many individuals or denominations together like pieces of a puzzle to get a larger whole. Paul's concept is that the whole defines the identity of the parts, and is more than the sum of the parts. This is a perspective of clan and tribe. Individuals have significance in themselves, but they derive their ultimate meaning from their place in the whole. As Paul expressed it in 1 Corinthians 12, a hand, ear, or eye has no significance, no task, no identity in itself. It takes on importance as a part of the whole body.

This concept of the body questions Western individualism as well as Marxist conformism. Persons are extremely important and unique, but only in and through their special participation in the whole by exercising their own unique gifts according to the grace given them. This is the sense in which to understand the old Cyprianic dictum, *extra ecclesiam nulla salus* (outside the church there is no salvation). Apart from the body no members can maintain their lives, their identities, or their purposes.

The oneness of the church is extroverted. The gifts are given for a purpose. The gifts are to equip the saints so that they may carry out *ergon diakonias* (the work of service, 4:12). And in this effort all the saints together work *eis oikodomēn tou sōmatos tou Xristou* (toward the upbuilding of the body of Christ). This is the oneness of *The Church Inside Out* (Hoekendijk 1964; 1966a). The members exercise their various gifts to prepare each other for mission and ministry in the world. This oneness is not an introverted club of like-minded enthusiasts. Here is a body of apostles, prophets, evangelists, pastors, and teachers who assist and enable each other in the proclamation of the gospel to the world around them. It is the body which exploded into action in those early years, going to all the nations to make disciples by preaching, teaching, and baptizing (Matt. 28:19–20). This body was known to hold all things in common (Acts 4:32), to be concerned about the sick, and to look after the widows, the orphans, the poor. This is an externalized oneness which searches the highways and byways of the world with an invitation to the great feast. Jesus emphasized this externalized perspective of oneness in his high-priestly prayer: "And the glory which Thou hast given Me I have given to them; that they may be one, just as We are one; I in them, and Thou in Me, that they may be perfected in unity, that the world may know that Thou didst send Me, and didst love them, even as Thou didst love Me" (John 17:22–23 NASB).

The overriding purpose here is that the church may grow to be one: "So shall we all at last attain to the unity inherent in our faith and our knowledge of the Son of God—to mature manhood, measured by nothing less than the full stature of Christ. . . . Let us speak the truth in love; so shall we fully grow up into Christ. He is the head, and on him the whole body depends. Bonded and knit together by every constituent joint, the whole frame grows through the due activity of each part, and builds itself up in love" (Eph. 4:13, 15–16 NEB). Growth is Paul's point.[3] This is growth in greater oneness through the incorporation of other members into the body (numerical growth), growth through the spiritual development of the members of the body as they exercise their gifts for the sake of the world (organic and spiritual growth), growth through the increased impact of the body of Christ in the world to which it has been sent (growth in diaconal service), and growth through an enhanced understanding of the lordship of Christ in the church, which will prevent us from being "tossed by the waves and whirled about by every fresh gust of teaching" (4:14 NEB—theological growth).

Mission and unity, then, are wedded in Paul's view of the church. One day we will have grown to such an extent that Christ will "present the church to himself all glorious, with no stain or wrinkle or anything of the sort, but holy and without blemish" (Eph. 5:27 NEB; see also Rev. 21:9–10, 25–26).

The Church's Mission as Holiness (Eph. 1:1–14; 4:17–5:5; 5:6–6:20; 3:14–21)

To speak of the holiness of the church is deeply disturbing. In ecclesiology we have had to create some careful distinctions such as visible/invisible, form/essence, real/ideal, institution/community, imperfect/perfect to make some sense out of the pain which we feel concerning the lack of holiness of the church. In Ephesians the idea of holiness flows deep and strong. As we have seen, the community of saints is a very dominant image in Ephesians. Further, the call to holy living, the call to being light in darkness, the exhortation to battle evil and the powers of the air as a soldier outfitted for war—all these constitute a reinforcement of our confession in the creed concerning the holiness of the church.

We accept on faith the fact of the holiness of the church (Eph. 1:1–14). We accept it because holiness is a gift of God, affirmed by God as his purpose for us. Paul opens his epistle with an ancient hymn extolling ten blessings. The hymn is a song of praise to the work of the three persons of the Trinity. What has God done for us?

> By the Father we are: (1) chosen (2) to be made holy, (3) predestined, (4) adopted—
> *Chorus:* To the praise of his glory;

---

3. Barth devotes a major section in his *Dogmatics* (1936–69, 4.2:641–60) to the upbuilding of the communion.

> By the Son we are: (5) redeemed, (6) pardoned, (7) made to know the
>   mystery, (8) united in Christ, and (9) heirs with him—
> *Chorus:* To the praise of his glory;
> By the Spirit we are: (10) sealed—
> *Chorus:* To the praise of his glory.

This is who we are as a holy people of God. We accept on faith the fact of
the holiness of the church, for we cannot see it. When we look into our individual lives, we do not see much holiness. With the mouth we confess that
we are saints (as in Eph. 1:1)—with the heart we feel that we are sinners
(Eph. 4:17).

Thus we are to strive individually and corporately to achieve the holiness
of the church (Eph. 4:17–5:5). Paul, the apostle to the Gentiles, calls into
question a whole series of practices of the Gentiles. He shines the searchlight
of the Word upon the cultural makeup of his followers and points out the
human practices which must be modified precisely because now his converts
constitute a new self, a transformed culture (4:24). Paul deals with some very
personal things here: sensuality, lust, immorality (4:19, 22; 5:3); greed (4:19;
5:3, 5); stealing (4:28); slothfulness in work (4:28); foul language (4:29; 5:4);
bitterness and anger (4:31); and lying (4:25).

Paul wants us to know that the church is directly affected by how we
speak, how we work at our jobs, how we use (or abuse) our bodies, how we
think and evaluate, how we relate to those in need. The holiness of the church
is directly related to the life of the new self in the world. How we pay our
income taxes, how we manage our family and business finances, how we vote
politically, and what we say in public and private all directly affect the holiness of the church. For when as members of the church we confess belief in
the holiness of the church, we make a commitment to our own holiness. This
involves righteous conduct which calls for the transformation of our culture,
our economics, our politics, our education, and even our lifestyles (Sider
1977; 1980).

In other words, Paul wants us to recognize that we exercise our holiness
as an expression of the holiness of the church (Eph. 5:6–6:20). As children of
light (5:8) the church carries illumination to the farthest reaches of the darkness of the world through the holiness of its members, individually and corporately (Matt. 5:14). Further, the holiness of the church encompasses worship (Eph. 5:19–20), church organization and accountability therein (5:21),
sexual relationships (5:22–33), the family (6:1–4), and work (6:5–9).

The church must be holy in society because we wrestle "not against
human foes, but against cosmic powers, against the authorities and poten-
tates of this dark world, against the superhuman forces of evil in the heav-
ens" (6:12 NEB). In the midst of great individual and corporate evil, the
church must never think that political and economic strength can replace the

strength of holiness in the Lord. The church must put on truth like a belt, righteousness at the heart of all its relationships, the gospel as its shoes, faith as a defense against oppression and pessimism, salvation as its helmet, the Word of God as a sword against evil, and prayer as the watchword which presents to God the needs of the world. Once the church is clothed in the armor described in Ephesians 6:10–20, it is ready to begin changing the world through the exercise of true missionary holiness.

True holiness is growth in love (Eph. 3:14–21). Paul pictures holiness here as "power through [the] Spirit in the inner man," as "Christ [dwelling] in your hearts through faith," as being "filled up to all the fulness of God" (NASB). And what is at the very center of that holy presence of God in his church? *Love.* "By this all [people] will know that you are My disciples," Jesus had said (John 13:35 NASB; see also 15:10–12). There is no other activity which so completely identifies Christians (and through them the church) with their Lord as does love. What is the sum of all the law and the prophets? Love of God and love of neighbor. The church in Ephesus is called to holiness by being "rooted and grounded in love," by "comprehend[ing] with all the saints what is the breadth and length and height and depth" of the love of Christ (Eph. 3:17–19 NASB). Love is the church's radically transforming power in the world. As Kenneth Scott Latourette (1953, 105–8; 1970, 163–69) has shown, love unleashed such tremendous energy in the disciples of Jesus that it eventually conquered the Roman Empire. "Greater love has no one than this, that one lay down his life for his friends" (John 15:13 NASB). And herein lies the missionary holiness of the church. "This I command you," Jesus said, "that you love one another" (v. 17 NASB). It is a sobering thought to say with the creed, "I believe the holy catholic church, the communion of saints."

The Church's Mission as Universality (Eph. 1:15–23; 2:1–22; 3:1–13)

Ephesians begins with a song of redemption and then follows in 1:15–23 with one of the most cosmic Christologies (apart from Col. 1, which parallels it) to be found in the New Testament. Paul wants us to know about the church by knowing about the head of the church. For the church derives her life, her nature, and her mission from the person of Jesus Christ. As Karl Barth (1936–69, 4.1:663) has put it:

> It is not the community which is called a body, or compared to it, but Christ Himself. He is a body. By nature He is not simply one (for a body is the unity of many members), but one in many. It is not that σῶμα [body] is a good image for the community as such, but that Jesus Christ is by nature σῶμα. . . . The community is not σῶμα because it is a social grouping which as such has some-

thing of the nature of an organism. . . . It is σῶμα because it actually derives from Jesus Christ, because of Him it exists as His body.

So when we read the full-blown Christology of Ephesians 1, the eyes of our heart should be enlightened (1:18) to recognize that we are being told something about the body, the church. And what we are told is fantastic! What was done in Christ is precisely the "surpassing greatness of His power toward us who believe" (1:19 NASB). Christ has been raised from the dead, seated at the Father's right hand in heaven, placed far above all rule and authority, power and dominion, and every name that is named in every age. All things have been placed in subjection under his feet; he is given to the church as ruler over all things; and he is the head of the body, the church. In him all fullness is manifested. He fills all in all.

Now if this cosmic Christology is applied to the body of which Christ is the head, we are faced with a far-reaching universality. We accept on faith the fact of the universality of the church because we recognize it as an expression of the universal intention of God in Jesus Christ (Ridderbos 1975, 387–92). In choosing a people, God intended to reach out to the whole world. As Johannes Verkuyl (1978, 91–92) has reminded us concerning Israel: "In choosing Israel as segment of all humanity, God never took his eye off the other nations; Israel was the *pars pro toto*, a minority called to serve the majority. God's election of Abraham and Israel concerns the whole world."

We accept on faith the fact of the church's catholicity, because we do not yet see it. True, there are more than a billion people around the world who may be counted within the Christian church in one way or another. And yet there are several billion others who are outside the Shepherd's fold. If the church is for everyone, why is not everyone in the church?

Because we confess the church's universality in Jesus Christ, we must strive to achieve it in the world (Eph. 2:1–13). Paul reminds us that at one time all of us were far from God, "dead in our transgressions," but we have been raised up with him in order that "He might show the surpassing riches of His grace in kindness toward us" who have been brought nigh (2:5–7 NASB). "Remember," Paul says, "that you were at that time [i.e., when Gentiles according to the flesh] separate from Christ, excluded . . . strangers . . . having no hope . . . without God." But now "you who formerly were far off have been brought near by the blood of Christ" (2:11–13 NASB).

Because it is for all people, the church may never cease to call, to invite, to draw everyone to Christ. The church catholic rightly belongs in the highways and byways as the messenger carrying a special invitation. The church catholic is a completely open fellowship, with its doors always spread wide, with its members' minds and hearts open to all. The church catholic is not to diminish its universality by exclusivism, be it social, economic, racial, gender, cultural, or national. The church catholic is by its very nature missionary, sent to all people precisely because the head of the church is he "who fills all in all" (Eph. 1:23 NASB).

Because we accept the church's universality on faith and strive to achieve it in the world, we understand that our Christian lives are an expression of the catholicity of the church (Eph. 2:13–22). Now we begin to see ourselves as world Christians. Christ in his flesh (v. 15) has demolished the middle wall of partition (vv. 13–14). Now all ethnic and social distinctions have been abolished in the fullness of one body, whose members have been reconciled through participation in the death and resurrection of Christ (2:16–18). We "are no longer strangers and aliens, but . . . fellow-citizens with the saints, and are of God's household" (2:19 NASB), the building God is constructing (2:20–22).

All of us have been drawn into the church catholic so that the church may become increasingly universal. Then we are sent out to make disciples of others. The church is not an exclusive club of privilege. Neither is the church a place to come and rest from our labors. We have been brought in so that we may gather others into this kingdom of grace. We have been drawn "in order that . . . He might show [to everyone else] the surpassing riches of His grace in kindness toward us in Christ Jesus" (2:7 NASB).

As the church's universality works itself out through the members of the body, the body grows toward the coming universality of the church catholic (Eph. 3:1–13). Paul's exposition of the missionary nature of the church in the Epistle to the Ephesians is at once profound and simple. Recognized by faith, the church's universality becomes something toward which the church strives through the life of each member of the body. The natural consequence is growth. As God's household, a holy temple (2:19, 21), the church continues to grow geographically, culturally, numerically, ethnically, and socially. And herein lies the mystery concerning the Gentiles that was revealed to Paul as a servant of the gospel (Eph. 3:2–12).

Taken prisoner by the universal intention of Christ Jesus, Paul is sent out "for the sake of you Gentiles" (3:1 NASB). Paul is made the steward of the mystery: "the Gentiles are fellow-heirs and fellow-members of the body" (3:6 NASB). The mystery revealed to Paul is in fact the catholicity of the church. He is to "preach to the Gentiles the unfathomable riches" of the cosmic lordship of Christ (3:8), so "that the manifold wisdom of God might now be made known through the church . . . in accordance with the eternal [universal] purpose which he carried out in Christ Jesus our Lord" (3:10–11 NASB). Living at the crossroads of Asia Minor in a cosmopolitan city filled with people of many races, colors, and languages, the Ephesian Christians, though formerly strangers, are now part of that great throng of the Father, "from whom every family in heaven and on earth derives its name" (3:15 NASB; see also Phil. 2:9–11).

We have studied the missionary nature of the church through the images afforded us by Paul in Ephesians, and have related those images to the creed. By so doing we have been confronted with a powerful vision of the local congregation in mission. By the very act of confessing our faith in "one holy catholic church, the communion of saints," we intentionally and unavoidably commit ourselves to participate in God's mission in the world.

6

The Missionary Church in Historical Perspective

Paul's energizing vision of the missionary church as one, holy, and catholic underwent significant modification during the ensuing centuries. Although the three words were affirmed, and a fourth ("apostolic") was added at Nicea, the church struggled, rather unsuccessfully, during the next millennium to maintain an organic, outward-directed, missional view of itself.

Paul had demonstrated that in its openness to God, humanity, and the future, the church stands in a tension between what it is and what it should be. But this tension itself can be the driving force to move the church to become what it really is, to emerge from seed to full-grown tree. As Christians who reflect on the nature and mission of the church, we are inquiring here about the essence of the church.

One would think this would be an easy matter. At least Martin Luther (1955, xi) seemed to think so when he wrote in the Smalcald Articles in 1537, "Thank God a seven-year-old child knows what the church is, namely holy believers and sheep who hear the voice of their shepherd (John 10:3). So children pray, 'I believe the one holy Christian Church.' Its holiness does not consist of surplices, tonsures, albs, or other ceremonies of [the papists] which they have invented over and above the Holy Scriptures, but it consists of the Word of God and true faith." More recently, Hendrik Kraemer came close to Luther's simplicity of definition when he said, "Where there is a group of baptized Christians, there is the Church."[1]

Yet the matter is not that simple. Even Luther seemed compelled to include the ancient confessional phraseology, "*I believe* the church." The ele-

---

1. Cf. International Missionary Council 1952.

ment of "believing the church" tells us there is more to the church than can be seen, more than exists at this moment, more than our feeble faith can encompass, and more than a list of its attributes can tell us about the church (Van Engen 1981, 48–94). As G. C. Berkouwer (1976, 7) points out:

> Whoever feels urged to reflect on the Church, on her reality for faith (*credo ecclesiam*), finds himself face to face with a long series of varied questions, all closely linked to the fact that there are so many churches as well as so many differing views of the essence of the Church. In our day, especially, still another question looms behind these questions: in view of the Church's place in the world today, is such reflection really relevant? . . . The more the Church claims to be, the more the question arises as to how obvious the statements made about the Church really are. Are such statements really credible?
>
> Even though one emphasizes that the Church may never be explained from her historical, psychological, and social components, one may still not deny that the intention of the *credo ecclesiam* is to point to nothing other than what is customarily called the "empirical" Church.

From Nicea to Vatican I

In the Apostles' Creed the church confessed, "I believe in the Holy Spirit, the [one] holy catholic church, the communion of saints." With the addition of "apostolic" at Nicea and Constantinople, these four words—"one," "holy," "catholic," "apostolic"—have spoken of the church's essence since its earliest beginnings.

The church has always understood that when these words refer to its nature, "they have to be visible qualities of the Church as it actually exists" (Dulles 1974, 126). We cannot capture the church's essence with abstract ideas out of touch with its life on this earth. And yet neither will we seek to describe the institution purely as it is. Rather we must search for the marks of the true community in its nature as a fellowship institutionally organized. "The only way we can measure a church is by what we can see" (Getz 1979, 16). And yet, paradoxically, we also know that the church is not what we see: she is holy but sinful, one but divided, universal but particular, apostolic but always steeped in the thought structures of her own time.

Originally the church made no distinction between the logical meaning of the four words and the visible reality to which they pointed. Thus J. N. D. Kelly (1960, 190) remarks, "The term 'holy,' the stock epithet of the Church, expresses the conviction that it is God's chosen people and is indwelt by His Spirit. As regards 'Catholic,' its original meaning was 'universal' or 'general,' and in this sense Justin can speak of 'the catholic resurrection.' As applied to the Church, its primary significance was to underline its universality as opposed to the local character of the individual congregations." Early theologians made no distinction between the visible and the invisible church. This universal fellowship or communion was almost always conceived of as an empirical, visible society. This was the real, existing fellowship of Christ, called by the Spirit, open to all people in all the world.[2] In the early church's self-perception unity, holiness, catholicity, and apostolicity were means by which to measure errors as they appeared. They were points of reference by which to detect heresy.

With time, however, the four terms began to be considered properties, then criteria, and finally *notae*—the recognizable marks of the Roman church which constituted the basis for defending the status quo. They were used to point out the holiness, perfection, completeness, and God-givenness of the Roman see, and constituted the basis for defending one institution called "church" over against another.

By the 1400s the Roman church believed that the gifts of unity, holiness, catholicity, and apostolicity were to be celebrated as its exclusive property. The ultimate function of the four words became self-justification rather than self-examination. Numerous apologists used the four classical attributes primarily as support for the authenticity of the Roman church. Eventually Vatican I was to state that the church is in itself "a great and lasting motive for its credibility and divine mission" (Küng 1968, 266).

From the Protestant Reformation to the Twentieth Century

Because of the static, self-justifying appropriation of the four terms by the Roman church, the Reformers felt that it was important to make a distinction between *attributes* and *notae*. G. C. Berkouwer (1976, 14) explains:

> Surveying the history of the Church, we meet with a striking distinction . . . between the attributes and marks of the Church. At first sight, the distinction is quite unclear, since one might expect that the Church can be known and precisely demarcated by means of her "attributes." However, closer inspection shows that there is an explicit motive underlying this distinction, which played a far-reaching role in the controversy between Rome and the Reformation and was related to the question of how one ought to view the Church's attributes. . . . In speaking of the marks of the Church, the *notae ecclesiae*, the Reformation introduced a criterion by which the Church could be, and had to be, tested as to whether she was truly the Church. This motif of testing in ecclesiology adds an entirely new and important perspective to the doctrine of the Church's attributes, and it is of decisive significance for the nature of the Church and her attributes.

2. Kelly 1960, 190–91, cites Clement of Rome, Justin, Ignatius, 2 Clement, and Hermas in this regard.

The issue at stake in this very important distinction is the function of the four words. In the Reformers' view, the Roman church treated them as attributes, static concepts reflecting an ecclesiology in which everything was decided simply on the basis that a church existed and that she necessarily possessed a number of specific attributes, regardless of whether they could actually be seen in the life of the church. The Reformers found this use of the words totally unacceptable. They felt the need to suggest something more profound, a test which would demonstrate the church's proximity to or distance from its center in Jesus Christ (Hendrikus Berkhof 1979, 409). This pushed the Reformers to search for a new paradigm which would help them verify whether the essence of the church was in fact present. Berkouwer (1976, 14–15) explains:

> It is striking in this connection that the four words themselves were never disputed, since the Reformers did not opt for other "attributes." There is a common attachment everywhere to the description of the Church in the Nicene Creed: one, holy, catholic, and apostolic. . . . Whether the Church is truly one and catholic, apostolic and holy, is not asked; rather, a number of marks are mentioned, viz. the pure preaching of the gospel, the pure administration of the sacraments, and the exercise of church discipline. . . . The decisive point is this: the Church is and must remain subject to the authority of Christ, to the voice of her Lord. And in this subjection she is tested by Him. That is the common Reformation motive underlying the *notae*.

Thus for the Reformers the three marks of the church were ways by which the church could ascertain her proximity to or distance from Jesus Christ, the one and only true center of the church's essence. Pure preaching of the Word, right administration of the sacraments, and proper exercise of discipline were tests by which the church could be measured as to her faithfulness to her Lord. The presence of the Lord in the midst of the church would test all the church's activities, dogmas, and postures of discipline. The Reformers wanted to point to something behind and beyond the four attributes, namely, the center, Jesus Christ, to whom the church owed her life and nature. Since the four attributes had lost their testing function, Word and sacrament were needed to bring back a focus on the ground of the church's being and truth, Jesus Christ. Jesus Christ would be the focal point as the gospel was proclaimed in word and deed in the life and worship of the church. Such an approach would redirect the church back to the testing function of the four attributes as well. As Avery Dulles (1974, 126–27) puts it, "The gospel, to be sure, is one and holy. Being directed to all men, it is catholic. Since it can never be changed into a 'different gospel' (cf. Gal. 1:6), it remains 'apostolic.' The Church, insofar as it lives out the gospel, would share these attributes. The Church, however, does not proclaim itself. . . . The Church is considered to stand under the gospel and be judged by it."[3] The Reformers felt that it did no good if the church claimed to be one, holy, catholic, and apostolic—and yet was not directed to the head of the body, Jesus Christ, the ground and goal of the four ancient words.[4]

Unfortunately, by the seventeenth century the Reformation marks themselves became means for destroying unity, true holiness, and catholicity. They too became dogmatic and polemical tools for differentiating one church as true over against another. In a sense they too ended up functioning as attributes because they lost their testing, self-examining, dynamic function. The struggle for a living and dynamic ecclesiology was again lost:

> First, it is clear that all definitions of the church written during the sixteenth century were influenced by social and religious factors prevalent at that time. . . . Secondly, the marks of the church carry one only so far, since their interpretation can vary considerably. Lutherans differ from Calvinists, some Lutherans from other Lutherans, and some Calvinists from other Calvinists, precisely because each group places its own connotation upon such words as "rightly" and "purely."
>
> Thirdly, although all Reformational definitions have their point of departure in Scripture, they are not necessarily "Scriptural," because Scriptural descriptions of the Church arise from the context of mission, whereas Reformational definitions arise from a given situation in society. . . . Lastly, the effect of Reformational thinking upon the present must be seen for what it is, and recognized wherever it appears. One effect is that anyone who adheres rigidly to Reformation concepts of the church stands in danger of having a stationary or static view of the Church. . . . The Church must look to God and to the world and find its reason for being as God's people in God's world. [Piet 1970, 28–29]

The upshot of this development in ecclesiology is that by the twentieth century neither Roman Catholics nor Protestants were very sure of the extent to which they embodied the essence of the church. The church had lost the ability to maintain a dynamic and constantly reforming ecclesiology. In addition, Christians continued to be troubled by the fact that they could not recognize the church's oneness, holiness, catholicity, and apostolicity in actual experience. There was also a growing suspicion about the inadequacy of a monophysitic perspective of the church which viewed the church as having only one nature, either divine or human.[5] So ecclesiologists began to seek a way to view the church as both divine and human, both organism and orga-

---

3. See also Küng 1968, 268.

4. See Calvin 1960, 282–86; Van Engen 1981, 237–39.

5. E.g., the Third World Conference on Faith and Order (1952) stated, "We are agreed that there are not two churches, one visible and the other invisible, but *one Church which must find visible expression on earth.*" See Vischer 1963, 103. Much earlier Abraham Kuyper (1883, 7–8) had defended a similar perspective in a section entitled "Waarom de ééne zelfde kerk op aarde tegelijk onzichtbaar en zichtbaar zij."

nization, both fellowship and institution. This in turn demanded that they look again at the Nicene attributes and the Protestant marks to find a way of perceiving them as both gifts and tasks.

A New Look at the Four Words

To remedy the situation, Hans Küng and G. C. Berkouwer, along with Avery Dulles, Hendrikus Berkhof, and Karl Barth called for a reexamination of the attributes, searching for a way of injecting into the four a testing and self-critiquing element which would make of them both gifts and tasks. Thus the gift that the church's nature is one entails the task of striving toward unity, living as one, uniting in the Lord. The gift that the church's nature is holy entails the task of striving toward holiness in its members, in its organizations, in its life in the world, in its reception and expression of the Word of God. The gift that the church is catholic entails the task of growing in catholicity—that is, in geographical, cultural, racial, spiritual, numerical, and temporal universality around the Lord of lords who speaks his Word to all creatures. Lastly, the gift that the church is apostolic entails the task of discovering the apostolic gospel, living in the apostolic way, and being sent as apostles to the world.

By adopting this perspective, the church which we confess by faith will become recognizable through its actual life in the world. There will also be exciting new possibilities for the church in mission:

> What seems clear is that we [have] both a profound consciousness of the utter futility of life without God, and at the same time an altogether new hunger and thirst for spiritual reality. What is equally clear is that the old order of the established and organized church, relying on its structures and traditions instead of the renewing of the Spirit of God, will not do. The formularies and creeds of the church, devoid of spiritual life, will never satisfy those who in their own different ways are searching for the living God.
>
> If, however, the church is able to rediscover its identity, as originally given by God in the Scriptures and made alive and relevant by the Spirit of God for every generation, we could be in the most exciting and exhilarating time in the history of the church that has ever been. Humanly speaking, everything depends on our ability to catch a new vision of the church as it ought to be, on our willingness to change where necessary, and above all on our determination to keep our lives continually open to spiritual renewal. [Watson 1979, 37–38]

In other words, we must move from our conception of what the church is toward a commitment to what the church must become (Moltmann 1977, 2).

Once we view the four classical words as both gifts and tasks, we find we are no longer restricted, enclosed, compressed within the confines of an institution which may not reflect the essential qualities of the church. Now we

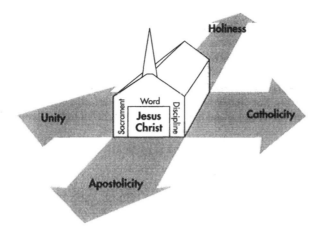

Figure 21
A Dynamic View of the Four Attributes of the Church

are thrown out beyond ourselves toward the far reaches of what could be, but we still maintain intimate contact with the central kernel of the church's nature. Actually, the center itself begins to expand. In its essence the church begins to reach out beyond itself. The church truly begins to be turned inside out, as Johannes Hoekendijk has advocated (1964, 1966a).

Figure 21 depicts dynamic outward movement of the attributes of the church. Jesus Christ is at the very center of the definition of the church, which is recognized in the Reformation marks and expressed through the four attributes. However, those attributes cannot express the presence of Christ in the church unless they are given an expanding direction as both gifts and tasks of the church's life. When this happens, they expand outward toward the periphery where church and world meet (Newbigin 1954, 47–60)

The Four Words as Missional Action

But missiologically we cannot stop there. We must look for a way of maintaining a dynamic missional understanding of the four words. The Küng-Berkouwer perspective of gift and task is deficient in this regard because it tends to look mostly inward at the church and ignores the world in which the church lives, for which the church exists, and to which the church is sent. Jürgen Moltmann (1977, 341–42) is among a number of more-recent ecclesiologists who call for a look outward to the world in which the church is to be the church:

> The matter . . . becomes difficult . . . when the one, holy catholic church gathered around word and sacrament considers its situation in our divided, fought

over, unjust, inhuman world. Is not the Christ proclaimed in the church the one who preached the gospel to the poor? Is not the Christ of its Eucharist also the brother of the one who is persecuted outside the church? . . . We cannot therefore merely give the marks of the church bearings that tend in an inward direction, understanding them in the light of word and sacrament; we must to the same degree give them outward direction and see them in reference to the world. They are not merely important for the internal activities of the church; they are even more important for the witness of the church's form in the world.

So Moltmann goes on to call for a radically missional perspective of the four words:

The church's unity is its unity in freedom. The church's holiness is its holiness in poverty. The church's apostolicity bears the sign of the cross and its catholicity is linked with its partisan support for the oppressed.

In *The True Church and the Poor* Jon Sobrino (1984, 98–121), following Moltmann's thinking, develops his own more strongly missiological view along the lines of the unity of the church of the poor, the holiness of the church of the poor, the catholicity of the church of the poor, and the apostolicity of the church of the poor: "I believe that the Church of the poor is an authentically missionary church dedicated to evangelization. Mission is much more important than in the past; it has changed the very being of the Church."[6]

The Latin American Roman Catholics have been echoed by Protestants as well. Across a wide spectrum of thought there is a growing sense that we must infuse the four ancient words with a new missiological emphasis. For example, Howard Snyder (1976, 133–34) does so as he comments about the unity of the church: "(1) The primary purpose of the unity of the Church is that God may be glorified. (2) The secondary purpose of the unity of the Church is the authentic communication of the Good News. (3) Unity in truth is unity with Christ and thus with the Trinity. (4) This unity in truth means both unity of belief and unity of life, both orthodoxy and orthopraxis."[7]

Maybe it is time we begin to see the four words not as adjectives which modify an entity we know as the church, but as verbals which describe the missionary action of the church's essential life in the world. This would make the four more than static attributes, more than testing marks, and even more than dynamic gifts and tasks. It would make them planetary orbits of the church's missionary life in the world.

6. Sobrino 1984, 117–18. See also Leonardo Boff 1986a; 1986b; Segundo 1985; Torres and Eagleson 1981; and Gutiérrez 1974, 255–85.

7. See also Míguez-Bonino 1981; Padilla 1987; Cook 1987; Costas 1982; Robert L. Wilson 1983; and Welsh 1986.

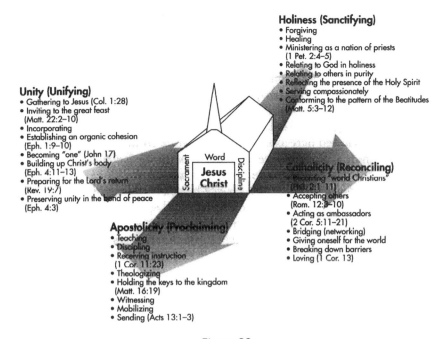

Holiness (Sanctifying)
• Forgiving
• Healing
• Ministering as a nation of priests
  (1 Pet. 2:4–5)
• Relating to God in holiness
• Relating to others in purity
• Reflecting the presence of the Holy Spirit
• Serving compassionately
• Conforming to the pattern of the Beatitudes
  (Matt. 5:3–12)

Unity (Unifying)
• Gathering to Jesus (Col. 1:28)
• Inviting to the great feast
  (Matt. 22:2–10)
• Incorporating
• Establishing an organic cohesion
  (Eph. 1:9–10)
• Becoming "one" (John 17)
• Building up Christ's body
  (Eph. 4:11–13)
• Preparing for the Lord's return
  (Rev. 19:7)
• Preserving unity in the bond of peace
  (Eph. 4:3)

Word

Sacrament

Jesus Christ

Discipline

Catholicity (Reconciling)
• Preparing "world Christians"
  (Matt. 21:11)
• Accepting others
  (Rom. 12:3–10)
• Acting as ambassadors
  (2 Cor. 5:11–21)
• Bridging (networking)
• Giving oneself for the world
• Breaking down barriers
• Loving (1 Cor. 13)

Apostolicity (Proclaiming)
• Teaching
• Discipling
• Receiving instruction
  (1 Cor. 11:23)
• Theologizing
• Holding the keys to the kingdom
  (Matt. 16:19)
• Witnessing
• Mobilizing
• Sending (Acts 13:1–3)

Figure 22
The Four Ancient Attributes as Missional Verbals

Adopting this perspective would provide us with a radically new way of affirming the congregation's missionary nature—and would give us very concrete means of understanding the church as an event, as a movement of missional existence in God's world (see figure 22). The "one" church of Jesus Christ would be seen as a *unifying* force. It would seek to invite, gather, and incorporate the world. The biblical images of organic cohesion, the life of the body, and wedding feast would be transformed into missionary action which would seek to "preserve the unity of the Spirit in the bond of peace" (Eph. 4:3 NASB). The "holy" church of Jesus Christ would be understood as a *sanctifying* event in the world. It would work toward forgiveness, healing, and the presence of the holy in the midst of the people. The tabernacle in the wilderness is a dominant image here, given fullest expression in Jesus Christ, Emmanuel, God with us. The "catholic" church of Jesus Christ would be understood as a *reconciling* event in the world. It would build bridges to gather fractured, alienated humanity into a common, renewed, changed fellowship of believers. Here is the church as ambassador, calling the world to be reconciled to God (2 Cor. 5). And the "apostolic" church of Jesus Christ would be seen as a *proclaiming* event in the world, the basis of truth and certainty, the offer of structure and stability, the fellowship of disciples who know, love, and serve each other because they know, love, and serve their Master. This is the witnessing, mobilizing, and teaching fellowship which, based on the teaching of the apostles and prophets, proclaims God's Word in the world.

Viewed as verbals, the four words are not only activities in which the church engages, but also descriptions of the essence of the church as it is found in the local congregation. What is the church? It is the unifying, sanctifying, reconciling, and proclaiming activity of Jesus Christ in the world. Mission is not viewed here as something separate from, or added to, the essence of the church. No! The essential nature of the local congregation is mission, or the congregation is not really the church.

Notice that our description is a far cry from the old saying, "Everything the church does is mission." Not so. As we shall see in chapter 8, what the church does internally with no intention of impacting the world outside itself is not mission. But when a local congregation understands that it is by its nature a constellation of missional activities in the world, and intentionally and carefully lives its life in the world as the embodiment of these activities—then it not only finds itself to be missionary, but discovers itself to have begun to emerge toward becoming authentically the church of Jesus Christ.

Part 4

Evangelical
and Conciliar
Mission Theologies

7

Forty Years
of Evangelical Mission Theology

The latter part of the twentieth century saw the explosive rise of the evangelicals as a religious force in North America, moving, as George Marsden (1975) has put it, "from Fundamentalism to Evangelicalism."[1] This growth has included an expanding role in sending missions coupled with very important developments in the way the evangelicals have articulated their mission theology.[2]

At the risk of oversimplification, this chapter presents a broad interpretive portrait of the historical development of evangelical mission theology from the birth of the National Association of Evangelicals (NAE) in 1942 to the triennial conference of the Interdenominational Foreign Mission Association

1. For help in defining what "evangelical" means, see Frank 1986; Wells and Woodbridge 1975; Marty 1970; 1984; Moberg 1972; Hoge 1976; Niebuhr 1937; Henry 1967; and James D. Hunter 1983. For a typological description see Quebedeaux 1978, 18–45, 53–54. Other definitions may be found in Bosch 1980, 30. Bosch is quoting from Beyerhaus 1975a, 307–8; he also mentions De Gruchy 1978 as giving a parallel description of five major groupings within evangelicalism. See also Murch 1956, 13; Kik 1958; and Webber 1978.

Martin Marty 1981, 9–10, gives an excellent definition of evangelicals. See also Ockenga 1960, which is quoted and enlarged upon by Bassham 1979, 173–74.

2. Some of the more accessible overviews of the evangelical mission theology of this period may be found in Bosch 1980; Handy 1984; Bassham 1979; Glasser and McGavran 1983; Glasser 1985; and Utuk 1986. See also Knapp 1977, 146–209; Harrell 1981; and Wagner 1981.

One of the most helpful treatments of this period and its historical roots, particularly with its 25-page bibliography, is Forman 1977; note, however, James Scherer's critique which follows Forman's analysis. See also Costas 1982, 135–61.

The relationship of modernity to the revitalization of evangelicalism is one of the major hidden dynamics behind the creation of mission theology during these years. See Marty 1981, 7–21; James D. Hunter 1983; Wells and Woodbridge 1975, 9–19; Marsden 1975; Carpenter 1984, 257–88; and Handy 1984.

(IFMA) and the Evangelical Foreign Missions Association (EFMA) which met with the Association of Evangelical Professors of Missions (AEPM) in Pasadena in 1984 (Allison 1985). Our thesis is that as North American evangelicals experienced (1) new sociocultural strength and confidence, (2) changes in the ecumenical theology of mission, and (3) developments in evangelical partner churches in the Third World, they responded with a broadening vision of an evangelical theology of mission which became less reactionary and more wholistic without compromising the initial evangelical élan of the World Missionary Conference at Edinburgh in 1910. This broadening took place in four general stages which we might call Reaction (in the 1940s and 1950s), Reassessment (in the 1960s), Reaffirmation (in the 1970s), and Redefinition (in the 1980s). To see the development more clearly, we will highlight four aspects of mission theology in each historical period: the context, the motivation, the goal, and the strategy. Although the story begins much earlier in the second half of the nineteenth century, we will pick it up after the two world wars had drastically altered people's perception of their world.

Reaction in the 1940s and 1950s

In the 1940s and 1950s the dominant characteristic of evangelical theology of mission seems to have been a continued reaction against the previous decades.[3] The war had solidified a certain pessimism concerning humanity, culture, the relevance of the Christian church to society, the condition of the world, and the old social gospel mentality. The threat of communism was always on the horizon during the Cold War era.

Evangelical reaction was expressed in two quite different formulations of mission theology. The contrasting responses to the liberal crisis[4] can be seen in the titles of two related but contrasting books published within two years of each other: Carl Henry's *Uneasy Conscience of Modern Fundamentalism* (1947) and Harold Lindsell's *Christian Philosophy of Missions* (1949). The revisionary and mutualist evangelicals have differed markedly from the reactionary and separatist fundamentalists up to the present day.[5] What, then, was the context to which these two groups were reacting in the late 1940s and early 1950s?

3. Carl Henry 1957, 33, says, "The fundamentalist movement became a distinctly twentieth-century expression of Christianity, characterized increasingly by its marks of reaction against liberalism."
    4. Lindsell 1962, 200, discusses the extent to which modernism had pushed the development of fundamentalist mission.
    5. A significant sociological study (Wilcox 1986) analyzed these two constituencies of the Ohio Moral Majority in 1986, and found marked differences.

The Context of Missions

On the one hand, the terrible world wars had shown that the kingdom of God would not be established immediately on earth. On the other hand, the passive constructionist era of Dwight Eisenhower was a high point for renewed church attendance and hopes of creating a brave new world, at least in America. Evangelical churches and missions in North America saw themselves in historic continuity with Edinburgh 1910, the early days of the International Missionary Council (IMC), and the Student Volunteer Movement (SVM), whose watchword had been propounded by John R. Mott: "the evangelization of the world in this generation."[6] But the dominant theme was one of reaction, of defining the evangelical movement in separatist categories.[7] Some fundamentalists referred to Protestant liberalism as "The Great Apostasy" and conceived the challenge as "The Battle of the Century" (Murch 1956, chs. 2–3). David Moberg (1972) has called this fundamentalist reaction to liberalism *The Great Reversal.*[8] It produced what Carl Henry (1957, ch. 2) termed "The Fundamentalist Reduction," which Charles Forman (1977, 103) describes as "a new, very conservative type of missiology . . . a defensive reaction to liberalism and the Laymen's Commission."[9]

After the war a host of new missionary recruits coming back from the trenches challenged the fundamentalists to join them in constructing a new conservative evangelicalism which was broader than fundamentalism (Donald Dayton 1976, 139–40). The result was "the emergence of a self-conscious new evangelicalism out of the original fundamentalist tradition and hence the clear division of that tradition into two major movements—evangelicalism and separatist fundamentalism" (Marsden 1975, 128). Earlier, when the NAE was formed in 1942, Harold Ockenga had made the point that the NAE would not be, in his words, "a reactionary, negative, or

6. In the late 1940s and 1950s the evangelicals had at their disposal the missiological thoughts of some of the greats like John Nevius, Robert Speer, Robert Glover, Samuel Zwemer, John R. Mott, and Roland Allen.

7. Joel Carpenter 1984, 267–68, writes, "Fundamentalism, according to George Marsden, has a paradoxical tension in its character. Sometimes it identifies with the 'establishment' and sometimes with the 'outsiders.' At times it presumes to speak for the 'mainstream' of American evangelical Christianity, seeing itself as the guardian of the 'faith once delivered to the saints.' . . . On the other hand, fundamentalists, like holiness groups, Pentecostal churches, and immigrant-based denominations, often acted like isolated, embattled sectarians." Carpenter has in view Marsden 1980, 6–7, 11–21, 124–31, 180–84, 192–93.

8. Moberg attributes this term to historian Timothy Smith (1962), though Moberg uses it as the title for his book. See also James D. Hunter 1983, 30.

9. Forman is referring here to William Ernest Hocking's work with the Laymen's Foreign Missions Inquiry and its subsequent report entitled *Re-Thinking Missions: A Layman's Inquiry after One Hundred Years* (1932), which mirrored the more liberal trends in North American public Protestantism. See Neill 1964.

destructive type of organization."[10] Even so, Harold Lindsell (1962, 192) has depicted the creation of the NAE as an evangelical reaction to the formation of the World Council of Churches (WCC). Three years later when the EFMA was organized, the emphasis fell on a more constructive note, the "primacy of evangelism in the self-understanding of the NAE" (Bassham 1979, 181).

Meanwhile the ecumenical Protestants were processing the postwar consequences of the social gospel. Richard Niebuhr's *Kingdom of God in America* (1937), the Hocking report on the Laymen's Inquiry, the International Missionary Council meetings (Jerusalem, 1928; Madras, 1938; Whitby, 1947; Willingen, 1952), and the official organization of the WCC in 1948 had convinced evangelicals that the ecumenical movement did not share their view of mission.[11] The strong influence of Johannes Hoekendijk at Willingen moved ecumenical theology away from an ecclesiocentric theology of mission toward a stress on the world's setting the missional agenda for the church, a stress which was particularly influential in the studies concerning the "Missionary Structures of the Congregation" (World Council of Churches 1968). The fundamentalists and evangelicals reacted vigorously by shaping and articulating their theology of mission in narrow, clearly definable categories. They carefully set forth their motivation, goals, and strategy for mission in the 1950s.

The Motivation for Missions

The reaction in the 1950s did not diminish the commitment of the evangelicals to preach the gospel to every creature (Marsden 1980, 181–82). Obedience to the imperative of the gospel became a major issue for them (David Johnson 1961, 152–54). Consistent with the evangelical perspective of the day, Harold Lindsell's *Missionary Principles and Practice* (1955, 28–50) suggested that the motivation for mission should include the Great Commission, the choice of Israel, the purpose of the church, realistic eschatology, and the need of the non-Christian world.[12]

In the midst of these imperatives, two overriding motifs stood out: the Great Commission (Matt. 28:18–20) and the coming millennium (Sandeen 1970). Focusing on Matthew 24:14, the premillennialists thought that once the church had preached the gospel of the kingdom to every nation, the millennium would begin. Their hopes for the second coming of Christ and the

10. Quoted in Marty 1984, 411. With regard to the formation of the NAE see Carpenter 1984, ch. 9.

11. See Bassham 1979, 15–36; Johnston 1974; Hoekstra 1979; Bosch 1980, 159–78; and Glasser and McGavran 1983, 113–19.

12. See also Lindsell 1961. Compare also with the themes presented at the IFMA Chicago conference of 1960, e.g., Walvoord 1961, 251–56, and with Bassham 1979, 177–79.

new kingdom he would establish on earth lent a strong, almost desperate urgency to gospel proclamation.

The Goal of Missions

Evangelicals articulated only one major goal of mission: the salvation of individual souls. Harold Lindsell (1962, 228) noted that this emphasis was specifically in response to the social aspects of the National Council of Churches–Division of Overseas Ministries (NCCC-DOM) missiology of the day. "Fundamental to a conservative philosophy of missions," Lindsell had said earlier (1961, 245), "is the assumption that man is a sinner." Whether these individuals lived in Los Angeles, London, or Lusaka, the eternal destiny of their souls was of utmost importance. The social, political, economic, and cultural aspects of the lives of the unsaved were relatively unimportant compared to the question of heaven and hell.

The Strategy of Missions

Interdenominational mission agencies arose with great strength and speed to form a significant force in conservative evangelical missiology after World War II. When the EFMA was founded in 1945, communications, means of travel, finances, and organizational structures were sufficiently in place for the evangelicals to begin to play a major role in sending missions. But there was little theoretical reflection. As Arthur Glasser (1985, 9) said of the period, "an elaborate theology of mission was not felt necessary."[13] The strategy amounted to one major command of Jesus to his disciples: Go!

It is instructive to note, however, that fundamentalist and evangelical missions actually carried out significant educational, medical, agricultural, and social projects in the Third World during this time.[14] Though the major goal was in theory the salvation of souls, the missionaries found that as they fell in love with the people to whom they had been sent, they yearned to help them in any way they could, and ended up doing work in such areas as education, medicine, agriculture, and translation.[15]

Carl Henry was on target when he spoke of "the uneasy conscience of modern fundamentalism." On the mission field many interdenominational fundamentalist and evangelical mission agencies found themselves far more socioeconomically and politically active than they would have considered

13. See also Lindsell 1962, ch. 7.
14. Harold Lindsell wrote in 1955 that the "means" of evangelism, education, medicine, and literature (1) "must be in harmony with the end" and (2) "must show themselves to be valid ones pragmatically" (p. 189).
15. Christian Weiss (1961) of "Back to the Bible Broadcast" made this point at the 1960 Chicago Congress of the IFMA.

being in North America. Was this because the North American environment had forced them into a "fundamentalist reduction" which could be overcome in other parts of the world? The ever-broadening vision kept calling the evangelicals to further and deeper reflection, and eventually drew them to making a careful reassessment of their mission theology.

Reassessment in the 1960s

Arthur Glasser has pointed out that "the year 1966 was truly crucial" for evangelical theology of mission. "Before it ended," he says, "a tremendous burst of dynamism had been released from within the evangelical wing of the church."[16] Harold Lindsell (1971, 91) wrote, "Affluence, in common with most of the churches, has overtaken evangelicals. They have never had it so good."[17] But the 1960s was also a time of tremendous challenge for evangelical mission agencies that were "seeking to engage a revolutionary world."[18]

The Context of Missions

In spite of North American peace, prosperity, and growing love of technology, world events were crying for new analyses and new vision. One of the major factors was the growth of the African nations during the 1960s. According to Charles Forman (1964, 17), in 1960 alone seventeen new African nations were born. Nationalism became a burning issue around the globe, although not as yet among Third World theologians and mission statesmen.

The Roman Catholic world was in an uproar. The Second Vatican Council met from 1962 to 1965, issuing documents like *Unitatis redintegratio*, *Lumen gentium*, and *Ad gentes divinitus* (Flannery 1975). These became indispensable reading for ecumenical and evangelical Protestants, who found some of their own perspectives articulated and stretched by Vatican II.

Evangelical mission theology responded to the dramatic changes going on in the ecumenical movement. One of the most influential happened in 1961 at New Delhi when the IMC was integrated into the WCC to become the Commission on World Mission and Evangelism (CWME).[19] Integration was

16. Glasser and McGavran 1983, 119. Similarly, Erling Jorstad (1981) has called the 1960s "a fundamental shift" in the development of North American evangelicalism.

17. See also Shelley 1967, 132.

18. Bassham 1979 uses this as the title of his chapter (5) dealing with this period.

19. Concerning the effects of this very controversial merger, see, e.g., *International Review of Mission* 70, no. 280 (Oct. 1981); Bassham 1979, 40–42, 210–12; Winter 1978; Warren 1974, 156–58; 1978; Neill 1964, 554–58; Nissen 1974. Evangelical assessments of the event may be found in Fife and Glasser 1961, 126–28; Johnston 1974, 240–42; Hoekstra 1979, 35–48; Costas 1982, 136; Henry 1967; and Lindsell 1966.

considered so important by its proponents that in 1961 Henry Van Dusen wrote an entire book (*One Great Ground of Hope*) dedicated to laying the historical and theological foundations for integration. About the same time Gerald Anderson edited *The Theology of the Christian Mission*,[20] which was to provide further foundations for ecumenical mission theory at New Delhi and afterwards.

The impact of integration on the evangelicals was overwhelming (Costas 1982, 136). In 1966 when the Congress on the Church's Worldwide Mission was convened by both the IFMA and the EFMA, the delegates stated, "The birth of the World Council of Churches and the pressures to integrate the International Missionary Council into the framework of that organization brought to the forefront the problem of conservative theological missionary cooperation."[21] So the fundamentalists and the new evangelicals found that they had to lay aside their differences and gather together to reassess their mission theology; they had to "wake up lest the foundations erode completely," as George Peters (1972, 28) expressed it. They held two major conferences in 1966: the Congress on the Church's Worldwide Mission (at Wheaton), and the World Congress on Evangelism (in Berlin). Although these conferences were far from identical, we will treat them here as complementary parts of a larger development of evangelical mission theology. Efiong Utuk (1986, 209) calls the Wheaton gathering a "minor miracle," considering that just six years before the IFMA had gathered in Chicago and had excluded the American Council of Christian Churches (ACCC), the EFMA, the NCCC-DOM, and the Pentecostals. As Harold Lindsell put it, "Perhaps who has been left out is as significant as who has been included."[22]

The Motivation for Missions

The motivations for mission were reassessed in 1966. At Berlin, John Stott presented an exegetical study of the Great Commission in Matthew and related passages in Luke and John, but the statement issued by the Berlin congress mentions the Great Commission only in passing. The Wheaton Declaration refers obliquely to "the evangelistic mandate," and also cites the eschatological theme, but no longer with frantic intensity.

20. In his introduction (p. 4) Anderson links the publication of this volume to the movement toward integration.
21. Lindsell 1966, 2. The link between the New Delhi integration and the move for a united reassessment of evangelical mission theology has been mentioned by others: Henry 1967, 85; Costas 1982, 136; and Shelley 1967, 103.
22. Lindsell 1962, 229. It is interesting to note that in this article Lindsell stated prophetically, "It is regrettable that fifty years after Edinburgh (1910) there cannot be a world congress for mission which transcends some of the unimportant differences dividing those of similar missionary aims. . . . Perhaps the faith missions may be able to enlarge this vision and provide a creative and dynamic leadership for a new age of missionary advance" (p. 230).

What comes to the fore most strongly in 1966 is an intentional continuity with the Edinburgh conference of fifty years before and the SVM watchword. The evangelicals at Berlin said, "Our goal is nothing short of the evangelization of the human race in this generation by every means God has given to the mind and will of men." At Wheaton they said, "The gospel must be preached in our generation to the peoples of every tribe, tongue, and nation. This is the supreme task of the church." But evangelicals were wrong in presenting themselves as the only viable descendants of Edinburgh 1910. The ecumenical movement was as well.

At Wheaton and Berlin the evangelicals began to discover other motivations for mission. The good news for lost humanity (One Gospel), the unity and reconciliation brought to all humanity in Christ through his lordship over the church (One Race), the call to set out God's Word in a broken world (One Task)—these broader, more integrating motivational foundations were quarried from the Scriptures.[23]

The Goal of Missions

The 1966 documents show a major shift from the strongly individualistic categories of previous decades to an increased emphasis on the church and its encounter with a multiplicity of cultures in the world. Berlin defined evangelism as proclamation for conversion, coupled with "serving the Lord in every calling of life" and participating in the "fellowship of his church." These were significant new steps toward broadening the goal of missions in line with the new mission emphases of the era.

When *Practical Anthropology* began publishing in 1953, Jacob Loewen, Eugene Nida, and Alan Tippett called the evangelical missionary force to take seriously the church's relation to culture. That same year Melvin Hodges (1953) encouraged evangelicals to reassess the importance of the Venn-Anderson "three-self theory" (self-government, self-support, self-propagation) and begin thinking of the indigenous church as a legitimate goal of missions. Further, the expanding influence of the Church Growth movement[24] with its stress on "people movements," along with the formation of new national churches, meant a whole new set of goals for evangelical mission. Amidst the optimism of a new-found unity of vision and cooperation in mission, there was nevertheless a mood of repentance, humility, and concern for a new impact of the gospel in the world.

23. See Lindsell 1966, 217–37 ("The Wheaton Declaration"); Henry 1967, 3–6; and Henry and Mooneyham 1967, 1:5–7.

24. In 1965 Donald McGavran moved the Institute of Church Growth from Eugene, Oregon, to Fuller Theological Seminary in Pasadena. The acceptance of the Iberville Statement gave great hope to the movement (McGavran 1977, 171–76; *International Review of Missions* 57, no. 227 [July 1968]).

The Strategy of Missions

New goals were both the product of and the incentive for developing new mission strategies, and Wheaton and Berlin were willing to experiment with untried forms of missionary cooperation, careful partnership with national churches, and timid openness to innovative methodology. The new evangelicals were experiencing a growing confidence in their role in world mission, and were becoming increasingly articulate of their own mission theology, as can be seen in their publications. *Evangelical Missions Quarterly* began in 1964, the same year the *Church Growth Bulletin* made its first appearance. Berlin was cosponsored by *Christianity Today* (along with Billy Graham), in part to celebrate the tenth anniversary of its founding.

The broadening vision brought new concern for unity in cooperative mission endeavors—among mission agencies and with younger national churches. Kenneth Strachan of the Latin American Mission and the Evangelism-in-Depth program was influential in this regard not only in North America but also in Africa and Asia (George Peters 1970). Beyond this, there was a strong affirmation at both conferences regarding the use of psychology, anthropology, sociology, business management, statistics, and technological advances for the sake of missions. The Wheaton delegates declared, "The best results come when, under the Holy Spirit, good principles of cultural and social patterns are applied to the proclamation of the Gospel" (Lindsell 1966, 232).

And yet in the midst of the new awakening, the vestiges of the old fundamentalist reactionism were also present. While a very strong anti–Roman Catholic sentiment was expressed in spite of Vatican II, the ecumenical movement came in for the sharpest attack. An observer from the WCC at Wheaton, Eugene Smith, noted that nine of the fifteen major papers carried attacks on the ecumenical movement. At Berlin the search for global evangelistic cooperation was very clearly divorced from anything that smacked of visible unity à la the WCC (Bassham 1979, 210–30).

This strong negativism colored the evangelical reassessment of mission for the next several years. It was especially evident in the way evangelical theologians and missiologists reacted to the Fourth Assembly of the WCC at Uppsala in 1968, and to a lesser degree the CWME meeting at Bangkok in 1973.[25] The need to deal with this negativism led to the most significant evangelical mission conference of these forty years: the International Congress on World Evangelization convened by Billy Graham in Lausanne in 1974 (Costas 1982, 136).[26] It was crucial that at Lausanne the new evangel-

25. See McGavran 1968; Beyerhaus 1971, 1972. The Frankfurt Declaration, which Beyerhaus spearheaded in 1970 in response to Uppsala, was a significant reaction by the German and North American evangelicals. See, e.g., McGavran 1977, 266–72; Glasser 1971.

26. Efiong Utuk (1986, 212) affirms, "Lausanne was to the Evangelicals what New Delhi was to the conciliarists—a turning point."

icals be able to go beyond reaction and reassessment to a reaffirmation of historic evangelical mission theology.

Reaffirmation in the 1970s

When delegates gathered at Lausanne, the world had been turned upside down, and it seemed imperative to evangelicals that they reaffirm their traditional faith. The hippies and the flower children had been questioning the most basic American values. An unprecedented exodus from the church had impacted primarily the mainline denominations.[27] The world which had seemed so large in 1966 had become a global village in danger of overpopulation and pollution. The Vietnam War cast into serious doubt the United States' ability to save the world. Martin Luther King and the Civil Rights movement had prompted quite a few changes in the United States.

The Context of Missions

The issues of the 1970s created a whole new context in which evangelicals needed to reaffirm their theology of mission. The evangelical world was experiencing what Donald Bloesch called *The Evangelical Renaissance* (1973),[28] a tremendous growth and development at all levels. Vietnam veterans were hurting, but their evangelical brothers and sisters were flooding the Urbana missionary conventions, and providing a host of new recruits for the burgeoning evangelical mission agencies (Coote 1982). The increasing influence of evangelical writers, preachers, and television evangelists was beginning to catch people's attention.

Moreover, North American evangelicals were suddenly encountering hundreds of very able evangelical leaders in the Third World churches. Out of the 2,473 participants at Lausanne, nearly one half were from non-Western countries. These Third World theologians who had not inherited the fundamentalist reduction would call Lausanne to a more wholistic reaffirmation of historic evangelical mission theology (Douglas 1975, 28–30).[29]

Lausanne marked the beginning of a new day. As C. Peter Wagner (1981, 90) put it, "The 'Great Reversal' was coming to an end."[30] Although some of the evangelical-ecumenical tensions of previous years were still evident, an atmosphere of greater tolerance and hesitant rapprochement with the evan-

27. Dean Kelley (1972, chs. 1–2) asked, "Are the Churches Dying?" and "Is Religion Obsolete?"

28. Cf. Bernard Ramm, *The Evangelical Heritage* (1973).

29. See also Padilla 1976, 8–11; and Pierard 1970.

30. At Urbana 1970 a growing awareness of the sociocultural and political dimensions of gospel proclamation had been quite evident in the main theme and the major addresses. See also Stott 1971.

gelicals had been evident at the Bangkok meeting of the CWME in 1973.[31] Although *Evangelii nuntiandi*, a major Roman Catholic exhortation on evangelization in the modern world, did not appear until late 1975, the reaction of the evangelicals to the documents of Vatican II had been sufficiently positive that the old anti–Roman Catholic rhetoric of the past was nearly silent at Lausanne (Attalah 1975). René Padilla (1976, 10–11) commented, "Evangelicalism on the whole is no longer willing to be identified as a movement characterized by a tendency to isolate evangelism, in both theory and practice, from the wider context represented by the nature of the Gospel and the life and mission of the Church." John Stott called this broadening perspective "evangelicalism with a face-lift" (Padilla 1976, 6).

Given the fantastic upheaval of the previous decade, it is no surprise that Lausanne was intentionally convened for the sake of reaffirmation. In the opening convocation Billy Graham explained:

> This Congress convenes to reemphasize those biblical concepts which are essential to evangelism. There are five concepts that both the evangelical and the non-evangelical world have been studying and debating during the past few years—concepts which we believe to be essential to true evangelism and which I expect we will reaffirm in this congress. . . . First, we are committed to the authority of Scripture. . . . A second concept we expect to reaffirm is the lostness of man apart from Jesus Christ. . . . Thirdly, we expect to reaffirm at this conference that salvation is in Jesus Christ alone. . . . Fourthly, . . . we expect to reaffirm that our witness must be by word and deed. . . . The last concept which we must reaffirm at this congress [is] the necessity of evangelism. [Douglas 1975, 28–30]

The Motivation for Missions

The hesitant broadening of motivational foundations for mission at Wheaton and Berlin became full-blown wholistic mission at Lausanne. The main figure at Lausanne in the construction of a broad biblical motivation for mission was John Stott. While maintaining continuity with the 1940s and 1950s by centering on the Great Commission, Stott himself broadened his understanding of it. Earlier at Berlin he had argued "that the mission of the Church . . . is exclusively a preaching, converting, and teaching mission." But after Lausanne Stott (1975b, 23) wrote, "Today . . . I would express myself differently. . . . I now see more clearly that not only the consequences of the commission but the actual commission itself must be understood to include social as well as evangelistic responsibility."[32] Stott was not alone in this. Peter Wagner (1981, 91), for example, having heard such speakers as

31. Arthur Glasser (1977) said he was a little encouraged, a little discouraged, but heartened enough to want to work at bridging the gap, listening and learning, bearing witness and serving.
32. See also Henry 1974; Bassham 1979, 231–32.

René Padilla, Samuel Escobar, and Orlando Costas at Lausanne, began to accept the concept of wholistic mission.[33]

A second foundational motivation for mission that was influential at Lausanne was the evangelical response to the *missio Dei* theology of the IMC meeting at Willingen in 1952 and the CWME meeting at Mexico City in 1963 (Vicedom 1965). John Stott articulated it this way: "Mission is an activity of God arising out of the very nature of God. The living God of the Bible is a sending God, which is what 'mission' means. He sent the prophets to Israel. He sent His Son into the world. His Son sent out the apostles and the seventy, and the Church. He also sent the Spirit to the Church and sends Him into our hearts today. So the mission of the Church arises from the mission of God and is to be modeled on it" (in Douglas 1975, 66).[34] Thus the motivation for mission was understood to lie in the trinitarian nature of God's character and, by extension, in the nature of the church.[35] With such broad foundations, Lausanne's vision and goals became wider and more wholistic.

The Goal of Missions

Three major goals were reaffirmed at Lausanne: church growth, the kingdom of God, and contextualization. The mark of the Church Growth movement on the proceedings at Lausanne is unmistakable (Douglas 1975, 32), being evident not only in the strategy papers and global surveys, but also in the plenary papers given by Donald McGavran and Ralph Winter. For the Church Growth enthusiasts the goal of mission involved the recognition of homogeneous cultural units, and the planting of the church in their midst. This meant that more attention had to be given to ecclesiology, and to the place of the local church both as goal and as instrument of world evangelization.[36]

Secondly, the goal of missions in relation to the kingdom of God was brought out by Peter Beyerhaus, Andrew Kirk, José Grau, and Billy Graham among others. This note was then echoed by the Ad Hoc Group on Radical Discipleship, composed primarily of persons from the Third World, including René Padilla and Samuel Escobar.[37]

33. Costas (1982, 158–59), Wagner (1981, 91–96), and Johnston (1978, 300–306) held an ongoing discussion of what the broadening of motivation means for interpreting the Lausanne Covenant and the consequent uneasiness of some North American evangelicals. See also Padilla 1976, 12; and Henry 1974.

34. See also Anderson and Stransky 1975, 6.

35. See Douglas 1975, 5; Snyder 1975; Runia 1975; Espinoza 1975; Newbigin 1963.

36. Howard Snyder, Francis Schaeffer, Henri Blocher, Hector Espinoza Trevino, and Jonathan T'ien-en Chao were among those who emphasized this at Lausanne.

37. See Beyerhaus 1975b; Kirk 1975; Grau 1975; Douglas 1975, 1294–96; cf. Escobar 1970.

The new evangelical theology of the kingdom of God also brought attention to contextualization as a goal of mission. At Lausanne the concept of contextualization as a natural step forward from indigenization was not really questioned. Rather, it was accepted and assumed, then strongly qualified and carefully distinguished from religious syncretism and cultural Protestantism (Douglas 1975, 1216–93).

The Strategy of Missions

Although Lausanne's agenda dealt with missiological reflection and theology, it was dominated by issues of strategy. The mood seemed to be one of pragmatism: "anything goes—if it works." That the Missions Advanced Research and Communication Center (MARC) of World Vision was a major consultant to the congress was a signal that the evangelicals were moving into the technological culture. Because of the prominence given to the Church Growth movement through Donald McGavran's and Ralph Winter's plenary papers, Church Growth strategies for cross-cultural church planting received major attention as well. In addition, Lausanne's aim of achieving unprecedented evangelical organizational unity for the sake of world evangelization meant that strategy was uppermost in everyone's mind (Costas 1982, 137).[38]

Given the emphasis on strategy, the relationship of missions to national churches became crucial, particularly in view of the growing maturity and restlessness of Third World churches in partnership with North American missions and denominations. So while the ecumenical movement was thinking in terms of moratorium, the evangelicals were seeking new cooperative strategies in education, literacy programs, interdenominational and intermissional evangelistic campaigns, leadership training, health programs, and even dialogue. Thus "visible unity" received a nod, but still remained within the arena of "cooperation in evangelism," the term used in paragraph 7 of the Lausanne Covenant (Douglas 1975, 5).

However, the new breadth had a limit. The relationship of evangelism and social action kept coming up for discussion, but was not resolved. Lausanne moved beyond Wheaton and Berlin by relating the two concepts in a positive way and overcoming the dichotomous perspective held before. Following John Stott's lead, Lausanne related the two ideas by viewing social action as a partner to evangelism. But Lausanne qualified that partnership by stating in paragraph 6, "In the church's mission of sacrificial service evangelism is primary" (Douglas 1975, 5). Whether this primacy relates to social action as a goal, as a means, or as a product of mission remained unclear. This hesi-

---

38. The official reference volume for Lausanne includes over 500 pages of strategy papers and another 150 pages of regional analyses.

tancy to engage global social problems squarely was decried by the Third World theologians in the Radical Discipleship group (Douglas 1975, 1294–96).[39] This issue more than any other served to highlight the ambivalence between the fundamentalist perspective of the 1940s and 1950s and the new evangelical viewpoint of the late 1960s. But this weakness of Lausanne does not minimize the importance of the conference. "The meeting itself symbolized the emergence of a worldwide community of evangelicals in which 50% of the participants . . . came from the Third World. Lausanne was one of the most geographically representative gatherings of Christians ever held. . . . The Covenant is the most mature and comprehensive statement produced by evangelicals" (Bassham 1979, 245).

Lausanne as an event and as the birth of a covenant demonstrated to the world the developing unity, growing confidence, increased enthusiasm, and broadened vision of the evangelicals in mission to the world. The ensuing decade would be one of tremendous activity, creativity, and production. It would take the next decade to process the implications of Lausanne. The fourth part of our story, then, deals with the process of redefining the basic issues raised at Lausanne.

Redefinition in the 1980s

We have arrived at the era of Ronald Reagan. The Vietnam War was neither forgotten, nor dealt with. Richard Nixon had been dethroned, creating a national disenchantment with politics. Then Jimmy Carter opened the way for new evangelical political power to fill the vacuum left by the Eastern establishment's demise (Robert Fowler 1982), as the young evangelicals began to articulate a new kind of activist word-and-deed synthesis.[40]

The Context of Missions

A major aspect of the post-Lausanne era was the rapid growth of evangelical strength in all arenas of North American life.[41] Who in the 1940s would have thought to see *Evangelicals in the White House* (Jorstad 1981)? On the heels of Lausanne the growth of evangelical influence was accompanied by some serious thinking about mission. In March 1976, a Consultation on Theology and Mission was held at Trinity Evangelical Divinity School (Hes-

39. See also Padilla 1976; Wagner 1981, 97–99.
40. See, e.g., Quebedeaux 1974; and Marsden 1984—an excellent overview in the form of a symposium.
41. See, e.g., Harrell 1981; Marsden 1984; Hutcheson 1981a; 1981b; Coote 1982; Henry 1980. In 1976 Carl Henry wrote a "sequel" to his *Uneasy Conscience of Modern Fundamentalism* (1947); in *Evangelicals in Search of Identity* he notes the tremendous rebirth of evangelical influence and its expression in the Chicago Declaration of 1974 (pp. 33–38).

selgrave 1978). The next year in Atlanta a Consultation on Future Evangelical Concerns was convened to "identify the problems and opportunities facing the evangelical church in the last quarter of this century" (Hoke 1978). Then in 1979 a second Consultation on Theology and Mission was held at Trinity Evangelical Divinity School (Hesselgrave 1979).

But the greatest influence on evangelical theology of mission during this time came from Third World evangelical theologians. By 1975 Third World members constituted the majority of the World Evangelical Fellowship (Scott 1979, 52–53). That influence was very clear at major conferences like the one at Pattaya, Thailand, in June 1980, and later at both the Consultation on the Theology of Development, held in 1980 in Hoddesdon, England, and the First Conference of Evangelical Mission Theologians from the Two-Thirds World, held in Bangkok in 1982.[42] Thus evangelicals found they had to deal in a new way with subjects like neo-Pentecostalism, contextualization, Catholicism, the Church Growth movement, dialogue with the non-Christian religions, and mission strategy and changing political situations.[43]

The hallmark year was 1980, the year of three major conferences. When 850 evangelical mission thinkers gathered in Pattaya, the complexities of doing mission in the modern world were highlighted by meeting in a country where hundreds of thousands of Indochinese refugees had sought protection.[44] The theology of liberation was growing in importance and influence in political affairs in Latin America, Africa was continuing its tortuous track in nation building, and Asian theologians were beginning to ask very important and unsettling questions. The Commission on World Mission and Evangelism had just met the month before in Melbourne,[45] and had reasserted the priority of the gospel's preferential option for the poor. Preparations were also under way for the World Consultation on Frontier Mission, which, organized by Ralph Winter and others under the rubric "A Church for Every People by the Year 2000," was to be held in Edinburgh in October 1980 (Starling 1981).

The Motivation for Missions

At Pattaya the motivations for mission represented a curious mixture of the old and the new. In some ways Pattaya was a step backward from Lausanne and a restatement of the SVM watchword which had figured so

42. See, e.g., Sider 1981; Samuel and Sugden 1984.
43. These are some of the subjects covered at the First Consultation on Theology and Mission, Trinity Evangelical Divinity School, March 22–25, 1976 (Hesselgrave 1978).
44. General reviews of the Pattaya conference may be found in Douglas 1980; Scott 1981b, 57–75 (see also the responses on subsequent pages); Stowe 1981, 23–25; Coggins 1980; "COWE: 200,000 by the Year 2000" 1980; and Winter 1980.
45. See *International Review of Mission* 69, nos. 275, 276, 277 (July 1980–January 1981).

strongly in 1966 at Wheaton and Berlin. Obedience to the Acts 1:8 form of the Great Commission was reasserted, stressing the element of witness. The writers of the Thailand Statement (1981) said, "As his witnesses [Christ] has commanded us to proclaim his good news in the power of the Holy Spirit to every culture and nation, and to summon them to repent, to believe and to follow him." This witness is motivated by four major truths: the primacy of evangelism, the urgency of the task, the lostness of humankind, and the coming of Christ (Coggins 1980, 225–27).

On the other hand, the Thailand Statement also reaffirmed Lausanne in saying, "We are also the servants of Jesus Christ who is himself both 'the servant' and 'the Lord.' . . . All God's people 'should share his concern for justice and reconciliation throughout human society and for the liberation of men from every kind of oppression.'" But then Pattaya went beyond Lausanne in stressing love, humility, and integrity as vital attitudes for the evangelization of the world. Again it appeared to be the Third World theologians and the North American evangelical social activists who called for a broader outlook on mission. Nearly a quarter of the 850 participants signed "A Statement of Concerns on the Future of the Lausanne Committee for World Evangelization," calling for serious consideration of social, political, and economic issues in relation to world evangelization.[46]

The Goal of Missions

Waldron Scott (1981b, 70) points out that the consultation at Pattaya was dominated by one theme: "For ten days it kept before a representative group of Christian leaders a world in which an estimated 16,750 people groups lie beyond the reach (proclamation *or* service) of any existing church—'hidden' people who will be evangelized only if cross-cultural missionaries are sent from one people to another." The issue of "unreached peoples" was a natural progression from the Church Growth stress on "people movements" at Lausanne. But the issue was also a controversial one, with representatives from the Third World arguing strongly against the "homogeneous unit principle." Their argument centered not so much on the strategy as on the goal of mission. Was it proper to hold up as the goal of missions a series of separate churches, each for its own ethnocultural people group? What did this say about the unity of the church and the unity of humankind under the lordship of Christ? Four months later at the Edinburgh Consultation on Frontier Mission, the other side of the spectrum would be emphasized.

The second major issue was again the relationship of evangelism and social action as goals of mission. Pattaya reaffirmed Lausanne's position that al-

46. See, e.g., Douglas 1980, 44. From the perspective of a participant, Orlando Costas (1982, 135–61) gives an excellent overview and critique.

though evangelism and social action are integrally related, evangelism is primary ("Thailand Statement" 1981, 30). Pattaya highlighted the social dimensions of the gospel, but then redefined them in terms of service. The last section of the Thailand Statement (1981, 31) said, "We pledge ourselves to SERVE the needy and the oppressed and in the name of Christ to seek for them relief and justice." We may say that Pattaya did not go beyond Lausanne in any significant way, leaving the question of "priority" to be solved later.[47]

The Strategy of Missions

In the area of strategy Pattaya wanted to be at the forefront of mission endeavor. North American evangelicals were anxious to use all the ethnolinguistic, cultural, sociological, statistical, and anthropological tools at their disposal in order to identify the 16,750 unreached peoples and mobilize the whole church to reach them. This led to a major stress on cooperative unity which was broader than Berlin and Lausanne. Pattaya said, "We joyfully affirm the unity of the Body of Christ and acknowledge that we are bound together with one another and with all true believers. While a true unity of Christ is not necessarily incompatible with organizational diversity, we must nevertheless strive for a visible expression of our oneness" ("Thailand Statement" 1981, 31). This emphasis was especially significant given the presence at Pattaya of many specialized parachurch missionary agencies and the increasing strength of Third World mission-sending organizations.[48]

But Pattaya also narrowed the focus. The "unreached peoples" were too narrowly defined as groups without a church in their midst—there was little or no reference to the sociopolitical and economic status of each people group. Was this a reaction to the overemphasis on socioeconomic issues at Melbourne? Clearly each conference needed the other, as Thomas Stransky (1981) rightly observed.[49]

Pattaya's focus was narrower than the redefinitions of evangelical mission theology articulated at the time. Major conferences had covered a wide range of related issues: "Evangelicals and Liberation" (Armerding 1977), "An Evangelical Commitment to Simple Life-style" (Sider 1982), "The Church and Peacemaking" (a 1983 conference in Pasadena), "Evangelicals and the Bishops' Pastoral Letter" (Curry 1984), the Glen Eyrie North American Conference on Muslim Evangelization (Glasser 1979a), and the Willowbank Conference on Studies in Christianity and Culture (Coote and Stott 1980). Thus Pattaya must be seen within the context of an evangelicalism come of

47. Whether the concept of priority itself is valid was discussed in 1982 at the Grand Rapids Consultation on the Relationship between Evangelism and Social Justice, sponsored by the Lausanne Committee for World Evangelization (LCWE) (Nicholls 1985).

48. See, e.g., Wong et al. 1973; Marlin Nelson 1976; and Keyes 1983.

49. See also Robinson 1984; Stott 1980; and Bosch 1988b, 467.

age, with young evangelicals like Tom Sine, Ronald Sider, Howard Snyder, and Jim Wallis calling for a broader social and political involvement. Meanwhile Third World theologians were advocating a more wholistic approach to mission, as, for example, in René Padilla's (1985) book of essays on the kingdom. The increasing strength of the evangelical churches in the Third World demanded better mission-church cooperation and translated into the rise of Third World mission-sending agencies, particularly from South Korea and Brazil.

Thus when the IFMA, EFMA, and AEPM met at the U.S. Center for World Mission in Pasadena in September 1984, they demonstrated both continuity and discontinuity with their heritage. David Hesselgrave and Donald McGavran called for a continuation of the great missionary élan of Edinburgh 1910, and a commitment to proclaiming the gospel of personal faith in Jesus Christ and radical transformation of each person's orientation to God, self, society, and world. At the same time Ray Badgero, John Gration, and representatives from MARC highlighted the need for careful cultural analysis, church and parachurch cooperation, and technological sophistication (Allison 1985; Gration 1985).

The story continues. In the midst of the complexities of mission in today's world, exciting new discoveries are possible for evangelicals in dialogue with Roman Catholic, Orthodox, and ecumenical perspectives. North American evangelicals will probably find one of those new discoveries to be the theology of the kingdom of God. Arthur Glasser (1985, 12), Howard Snyder (1983), René Padilla, and John Stott (1985) are among those who have called for an analysis of the kingdom motif for evangelical theology of mission. The kingdom motif could provide a vehicle for greater breadth of vision, including wiser and more careful use of technology, better understanding of other Christians, and increased cooperation between churches. Evangelicals might find the gospel to be a transforming force in society without losing the missionary élan of Edinburgh 1910 and the drive of the Student Volunteer Movement, which have been at the heart of evangelical mission theology for many years (Harder 1980).

8

Conciliar Mission Theology, 1930s–1990s

This chapter will illustrate how ecumenical theology of mission over the last sixty years has proven the truth of Stephen Neill's axiom, "When everything is mission, nothing is mission" (1959, 81). The purpose is to call us to search again for a dynamic and contextually appropriate balance between church and mission in both theory and practice. There is space here for only three brief snapshots of the last sixty years: (1) the 1930s—recognition of the need for a close relation between church and mission; (2) the 1960s—the articulation of a close relation between church and mission; and (3) the 1990s—the two-pronged loss of both church and mission. We will conclude with some implications for future ecumenical missiology.[1]

The relation of church and mission has been one of the most difficult issues vexing missiology during the last sixty years.[2] It is essential that we be very clear about this relation, for it affects all other aspects of both our theology of church and our theology of mission. My introduction to the importance of this relation came through the ministry of John Piet in *The Road*

---

1. Because of limits in space here, we will not attempt to explain or document many of the observations that follow. The reader may consult, among others, Bassham 1979, 15–121; Bosch 1980, 159–201; 1991, 368–408; Scherer 1987, 93–163; *International Review of Mission* 67, no. 267 (July 1978); 70, no. 280 (October 1981); and 77, no. 307 (July 1988); Gerald H. Anderson 1961; Anderson and Stransky 1974; and, from an evangelical perspective, Johnston 1974; Hoekstra 1979; McGavran 1977; Hedlund 1981; and Glasser and McGavran 1983.

2. Note that we are not referring here to the relationship of an institutional church or denomination to another institution like a mission society or agency. This more structural problem is affected by the subject of this chapter, but is subsequent to it. The first question must be how we relate the two *ideas* of church and mission. Subsequently, we can begin to see how this ideational relation affects the way institutions react to each other.

Ahead (1970). What Piet wrote there has affected both my ecclesiology and my missiology ever since.

The Road Ahead contains a foreword by Stephen Neill, and derives naturally from Piet's and Neill's context of the church in India. In two ways the Indian connection gave urgency and impetus to the issue of the relation of church and mission. First, one must consider the influence that persons like Neill and Lesslie Newbigin had on the "ecumenical"[3] movement associated with the World Council of Churches (WCC), with both of them offering their contribution out of what they had learned from and in the Indian context. Especially significant was the global impact of the movement toward unity in the formation of the Church of South India, a phenomenon that affected both Neill's and Piet's denominations and mission agencies. Secondly, we must remember that the missiological significance of the relation of church and mission was first articulated in Madras, India, at the International Missionary Council (IMC) meeting in 1938.[4]

In *The Road Ahead* Piet is concerned with developing an ecclesiology that is missionary. Thus Neill says in the foreword that Piet's intention is to offer "a dynamic as against a static interpretation of the nature and being of the Church" (1970, 5). In this effort Piet joined a number of other theologians and missiologists.[5] He shared with them a "desire to . . . point the church away from its introversion outward toward its reason for being, its apostolicity in the world, and in this sense, its 'Road Ahead'" (Van Engen 1984, 187; cf. Piet 1970, 12). So Piet (1970, 9) begins his work by quoting Neill (1959, 112). "What we need," Neill had said, "is a true theology of the Church. All our ecclesiologies are inadequate and out of date. . . . The one central purpose for which the Church has been called into existence is that . . . it should preach the Gospel to every creature. Everything else—ministry, sacraments, doctrine, worship—is ancillary to this."

When I first read *The Road Ahead*, the ecclesiological issues made sense to me. But I was unaware that in the volume from which Piet had quoted,

---

3. Although we all know that the word *ecumenical* does not exclude those holding to an evangelical theology, in this chapter we will use the words *ecumenical* and *conciliar* to mean predominantly the persons and perspectives associated with the World Council of Churches. This does not mean that the WCC has a monopoly on the ecumenical movement or on ecumenicity. Clearly the terms *ecumenical* and *evangelical* are not mutually exclusive, yet they usually are understood to refer to rather distinct perspectives. I consider myself an ecumenical-evangelical: I belong to the Reformed Church in America, a charter member of the WCC, and I cooperate with, teach, and work alongside members of a host of various churches from all over the *oecumene*. Yet I hold to an evangelical theology, articulated most clearly in the Lausanne Covenant of 1974. Bosch, 1980, 28–30, is a helpful discussion of this matter. See also Van Engen 1981, 379–85.

4. For the record of this conference see International Missionary Council 1938.

5. Others who have emphasized similar concerns are Küng 1968; Berkouwer 1976; Hendrikus Berkhof 1979; Segundo 1973; Moltmann 1977; Griffiths 1975; Dulles 1974; Leonardo Boff 1986b; Snyder 1977; Sobrino 1981; Van Engen 1984 and 1991b.

Neill also had offered a cryptic statement (an axiom, if you will) highlighting the missiological dilemma that would plague ecumenical mission thinking for decades, a statement Neill would repeat often in subsequent years: "When everything is mission, nothing is mission."[6]

Here is the dilemma involved in Neill's axiom: On the one hand, we find it necessary to affirm that the church of Jesus Christ finds its fullest expression only as it lives out its nature as a missionary people sent by God as ambassadors for the reconciliation of the world (2 Cor. 5). As Emil Brunner said, "The Church exists by mission as fire exists by burning" (quoted in Griffiths 1975, 135). But on the other hand, we also know that church and mission are not synonymous. We might define the church as "the one, holy, universal, and apostolic community of the disciples of Jesus Christ, gathered from all the families of the earth around Word, sacrament, and common witness." And we could define mission with Neill (1984) as "the intentional crossing of barriers from church to nonchurch in word and deed for the sake of the proclamation of the gospel." The fact remains that in the minds of many, church and mission are distinct and sometimes conflicting ideas. As Lesslie Newbigin (1954, 164–65) said earlier:

> In the thinking of the vast majority of Christians, the words "church" and "mission" connote two different kinds of society. The one is conceived to be a society devoted to worship and the spiritual care and nurture of its members. . . . The other is conceived to be a society devoted to the propagation of the gospel, passing on its converts to the safe keeping of "the church." . . . It is taken for granted that the missionary obligation is one that has to be met AFTER the needs of the home have been fully met; that existing gains have to be thoroughly consolidated before we go further afield; that the world-wide church has to be built up with the same sort of prudent business enterprise.

Although the two ideas are distinct, we are also aware that it is impossible to understand one—or to be part of one—without being a part of the other. Mission activity is supported by the church, carried out by people from and in the church; and the fruits of mission are received by the church. On the other hand, the church lives out its calling in the world through mission, finds its essential purpose in its participation in God's mission, and engages in a multitude of programs whose purpose is mission.

So we cannot understand mission without understanding the nature of the church, and we cannot understand the church without looking at its mission. As Newbigin (1954, 169) has said, "Just as we must insist that a Church which has ceased to be a mission has lost the essential character of a Church,

---

6. Neill repeated this statement in one of his last public lectures, "How My Mind Has Changed about Mission," offered in 1984 at the Overseas Ministries Study Center when it was still in Ventnor, New Jersey.

so we must also say that a mission which is not at the same time truly a Church is not a true expression of the divine apostolate. An unchurchly mission is as much a monstrosity as an unmissionary church."[7] But we must also hasten to qualify the relationship between the concepts of church and mission by affirming Neill's axiom: "When everything [in the church] is mission, nothing is mission."

The 1930s: The Recognition of the Need for a Close Relation between Church and Mission

David Bosch (1991, 369) points out that "for an understanding of the shifts in Protestant thinking regarding the relationship between church and mission, the contributions of the world missionary conferences are of primary importance." And, for our topic, probably the most important of the twentieth century was the 1938 meeting of the International Missionary Council in Tambaram, Madras, India. At Tambaram, and for the first time in the history of the missionary movement, an urgent global consensus began to form that mission and church somehow belonged together. Although Tambaram is presently remembered mostly for its impact on the discussion concerning Christian faith and other religions,[8] its most significant contribution had to do with the relation of church and mission.

At the time two major forces were pushing church and mission together. First, there was increasing concern that the concept of church needed something more. Early in the twentieth century North American (and to a lesser extent European) mainstream Protestant churches had basked in the euphoria of high optimism regarding the *Kingdom of God in America* (Niebuhr 1937). There was great hope in the new creation that would be the grand result of secularization, Western civilization, and the North American way. But after the First World War the optimism dampened, and there was a suspicion that Christians needed to rethink the perspectives offered by the social gospel (e.g., in Rauschenbusch 1917). Thus already in the 1930s people began questioning the close identification of culture and Protestantism in Europe and North America. The heart of the question actually had to do with the mission of the church, its reason for being, and its relationship to the world if the church was no longer to be seen as synonymous with Western civilization.

The support of Hitler by the German state churches, Karl Barth's efforts in the Barmen Declaration to dissociate the church from political movements, the chaos of World War II, and Dietrich Bonhoeffer's concept of reli-

---

7. See also Van Engen 1991b, 29–30.

8. E.g., the articles in the July 1988 issue of the *International Review of Mission* 77, no. 307, entitled "Tambaram Revisited," deal almost exclusively with interreligious dialogue and contain scant references to the matter of church and mission. See also Hogg 1952, 290–353.

gionless Christianity added urgency to the question of the mission of the church, which had begun to be explored at Tambaram. The idea of church needed some concept of mission in order to be able to fill out its relationship with the world. By the late 1950s the search for relevance would replace the optimistic identification of culture and Christianity that prevailed at the beginning of the century.

Meanwhile, on the other side of the fence, the people involved in mission were beginning to suspect that they needed the churches. During most of the nineteenth century, mission had been predominantly a voluntary affair; though involving church people, it operated alongside of (or even apart from) denominational structures. But by the 1930s the women's missionary movement was slowly being taken over by the men; independent or semi-autonomous mission agencies began to be controlled by their denominational structures;[9] and younger churches in Africa, Asia, and Latin America were beginning to wonder what their relationship was to a world Christendom that seemed to operate on two planes: mission organizations and church structures.[10] Thus the International Missionary Council convened at Tambaram, although a council of mostly mission organizations, was increasingly related to older denominations in Europe and North America and to younger churches in Africa, Asia, and Latin America.

From both perspectives—the church needing to discover its mission, and mission needing closer ties with the churches—it seemed urgent that a new paradigm of the relation of church and mission be discovered. As Carl Hallencreutz (1988, 354) sums it up: "The integrating theme of the Tambaram report is the *Church in Mission* and this reflects a powerful convergence with the subject matter of the second World Conference of Life and Work, in Oxford 1937, which coined the slogan, 'let the Church be the Church,' and the World Conference on Faith and Order, in Edinburgh the same year, which explored *The Unity of the Church in Christ*."[11]

The questions being asked in the 1930s were right and necessary. The concerns were appropriate. Fifty years later parallel forces were operating in North American evangelical missiology. As parachurch mission agencies successfully planted new churches worldwide, and as their staff members became more integrated personally and structurally in the churches of North

---

9. An excellent illustration of this development, though with a slightly different time-line, is the London Missionary Society's transformation into the Congregational Council for World Mission (1966) and then the Council for World Mission (1975); see Thorogood 1994.

10. Newbigin 1981b, 247, wrote of the impact of these forces on him as a minister in an Indian church; these existential difficulties brought him to support the integration of the IMC into the WCC in 1961.

11. Actually, it was John Mackay (1935, 195) who coined the phrase: "The supreme need is that the Christian church be a fellowship. Let the church be the church, let it be true to its inmost self."

America, these agencies also felt the urgent need to find their own ecclesiological nature and relationships. So much so that the theme of Lausanne II (Manila, 1989) was "the whole church taking the whole gospel to the whole world."[12] Few seemed to note that the identical phrase had been used nearly forty years earlier (1951) by the Central Committee of the World Council of Churches meeting in Rolle, Switzerland.[13]

The original impetus toward making everything mission by affirming that the church is mission was an appropriate and necessary search for a closer relationship of church and mission. This search led naturally toward the rather amazing consensus that developed in ecumenical missiology in the 1960s.

The 1960s: The Articulation of a Close Relation between Church and Mission

The late 1950s and the 1960s were times of amazing change, exploration, re-evaluation, and openness. For ecumenical mission theology this period was a watershed that changed the direction and paradigm of mission. The implications of this radical change are still being played out. We can highlight three major factors which sought to bring church and mission so close as to make them nearly synonymous.

The first major influence was apparently structural, but in fact had deep theological roots—the integration of the International Missionary Council into the World Council of Churches.[14] The prevailing mood in both the older IMC and the newly formed WCC was that neither organization (thus, neither mission nor church) was complete without the other. This sentiment was probably helped by the fact that a significant number of individuals from Europe and North America were personally involved in both organizations. Be that as it may, the union was given birth at the Third Assembly of the WCC, meeting, again, in an Indian context, in New Delhi in 1961 (World Council of Churches 1962).

Whether this union meant in fact the death of the IMC depends on how one reads the rest of the story. One thing is certain. This union gave a tremendous boost to North American evangelical missiology, for much of the

12. For documentation of this conference see Douglas 1990.

13. For quotes from the minutes and reports of this meeting see Mackay 1963, 13. See also Hoekendijk 1966a, 108; Van Engen 1981, 382.

14. Space is too limited here for a discussion of this highly controversial matter. The October 1981 issue of the *International Review of Mission* (70, no. 280) contains some excellent reflection on the twenty-year anniversary of the event. See also Newbigin 1958; Van Dusen 1961; Warren 1974, 156–58; 1978, 190–202; Bosch 1980, 180–81; 1991, 369–70. For evangelical assessments of the event see Fife and Glasser 1961, 126–43; Bassham 1979, 40–42, 210–12; Winter 1978; Lindsell 1962, 200; 1966; Costas 1982, 136; Glasser and McGavran 1983, 113–25; Johnston 1974, 240–42; Hoekstra 1979, 35–48; Henry 1967; and George Peters 1972, 28.

energy, enthusiasm, and personal involvement that had once been part of the IMC left the conciliar fold and joined forces with evangelical missiology at the 1966 meeting (Wheaton) of the Congress on the Church's Worldwide Mission. From that point on, evangelical missiologists have considered themselves to be the true heirs of the vision of the IMC.

At the time of the union, integration was thought by the majority in both the IMC and the WCC to be an appropriate expression of deeply held theological convictions regarding the relationship of church and mission. The effects on the member churches of the World Council—John Piet's denomination, the Reformed Church in America, being one of them—were wide and long-lasting.[15] One's evaluation of those effects will be closely related to one's view on the rise of two major missiological ideas that paralleled the integration: the concept of *missio Dei* as the motivation and basis for mission,[16] and the concept of the missionary nature of the church.[17]

The second major influence, then, was the birth of the trinitarian concept of the *missio Dei*. Strongly affirmed at the first meeting (Mexico City, 1963) of the reconstituted IMC as the Commission on World Mission and Evangelism (CWME) of the WCC,[18] the *missio Dei* perspective was clearly articulated in and widely popularized by Georg Vicedom's book *The Mission of God: An Introduction to a Theology of Mission* (1965). This perspective affirmed that mission is in the final analysis God's mission. It derives from the trinitarian being and action of God. God's decision to use human agency (*missio hominum*) and God's willingness to work by means of the missions of the churches (*missiones ecclesiarum*) are secondary to, and derivative from, God's mission.[19] Thus all human, ecclesiastical, and structural reflection and action in the area of mission must first be tested with regard to their proximity to (or distance from) God's mission.[20] David Bosch (1991, 390–91) has emphasized the pervasive influence that this new perspective had on missiology as a whole:

15. The impact on the Reformed Church in America can be seen in the formation of the General Program Council (1968), an agency that integrated all denominational programs within one structure, which was nearly a carbon copy of the larger IMC-WCC. See Hoff 1965, 148–99.

16. For an excellent overview of the implications for mission theology see Scherer 1993a.

17. For two contrasting perspectives see Johannes Blauw's *Missionary Nature of the Church* (1962) and Johannes Hoekendijk's *Church Inside Out* (1966). Unfortunately, the former was ignored in conciliar circles and the latter was given pride of place.

18. For the documents from this conference see Orchard 1964.

19. Coupled with Vicedom's book, one of the best articulations of this perspective can be found in Newbigin 1978. For an excellent overview of the origins of the *missio Dei* perspective (Karl Barth, Karl Hartenstein, and the Willingen conference), see Bosch 1991, 389–93; see also Goodall 1953; and West and Paton 1959.

20. This is the missiological thread that weaves its way throughout Karl Barth's *Church Dogmatics*, vol. 4 (1958).

Since Willingen, the understanding of mission as *missio Dei* has been embraced by virtually all Christian persuasions—first by conciliar Protestants,[21] but subsequently by other ecclesial groupings, such as the Eastern Orthodox[22] and many evangelicals.[23] It was also endorsed in Catholic mission theology, notably in some of the documents of the Second Vatican Council. . . . For the *missiones ecclesiae* (the missionary activities of the church) the *missio Dei* has important consequences. "Mission," singular, remains primary; "missions," in the plural, constitutes a derivative.

Tragically, the meaning of "mission" and the theological understanding of *missio Dei* underwent a radical shift very soon after this initial expression— a shift that brought about the opposite of what was originally intended. But we are getting ahead of our story.

The third major influence coursing through ecumenical missiology at this time had to do with a series of study groups examining the missionary structure of the congregation. These groups included representatives from the National Council of Churches of Christ in the United States as well as from the World Council of Churches in Europe (World Council of Churches 1968). Their studies brought church and mission very close together.

Support came from two sources a decade apart. The first was the 1952 Willingen conference of the IMC, which nearly identified the church with mission (International Missionary Council 1952). The second was Johannes Blauw's *Missionary Nature of the Church: A Survey of the Biblical Theology of Mission* (1962), which had been commissioned by the IMC at its Ghana Assembly in 1958. Together, Willingen's documents and Blauw's biblical acumen offered ecumenical missiology a very strong foundation for bringing church and mission so close as to nearly eclipse each other. This emphasis was strengthened even more by parallel developments in Roman Catholic missiology at Vatican II (Flannery 1975), by the Orthodox churchcentric perspective on mission,[24] and by the world church's growing awareness of Pentecostal missiology, in large part a missiology of the local congregation.[25]

Together the three major influences (integration of the IMC and WCC, the concept of *missio Dei*, and studies of the missionary nature of the church) helped to shape a consensus that united church and mission in a way never before accomplished. Taken together, the three declared, "The church *is* mission." The intention of the players in this drama was laudable. But thirty years later we face some disastrous consequences of their perspectives.

21. See Bosch 1980, 179–80, 239–48; and Lutheran World Federation, n.d.
22. See Anastasios of Androussa 1989.
23. See Costas 1989, 71–87.
24. See, e.g., Meyendorff 1962; 1974; Patelos 1978; Schmemann 1979; Bria 1980; 1991; Stamoolis 1987.
25. See, e.g., Hodges 1953; 1972; 1977; 1978; McGee 1986b; 1989; 1993; and Dempster, Klaus, and Petersen 1991.

Stephen Neill's axiom has proven to be true. Never was there a time when one could say so confidently that everything is mission. But by the same token, never has there been a time of such massive confusion about mission. Unfortunately, Neill was right: "When everything is mission, nothing is mission." In such a situation both church and mission can get lost.

The 1990s: The Two-Pronged Loss of Both Church and Mission

Almost as soon as the three major factors had an appreciable impact, they began to undergo radical reconceptualization.[26] The primary source of this change was the influence of Johannes Hoekendijk on ecumenical mission thinking.[27]

The impact of Hoekendijk's thinking on the WCC began with the publication in 1948 of his dissertation, *Kerk en volk in de Duitse zendingswetenschap*. In this work Hoekendijk "radically tested against the biblical norms the *Volkstumideologie* that had been so prominent in German missiology from Gustav Warneck to Christian Keysser. . . . He principally rejected any idea of a church which is based on *Volk*, or, as it is sometimes called in Dutch literature, a *taalkerk* (a church whose language is its chief identity)" (Verkuyl 1978, 51). Considering how few of his works were available in English, Hoekendijk's influence on ecumenical missiology is truly remarkable.[28] It increased substantially in 1950 when Hoekendijk was "in charge of the WCC's study department on mission and evangelization" (Bockmuhl 1977, 351). Rodger Bassham (1968) has noted Hoekendijk's marked influence in the preparatory documents for "The Missionary Obligation of the Church" project, through which his thought was allowed to impact the discussions at Willingen in 1952.[29] There Hoekendijk began to move ecumenical missiology away from ecclesiocentric mission toward an eschatological and world-directed mission. His influence at Willingen is unmistakable.[30]

The perspective that captured Willingen continued to be developed, especially in the project later published as *The Church for Others and the Church for the World* (World Council of Churches 1968).[31] As late as 1977, Klaus Bockmuhl rightly perceived this document as still being "the manual for

26. For the radical redefinition of the concept *missio Dei,* see, e.g., Rosin 1972; Aagaard 1974; Scherer 1993a; and Shenk 1993b.

27. Our discussion of Hoekendijk is based on the fuller treatment in Van Engen 1981, 305–7.

28. For his best-known writing see Hoekendijk 1950; 1952; 1961; 1964; 1966a; 1966b.

29. Bassham here refers to the study that was later published as *The Missionary Obligation of the Church* (International Missionary Council 1952).

30. See, e.g., Andersen 1961, 309; Horner 1968, 40–42; Bosch 1980, 179–80; 1991, 392; Bassham 1979, 67–71; and Scherer 1987, 95–117.

31. See, e.g., Hendrikus Berkhof 1979, 345; Newbigin 1978, 10, 20–23; and Bockmuhl 1977, 352.

understanding ecumenical theology" (1977, 352). In fact, the influence of Hoekendijk's ecclesiology and missiology as expressed in this document can be clearly seen in the publications of, for example, Hans J. Margull (1971) and Colin Williams (1963, 1964, 1966, 1968). It was also evident at the CWME meeting in Mexico City in 1963 and particularly strong in "the interim report on the 'Missionary Structure of the Congregation' as presented in 1965 to the WCC Central Committee" (Scherer 1987, 111). Hoekendijk's perspective received added impetus at the Fourth Assembly of the WCC (Uppsala, 1968), as well as the CWME gathering in Bangkok in 1973. Although not everything in Hoekendijk's missiology became official WCC thinking, still his influence has been both deep and broad right up to the present. The emphasis, for example, at the CWME conference in San Antonio on "acts of faithfulness" is consistent with Hoekendijk's thought.

But Hoekendijk's thought led ecumenical mission theology astray. It reinterpreted the meaning of *missio Dei*, it reoriented the results of integration, and it redefined the mission of the congregation. Early on, Lutheran theologians and missiologists had seen this danger (Scherer 1987, 114–17; 1993a). Rather than remaining faithful to a biblical concept of church, of mission, and of church and mission, ecumenical theology was in fact pulled in two directions that ended up fulfilling Neill's prediction, "When everything is mission, nothing is mission."

Once everything became mission, both church and mission got lost. In the first place Hoekendijk's strongest emphasis involved a deep negativity with regard to the church. "A church-centric missionary thinking is bound to go astray," Hoekendijk (1952, 332) would say, "because it revolves around an illegitimate center." Hoekendijk's influence was pervasive because his voice was being heard in a time of great pessimism about the church, especially in Europe and North America. In Europe the church's inability to respond appropriately to Hitler made many ecumenists talk about some ethereal concept of the church, but not have much to do with the churches themselves. In North America, the baby boomers, the advocates of the Peace Corps, and the army of young social workers in Lyndon Johnson's Great Society had no patience for a church that did not respond appropriately either to the Vietnam War or to the socioeconomic crises of the world. Hoekendijk's personal disillusionment with the church struck a responsive chord.

Missiologically this antichurch bias brought about a change in the mission order, from God-church-world to God-world-church. What mattered was the presence of *shalom* in the world: "World and kingdom are correlated to each other; the world is conceived of as a unity, the scene of God's great acts; it is the *world* which has been reconciled (2 Cor. 5:19), the *world* which God loves (John 3:16) and which He has overcome in His love (John 16:33); the *world* is the field in which the seeds of the kingdom are sown (Matt. 13:38)— the *world* is consequently the scene for the proclamation of the kingdom"

(Hoekendijk 1952, 333). Thus Hoekendijk developed a series of couplets: kingdom and world, gospel and apostolate. In all this grand vision there was no mention of, and no room for, the church or the churches.[32] "Hoekendijk wanted the Kingdom of God, shalom, and service in the world to replace the Church as the central locus of mission and evangelization" (Van Engen 1981, 311). Thus there was a need for a *Church Inside Out* (Hoekendijk 1966a), which essentially amounted to the euthanasia of the church.

So the church gets swallowed up in mission. Everything becomes mission. This emphasis flows consistently throughout ecumenical missiology from Willingen to Canberra (the Seventh Assembly of the WCC, 1991). Whether involved with socioeconomic "acts of faithfulness," political changes, or a growing universalist orientation to other religions, ecumenical mission has had little space for the church as God's instrument of grace and reconciliation. Rather, as God is doing things in the world, the church is a bystander, applauding God's activities in the world. The churches are essentially irrelevant to God's mission. How ironic that the World Council of *Churches* would adopt Hoekendijk's view, and exclude the church as the primary locus of the kingdom and the primary agent of God's grace in the world. In other words, once the church was engulfed within mission ("When everything is mission, . . ."), the mission of the church was essentially lost.

But there is another side of the same coin. Hoekendijk's emphasis also gave strength to a growing awareness of the possible role the churches might play in socioeconomic and political liberation. Once the church became aware of what God was doing in the world, the church was called to begin to act in ways that would support this "mission" of God. In other words, if there was any role for the church at all, it was to be a utilitarian one. The church could be accepted if it was willing to become an appropriate instrument, a useful tool in bringing about revolutionary change. This utilitarian ecclesiology was particularly strong in Latin American theologies of liberation.

Given Hoekendijk's perspective, the sociopolitical usefulness of the church overshadows any biblical concept of mission (in the sense in which we have defined it in this chapter). Subsumed under the church, mission becomes equated with the church's usefulness in producing social revolution. And the church (as the unique company of believers in Jesus Christ) gets lost in the jungle of sociopolitical and economic agendas. This is precisely the recent problem of the base ecclesial communities in Latin America. There are those who are beginning to question their *ecclesial* nature. Are they now mostly cell groups for political activism? In that case, are they any longer church? Once everything is mission, and mission is subsumed under the

---

32. For an extended critique of Hoekendijk's ecclesiology as it impacts theology of church growth, see Van Engen 1981, 308–23.

heading of the churches as useful instruments for social change, both mission and church get lost.

Ecumenical mission theology that has followed Hoekendijk has fallen prey to the built-in contradiction in Hoekendijk's missiology, which is so aptly expressed in Neill's axiom. On the one hand, when the church is buried under a redefinition of mission, both church and mission get lost. On the other, when mission is overlaid with a strongly sociopolitical view of the usefulness of the church for revolutionary change, both church and mission are again lost.

As we enter the third millennium, many of us will need to struggle to understand more completely, and shape more clearly, the postmodern "ecumenical missionary paradigm" of which David Bosch spoke (1991, ch. 12). Let us pray that as we work with the elements Bosch highlighted for us, we will begin to find ways to finally break the stranglehold of Hoekendijk's thought on ecumenical mission theology. Only then will we be able to rethink our mission theology and find new ways to relate church and mission.

Our brief survey has shown that it is absolutely imperative for us to discover new ways of relating church and mission amid our widely diverse contexts. As John Piet showed us, and we now know, in our missiological paradigms church and mission must remain in close proximity. We have resonated with the attempts to articulate this closeness in the 1960s. But we have also taken note of the dilemma this proximity produced in ecumenical mission theology.

The dilemma may not be inherent to an intimate relation of church and mission. I suspect that if the WCC had followed Johannes Blauw's lead rather than Hoekendijk's, the results would have been radically different. For there have always been lights to show us another way. *Mission and Evangelism: An Ecumenical Affirmation* (1983), the Stuttgart Declaration, the *Manila Manifesto* (1989), *Evangelii nuntiandi* (1976), and *Redemptoris missio* are but a few recent examples of attempts to maintain a close relationship between church and mission without getting caught in Hoekendijk's dilemma.[33] I began to explore ways to do this in *God's Missionary People: Rethinking the Purpose of the Local Church* (1991). It is the part of wisdom for all of us, in our various contexts of mission, to heed Stephen Neill's call and warning, "When everything is mission, nothing is mission."

---

33. James Scherer and Stephen Bevans (1992) have done us all a wonderful service by compiling many of these documents in one reader.

Part 5

Mission Theology and Religious Pluralism

9

The Effect of Universalism
on Mission Theology

The relationship between pluralistic universalism and mission effort has been predominantly negative. Universalists have tended to caricature and undermine mission effort, while the practitioners of mission have felt threatened and responded strongly against universalism. The disagreements are real, serious, and far-reaching in their impact upon the way the church relates to the people of other faiths. However, the negative effect of pluralistic universalism on mission effort may be diminished by recognizing that the gospel of the kingdom is culture-universal and faith-particular, as understood through the biblical record of the death, resurrection, and ascension of Jesus Christ.

Universalism and mission would seem to be mutually exclusive terms—or are they? Certainly the ideas represented by the two camps have not been seen as compatible with each other. Those espousing a universalist perspective tend to express rather negative views on traditional missionary practice. For example, when John Hick called for a Copernican revolution in theology, he began by degrading the idea of *extra ecclesiam nulla salus* (outside the church there is no salvation) by referring to it with terms like "arrogant," "cruel," "entirely negative," "ignorant," "blinded by dark dogmatic spectacles," and an "attitude of rejection" which comes from a "radically questionable" concept of God:

> The first phase—the phase of total rejection—was expressed in the dogma that non-Christians, as such, are consigned to hell. As the expression of an attitude to other human beings the dogma is as arrogant as it is cruel; and it is a sober-

ing thought that such a dogma was at one time almost universally accepted among Christians. . . . The Roman Catholic Church today has passed decisively beyond this phase, but the earlier dogma still persists within evangelical-fundamentalist Protestantism. For example, one of the messages of the Congress on World Mission at Chicago in 1960 declared: "In the years since the war, more than one billion souls have passed into eternity and more than half of these went to the torment of hell fire without even hearing of Jesus Christ, who He was, and why He died on the cross at Calvary. . . ."

This entirely negative attitude to other faiths is strongly correlated with ignorance of them. . . . Today, however, the extreme evangelical Protestant who believes that all Muslims go to hell is probably not so much ignorant . . . as blinded by dark dogmatic spectacles through which he can see no good in religious devotion outside his own group.

But the basic weakness in this attitude of rejection lies in the doctrine of God which it presupposes. If all human beings must, in order to attain the eternal happiness for which they have been created, accept Jesus Christ as their Lord and Savior before they die, then the great majority of humanity is doomed to eternal frustration and misery. . . . To say that such an appalling situation is divinely ordained is to deny the Christian understanding of God as gracious and holy love. . . . Thus the attitude of total rejection, expressed in the dogma that outside Christianity there is no salvation, implies a conception of God radically questionable from the standpoint of Christian faith.[1]

Missionary spokespersons, on the other hand, have reacted strongly against the undermining of missionary motivation by such universalist perspectives. Already in the 1930s Hendrik Kraemer responded to William Hocking and the Laymen's Foreign Missions Inquiry by strongly affirming a deeply biblical missionary motivation. Opposing the religiously pluralistic position advocated by Hocking and Protestant liberalism of the day, Kraemer stated, "The only valid motive and purpose of missions is, and alone can be, to call men and peoples to confront themselves with God's acts of revelation and salvation for man and the world as presented in Biblical realism, and to build up a community of those who have surrendered themselves to faith in and loving service of Jesus Christ."[2]

During the past several decades mission theorists and practitioners have warned that universalism undermines the motive and urgency for mission. Michael Griffiths (1980, 116, 129) has even called it a Trojan horse:

---

1. Hick 1982, 29–31; see also Hillman 1968, 25–27. Hick's antimissionary assessment is an echo of Ernst Troeltsch's negative perspective (1980, 26–28) in a lecture intended for Oxford University in 1923.

2. Kraemer 1938, 292. Kraemer was writing against Hocking's *Re-Thinking Missions* (1932). A good source here is the July 1988 issue of the *International Review of Mission* (77, no. 307), which commemorated the fiftieth anniversary of the International Missionary Council conference at Tambaram, India. For a response to this issue see Newbigin 1989b. See also Bosch 1980, 159–75; and Samartha 1981, 19.

This "Trojan Horse" has gained entrance into Christendom and threatens to destroy missionary motives and hinder the effectiveness of Christ's soldiers and their readiness to continue the battle . . . perhaps there is no battle! . . . If all men are to be saved in the end why bother to urge men to repent now? They will later in any case. Why bother to be converted oneself for that matter? But the urgency which has characterized missionary endeavor derives not merely from the fear of hell, but from the consciousness that to live even this life without Christ is to be condemned to an alienated, meaningless existence estranged from God.

After citing D. T. Niles (1959, 32–33) and Douglas Webster (1958) to support his contention that the universalist position destroys missionary urgency, Griffiths (1980, 119) concludes, "It is this viewpoint which appears to underlie the present swing away from soteriological concern to social concern. Indeed, it is precisely because many leaders in the World Council of Churches believe that God will save all men anyway that 'salvation has been given such a firm this-worldly orientation and evangelism often becomes simply irrelevant' [N. T. Wright 1975, 204]."

Significantly, as recently as 1989, both Lesslie Newbigin (1989b, 54) and Johannes Verkuyl (1989, 55) expressed concern that if the present universalist/ pluralist current in the World Council continues, the council may become irrelevant to the missiological issues which face us in the future. Clearly universalism has a negative effect on missionary motivation and urgency.[3] The universalist perspective threatens missionary motivation, reduces missional urgency, and emasculates the biblical message. This matter is especially critical today when Christians on every continent are rubbing shoulders with neighbors representing a whole range of different religious allegiances.

And yet we must be cautious in assessing the polemics between the two camps from a missiological point of view. A historical case can be made that the introduction of pluralistic viewpoints into the International Missionary Council from 1938 on (along with the subsequent impact of the Comparative Religions movement in North American mainline Protestantism) reduced missionary sending in some churches. Secondly, a theological argument can be offered that religious pluralism reduces the Christian sense of missionary urgency.[4] However, these arguments alone do not prove that the universalist perspective inevitably reduces evangelism and should on that account be disavowed.

In the first place, religious movements other than Christianity (even relatively pluralistic ones) have been evangelistic in their own right. The Crusades and the Spanish conquest of the Americas could be added to a list

---

3. See, e.g., Lindsell 1962; Stott 1975b, 64–69; Punt 1987; Harold Brown 1987; Braaten 1987–88; Brownson 1988; and Chapman 1990.
4. In 1 Cor. 15 Paul follows a similar line of argument with reference to the resurrection.

which would include Marxism in the 1950s, transcendental meditation in the 1960s, militant Islam in the 1970s, the New Age movement in the 1980s, and even the Unitarian universalism of the last fifty years as perspectives which have been quite committed to furthering their viewpoints even though they did not represent a biblical understanding of either the gospel or God's mission. To adopt a universalist perspective may not of itself mean the loss of evangelistic energy. The historical argument also ignores numerous other theological and nontheological factors which have discouraged North America from sending missionaries (the world wars, for example).

Secondly, the presence of strong missionary motivation does not itself guarantee the truth of the message being advocated. The examples given above demonstrate that movements we might consider unbiblical may be strong proselytizers. Militancy often goes hand in hand with belief in one's unique (triumphalistic?) perspective, but the militancy itself does not prove the beliefs which form the foundation of such activism. The truth or falsehood of the universalist perspective must be decided by reference to Scripture—not Christian activism. As Newbigin (1981a, 4) has said, "The Christian goes to meet his neighbor of another religion on the basis of his commitment to Jesus Christ. There is no dichotomy between 'confession' and 'truth-seeking.' His confession is the starting point of his truth-seeking." A Christian approach to other religions, then, must begin and end with Scripture. We cannot afford to follow the lead of some of the universalist literature which moves away from its scriptural foundation simply because persons of other faiths do not recognize our Scriptures. This is precisely the point at issue. Our affirmation of Christian truth is based on our experience of Jesus Christ, and grounded on the revelation of God as found in Scripture.

Against this background our study of the relation of universalism and mission will include a recognition of the wide variety of topics falling under the concept of universalism, a careful distinction between faith and culture, and an analysis of Paul's twin concepts of culture-universalism and faith-particularism.

The Variety of Topics within Universalism

When we speak of universalism, we in fact mean an entire constellation of topics which have been discussed for centuries. No one topic by itself covers the whole range of issues involved in universalism.[5] Each topic in fact relates

---

5. *The Oxford Dictionary of the Christian Church* defines universalism (s.v. "apocatastasis") as "the doctrine that ultimately all free moral creatures—angels, men, and devils—will share in the grace of salvation. It is to be found in Clement of Alexandria, in Origen, and in St. Gregory of Nyssa. It was strongly attacked by St. Augustine of Hippo and formally condemned in the first anathema against Origenism, probably put out by the Council of Constantinople in AD 543."

to a different group of scriptural verses and ideas. The following list is by no means intended to be exhaustive:[6]

1. Christianity's view of other religions past and present
2. Ultimately will all be saved? Is there a second chance?
3. The uniqueness of Christ
4. Eternal punishment, hell, torment, annihilation
5. Universal/local, objective/subjective views of truth
6. Restoration of all things in Christ
7. Everyone already an anonymous Christian
8. The necessity of God's love to save all human beings
9. Confusion of the doctrines of creation and redemption
10. Urgency of evangelism and missionary motivation
11. Sociological usefulness of other religions
12. Theocentric world religion—"Copernican revolution"
13. Theocentric Christology—reductionist local Christologies
14. Panentheistic perspectives on the Holy Spirit
15. Soteriological approaches to other faiths
16. Cultural pluralism equated with religious pluralism[7]

Clearly we do not have space or time here to develop each of the topics listed above. However, to enumerate them helps us to see how complex the subject is and to understand the number of ways in which it may be approached, particularly in relation to the mission of the church. The complexity of the list is also a warning to us to be careful and critical in our reading. We must be mindful that a person who brings new questions to bear upon one of the topics is not necessarily universalist in relation to all the other topics. In the evangelical world, and especially in mission, we have too quickly tended to categorize as universalist someone who may be asking questions with regard to only one of the topics—and who may be biblically particularist with regard to the others. For example, when Karl Barth offered the hope that one day all humanity would be gathered to God, he did not mean to question the uniqueness of Jesus Christ, the doctrine on which his whole dogmatic theology stands.[8] So also when John Stott (1989) asked whether annihilationism is compatible with the biblical concept of hell, he was not necessarily suggesting that there is more than one salvific path to God. In other words, as evangelical Christians we need to be very specific as to the topic

---

6. For excellent reviews covering some of the more recent works on the subject see *Religious Studies Review* 15.3 (July 1989): 197–209.

7. An excellent short survey of Christian attitudes to other religions over the last century is given in Bosch 1988a; cf. Hesselgrave 1990; and Braaten 1981, 69–89.

8. For a good synopsis of this matter see Bauckham 1979.

under consideration, and very clear as to how the various topics relate to each other with regard to the larger question of universalism.

A Distinction between Faith and Culture

As the church becomes more and more a global community, it is becoming increasingly clear that faith and culture cannot be entirely separated from each other. The gospel does not take place in a cultural vacuum, but is always incarnated in a specific cultural context. And yet we must also affirm that culture and faith are not identical. As Charles Kraft (1979, 115) has said:

> We deduce, then, that the relationship between God and culture is the same as that of one who uses a vehicle to the vehicle that he uses. But this relationship between God and culture is not a required relationship in the sense that God is bound by culture. On the contrary, God is absolute and infinite. Yet he has freely chosen to employ human culture and at major points to limit himself to the capacities of his interaction with people. . . . Any limitation of God is only that which he imposes upon himself—he chooses to use culture, he is not bound by it in the same way human beings are.

Not only is God to be seen in distinction from culture, but the faith of the individual must also be separated from the individual's culture. We need to affirm matters of contextualization which take seriously the culturally appropriate shape for the gospel in each time and place. But that is a far cry from equating culture and faith. We all know that various persons within the same culture may espouse radically different faiths. And persons of many cultures may share the same faith. At the outset this would seem to be a truism. It is not always so obvious.

One of the most disturbing aspects of the literature on universalism is the very close (nearly synonymous) relationship between faith and culture. This can be seen clearly in Ernst Troeltsch's dictum (1980, 27) that "in relation to the great world religions we need to recognize that they are expressions of the religious consciousness corresponding to certain definite types of culture." There is a disturbingly close relationship drawn between faith and culture in the writings of Wilfred Cantwell Smith, Karl Rahner, Paul Knitter, John Hick, John Cobb, and Wesley Ariarajah.[9] It is noteworthy that the strongest proponents of religious pluralism also seem to represent the strands of Christendom which tend to be the most culture-affirming, where faith and culture are most closely intertwined.

9. See, e.g., Ariarajah 1990, and the representative articles in the very fine reader compiled by Hick and Hebblethwaite 1980.

Yet the relationship between faith and culture is part of the question—it should not be unquestioningly assumed. Karl Barth demonstrated the importance of this when he drew a radical distinction between religion and faith.[10] Creation and redemption, as understood in Scripture, are not the same thing for the Christian. God is the creator of all human beings, but it is only in Jesus Christ, by the power of the Holy Spirit, through faith, that they are given the "power to become children of God" (John 1:12 RSV). It is only through God's grace that we are predestined to be "adopted as [God's children] through Jesus Christ, in accordance with his pleasure and will—to the praise of his glorious grace" (Eph. 1:5–6).

More recently, Lesslie Newbigin in *Foolishness to the Greeks* (1986) and *The Gospel in a Pluralist Society* (1989a) has shown that faith and Western culture cannot and must not be equated.[11] We must carefully and incisively distinguish between faith and culture, no matter if that culture is Jewish, Greek, Roman, European, North American, Asian, African, or Latin American. Unless we draw a radical distinction between faith and culture, Christian mission cannot get past the accusation of cultural imperialism. But when we do come to recognize a difference (though close interrelationship) between our faith and our culture, we will be prepared to deal more creatively with the impact of universalism upon mission effort.

Culture-Universality and Faith-Particularism in Paul

The distinction between faith and culture lies at the heart of Paul's concept in Romans of the particularity of a universal gospel. In fact, maintaining a radical distance between faith and culture may be the key to a missiological reading of the "all" passages in Romans, so often cited by universalist authors as scriptural support of their position.[12] What follows is a cursory, suggestive outline of Romans which may serve to illustrate the implications of Paul's unique perspective for universalism and mission. Paul certainly has a universal perspective. The confusion lies in the overlapping of faith and culture. Paul in Romans advocates a culture-universality together with a faith-particularity.

Romans: The Message of a Missionary Team-Leader to a Mission Church

The theme: The universality of the gospel of faith in Jesus Christ; it is for Jews and Gentiles, Greeks and non-Greeks, wise and foolish, that is, for *everyone who believes* (Rom. 1:14–17; 15:8–9, 15–16; 16:26)

10. See, e.g., Barth 1980; cf. J. Robert Nelson 1967.
11. See also Coote and Stott 1980.
12. N. T. Wright 1979 helpfully identifies these passages.

The underlying agenda: A proposed missionary journey to Spain

Paul begins with the worldview of his readers, who held that there are two kinds of people in the world—Jews and Gentiles.

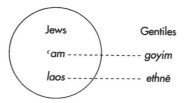

Figure 23
Two Kinds of People

I. The unrighteousness of *all* demonstrated by general revelation (1:18–32)
II. The sinfulness of *all* demonstrated by special revelation
    A. The sinfulness of all humans in general (2:1–16)
    B. The sinfulness specifically of the Jews also (2:17–3:8)
    C. The universality of judgment (3:9–20)

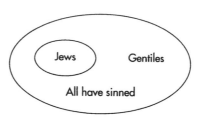

Figure 24
The Sinfulness of All

III. Special grace in Jesus Christ
    A. The element of universality: the offer of grace to *all who believe* (3:21–31)
    B. The element of particularity: the response of specific faith (4:1–5:21)
    C. The completeness of the transformation (6:1–23)
        1. The divine-human tension in the transformed individual—faith and culture are, after all, not the same (7:1–25)
        2. The Holy Spirit's role in the transformation (8:1–27)
        3. The universal scope of the transformation (8:28–39)
    D. The matter of Israel after the flesh—a question occasioned by Paul's re-definition of universality and particularity (9–11)
        1. Rejection of a new exclusivity
        2. The God who acts in history as a God of compassion
        3. The instrumentality of the new people of God for the nations—and for Israel's salvation as well

Figure 25
Paul's New Universality

IV. The special life of the unique people of God in the world ("renewing of the mind" deals with the difference between faith and culture)
  A. The life of the community of faith in the world (12:1–15:13)
  B. Paul, a minister of Christ Jesus to the Gentiles (the newly created universal/particular people of God) (15:14–22)
  C. Paul's long-range plans for Spain (15:23–33)
  D. Paul's concept of teamwork-in-mission illustrated (16:1–24)

Figure 26
Mission Nature of God's People

Conclusion: "Now to him who is able to establish you by my gospel and the proclamation of Jesus Christ, according to the revelation of the mystery hidden for long ages past, but now revealed and made known through the prophetic writings by the command of the eternal God, so that *all nations* might believe and obey him—to the only wise God be glory forever through Jesus Christ! Amen!" (16:25–27 NIV, emphasis added)

There are two final observations we need to make. First, the reader should notice that in the final analysis the center around which the new universal particularity is constructed is the confession "Jesus is Lord" (Rom. 10:9). This calls into question all the layers of cultural accretions that have been added to that confession down through the centuries by the Christian church. For the gospel to be culturally universal, all Christians must be willing to divest themselves of everything except that confession. There has been no time in history when the church's cultural universality has been more evident than in this new day of the world church. Surrounding the globe and its multitude of cultures, the church demonstrates its "translatability" in a myriad of new and unexpected ways.[13] Paul Knitter's thesis is untenable. The fact of numerous religious traditions does *not* make them normative. Instead, the apostle Paul offers God's love and grace to all human beings, representing any and every religious background. By faith in Jesus Christ, God's love gathers all people at the foot of the cross, calling them to experience new life in the Spirit.

Secondly, this culture-universality develops within a faith-particularity that creates a new Israel by faith. Not only does this represent a continuity with Abraham (by faith), it also represents a new missional instrumentality by the church for the sake of all people. These new people of God are now called to be "ambassadors" (2 Cor. 5:11–21) in the midst and for the sake of the nations. This instrumentality stresses the faith relationship which transcends all cultural barriers, breaks down the middle wall of partition (Eph. 2), and challenges every form of cultural particularism (even Gentile particularism against the Jews; see Rom. 11). This biblical universalism disavows all other forms of exclusivity: ethnic, gender, social, educational, economic, political. "Jesus is Lord" is for all persons. This type of biblical universalism represents a common perspective evident in the latest mission documents of a variety of Christian traditions.[14] Such a culturally universal faith calls for "the whole church to take the whole gospel to the whole world."[15]

Are universalism and mission mutually exclusive? If by universalism we mean the range of topics used to defend religious relativity and pluralism, the answer is yes. But if we mean a Pauline culture-universality coupled with faith-particularity, the answer is that they in fact support and encourage each other. The invitation which Jesus Christ extends for salvation in him is extended to all people. If we take seriously Pauline universality in all its human, cultural, and relational dimensions, our mission effort will be revolutionary. Then we will be truly universal, seeking to bring together all peoples, all tribes, all nations confessing in one common faith that "Jesus is Lord."

---

13. Lamin Sanneh 1989 masterfully shows this element of the church's missionary nature.

14. See, e.g., Visser 't Hooft 1963; *Ad gentes* and *Lumen gentium* in Flannery 1975, 350–426, 813–56; "The Lausanne Covenant" 1974; *Evangelii nuntiandi* 1976; *Mission and Evangelism* 1983; *The Manila Manifesto* 1989; cf. *The San Antonio Report* 1990.

15. This was the theme of the Lausanne II meeting in Manila (1989), the largest missionary gathering in history.

10

The Uniqueness of Christ in Mission Theology

The subject of this chapter is the ramifications of the confession that "Jesus Christ is Lord." This essential, biblical, personal confession of faith questions the traditional pluralist, inclusivist, and exclusivist positions held by Christians concerning other religions and calls God's missionary people to be mobilized by the Holy Spirit to participate in Christ's mission, which is culturally pluralist, ecclesiologically inclusivist, and faith-particularist.

Several years ago Colin Chapman (1990, 16–17) pointed out that "to speak of 'other religions' is ultimately to refer to two-thirds of the human race. The world's other religions present a challenge to Christians not only because they have world views that conflict at many points with our own, but also because their influence is growing. . . . We must do more . . . than simply reassert the uniqueness of Christ in old categories, more than just produce strategies for reaching people of other faiths. We must first do some hard thinking about religions."[1]

Apparently Chapman's sense of urgency about this issue is increasingly being shared by other evangelicals. Most of us might agree with Clark Pinnock (1992, 7) that "by all accounts the meaning of Christ's lordship in a religiously plural world is one of the hottest topics on the agenda of theology in the nineties."[2]

---

1. Chapman's article in *Christianity Today* developed some of the themes of his address delivered at Lausanne II (Manila, 1989). Robert Coote 1990, 15, reported that "only Colin Chapman . . . dared to broaden the examination of what the gospel means for those who have never heard of Jesus Christ."

2. Ralph Covell 1993, 162, echoed this urgency when he affirmed that "no doctrine is more important for the Kingdom of God than the unique person of its King and the obedience of his

Not that the topic itself is new. It has in fact been a matter of the church's reflection since the first century. During the last five centuries of missionary expansion (both Roman Catholic and Protestant), conquest, accommodation, adaptation, indigenization, acculturation, contextualization, and inculturation have all been tried at various times in terms of Christianity's relationship to other religious traditions. At the International Missionary Council's meeting in Tambaram, Madras, India, in 1938,[3] Hendrik Kraemer replied to William Hocking's earlier criticism of the missionary movement (the Laymen's Foreign Missions Inquiry). Kraemer offered his perspective on *The Christian Message in a Non-Christian World*, which was based on his missiological interpretation of Karl Barth.[4]

The matter also received increasing attention from the Roman Catholics after the Second Vatican Council,[5] and from the World Council of Churches after the Second World War.[6] In 1990 Gerald Anderson listed 175 books published in English between 1970 and 1990 that dealt with the subject of "Christian Mission and Religious Pluralism." Three years later Anderson (1993, 200) wrote, "No issue in missiology is more important, more difficult, more controversial, or more divisive for the days ahead than the theology of religions."[7]

Evangelicals have only recently begun to give attention to this matter. As Ralph Covell (1993, 162–63) says, "Evangelicals as a group have long neglected to analyze these issues [of Christian attitudes toward other religions]." By way of recent example, at the 1979 Evangelical Consultation on Theology and Mission, held at Trinity Evangelical Divinity School, no major presentation dealt with the topic of other religions, even though the papers were published under the title *New Horizons in World Mission* (Hesselgrave 1979). However, during the 1980s and 1990s several evangelicals representing differing viewpoints made significant contributions to the conversation.[8]

---

subjects to witness for him in all the world (with special reference to adherents of other religious faiths)." Harold Netland 1991, 9, says, "The most critical aspect of the task of forging a viable theology of mission today 'deals with the Christian attitude toward religious pluralism and the approach to people of other faiths'" (quoting Gerald H. Anderson 1988, 114).

3. See International Missionary Council 1938. An excellent series of articles on Tambaram appeared in the *International Review of Mission* 77, no. 307 (July 1988); see also Hallencreutz 1969.

4. An excellent sample of Barth's thought on this matter can be found in Hick and Hebblethwaite 1980, 32–51.

5. A helpful discussion of more-recent Roman Catholic approaches to the subject can be found in Roukanen 1990.

6. See, e.g., Samartha 1977; 1981; Ariarajah 1990; Wilfred Cantwell Smith 1980; Cragg 1986; Forman 1993; Song 1975; 1987; Gort 1992; Mulder 1985; Wessels 1992; Tillich 1980; and Watson 1990.

7. Excellent review essays covering some recent works on the subject may be found in *Religious Studies Review* 15.3 (July 1989): 197–209.

8. Clark Pinnock 1992; John Sanders 1992; John Stott 1975b; 1981; 1989; Harold Netland 1991; David Hesselgrave 1981; 1988; Michael Green 1977; Carl Braaten 1981; Ajith Fernando

Key to the subject of Christians' attitudes to other religions is the area of Christology. In one sense, one's beginning point in Christology affects all else, as Robert Schreiter rightly pointed out in his play on words ("The Cruciality of Christology") at the 1990 gathering of the American Society of Missiology. But it is equally true that missiological results can best be assessed by looking at the Christologies produced. Thus Christology is both the source for Christian approaches to other religions and the result of those approaches.

The Three Paradigms (and a Fourth) of Christian Attitudes to Other Religions

The attitudes of Christians toward other religions are generally classified in three broad categories: pluralist, inclusivist, and exclusivist (or restrictivist).[9] By 1992 this three-part typology had become common currency among evangelicals at least (Pinnock 1992, 14–15).[10] Harold Netland (1991, 8–35) follows this structure, but qualifies his acceptance of it: "The use of the term 'exclusivism' is somewhat unfortunate since it has for many people undesirable connotations of narrow-mindedness, arrogance, insensitivity to others, self-righteousness, bigotry, and so on. In the context of the current debate, however, the term is unavoidable, because of the widespread use today to refer

---

1987; Ken Gnanakan 1992; J. Andrew Kirk 1992; Mark Heim 1985; Bruce J. Nicholls 1990; and William Crockett and James Sigountos 1991—along with J. I. Packer, Carl Henry, and Kenneth Kantzer—have begun to offer us some very substantial food for thought. This list is not intended to be exhaustive, just a sampling of those works that stand out. (See also Jack Cottrell and Stephen Burris 1993.) David Bosch, Gerald Anderson, and Lesslie Newbigin, along with John V. Taylor, Max Warren, Johannes Verkuyl, and Arthur Glasser, are among those who have consistently kept before all missiologists, including us evangelicals, the importance of continued and careful reflection on the subject. For an excellent survey of Christian attitudes to other religions over the last century see Bosch 1988a; see also Hesselgrave 1990; Braaten 1981; and Bauckham 1979.

9. The use of these particular terms seems to be a rather recent phenomenon. In *No Other Name?* (1985) Paul Knitter spoke of "models" of Christian attitudes to other religions: the conservative evangelical, the mainline Protestant, the Catholic, and the theocentric. In doing so, he downplayed the pluralist, inclusivist, and exclusivist typology. In *God Has Many Names* (1982) John Hick referred to the three major types of approaches, but the words themselves as typological categories are not strongly emphasized (Netland 1994). On the evangelical side Mark Heim in *Is Christ the Only Way?* (1985) and Ajith Fernando in *The Christian's Attitude toward World Religions* (1987) did not structure their work around these three perspectives. In a good reader on *Christianity and Other Religions* (1980) John Hick and Brian Hebblethwaite mentioned "religious pluralism" and "Christian absolutism," but did not use the three-part typology. Among the earliest uses of this three-part typology were Paul Knitter's and Francis Clooney's articles in *Religious Studies Review* 15.3 (July 1989): 197–209, surveying significant new books in the field. Carl Braaten seemed to accept the threefold typology in 1987, mentioning Gavin D'Costa and Alan Race as utilizing it, but he did not indicate where it came from (1987, 17).

10. John Sanders 1992, 1–7; Erickson 1991, 27–33; Kirk 1992, 9–15; and Gnanakan 1992 all follow this classification. David Bosch 1991, 478–83, follows a similar typology, but uses the words *relativism*, *fulfillment*, and *exclusivism* to describe the three major perspectives.

to the position represented by the Lausanne Covenant" (pp. 34–35).[11] Have we given away too much by too easily accepting these terms?

First, notice that two of the words are essentially positive. "Pluralist" is positive in terms of a multicultural and multireligious world of which we are all increasingly conscious. "Inclusivist" is positive in terms of opening our arms to receive all those who are loved by God. But "exclusivist" is a negative word. Is this by accident or by design? The pluralists and inclusivists feel quite negative about the content of the so-called exclusivist position. In fact, few of us would like to be accused of being individually, institutionally, culturally, economically, politically, or socially exclusive.

Secondly, consider the basis on which these words are being compared. If the basis is tolerance, the pluralist and inclusivist would seem to espouse tolerance, the exclusivist intolerance. If the basis is love? The pluralist loves everyone, as does the inclusivist, for they refuse "to limit the grace of God to the confines of the church" (Pinnock 1992, 15). It is the so-called exclusivist who "restricts hope" and therefore relegates people of other religions to "zones of darkness," refusing to love all peoples enough to offer them a "wider hope" (Pinnock 1992, 14). If the basis of comparison is global openness versus parochialism, the exclusivist position looks ancient and out-of-date, narrow and parochial. If the basis of comparison is optimism versus pessimism, the inclusivist position is, in Pinnock's (1992) words, "optimistic of salvation" (p. 153), while the so-called restrictivists demonstrate a "negative attitude toward the rest of the world" (p. 13), a "pessimism of salvation, or darkly negative thinking about people's spiritual journeys" (p. 182). Pinnock asserts that "we have to confront the niggardly tradition of certain varieties of conservative theology that present God as miserly, and that exclude large numbers of people without a second thought. This dark pessimism is contrary to Scripture and right reason. Not only does it contradict the prophetic hope of a large salvation, it is a cruel and offensive doctrine. What kind of God would send large numbers of men, women, and children to hell without the remotest chance of responding to his truth?" (p. 154).

I'm not sure I want to be an exclusivist or restrictivist. I'm even less inclined to be an exclusivist when I hear what the open, accepting, loving, and tolerant pluralists say about me! As we saw earlier (p. 160), John Hick (1982, 29–31) argues that the exclusivist's

> entirely negative attitude to other faiths is strongly correlated with ignorance of them. . . . Today, however, the extreme evangelical Protestant who believes

11. Later Netland 1994, 1, commented, "It is probably safe to assume that the term 'exclusivism' was not first introduced into the discussion by adherents of that perspective, but rather is a pejorative term first introduced by those who did not accept that view, who wished to cast it in a particularly unappetizing light. Unfortunately, by default, we Evangelicals have allowed others involved in the debate over religious pluralism to define the category of 'exclusivism,' and to do so in unacceptable terms."

All Humans Are Loved by the Same God

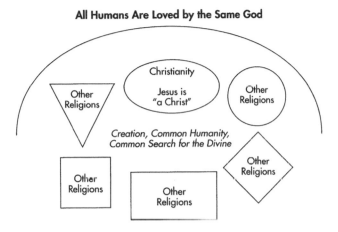

Figure 27
**The Elements of Pluralism—
A Creation Paradigm**

1. Starting point: creation and the fact of religious pluralism
2. Relativism as to both culture and faith
3. Prior choice: common humanity
4. Concern about peoples of various faiths coexisting together
5. Understanding of Romans 5:12–19: "in Adam" all were created good[12]
6. Predominantly horizontalist orientation
7. Religion regarded as expression of individual subjectivity or culture
8. Weak theology of the fall and sin[13]
9. Optimism about culture/faith
10. Bible regarded as only the Christian's book (one of many holy books)
11. Jesus Christ regarded as equal to the leaders of other religions
12. No conversion, no transformation
13. No concern for personal relationship with Jesus Christ
14. Holy Spirit viewed as working everywhere in the world, but with no relation to Christ or to the church
15. Pessimism about the church
16. No recognition of the kingdom of darkness or demonic
17. Ultimately an illogical view (pluralists cannot dialogue so conversation stops)
18. Little relationship to issues in folk religions
19. Close relationship to academic views of world religions
20. Mission regarded as irrelevant, unnecessary, demeaning, disrespectful

12. The question of what Paul meant in Rom. 5:12–19 as to the extent and nature of the symmetry between Adam and Jesus is beyond our scope here. Yet the implications of one's hermeneutic of that passage are profound and deep for our subject.
13. See, e.g., Griffiths 1980, 128–30.

All Humans Are Loved by the Same God

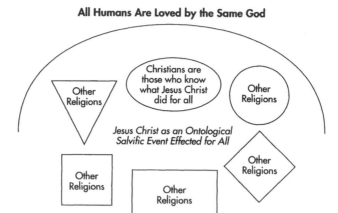

Figure 28
The Elements of Inclusivism—
A Paradigm of Universal Soteriology

1. Starting point: the unique Christ event as ontologically affecting all people
2. Absolutism about Jesus Christ, but weakness in personal relationship to the living Jesus Christ, and relativism about the form of universal christological soteriology
3. Prior choice: ultimate salvation of all by a loving God (Hick 1982)
4. Concern about peoples of various faiths coexisting together
5. Understanding of Romans 5:12–19: "in Christ" all are saved
6. Rather strongly verticalist soteriology, weakly horizontalist
7. Many religious forms regarded as ultimately based on the Christ event
8. Weak theology of the fall and sin
9. General optimism about culture/faith
10. Bible regarded as God's inspired revelation for all
11. Strong concern about the ontological uniqueness of Christ
12. Conversion regarded as good, but not necessary; transformation de-emphasized
13. Personal relationship to Jesus Christ regarded as desirable, not normative
14. Holy Spirit separated from Christology (Bradley 1993)
15. Pessimism about the institutional church
16. No recognition of the kingdom of darkness or demonic
17. Ultimately a patronizing attitude—all are saved in the Christ event whether or not they know or want it
18. Little relationship to issues in folk religions
19. Close relationship to academic views of world religions
20. Mission defined as telling people they are already saved in Jesus Christ

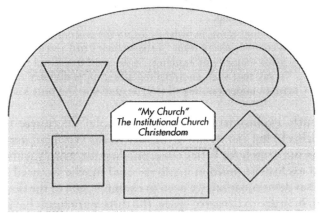

All Humans Are Loved and Judged by the Same God

"My Church"
The Institutional Church
Christendom

Figure 29
The Elements of Exclusivism—
An Ecclesiocentric Paradigm

1. Starting point: the church as the ark of salvation
2. Absolutism regarding personal allegiance to Jesus Christ *in the church* (a rather medieval, institutional understanding of *extra ecclesiam nulla salus*)
3. Prior choice: salvation only in the (my) institutional church
4. Concern that all non-Christians become Christians in the church
5. Understanding of Romans 5:12–19: "in Adam" all sinned
6. Strong verticalist orientation
7. All religious systems and cultures outside the church regarded as sinful (religious coexistence is possible only as people become Christian and part of the institutional church)
8. Heavy emphasis on theology of the fall and sin
9. Pessimism about culture/faith
10. Bible regarded as God's inspired revelation proclaimed through the church
11. Strong concern about uniqueness of Christ
12. Strong emphasis on conversion and transformation in and through Jesus Christ (and the church)
13. Personal relationship with Jesus a necessity
14. Holy Spirit predominantly mediated in word, worship, sacrament
15. Great optimism about the church—ecclesiocentric focus[14]
16. Overemphasis on kingdom of darkness; not much about the demonic
17. Ultimately a triumphalistic, dominating, self-serving approach
18. Success among folk religions
19. Lack of success among world religions
20. Mission defined as rescuing people out of sinful cultures into the church

14. Wilfred Cantwell Smith 1980, 90, argues that "traditional missions are the exact extrapolation of the traditional theology of the church."

that all Muslims go to hell is probably not so much ignorant . . . as blinded by dark dogmatic spectacles through which he can see no good in religious devotion outside his own group. . . .

If all human beings must, in order to attain the eternal happiness for which they have been created, accept Jesus Christ as their Lord and Savior before they die, then the great majority of humanity is doomed to eternal frustration and misery. . . . To say that such an appalling situation is divinely ordained is to deny the Christian understanding of God as gracious and holy love.

Apparently exclusivists are not nice people! Of course I'm speaking tongue-in-cheek! But can we not do better? At the very least it seems we need to continue our search for better conceptualization and articulation of what a so-called exclusivist position involves—and maybe we need a new word. To make that determination, we need to examine each of the three paradigms separately. In order to conserve space, the three paradigms have been graphically represented and their overall theological and missiological contours summarized in figures 27–29.[15] Should this presentation prove to be an oversimplification, I beg the reader's indulgence.

Let me now suggest a fourth perspective: the "evangelist" paradigm. I have chosen this name because I want to present a paradigm whose starting point and center is the evangel, the confession by the disciples that "Jesus is Lord."[16] As Lesslie Newbigin (1978, 190–91) said:

The Christian goes to meet his neighbor of another religion on the basis of commitment to Jesus Christ. There is no dichotomy between "confession" and "truth-seeking." His confession is the starting point [for] truth-seeking. He meets his partner with the expectation and hope of hearing more of truth. . . . Confessing Christ—incarnate, crucified, and risen—as the true light and the true life, [the Christian] cannot accept any other alleged authority as having right of way over this.

15. For a helpful definition of each viewpoint the reader may consult the evangelical sources listed in n. 10.

16. I have been helped here by an article by John Howard Yoder, "'But We Do See Jesus': The Particularity of Incarnation and the Universality of Truth," in which he calls for the use of the word *evangelical* to refer to an "apostolic example . . . of relating the wider [world—the universal truth of Christ's cosmic sovereignty over all] and the smaller world [of pluralism/relativism . . . in which truth claims. . . find their credibility challenged]. . . . I take the term in its root meaning. One is functionally evangelical if one confesses oneself to have been commissioned by the grace of God with a message which others who have not heard it should hear. It is *angelion* ('news') because they will not know it unless they are told it by the message-bearer. It is *good* news because hearing it will be for them not alienation or compulsion, oppression or brainwashing, but liberation. Because this news is only such when *received* as good, it can never be communicated coercively; nor can the message-bearer ever positively be assured that it will be received" (1983, 59, 66–67).

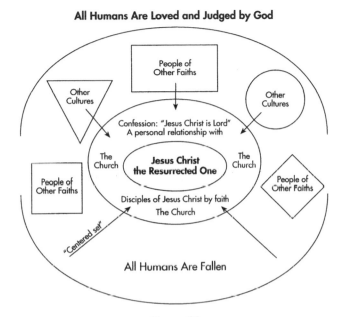

All Humans Are Loved and Judged by God

Figure 30
The Elements of "Evangelism"—
A Fourth Paradigm

1. Starting point: the confession "Jesus Christ is Lord"[17]
2. Absolutism regarding a personal faith relationship with the risen Jesus Christ as Lord; relativism in terms of the shape this takes in church and culture
3. Prior choice: personal faith in Jesus Christ (he was born, lived, ministered, died, rose, ascended, and is coming again) by grace and in the power of the Holy Spirit
4. Concern about human coexistence amidst multiple cultures and religions
5. Understanding of Romans 5:12–19: "as in Adam . . . so in Christ" is not completely symmetrical
6. Equally verticalist and horizontalist orientation
7. All cultures (including our own) regarded as fallen, but also as able to teach us something new about how "Jesus Christ is Lord"[18]
8. Seriousness regarding the consequences of the fall and of sin
9. Some optimism about cultures—affirmation of culture yet pessimism about human sinfulness
10. Bible regarded as God's inspired revelation for all humanity—it has new things to say to each new culture where the gospel takes root

17. For some discussion of this most essential kerygmatic confession by the early church and some of its missiological implications, see Van Engen 1991b, 92–94.
18. See Van Engen 1989a for some initial insight into how this seems to work through time in the midst of multiple cultures; see also ch. 3.

11. Strong emphasis on confessing anew in word and life, "Jesus is Lord"
12. Strong emphasis on conversion and sometimes on transformation
13. Personal relationship with Jesus Christ a necessity
14. Holy Spirit viewed as working simultaneously but differently in the world, in and through the church, and in the believer for mission in the world
15. Moderate optimism about the institutional church—the orientation is more toward the kingdom of God
16. Consciousness of the kingdom of darkness and the demonic both in the world and in the church
17. Ultimately creative, ever-changing theology-on-the-way approach that calls for new Christologies in new cultural settings
18. Success among folk religions
19. Tendency to be confrontational with other global religious systems
20. Mission defined as calling people in multiple cultures to conversion, confession, and new allegiance, personally and corporately, to Jesus Christ as Lord

Presuppositions Distinguishing the Four Perspectives

The Relation of Faith and Culture

Before we look at the missiological implications of our fourth paradigm, we need to examine some of the presuppositions that underlie all four paradigms. First, we need to ask about their respective views of the relation of faith and culture. We saw earlier (p. 164) that while faith and culture cannot be entirely separated from each other, that is a far cry from equating them:

> The gospel must be distinguished from all human cultures. It is divine revelation, not human speculation. Since it belongs to no one culture, it can be adequately expressed in all of them. The failure to differentiate between the gospel and human cultures has been one of the great weaknesses of modern Christian missions. Missionaries too often have equated the Good News with their own cultural background. This has led them to condemn most native customs and to impose their own customs on converts. Consequently, the gospel has been seen as foreign in general and Western in particular. People have rejected it not because they reject the lordship of Christ, but because conversion often has meant a denial of their cultural heritage and social ties. [Hiebert 1985, 53]

That there is a difference between faith and culture is supported not only anthropologically, but also historically and biblically. Historically, one need only review the history of the church to realize that the gospel of faith in the lordship of Jesus Christ has always tended to break out of the cultural molds that would imprison it. Originally the gospel was not Western at all—it was Middle Eastern. It began among Aramaic-speaking Jews. Then it took shape in all the cultures surrounding Jerusalem that are referred to in Acts 2—in Greek culture, in Roman culture, in North African cultures, in Ethiopia, in India, in Near Eastern cultures, in Arabic cultures. It expanded to the Franks, to Scandinavia, to the British Isles, and on and on. To closely associate any culture with biblical faith is to ignore the historical expansion of the church.

But even more profoundly, the distinction between faith and culture is biblically essential. This issue is at the heart of Acts and Romans.[19] In Acts and Romans the issue is precisely how a single faith in Christ's lordship can take shape in a variety of cultures. The difference between faith and culture is also essential for our understanding of Galatians, Ephesians, and Colossians. Paul speaks, for example, of the mystery "that through the gospel the Gentiles [the *ethnē*, comprising a multiplicity of cultures] are heirs together with Israel, members together of one body, and sharers together in the promise in Christ Jesus" (Eph. 3:6). First Peter and Revelation would also be difficult to understand were there no distinction between faith and culture.

Now this issue is even more important than it may yet seem. We noted earlier (p. 164) that the literature of pluralism assumes a nearly synonymous relationship between faith and culture. It is disturbing that a close examination of the writings of inclusivists like Clark Pinnock, John Sanders, and David Watson reveals a similar almost total identification of culture with faith. However, please take note that the so-called exclusivists also tend to closely equate culture and faith—and in that case, conversion to Jesus Christ sometimes too easily becomes conversion to a particular version of culture Christianity.

Now the nature of the world in which we live has made the equation of faith and culture more dangerous than ever. Christians and non-Christians, pluralists, inclusivists, and exclusivists are beginning to share one thing in common. We are all being radically impacted by the largest redistribution of people the globe has ever seen. And the multiculturalness of our new reality is so staggering that we are reeling between rising new protectionist racism, rampant individualization and balkanization, and a radical postmodern embrace of cultural relativism that calls into question many of our most cherished values. In this new reality, all of us are being called on to find ways to affirm cultural relativity: tolerance, understanding, justice, equality, and coexistence within the new multiculturalism. The cities of our world are being especially impacted, and the church in the city knows very little, and seems to care even less, about how to present the gospel in this new reality.

---

19. See pp. 165–67 for an outline of the faith-culture dynamic in Romans, as seen from a missiological point of view.

If one views faith and culture as nearly synonymous and also begins to be open to *cultural* relativism, the next step is some form of *religious* pluralism.[20] If one goes all the way with this process, one arrives at the pluralist position. If one cannot go that far, feeling strongly constrained to hold tightly to the uniqueness of the cosmic Christ-event, one arrives at the inclusivist position. If one refuses to accept cultural relativism, but holds faith and culture to be synonymous, one arrives at an exclusivist position reminiscent of the cultural Protestantism of the nineteenth century. Is it not enlightening that the strongest proponents of religious pluralism (or exclusivism) also seem to represent the strands of Christendom that tend to be the most culture-affirming (or culture-bound), where faith and culture are most closely intertwined? As the evangelical community has become more culture-affirming in the way it lives out the gospel, the distinction between faith and culture has become harder to maintain.

The Forms of the Soteriological Question

Secondly, we need to examine the form of the soteriological question being asked by the four paradigms. We need to be conscious of the radical difference in the form the question takes among pluralists and inclusivists on the one hand, and the exclusivists and "evangelists" on the other. The bottom-line question of the pluralist and inclusivist positions is, "Given the fact that humanity is basically good, and God is a God of love, how is it possible that God could condemn so much of humanity to eternal punishment?" The exclusivists and evangelists would ask the question differently. We would ask, "Given the fact of the fall, and that 'all have sinned and fall short of the glory of God' (Rom. 3:23), how is it possible that so much of humanity can be saved?"

We cannot pursue this issue further here. But it is imperative that our theological work concerning Christology and relation to non-Christian faiths expand beyond the soteriological questions to questions about creation, the nature of humanity, the fall, and the nature of sin and holiness. Without examining these questions, we cannot fully clarify the issues at hand. This is where Pinnock and Sanders are both quite unrealistic about their christological rethinking. One cannot make such a substantive change in one's Christology without its being either the beginning of a change in all the other loci of one's theology, or the result of changes already made or assumed. James Bradley (1993, 20–22) points this out in relation to ecclesiology and popular faith:

20. W. A. Visser 't Hooft emphasized the importance of the distinction between faith and culture already in 1963 (p. 85): "To transform the struggle between the religions concerning the ultimate truth of God into an intercultural debate concerning values is to leave out the central issue at stake . . . the central affirmation of the faith, that God revealed himself once for all in Jesus Christ."

Pinnock has failed to reckon with how the various topics of Christian doctrine cohere: one cannot make such a fundamental shift in Christology without changing (in this instance, for example) ecclesiology as well. . . . A Christology that has no relation to ecclesiology will fall short of the biblical norm and it will inevitably underplay the importance of fellowship and enervate the will to evangelism. . . . Another test for any Christian doctrine is its universal applicability to all classes of people. . . . The dialogue with world religions is not only a discussion among intellectuals, but it must have bearing upon the way that the common person and the oppressed are met in concrete encounter. . . . The abstract characterization of Christ and the idea of cosmic revelation thus not only present us with theological problems, they present us with practical problems as well. The particular human nature of Christ is not sufficiently emphasized, and salvation from sin and oppression seems to be suspended in the air. "Salvation" for Pinnock tends to be reduced to the bare notion of escape from final judgment. In the crushing modern world of dehumanization, people require a tangible sense of God's solidarity with them in Christ's humanity. It is ironic that in the name of dialogue with world religions, *Logos* Christology fails to offer us the humanity of God that alone can relieve the oppressions of the downtrodden.

Missiological Implications of the "Evangelist" Paradigm

Having examined some of the basic presuppositions of the four paradigms, we must, before developing the major missiological implications of the "evangelist" paradigm, clarify a foundational commitment from which all else derives. We are making a conscious choice here to highlight the Christian's personal relationship with the historic Jesus Christ who was born, lived in Palestine during a specific historical time, ministered, died, rose, ascended, and is coming again. The absolutely radical claim of the canonical text of the Bible is that this Jesus lives today, and is the one with whom the Christian disciple relates personally by faith. Even John Hick (1982, 122–23) recognized the viability of this perspective:

In allowing for significant change in the Christian as a fruit of his dialogue with non-Christians it is customary to draw a very important distinction (suggested by that of Karl Barth) between, on the one hand, the historical phenomenon called Christianity, which is one of the religions of the world, and on the other hand, personal discipleship and devotion to Jesus Christ. This implies an entirely proper and helpful distinction between Jesus—the actual Jesus who lived in Palestine in the first third of the first century, the reports and rumors of whose life and teaching have inspired millions ever since to try to live as his disciples—and the historical development of Christianity, the latter being recognized to be a human, and often all-too-human, affair. And the contemporary confessionalist often suggests that we should engage in dialogue, not primarily as adherents of historical Christianity, but simply as disciples of Jesus. This is, I think, a very fruitful approach.

Hick himself (1982, 19) recognized the implications of this position: "If Jesus was literally God incarnate, the second Person of the holy Trinity living a human life, so that the Christian religion was founded by God-on-earth in person, it is then very hard to escape from the traditional view that all mankind must be converted to the Christian faith."

Of course, this is the crucial point. But Hick opted to understand the narrative about Jesus Christ as "metaphorical" rather than literally descriptive of a verifiable historical fact (1982, 19). That decision was coupled with his prior conclusion that "any viable Christian theodicy must affirm the ultimate salvation of all God's creatures" (1982, 17). The combination of these two factors leads logically to a pluralist position. Thus the reader needs to notice that we are affirming here our own prior commitments: to Jesus Christ as a historical person, and to faith in Jesus Christ as a personal relationship of covenantal discipleship in the power of the Holy Spirit.

In developing the missiological implications of the evangelist paradigm, we will try to present a trinitarian and kingdom-oriented perspective that may help us listen to the other three paradigms and critique them as well. In so doing, we need to be able to move past the pessimism about mission, faith, and the church exhibited by pluralists and inclusivists alike. That is, we need to be able to get "Beyond Anti-Colonialism to Globalism," to use Paul Hiebert's words (1991). At the same time, we need to become open to a modern global village of interreligious encounter and multicultural diversity where we can no longer afford to create, protect, and preserve our own seemingly safe sanctuaries of religious exclusivity.

We live at the dawn of the most exciting missionary era ever. Never before could we say that there are Christians in every nation on earth. With about 1.5 billion Christians circling the globe, the Christian faith now has the potential of evangelizing the other 4.5 billion people in a way never before possible. The global reawakening of interest in spirituality, in the spirit world, and in religious phenomena provides an unprecedented opportunity for calling people to faith in Jesus Christ. And so the subject at hand is timely, urgent, and essential. For "the uniqueness of Jesus Christ is not an exclusive claim purely for the Christian community, or for the disciple of Jesus Christ. It has universal validity. . . . Any casual reader of the Bible will be convinced that very central to the Christian revelation is its historic and universal claim for salvation for all the world" (Gnanakan 1992, 126). And so the particularity of Jesus Christ's incarnation, ministry, death, and resurrection in history continues to stand in dialectical tension with the universality of Jesus Christ's claims to be the Savior of the world. In the midst of this universal particularism, the disciples of Jesus confess that "Jesus Christ is Lord."

Faith-Particularist	*Culturally Pluralist*	*Ecclesiologically Inclusivist*
"**Jesus** Christ is Lord"	"Jesus **Christ** is Lord"	"Jesus Christ is **Lord**"
(God the Son)	(God the Father)	(God the Holy Spirit)

Figure 31
The Missiological Implications of the Evangelist Paradigm

Jesus Christ is Lord: Faith-Particularist

Our study of the implications of the evangelist paradigm will be limited to three basic categories. This paradigm of Christian attitude to other religions offers a perspective that is (1) faith-particularist, (2) culturally pluralist, and (3) ecclesiologically inclusivist (see figure 31).

The first element of this new paradigm that we need to stress is that it is personal. It deals not with religious systems, or theoretical religions as such, but with people and personal faith (Taber and Taber 1992). It has to do with personal faith in and allegiance to Jesus, who lived and ministered in Palestine at a specific time in history (Hiebert 1979b; 1983, 427; 1994, 125–30). As Ken Gnanakan says, "God's revelation has a historicality and a universality that will need to be reconciled" (1992, 19). And such reconciliation is to be found, first of all, in a personal relationship of the Christian with the resurrected and ascended Jesus Christ of history. The only truly unique, truly distinctive aspect of Christian faith is "a personal relationship between the Christian and the living Christ" (Heim 1985, 135).

In the evangelist paradigm, confession of Jesus as Lord involves a personal relationship that breaks the bonds of all religious systems. This relationship involves all of life with all its contradictions. It is not neat, logical, coherent. It is not exclusive, nor arrogant, nor triumphalistic. Rather, it is humble confession, repentance, and obedience. Thus the major question is not to what religious system a person belongs. Rather, the crucial issue is one's center. The ultimate question is the question of discipleship, of one's proximity to, or distance from, Jesus the Lord.

The evangelist paradigm calls into question the institutional structures of all churches, and especially of Christianity as a religious system, for the churches are now seen to be the fellowship of disciples whose allegiance is to Jesus more than to a particular institution (contra the exclusivist perspective). The evangelist paradigm also calls into question the inclusivist perspective that the cosmic Christ-event is salvific for all persons regardless of their personal relationship with Jesus Christ. And it questions the pluralists' relativistic reduction of the confession to Jesus' being only "a christ" among many.

On the other hand, the confession of Jesus as Lord also signals all that cannot be called "lord" by the Christian. The confession calls for stripping away all the layers of the artichoke[21] of cultural accretions that Christians have added to the basic confession. As Paul declares in Romans, and we see modeled in Acts, to confess with one's mouth and believe in one's heart that Jesus is Lord—that is all there is. Nothing else really matters. All else is to be held lightly. Everything else is negotiable. Thus when we call people of other cultures and faiths to confess "Jesus is Lord," it is not *our* Jesus (exclusivist), nor is it *a* Jesus (pluralist), nor is it the cosmic amorphous idea of Jesus Christ (inclusivist). Rather, it is Jesus *the Lord*, who calls for conversion and transformation of all who confess his name. Thus, again, only in humility, in personal repentance and prayer, and with the expectation of a great diversity in cultural forms may we invite others to join us in confessing *Jesus* as Lord. Many evangelical theologians and missiologists have affirmed this.[22] Such broad agreement, however, does not minimize the radicalness of the affirmation.

Jesus *Christ* is Lord: Culturally Pluralist

Along with the historicity and relationality of Jesus Christ, we must also affirm the universality of Christ's messianic lordship. As John 1, Ephesians 1, and Colossians 1 state, Jesus the Christ is the creator and sustainer of all the universe. Here we are listening carefully to pluralist concerns. For we too are concerned about the whole of humanity and about the care of God's creation. We are concerned about how humans can live together in peace and justice, especially in the midst of increasingly difficult clashes between conflicting religious allegiances.

Given our universal concerns, we need a trinitarian missiology that is kingdom-oriented, as Johannes Verkuyl has masterfully pointed out (1993). We need to remember that Christ's lordship is not only over the church (contra the exclusivist), but also over all the world. The pluralist and inclusivist perspectives confuse the manner, scope, and nature of Christ's kingly rule over the church (the willing subjects), over all humanity (many unwilling subjects), and over the unseen world. These need to be differentiated.[23]

However, differentiating the categories of Christ's kingly rule does not warrant our ignoring all peoples. Rather, Christ's lordship will radically question the exclusivist position on other cultures and religions, and will instead open up a much greater breadth for contextualized encounter between Christians and the multiple cultures. Not all so-called non-Christian culture

21. At one time I used the onion as a metaphor. But onions have no center—artichokes do.
22. See, e.g., Verkuyl 1989; Glasser 1989; Thomsen 1990; Michael Green 1977; Braaten 1981; Taylor 1981; Scott 1981a; Norman Anderson 1950, 228–37; Heim 1985, 135; Yoder 1983; Neill 1970; Pickard 1991; and Gnanakan 1992.
23. See Van Engen 1981, 277–305; 1991b, 108–17.

is sinful (contra the exclusivist). But neither is it all relative (contra the pluralist). For all is brought together under the lordship of Christ. Neither are all humans ontologically determined to be included in Christ's salvation against their will (contra the inclusivist). Rather, we are called to "test the spirits" (1 John 4:1–3). Those who confess "that Jesus Christ has come in the flesh" are to be recognized as coming from God.

This broad, all-encompassing Christology means that we need to continue to listen carefully to the new Christologies that are arising in Asia, Africa, and Latin America. All that which does not contradict the biblical revelation concerning the historical Jesus Christ our Lord is open for consideration. We are becoming aware that even in the New Testament a multiplicity of Christologies draw from the greatness of Jesus Christ and shape themselves for specific cultural and historical contexts (Gundry 1994).

Thus John Levison and Priscilla Pope-Levison (1994) have called us to join them in a search for "An Ecumenical Christology for Asia" that is neither so cosmic that it loses touch with real life, nor so focused on the suffering Jesus that there is no possibility for transformation. Latin America has stressed the impotent Jesus hanging on the cross and the powerless baby Jesus in the manger.[24] Such truths can enrich and in turn be enriched by our Christologies. "That Christ is *the* truth does not mean that there are no truths to be found anywhere outside of him, but it does mean that all such truths are fragmentary and broken unless they become integrated in him as the center" (Hendrikus Berkhof 1979, 48). Clearly, we need to be very careful here, and must follow a very sensitive process that Paul Hiebert has called "Critical Contextualization" (1987). David Hesselgrave warns that we are constantly faced with twin dangers: "the risk of going too far" and "the risk of not going far enough" (1988, 152).[25]

Jesus Christ is *Lord:* Ecclesiologically Inclusivist

The third missiological implication of the evangelist paradigm has to do with the kingdom of God and the church:

> A theology and missiology informed by the biblical notion of the rule of Christ will never fail to identify personal conversion as one of the inclusive goals of God's Kingdom. . . . The good news of the Kingdom also has to do with the formation and in-depth growth of the Body of Christ throughout the world and to the end of time. . . . The Kingdom is, of course, far broader than the Church

24. In Latin America the development of new Christologies has been extensive and creative—too much to be treated well here. See, e.g., Escobar 1991; Padilla 1986; and Mackay 1933. New christological formulations have been especially important in the development of liberation theology.

25. See also Kirk 1992, 171–87; Fernando 1987, ch. 6; Nicholls 1979; 1984; Newbigin 1978; and Henry 1991, 253.

alone. God's Kingdom is all-embracing in respect of both point of view and purpose; it signifies the consummation of the whole of history; it has cosmic proportions and fulfills time and eternity. Meanwhile, the Church, the believing and active community of Christ, is raised up by God among all nations to share in the salvation and suffering service of the Kingdom. The Church consists of those whom God has called to stand at His side to act out with Him the drama of the revelation of the Kingdom come and coming. [Verkuyl 1993, 73]

So the kingdom leads us to the church, the disciples of Jesus Christ the Lord. For the church is not only a gathering of individuals, it is much more. "Though faith may be intensely personal," comment Charles and Betty Taber, "religion is irreducibly social" (1992, 76). Jesus Christ is not only Lord of creation, he is also head of the church (Col. 1). Thus Jesus Christ sent his Spirit (contra Pinnock's *Logos* Christology) at Pentecost to establish the church. Because Jesus Christ is head of the church, no one else is. The church belongs to no human person, and church growth must be growth in the numbers of disciples of Jesus, as Donald McGavran always affirmed—not proselytism with a view to expanding someone's little ecclesiastical kingdom. The evangelist paradigm seeks to correct the triumphalism and arrogance of which the exclusivists have sometimes been accused (Gnanakan 1992, 154).

Because Jesus Christ the Lord is the head of the church, the church's mission is therefore to participate in the mission of Jesus the Christ. This means that it is no less than that which Jesus declares in Luke 4. And it is as much as what Paul in Acts 13 says it is: Christ's disciples, the church, are commanded to be a "light to the nations." The church is therefore to focus on the whole of humanity. There is always room for one more forgiven sinner. But this also means (contra the inclusivists) that it is the church and not some cosmic idea that gathers disciples. This also signifies (contra the pluralists) that the church of which Christ is head is called to proclaim that Jesus is the Lord of all humanity, not just "a christ" for the Christian:

> The Church cannot escape the fact that to confess Jesus as Lord moves it profoundly toward its own universality—a movement outward to the nations. This is climactically presented to us in the Great Commission of Matthew 28:19–20: "Full authority in heaven and on earth has been committed to me. Go forth therefore and make all nations my disciples.". . . Thus the mission of Jesus becomes inescapable and utterly binding for all of his disciples. They cannot confess Jesus is Lord without at the same time proclaiming his lordship over all people. . . . So Jesus Christ, the Lord of all people, all creation, and Lord of the Church, sends his people to a radical encounter with the world. [Van Engen 1991b, 93–94]

This world-encountering church is as broad as all humanity (pluralist), as accepting as Christ's cosmic lordship (inclusivist), and as incorporating and gathering as Christ's disciples (exclusivist). Clearly, the scandal associated with this church is that it is *simul justus et peccator*. Yet it is still the church of Jesus Christ. And just as clearly, in today's world of multiple religions and cultures the shape of this church needs to be reconsidered. We need new ecclesiologies for new contexts—and many new ecclesiological endeavors are being suggested. Yet in another sense the church is always the same: it is the disciples of Jesus Christ, the Lord of creation, of all peoples, and of the church.[26]

This chapter has not said much that is new—that was not the intent. Ultimately our conviction, reflection, and proclamation involve only a restatement of the mystery of the gospel for all people, a mystery that "for ages past was kept hidden in God, who created all things. His intent was that now, through the church, the manifold wisdom of God should be made known . . . according to his eternal purpose which he accomplished in Christ Jesus our Lord. In him and through faith in him we may approach God with freedom and confidence" (Eph. 3:9–12). If Paul and the early church could so emphatically state such a conviction in the midst of their amazing cultural and religious diversity, we can feel confident in doing so as well.

So then, although our subject is incredibly complex, yet it is really quite simple. "Jesus is Lord." In the midst of many cultures and people of many faiths, we must be bold. We must learn more profoundly how to be evangelists: faith-particularist, culturally pluralist, and ecclesiologically inclusivist.

---

26. Among a number of helpful guides for "evangelistic" dialogue with people of other faiths are Verkuyl 1978, 354–68; 1993; Bosch 1991, 474–89; Nicholls 1984, 131–35; 1990; and Kirk 1992.

Part 6

Modernity and Postmodernity in Mission Theology

11

Mission Theology in the North American Context

The circle is being completed, and we in North America now need the perspectives and advice of our brothers and sisters from the Two-Thirds World to give us new insight into and urgency in bringing the gospel to our people in a fresh and exciting way. Now *we* are in need of receiving from others that which we previously shared with the world. This chapter is a series of musings and reflections concerning evangelism in the North American context as viewed through the eyes of our brothers and sisters in the Two-Thirds World. Here we are interested in reflecting on proclaiming the gospel in North America and the implications for mission theology. We will begin with some observations, acknowledge the obstacles, make a note of the opportunities, and set forth some objectives for evangelizing North America.

Observations

The United States has been the spawning ground of some of the world's greatest evangelists and evangelical movements. Just a glance at Paulus Scharpff's definitive work on the *History of Evangelism* (1966)[1] brings to mind such people as Theodore Frelinghuysen,[2] Jonathan Edwards, Charles Finney, Dwight L. Moody, Billy Sunday, and Billy Graham. These evangelists were influential because they were catalysts for and harvesters of the great movements of revival and spiritual awakening which are a part of the

1. See also Terry 1994.
2. Concerning Frelinghuysen and the history of Reformed revivalism see Brouwer 1977, 48–51.

history of religion in America. The Great Awakening of the 1720s, the Second Great Awakening of the 1790s, the Revival of 1830, the Prayer Revival of 1858, the Revival of 1905, and lesser regional revivals of the 1880s, 1900s, and 1940s have left an indelible stamp on the culture and religious life of the United States.[3] Founded to some extent because of religious issues, never having had an established state church, and affected over her history by evangelistic people and movements, the United States has taken on a certain peculiar religious flavor which influences the doing of evangelism. As James McCord, president of Princeton Theological Seminary (1959–83), said, "I think that [the strength of the present religious revival in America] is in the deep, evangelical piety that has characterized Americans' religion from the very beginnings. It's like a subterranean stream that surfaces and resurfaces again and again from generation to generation. And it's surfacing now, just as the mainline churches have flattened out. But it makes one realize the deep evangelistic spirituality of the American people" (quoted in Gallup and O'Connell 1986, 77).

Leaders of churches in the Two-Thirds World (Africa, Asia, Latin America, Oceania) who have looked from outside our culture at the role and significance of religion in North America are well aware of the impact which the deep evangelistic spirituality of the American people has had upon the rest of the world. The rise of the North American Protestant missionary movement from the early 1800s on, the formation of the YMCA and YWCA, the Student Volunteer Movement, the International Missionary Council, the formation of the World Council of Churches, and the recent rise of evangelical foreign mission agencies have all been strongly influenced by this characteristic of American religious life. For the past 150 years churches in the Two-Thirds World have been strongly impacted by this North American evangelistic fervor, a recent example of which is the series of congresses for itinerant evangelists which the Billy Graham Association has sponsored in Amsterdam.

Given this historical and national context, members of churches in the Two-Thirds World find it perplexing that evangelism in North America is presently not a high priority for most North American Christians, and in fact has been the neglected child of much of mainline Protestantism during the past several decades.[4] They find it hard to understand why the mainline de-

---

3. For some of the best literature on revivals in America, see the writings of J. Edwin Orr, the histories by Kenneth Scott Latourette, along with Lovelace 1979; Beardsley 1912; Stoeffler 1976; De Jong 1978; Marty 1984; McLoughlin 1978; and Cairns 1986.

4. In a study done by Schuller Ministries and the Gallup organization, people were asked, "Of the statements on this card, which four do you think are the most important if someone is trying to be a follower of Jesus?" The sixteen possible responses that were listed represent a fairly wide range: "Obeying the Ten Commandments, Forgiving those who have wronged you, Putting others' needs before your own, Living in such a way as to draw others to Jesus, Person-to-person charitable activities among the underprivileged, Consoling those in sorrow or

nominations, which have been their historic mothers, sisters, and now ecclesiastical partners, have a consistently declining membership. They wonder why we who have helped them evangelize their parts of the world cannot impact our own culture for the gospel. Most perplexed are those Christians in the Two-Thirds World who labor under tremendous pressure from other religions, severe restrictions on their evangelistic activities, and radical shortages of personnel, materials, and finances. As a pastor from India and student at Western Theological Seminary asked me once, How is it that with such liberty, wealth, and popular openness to the Christian religion many Christian churches in North America are not evangelizing their people? According to the *World Christian Encyclopedia* (1982), over half of all Christians now live in the Two-Thirds World, and their numbers are rapidly growing while the percentage of Christians in Europe and North America continues to dwindle. Maybe it is time we let the Two-Thirds World help us.

Christians from the Two-Thirds World can help us because of their experience with similar situations. For example, Christians in Latin America have struggled with widespread nominalism for three centuries now and readily recognize it in our own Protestant situation. They are immediately struck by the lack of commitment of church members to the life and activities of the church, and particularly to participation in the evangelization of North America.

Christians in Asia have dealt for a very long time with movements offering mystical experiences and quickly recognize them in the latest fads here. So when newspaper headlines announce, say, "Cosmic age believers gather for 'harmonic convergence,'" Asian Christians could help us offer a Christian response.

Christians from Africa have been dealing with a proliferation of new religious movements and the prophets, healings, spiritism, exorcisms, and spiritual power which usually accompany these movements.[5] The new interest in this kind of spiritual phenomenon in North America calls us to seek the Africans' advice when we bring the gospel to bear upon such movements in our midst. As an African pastor said to me recently, "We have had our spiritual sensitivities sharpened over the last several decades, and can assist North American Christians to discern the true from the false."

Christians in the Middle East, Indonesia, and northern Africa have lived side by side with Islam for many centuries. They could certainly enrich our

---

affliction, Telling people about Jesus, Being active in a local church, Studying the Bible daily, Having a regular prayer time, Receiving Holy Communion, Becoming involved in community activities . . . ." Only 22 percent cited "Telling people about Jesus" as one of the four most important activities of a follower of Jesus (Gallup and O'Connell 1986, 45).

5. At Selly Oak Colleges in Birmingham, England, Harold Turner established an institute which seeks to study new religious movements around the world and then aid Christians in communicating the gospel in the context of these new movements.

own approach to the large Islamic population of the United States if we were to seek their advice and guidance.

And what of issues like secularism which European Christians have been facing? What of the materialist reduction of life with which Christians in Marxist societies have been struggling for some time? And what of those nations and governments organized around new ideologies to which Christians in the Two-Thirds World have had to respond? And what of the Christians in places such as South America, South Africa, Nicaragua, Guatemala, and El Salvador who have been carefully and seriously dealing with the issues of evangelization in the context of liberation and justice? Are there not similar issues in our context? It seems that we will urgently need the input of Christians in other parts of the world if we are to be able to speak the gospel in a meaningful way to our people. Although many of us might tend to think of ours as a Christian nation, others looking in see the beam in our eye because it is so obviously similar to phenomena they encounter in their contexts. When these kinds of issues are all combined, we begin to understand that our evangelistic task is really one of *Evangelizing Neopagan North America*, as Alfred Krass (1982) has put it.[6] In fact, if we take the gospel seriously in all its biblical breadth, we will find it radically questioning some of the most basic presuppositions of our culture.[7] Although at the outset we might consider the evangelization of North America a simple task, on more careful consideration we will find significant obstacles which make our context one of the more difficult ones to impact with the claims of Jesus Christ.

Obstacles

We need to consider soberly the unique obstacles facing us in the evangelization of North America. We will broadly highlight some of the obstacles most often identified by Christians from the Two-Thirds World as being especially true of our situation in North America. These tend to fall into two major categories: obstacles in our culture and obstacles in our churches.

Obstacles in Our Culture

The Perception That God's Help Is Not Needed

There are certain built-in obstructions in our cultural setting which must be squarely faced, understood, dealt with, and overcome in order for the gospel to impact North America. First is the perception that we do not need God's help.

6. For a similar appraisal of the European scene see Visser 't Hooft 1974; 1977.

7. Newbigin 1986. As a result of Bishop Newbigin's work, the British Council of Churches established a program "to examine how the Christian Church can effectively confess its faith within the public life of the world," and specifically in the context of Western culture. Wilbert Shenk of Fuller Theological Seminary continues to head up this project.

I remember crossing the United States–Mexico border in the spring of 1983 on the way to a women's triennial conference at Hope College. In the car were two women from Chiapas, Mexico, who had been very active in evangelism there over the past several decades. As we rode through the luxurious cities and countryside of southern Texas, one of their comments was, "It appears that these people don't need God." I asked them what they meant. They responded that compared with their own situation where they daily deal with the presence of extreme poverty, the lack of physical safety, constant job insecurity, uncertainties regarding housing and food, family crises, and a general lack of control over one's destiny, the people of the United States do not appear to need God. Insurance companies take care of accidents and other crises, workers' compensation cares for the unemployed, and school systems look after nearly everyone's basic education. In short, concerns about health, welfare, and the pursuit of happiness are given secular answers, though they in fact entail spiritual questions.

As we rode, we talked more. One of the women went on to observe, "It appears that in this culture there is no space for God." People appear busy with family, work, recreation, social life, and the personal pursuit of wealth. Where, then, is there space for God? It appears that God is restricted to a narrow part of life which has to do with illness and personal crises. Amelia said, "It is no wonder so many people in this country seem to think they can do without God."

Since seeing our culture through Mexican eyes, I have carefully taken note of the arenas of life mentioned during congregational prayers. Is it not true that our need for God is narrowed to matters of health and personal crisis—with a political or global issue thrown in once in a while? Whole arenas of life like food, clothing, housing, education, work, recreation, social relationships, finances, and personal moral choices—matters which are commonly subjects of prayer in other cultures—are seldom mentioned in our own prayers. Even less are they considered to be religious issues in our North American culture. It is no wonder that when we begin to deal with issues of evangelism and God-talk, we seem rather tongue-tied and embarrassed. Our culture seems to push us to speak of religious faith and commitment as something separate from the daily life of the people of North America. But a careful reading of Scripture teaches otherwise. God in Jesus Christ through the Spirit is interested in permeating all arenas and transforming every aspect of our lives.

The Privatization of Faith

Issues of faith are separated from public life in North America. In 1980 I attended an ecumenical consultation convened by my denomination in New York City. While there, an Arab Christian emphasized to me that in the Middle East "religious affiliation is a public matter, highly visible, politically significant, and publicly demonstrated. Islam forces us in that direction. Though that creates severe religious, social, and political tensions, I sometimes think that they are easier to deal with than this culture, where in terms of public demonstration you cannot guess the religious affiliation of many of the people around you."

What a different perspective from that of my friend Dirk, a milkman from Monnickendam, the Netherlands. I sat in his living room in 1981 and listened to him expound at length on how faith and religious affiliation are a matter of taste and personal preference. Influenced strongly by a Western worldview, Dirk showed me two bottles of wine, one white and one red: "Some people like white wine, others like red. You like Reformed Christianity, my brother Hans likes the Seventh-Day Adventists, I like no religion at all. You see, each individual should be free to choose, and we should respect each other's choice."

This "live-and-let-live" attitude is highly valued in our North American culture, and we would probably find people inside and outside the church giving very strong support to it. In fact, however, it is a contradiction of the very heart of the gospel, which speaks of one God who created all people, one Jesus Christ who has authority over all creation and at whose name every knee shall one day bow, and one Spirit who convicts the world of sin, righteousness, and judgment (see, e.g., Matt. 28; Col. 1; Rom. 5–6; Phil. 2; John 16:8).

In a masterful philosophical analysis Lesslie Newbigin (1986, chs. 1–2) points out that the Western worldview has created a dichotomy between two spheres—our culture and the gospel. On the one hand is the public sphere of scientific rationality, cause-effect explanation, observable and demonstrable facts, and truth claims measurable by an appeal to a rational and contingent (constantly changing) universe. On the other hand, the culture has relegated religious experience to the private sphere of personal opinion and values, inward concepts of faith, and individual choice of a religious lifestyle. But in fact the gospel is unavoidably public! The spiritual is an integral part of our history. Our message is one of hope: there are reason, purpose, and direction to our history because God is in control. And this message is public truthful fact! The gospel must be allowed to impact, question, shape, and transform science, economics, politics, logical reasoning, and Western cultural values.

The privatization of religious belief constitutes a major obstacle to the evangelization of North America. Particularly strong in culture-affirming denominations, it takes away the vitality and robs us of the urgency of communicating the gospel in our context. Our desperate fear of anything that smacks of propaganda and proselytism is a direct result of the privatization of our religion. Other religious movements in our midst seem to have no such fear. We who worship the God of the universe and Jesus Christ in whom all things subsist need not fear a public demonstration of our faith.

The Absence of Radical Conversion

A third obstacle is even more pervasive and subtle. A non-Christian medical doctor in Tapachula, Chiapas, Mexico, who had done extensive study in the United States once observed to me that in the United States people seem to be constantly bombarded by religious literature, radio and television programs, and church presentations. He then spoke of the law of diminishing returns and of deafness caused by too much noise, of blindness caused by too much light. "I believe," he said, "that religious overkill in the U.S. has produced similar reactions on a personal and spiritual plane." He was pointing to a very significant obstacle resulting to some extent from our own evangelistic and revivalist history.

If we turn on the radio or television on Sunday morning, we are bombarded by evangelist preachers. In studying the general population of the unchurched in North America, we discover that their contact with the church may have been quite extensive—but mostly negative. Many may have gone forward in an evangelistic crusade and even signed a decision card. But they have little personal faith and seldom attend church. The left-outs, the dropouts, the locked-outs, and the opt-outs all had contact with the church at one time or another—but do not live out their faith in any meaningful way at the present time.[8] Many of the unchurched in fact have quite good and understandable reasons why they essentially have given up on the church. Indeed, there is ample cause for disillusionment with the church in North America:

> We boast Christianity as our faith, but many of us have not bothered to learn the basic biblical facts about this religion. Many of us dutifully attend church, but this act in itself appears to have made us no less likely than our unchurched brethren to engage in unethical behavior.
>
> We say we are Christians, but sometimes we do not show much love toward those who do not share our particular religious perspective. We say we rejoice in the good news that Jesus brought, but we are often strangely reluctant to share the gospel with others. . . .
>
> We say we are *believers*, but perhaps we are only *assenters*. [Gallup and O'Connell 1986, 88–89]

The problem in North America is that mainline religiosity has been strongly culture-affirming, blurring the distinction between Christian and non-Christian and lessening the impact of conversion in the life of the individual and the church. In other cultures conversion to Jesus Christ often means a radical change in the life of the individual, a radical distinction between church and society, and a strong differentiation between those who are Christian and those who are not. These distinctions aid the impact of

8. For two helpful studies of the unchurched in the United States see Hale 1977; Dale and Miles 1986. The categories of left-outs, etc., are taken from the former.

evangelization as long as they are positively transformational rather than being so sectarian and countercultural that they are foreign or irrelevant to the surrounding culture.[9]

Obstacles in Our Churches

Lack of Clarity in Defining Our Task

In evangelizing North America we need to be aware of obstacles found in our churches as well. Here we will highlight two: a basic lack of clarity both in defining our task and in understanding our faith. These deficiencies further obscure our presentation of the gospel amidst North American neopagan culture.

Some time ago a pastor from Taiwan and student at the seminary where I was teaching observed that North Americans do not seem to know what the word *evangelism* means. He questioned how we can speak about evangelizing North America without having a clear definition of the task. I think his question is important. One of our greatest internal obstacles during the last several decades seems to have been our lack of clarity in defining evangelism. Ever since the fundamentalist-modernist debates of the 1920s and 1930s arguments have raged in North America concerning the meaning, means, and message of evangelism. "The term 'evangelism' has become highly misunderstandable, precisely because of all the meanings attached to it. It creates barriers for some and awakens such concrete associations for others that discussion of it almost always requires a long process of terminological clarification" (Guder 1985, 134). The uncertainty has been severely detrimental to enthusiasm, commitment, and cooperation in the practice of evangelism, particularly among mainline denominations. The misunderstanding continues up to the present.[10]

Our uncertainty with regard to a definition has contributed to strong negative images on the part of the members of our churches. Whenever I ask pastors and seminary students to describe the feelings, impressions, and memories which the word *evangelism* conjures up for them, their responses have been overwhelmingly negative. Images of manipulative techniques, of decision cards never followed up, of door-to-door intruders, of sidewalk confrontations, and of ranting television and radio evangelists have produced a

9. There has been a lot of discussion around this point ever since Richard Niebuhr published *Christ and Culture* (1951). In fact very few clear conclusions have emerged. For differing perspectives see, e.g., Dean Kelley 1972; Hoge and Roozen 1979; Kraft 1979; Roozen, McKinney, and Carroll 1984; and Hoge, Johnson, and Luidens 1994.

10. An example of an attempt at clarification can be found in the April-June 1987 "Monthly Letter on Evangelism" from the World Council of Churches. There a portion of an address given in 1985 by James Burtness is reproduced. Reflecting on Matt. 16:13–16, Burtness suggests, "1. Jesus is the question," and "2. Christ is an answer."

strong negative reaction to the concept of doing evangelism, and a strong deterrent to participation on the part of our pastors and church members. There is evidence from seminary courses in the subject, however, that when people are helped to get beyond those negative images to gain a positive and biblical view of evangelism, they become overwhelmingly positive, participatory, and activist.

There is hope for future clarification. It appears that a major convergence is beginning to form between the ecumenical movement, the Roman Catholic Church, and the conservative evangelicals. One need only compare, for example, the fine statement on evangelism issued by the World Council of Churches, *Mission and Evangelism: An Ecumenical Affirmation* (1983), with the Reformed Church in America's *Evangelism in Reformed Perspective: An Evangelism Manifesto* (1977),[11] "The Lausanne Covenant" (1974), and the papal exhortation *Evangelii nuntiandi* (1976)[12] to see this convergence beginning to take shape.

In 1987 theologians representing the Commission on World Mission and Evangelism of the World Council of Churches, the Lausanne Committee for World Evangelization, and the World Evangelical Fellowship met in Stuttgart, West Germany, to discuss the matter—and ended up issuing a very significant nine-page joint statement on evangelism. This statement quoted *Mission and Evangelism: An Ecumenical Affirmation*:

> The Church is sent into the world to call people and nations to repentance, to announce the forgiveness of sin and a new beginning in relation with God and with neighbors through Jesus Christ. This evangelistic calling has a new urgency today. . . . The proclamation of the Gospel includes an invitation to recognize and accept in a personal decision the saving lordship of Christ. It is the announcement of a personal encounter, mediated by the Holy Spirit, with the living Christ, receiving his forgiveness and making a personal acceptance of the call to discipleship and a new life of service. [World Council of Churches 1987, 1]

One of the participants at Stuttgart, David Bosch from South Africa, shortly thereafter set forth one of the most clearly articulated perspectives of this convergent view of evangelism (1987, 103): "Evangelism may be de-

---

11. Written by William Brownson and Carl Kromminga, the manifesto was published by both the *Church Herald* and the *Banner* in 1977. See also "The Call to Evangelize" in the Minutes of the General Synod of the Reformed Church in America, June 17–21, 1985, pp. 223–26, which draws heavily from the manifesto.

12. This exhortation was issued by Pope Paul VI in December 1975 and entitled "Evangelization in the Modern World." Strongly reflecting the documents of Vatican Council II, it is considered by Roman Catholics and Protestants alike to be basic to the present Roman Catholic understanding of evangelization. (See also *Lumen gentium, Unitatis redintegratio*, and *Ad gentes divinitus* in Flannery 1975, 350–426, 452–70, 813–56.)

fined as that dimension and activity of the church's mission which seeks to offer every person, everywhere, a valid opportunity to be directly challenged by the gospel of explicit faith in Jesus Christ, with a view to embracing him as Savior, becoming a living member of his community, and being enlisted in his service of reconciliation, peace, and justice on earth."[13] Bosch's definition could be accepted by people from all three perspectives—Roman Catholic, ecumenical, and evangelical. If such a convergence became a reality in the thinking of North American Christians as a whole, a major internal obstacle to the evangelization of North America might be removed.

Lack of Clarity in Understanding Our Faith

After attending a seminary in western Michigan, a pastor from the National Presbyterian Church of Mexico commented that he found church members in North America to be weak in their knowledge of the Bible, uncommitted to the church's programs, and passive in their evangelistic outreach. At first I thought his critique rather severe. But the last few years have taught me otherwise. We seem to be suffering from a kind of biblical anorexia, a loss of appetite often due to prolonged periods of not eating properly. A survey conducted by Schuller Ministries and the Gallup organization found a general "lack of knowledge of basic Biblical facts, a lack of love toward those who do not share our religious perspective, a reluctance to share the good news with others, and a failure to do much about the problems of poverty and hunger" (Gallup and O'Connell 1986, 88–89). And a similar survey of the membership of the Reformed Church in America indicated that the unique beliefs expressed in the confessional standards of that church are considered unimportant by a large portion of the membership (Luidens and Nemeth 1987).

It is a given fact in evangelism that we cannot share what we do not have. Lack of clarity in matters of Scripture and faith produces a lack of enthusiasm and in fact a real avoidance of personally sharing our faith. Our reluctance to participate in evangelism is obvious. Few pastors in the Reformed Church in America consider their primary calling to be evangelizing the unchurched, and few members view sharing their faith to be their major spiritual activity. A look at our congregational budgets readily illustrates the low priority assigned to evangelism. Staff salaries, building maintenance, and programs for the members themselves far outweigh the amount of time, effort, and money allocated for evangelism. Major congregational programs like the Bethel and Stephen ministries are targeted primarily for church members rather than the unreached. Kenneth Chafin, a Southern Baptist pastor

---

13. For a list of twenty different definitions of evangelism and a very helpful chapter dealing with this issue see Armstrong 1984, 21–51.

and dean of the Billy Graham Schools of Evangelism, put it bluntly, "The average congregation has little meaningful contact with those who are not Christian" (1978, 120). It seems that concern for the preservation of our history, traditions, and church life obscures our commitment to the fact that "God so loved the world [N.B., it does not say 'the church'] that he gave his only begotten Son" (John 3:16 KJV).

The obstacles we have noted are not new, nor are they insurmountable. Neither should they discourage us. Instead, they can teach us that effective evangelism is neither magical nor miraculous—but just plain hard work. The obstacles point to the urgency of maximizing the potential provided to us by magnificent opportunities for evangelism in the North American context. Nowhere in the world are such opportunities so readily available to local congregations as they are in North America. Nowhere are there greater possibilities for impacting a culture with the gospel.

Opportunities

Christians from the Two-Thirds World often remark about the fantastic range of evangelistic resources available to us in North America. These opportunities may be found both in the culture at large and in the church.

Positive Cultural Receptivity

In 1985 a very significant sociological study pointed to the potential role that Christianity could play in American culture: "Basing their research on a massive five-year study of various American communities, the authors conclude that Americans, largely confined to a vocabulary of individualism, have lost the language needed to make moral sense of their lives." As a result, personal faith in its various expressions is essential for North American society and is sought by many as a source of meaning in their lives (Bellah et al. 1985, back cover, 246–48).

The study done by Schuller Ministries and the Gallup organization which we noted earlier also points to the incredible potential of evangelism in North America:

> The prospect for deepening America's spiritual commitment is far from hopeless. Virtually all Americans are, in some measure, drawn to the person of Jesus Christ. . . . Many believe he is the Son of God, and even many among the non-devout feel that Jesus' life and person tell us something profound about the meaning of existence. And, remarkably, as many as 9 in 10 say that Jesus as a moral and ethical leader has had at least some impact on their lives.
>
> Furthermore, at least half of Americans wish their religious faith were stronger, and a perhaps surprising one fifth of non-believers say they would like to believe in the divinity of Jesus Christ. . . .

A remarkable 4 in 10 Americans have an intuitive or experiential basis for their belief and report a dramatic religious experience. . . . And 7 in 10 of all survey respondents feel that their relationship with Jesus Christ is deepening. [Gallup and O'Connell 1986, 89][14]

Christians in the Two-Thirds World do not have this kind of positive cultural background for evangelism. On the contrary, invariably their contexts call for radical encounter with other faiths that do not accept belief in Jesus Christ. Why are we not capitalizing on such remarkable receptivity?

Freedom, Finances, and Forms for Mass Evangelism

The general cultural receptivity looks even brighter when we consider the freedom of proclamation found in North America coupled with the freedom of individuals to change their faith. Add to this the money, people, and programs available to us for Christian literature, videos, the mass media, and so forth—and the possibilities skyrocket. The multimillions handled by television evangelists not only are a scandal. They also demonstrate the fantastic potential open to evangelists, pastors, and churches that wish to impact North America for Jesus Christ.

Compare that with a little radio program in Tapachula, where my wife and I served as missionaries. For a couple of years we were able to have a one-half-hour program of Christian music and a brief sermon which I sometimes was invited to preach. What a tremendous amount of energy it took for Pascual, the brother in charge of the program, to gather the necessary money and people to cover that one-half-hour! Then came the fateful day when the radio station told Pascual that the government had decreed that no radio stations in Mexico would again be allowed to broadcast religious programs. All Protestant radio broadcasts were silenced that day and have only recently resumed. How well I remember Pascual lamenting that the freedoms and resources available to Christians on this side of the border were not available to him or the churches on that side. "What couldn't we do here if we had the resources and freedom available to Christians there?" he asked.

Myriad Relational Bridges

In addition to the general cultural receptivity and potential resources, a third major opportunity is being increasingly emphasized by evangelists in North America. Every congregation has close ties with its target population. The key is to be found in the thousands of close and casual, formal and informal personal relationships which church members have with the un-

---

14. Bob Bast 1987, then minister of evangelism and church life in the Reformed Church in America, made similarly positive observations.

churched in the community. It does not take much work to identify the businesses, recreational arenas, neighborhoods, schools, and networks of friendships impacted by the members of a congregation. Here are the most fruitful bridges for evangelizing North America. It is a proven fact that about 80 percent of all new church members originally came to their church because of previous friendship with a member of the congregation. Here, then, are the networks through which the gospel can be communicated naturally, lovingly, openly, personally, and effectively. We need to maximize the potential of our natural relationships.[15]

Research, Data, Consultation, and Training

A pastor from Kenya who had been in the United States only a short time made a telling comment regarding the research and consulting resources which North American churches have to aid them in evangelism: "If we only had usable data to know who lives where in our country, how many there are, what needs they have, and how we can serve them. If we had such data I'm sure our church would be growing ten times faster than it is." And yet his church is growing by about 30 percent each year because the members share their faith with others. What would the growth rate be if the pastor in fact had the kind of data he desired?

We have those kinds of resources at our fingertips. Church consulting and training groups like the Alban Institute, the American Institute of Church Growth, the Yokefellow Institute, the Fuller Evangelistic Association, and the Billy Graham Schools of Evangelism are there to be tapped for guidance and research. Evangelism programs like Evangelism Explosion, Good News People, Life-Style Evangelism (Joseph Aldrich), and Night of Caring/Sharing (Paul Cedar) are but a few of the many resources available to churches. There is no reason why a congregation that wants to reach out in evangelizing North America cannot do so. There are plenty of consultants willing to help. Much depends on whether the members of a congregation are personally committed to live out their evangelistic calling. George Hunter (1987, 31) regards "faithful, reproducing congregations [as] the laboratories of the living God. In such churches, the God who acts in history is showing his whole church the ways forward. . . . Through data collection and case studies, we can discover the approaches and methods God is blessing to reach the undiscipled, and we may barely have scratched the surface. More reproducible principles and strategies are waiting to be discovered in churches already experiencing apostolic growth."[16]

15. The vast potential of the relational networks of our church members has been emphasized by George Hunter 1987, ch. 4; Calver et al. 1984, ch. 3; Hinson 1987, ch. 6; Aldrich 1981, part 2; and Van Engen 1992c.

16. A very helpful resource for congregational evangelism is George Hunter 1979.

Objectives

Hunter (1987, 16) also affirms that "the work of evangelistic mission is only done by Christians and churches who (a) see their identity in continuity with the apostles, (b) see the mission fields in which their churches are placed, (c) are open to the empowerment of the Spirit, and (d) desire above all else to join the Lord of the Harvest in finding the lost and in building that church against which the gates of hell and powers of death will not prevail." The deficiencies in personal faith and church attendance which we observed earlier (p. 197) can be allayed only by Christians in local congregations who become the incarnation of the body of Christ in that place. After all is said and done, Christ addressed no one else but his disciples when he said, "You will be my witnesses" (Acts 1:8).

In addition to helping us understand and analyze, Christians from the Two-Thirds World can also exhort and challenge. The fantastic growth of the church in China under incredible oppression and seemingly insurmountable odds has called all of us to reexamine not only our methods, but also our commitment. The explosive growth of churches in Africa could challenge the effectiveness of our own response to the opportunities before us. The rapid growth of base ecclesial communities, of Pentecostal fellowships, and of suffering Protestant churches in Latin America might be an example to us of the tremendous effect which vibrant Spirit-filled and Spirit-led churches can have on their society.

The churches of North America stand in need of drawing sap from their roots and receiving sustenance from the evangelical and revivalist foundations of their history. We need to allow the deep evangelistic spirituality of American Christianity to resurface in our midst. Revival and renewal are as essential to evangelization as are resources and strategies. Christians from the Two-Thirds World like René Padilla, Orlando Costas (1989), José Míguez-Bonino, Leonardo Boff, Emilio Castro, Raymond Fung, Juan Carlos Ortiz, and Juan Luís Segundo have stressed various aspects of this renewal in their exhortations to North American churches. We are called to heed what Paul said to the Corinthian church: we need to experience being made "new creatures," reconciled to God through Christ, called to the "ministry of reconciliation," moved to participate actively in Christ's work of "reconciling the world to Himself." This renewal of ourselves then empowers us to be "ambassadors for Christ, as though God were entreating through us; we beg you on behalf of Christ, be reconciled to God." This involves us in a revolutionary movement of radical transformation! "He made Him who knew no sin to be sin on our behalf, that we might become the righteousness of God in Him!" (2 Cor. 5:17–21 NASB).

Such newness would impact a number of areas of our life as Christians in North America. It would begin by calling us to *new purpose*. It would remind us that the purpose of the church, its reason for being, is not so much to preserve a tradition, not really to maintain a building, not essentially to serve its members, nor to pay the bills. The church's purpose is to be the covenant people of God who seek the reconciliation of people with God and with each other so that through the church "all the families of the earth shall be blessed" (Gen. 12:1–3 NASB).

The newness involves a *new heart*—a heart of compassion and love which yearns deeply for the transformation of the world and the coming of the kingdom of God. This love is the heart of the gospel and the central essence of the body of Christ (Jer. 31 and John 13). The new heart seeks to be God's instrument (ambassador, servant) in the world for Jesus' sake through the power of the Spirit.

The newness entails a *new urgency* which will not rest as long as there are people who have not been impacted by the gospel. We will have a sense of being debtors—that we owe it to the people of the world to present them the gospel. The urgency comes from understanding that the world will not hear without preachers, and the preachers will not proclaim unless they be sent—and it is in the sending that we find our true nature as the people of God (Rom. 1:14–15; 10:1–15).

The newness calls for *new programs* and *new methods*. As someone asked once, "If the church is for everyone, why is not everyone in the church?" Do we believe that the gospel of Jesus Christ is really good news? Do we have the confidence that the wholistic perspective embodied in Reformed theology has a major contribution to make to the people and society of North America? Are we sure that what we have to offer is like a "treasure hidden in a field" (Matt. 13:44)? Do we believe that "there is no other name under heaven . . . by which we must be saved" (Acts 4:12)? If our answer is positive, we will constantly search for the most effective means by which we may carry out our calling to a ministry of reconciliation.

Finally, the newness means a *new conversion*—conversion to God, conversion to the church, and conversion to the world. The need to evangelize North America calls us to a new examination of our own conversion. For many of us the process of conversion has been shortchanged. Our Western individualism, the ecclesiastical captivity of the gospel, the stress on preserving past traditions, our history of campaign evangelism, and the public/private split of North American religion have all contributed to some degree to holding us back from the full range of our spirituality and conversion. Reporting new discoveries concerning spirituality, James Fowler in his *Stages of Faith* (1981) and Henri Nouwen are voices joined to those of the Two-Thirds World calling us to a radical threefold conversion to God, to church, and to the world for whom Christ died.

The evangelization of North America is not optional—it is the reason why we exist, it is commanded by our Lord, and it is urgently needed for the sake of righteousness and reconciliation. What a marvelous gift from God! Our participation in God's mission makes us instruments through whom the nations of the earth may be blessed. In the final analysis evangelism is people sharing with people the love and grace of God in the power of the Holy Spirit. Christians in the Two-Thirds World live this out in marvelous ways under severe pressures. Already more than half of all Christians live in Asia, Africa, and Latin America. Many predict that by the year 2000 the percentage of Christians on those continents will have risen dramatically, while the percentage of Christians in Europe and North America will have dwindled even further. Is there a way of responding to and offsetting the latter prediction? Can we in North America learn enough from Christians in the Two-Thirds World to reverse the trend? Will we allow them to challenge us to evangelize our neopagan continent? Christians in Africa, Asia, and Latin America labor against tremendous economic, social, political, and religious odds, and still continue to evangelize increasing numbers of people. Can we do less? Will we let them help us?

12

Mission Theology in the Light of Postmodern Critique

We are currently living through what is generally labeled a transition from modernity to postmodernity, a transition that many, including Peter Drucker (1993, 1) regard as of momentous significance:

> Every few hundred years in Western history there occurs a sharp transformation. We cross what . . . I have called a "divide." Within a few short decades, society rearranges itself—its worldview; its basic values; its social and political structure; its arts; its key institutions. Fifty years later, there is a new world. And the people born then cannot even imagine the world in which their grandparents lived and into which their own parents were born.
>
> We are currently living through just such a transformation.

The thesis of this chapter is that a Christian critique of modernity[1] would include an examination of ourselves as Christ's church to see how we may

---

1. The matter of defining what is meant by "modernity" and "postmodernity" is not a simple thing. Bryan Turner (1990, 4) says, "Modernity is broadly about the massive social and cultural changes which took place from the middle of the sixteenth century, and it is consequently and necessarily bound up with the analysis of industrial capitalist society as a revolutionary break with tradition and social stability founded on a relatively stagnant agrarian civilization. Modernity was about conquest—the imperial regulation of land, the discipline of the soul, and the creation of truth. . . . The question of postmodernism is a question about the possible limits of the process of modernization. . . . Postmodernism has encouraged the view that the various fields and specialties in the sciences are primarily strategies or conventions by which 'reality' is divided up, partly as a consequence of the intense struggle over truth by social groups in the quest for power."

Mike Featherstone (1988, 197–98) says it this way: "Modernity is contrasted to the traditional order [of antiquity and medievalism] and implies the progressive economic and administrative rationalization and differentiation of the social world. . . . Consequently, to speak of become authentic, contextually appropriate hermeneutical communities of the gospel in a postmodern world (Newbigin 1989a, 222–33).

There seem to be at least three ways we could go about reflecting on the present crisis of the transformation of modernity to postmodernity with reference to the church. First, we could follow the predominant tendency found in philosophical analysis of modernity and postmodernity, and deal with ecclesiology from the point of view of epistemology. In this case we might examine modernity and the church in terms of the church's presuppositions with regard to knowing: how we know, how we know with certainty, and how we know that what we know with certainty is true.[2]

---

postmodernity is to suggest an epochal shift or break from modernity involving the emergence of a new social totality with its own distinct organizing principles."

David Harvey (1989, 42–43) asks some penetrating questions in relation to a definition of postmodernism: "Does postmodernism . . . represent a radical break with modernism, or is it simply a revolt within modernism against a certain form of 'high modernism'? . . . Is postmodernism a style, . . . or should we view it strictly as a periodizing concept? . . . Does it have a revolutionary potential by virtue of its opposition to all forms of meta-narratives (including Marxism, Freudianism, and all forms of Enlightenment reason) and its close attention to 'other worlds' and 'other voices' that have for too long been silent? . . . Or is it simply the commercialization and domestication of modernism, and a reduction of the latter's already tarnished aspirations? . . . And do we attach its rise to some radical restructuring of capitalism, the emergence of some 'postindustrial' society . . . or [do we view it] as the 'cultural logic of late capitalism'?" Harvey goes on to offer an excellent comparative schematic to show how different, at least apparently in his view, postmodernism is from modernism.

One of the most helpful essays I have found for seeing the difference between modernism and postmodernism was written by Nancey Murphy and James McClendon (1989). Their comparison envisions three axes: (1) an epistemological axis, (2) a linguistic axis, and (3) a metaphysical axis. At the modernist end one would find, respectively, (1) a foundationalist agenda that searches for indubitable beliefs that can respond to the modernist's skepticism; (2) a referential and representational view of language; and (3) ontological priority of the individual over the collective. Postmodernist thought lies at the other end of each of these axes: epistemologically, postmodernism means the rejection of all forms of foundationalism (even of the need for foundations at all); linguistically, representationalism is discarded, and it is language itself that makes ideas, experience, and meaning possible; and, metaphysically, postmodernism affirms a notion of wholism: "society is no mere collection of similar individuals; rather, individuals participate in [society] through complementary interaction. It is the individuals' differences rather than their similarities that enable them to contribute to society" (p. 203).

Given these and other attempts at definition, I am inclined to see postmodernity as primarily a reactive viewpoint against modernity rather than a radically new, discontinuous option that rescues us from modernity. Bryan Turner (1990, 2) says, "Whether . . . postmodernism is reactionary or progressive will depend a great deal on whether we view postmodernism as antimodernism or beyond modernism." On this point I believe Philip Sampson (1993, 5) is correct when he states that "modernity is the creation of postmodernity in that it only became visible qua *modernity* within a self-conscious postmodern debate; modernity itself emerges as a postmodern phenomenon." Or as Turner (1990, 6) has asked, "Can anti-foundationalism exist without foundations?" See also Centore 1991, 1–20; Gellner 1992, 2–23; Harvey 1989, 113–18; Berger et al. 1973, 181–200; Cooke 1988, 475–79; Roxburgh 1993, 12–15; Hiebert 1991; and Mouw and Griffioen 1993, 53.

2. Although discussions of modernity and postmodernity emanate from a whole range of disciplines like art, architecture, philosophy of language, and ethics, an inordinate amount of

Secondly, we could approach the topic through a more accommodational or apologetic focus, standing with our feet placed in what we consider to be the church and looking outward at the modern/postmodern world in which we live. This would lead us to discuss the ways in which the postmodern critique of modernity may or may not offer the world the answers that humanity seeks—answers that perhaps the church could supply.[3] In his magnum opus David Bosch (1991, 349) spoke of the emergence of a postmodern paradigm: "A time of paradigm shift is a time of deep uncertainty—and such uncertainty appears to be one of the few constants of the contemporary era and one of the factors that engender strong reactions in favor of hanging on to the Enlightenment paradigm, in spite of signs from all quarters that it is breaking up."[4] To deal with this uncertainty Bosch called for a reorientation of mission.

Clearly both the epistemological and accommodational approaches are valid, important, and urgent. As Wilbert Shenk (1993a, 192) affirms, "Although the culture of modernity has yet to be taken seriously as a subject of sustained missionary concern, my argument will be that this represents one of the most urgent frontiers facing the church in the twenty-first century." But this chapter will follow a third approach, which calls for us to examine ourselves in terms of the impact that modernity has had on us. If we can see

---

reflection on this matter seems to have come from philosophy of religion and philosophy of science. Much of this philosophical thought seems most interested in the epistemological issues dealing with knowing, certainty, and truth claims. This is acceptable and necessary, but should not restrict the range of our inquiry when we examine the critique of modernity offered by postmodern thinkers. See Bosch 1991, 349–62; Küng and Tracy 1989, 3–33; Kuhn 1962; 1977; Barbour 1990; Fetzer 1992a, esp. 147–78; 1992b (an excellent reader). Of influence here we could note, among others, Polanyi 1958a; 1958b; 1969; Polanyi and Prosch 1975; Hempel 1965; 1966; Toulmin 1961; Popper 1965; 1972; and Lakatos 1978. For a superb treatment of some of the very technical matters involved in this discussion of epistemology see Murphy 1990.

3. Alan J. Roxburgh states, "Christian thinkers as diverse as Lesslie Newbigin, Richard Neuhaus, Stanley Hauerwas, Langdon Gilkey and Hans Küng all speak of an important cultural turning point—a transformation that requires us to find new ways of reaching a new generation." Roxburgh follows this direction in laying out the purpose of his book *Reaching a New Generation: Strategies for Tomorrow's Church* (1993, 10): "Beginning in a local context, this book examines how change and transformation challenge the church to rethink its mission in the modern world. I will argue that important elements of modernity are being rejected by the culture, and that a search for alternative values is gaining momentum." It might be said that Lesslie Newbigin's works (1986, 1989a, and 1991) along with both the Gospel and Culture Network in England and the Gospel and Our Culture Network in North America are some of the finest examples of this search for a new apologetic vis-à-vis the discussion of modernity and postmodernity. Though we do not have space to critique them here, there has been a wide range of attempts to do theology from a postmodern perspective, some less biblically based than others. See, e.g., Walsh 1990; Edgar V. McKnight 1988; Breech 1989; Gellner 1992; and Cupitt 1990.

4. MacNulty 1989 demonstrates how widely pervasive and deeply transformational is the transition in which we now find ourselves, a transition from what he calls the "industrial paradigm" to the "consciousness paradigm."

more clearly how modernity has clouded our own embodying of the gospel, could we offer our postmodern world "a more excellent way" (1 Cor. 12:31 KJV) than that which postmodernity wants to create?

A testing approach is consistent with trends in twentieth-century ecclesiology. Already before the turn of the century, Abraham Kuyper (1883) had spoken about the possibility of the church's "deformation."[5] It is the possibility of such deformation, not only in terms of the sinfulness of individuals, but also in terms of the church itself as an organic unity, that calls us to test the church against what Scripture intends for us to become. Such testing involves a rethinking, a reorientation of what it means for us to be the church in a postmodern world.[6]

So in addition to looking outward at the increasingly non-Christian Western culture of modernity, we should also be willing to look inward and ask about our own authenticity and faithfulness to the biblical gospel. In other words, maybe we could allow the postmodern critique of modernity to help us see more clearly where we as evangelicals have syncretized the gospel by accepting the content and method of modernity—a syncretism that may distort both the messenger and the message of the gospel that we have wanted to present.[7]

The remainder of this chapter will offer some very brief and preliminary reflections of what this kind of self-examination might look like. We have space for only four major elements of the critique of modernity: the issues of individualism, rationalism, scientific positivism, and technology. We will relate them respectively to the four ancient credal marks of the church, exploring their implications for a new paradigmatic understanding of our being the

5. See, e.g., Veenhof 1977; Berkouwer 1976, 182; and Van Engen 1981, 62–79.

6. This testing element is perhaps the strongest and most pervasive element in recent ecclesiology. See, e.g., Herman Bavinck 1967, 493–95; Bonhoeffer 1963; Barth 1936–69, 4.1:643–739; Flannery 1975; Küng 1968, 69; 1987, 263; Dulles 1974, 128–29; 1982, 48–52; Berkouwer 1976, 7–25; Hendrikus Berkhof 1979, 409–10; Moltmann 1977; and Van Engen 1981, 74–75.

7. Is it possible that the critique of modernity in fact strikes at the heart of the content and method of our own theologizing as evangelicals? Miroslav Volf (1992a; 1992b, 7) has made a good case that while the North American fundamentalism of the 1920s may have been "one of the most significant conservative Protestant responses to modernity," fundamentalism's way of responding was itself developed by using the rationality of modernity.

James D. Hunter (1987, 51–52) has observed, "One could hypothesize that Evangelicals have made concessions to modernity. With the growing plausibility of the modern worldview resulting from the extension of the modernization process in American society came an increased pressure to accommodate. The founding of the NAE marks the point in the history of American conservative Protestantism at which yielding to those pressures began—the point at which a more positive and constructive, or perhaps more conciliatory, approach to modernity was taken. Efforts to develop a rational apologetic for Protestant orthodoxy, and to establish stable institutional structures within the Evangelical community, are evidences of the accommodation. Evangelicals embraced modern technology and modern (middle class) forms of cultural expression for the same reason."

one, holy, catholic, and apostolic community of faith in a modern/postmodern world. This in turn will call us to search for a new plausibility structure[8] that, though not based on modernity's assumptions, might offer us an alternative to the nihilism, meaninglessness, valuelessness, and atomization that postmodernity has advanced.

Individualism

Modernity

The dominance of individualism in modern Western culture is well known:

> In American society today, the unquestioned assumption is that the individual takes precedence over the group. Freedom means individual independence. Civil rights means the individual's right to "life, liberty, and the pursuit of happiness." . . .
>
> The concept of organic community has been heavily eroded by technology, urbanization, political ideology, and legal definition. Even marriage and family are increasingly accepted as matters of individual contract and convenience. The group has become for us a collection of individuals created *by* individuals *for* their own individual advantages. [Kraus 1993, 31–32]

> Modernity is characterized by its commitments to technical rationality and individualism. We highly value the right of individuals to choose for themselves their direction in life, untrammeled by hierarchy and authority. This is a canon of our culture: the individual rights of every human being are sacred so long as they do not trample on the rights of others. Our liberal democracies are built upon this fundamental presupposition of modernity. [Roxburgh 1993, 14–15][9]

Indeed, individualism is so pervasive that its influence on religion in the West has not been taken seriously enough. But "religion can never be successfully reduced to a private concern," as Richard Mouw and Sander Griffioen (1993, 51) point out: "Since religion has to do with our relationship to the ultimate meaning and value found in every aspect of human existence, and since public life is ineluctably drawn to matters of ultimate concern, religion is bound to reassert itself in the public sphere."

The Postmodern Critique of Individualism

The postmodern critique has been strident with regard to modernity's penchant for atomized individualism. Nancey Murphy and James McClen-

---

8. See Newbigin 1987, 2; and Berger 1980.
9. See also Roof and McKinney 1987, 7–8; and Barna 1991, 210–12.

don (1989, 203–5) point out that Alasdair MacIntyre's work in postmodern ethics "transcends the individualism of the modern period without falling back into premodern modes of thought." MacIntyre instead argues for "recovering a corporate or organic view of society that will support the notion of the common good. . . . Individual good is unintelligible apart from the good inherent in practices that are essentially communal." Murphy and McClendon then take the matter a step further: "Both holism in epistemology and the new understanding of language and utterance [in postmodern thought] cut against the individualism of the modern period. . . . In postmodern thought the community itself plays an indispensable role."

The more collective perspective is especially clear in the postmodern epistemology of philosophy of science. This has to do with the way a scientific community brings about the creation of new plausibility structures on the way to a possible paradigm shift, as envisioned (albeit in differing ways) by Michael Polanyi, Karl Popper, Stephen Toulmin, Thomas Kuhn, Ian Barbour, and Imre Lakatos. The common thread running through this process is the corporateness of the scientific community's work.

But the postmodern agenda is not quite as simple as it would appear. The other side of the coin is postmodernity's atomization of ethical and moral values into competing and conflicting interest-groups, especially in the arena of the social sciences and ethics. Once foundationalism has been discarded, one is left with nothing but endless relativism that creates a confusing and anarchic multiplication of perspectives where only matters of difference and diversity are celebrated.

Evangelical Individualism

One might think that we evangelicals would have tried to speak to modernity's rampant individualism. But we have not done so. To the contrary, we have fostered a strong sense of individual salvation, particularly in terms of our perspective on conversion. We have multiplied denominations as we compete for those whom we can win to our church. We create large "shopping-center" churches that cater to the individual tastes of each one who comes. In fact, our emphasis on individual evangelism and conversion may have fostered even greater individualization of faith than we ever intended:

> In the nineteenth century, . . . [North American] people adopted a new working definition of the church. Whereas Christians previously had seen the church as God's primary agent of activity in human history, the new view saw it as a voluntary association functioning to aid the individual Christian in practical goals such as spiritual growth and the gaining of converts. In the new perspective no institution had an inherited or traditional authority; instead, all human organizations found their basis in the uncoerced consent of the individual. . . .

> The will of the individual was the primary foundation for human organization, and the church was no exception. [Woodbridge, Noll, and Hatch 1979, 175]

This direction toward individualization and atomization of American religion has continued unabated. Consider the following illustration as related by Robert Bellah and his associates (1985, 221):

> Today religion in America is as private and diverse as New England colonial religion was public and unified. One person we interviewed has actually named her religion (she calls it her "faith") after herself. This suggests the logical possibility of over 220 million American religions, one for each of us. Sheila Larson is a young nurse who has received a good deal of therapy and who describes her faith as "Sheilaism." "I believe in God. I'm not a religious fanatic. I can't remember the last time I went to church. My faith has carried me a long way. It's Sheilaism. Just my own little voice." Sheila's faith has some tenets beyond her belief in God, though not many. In defining "my own Sheilaism," she said: "It's just try to love yourself and be gentle with yourself. You know, I guess, take care of each other. I think He would want us to take care of each other." Like many others, Sheila would be willing to endorse few more specific injunctions.

To what extent have we evangelicals in the West contributed to, or at least mirrored, this phenomenon? Far from adopting a missionary stance toward our culture, we may have instead aided in entrenching modernity even further. As Wilbert Shenk (1993a, 197) points out, "The traditional distinction between mission and evangelism played on the assumption that the church *knows* its own culture profoundly. What remains is to employ certain techniques or methods in recruiting people back to the church. This stereotyping of evangelism had implications for both message and method. It had a reductionistic effect on both. . . . Secularized modes of evangelism are sources of alienation rather than means of personal and social reconciliation."

The Church as *One* Global Communion of Disciples of Jesus

Maybe what we need is to recapture the biblical notion of the church as a *Communion of Saints* (Bonhoeffer 1963), a corporate body of believers involved in what Donald Messer has called *A Conspiracy of Goodness* (1992). A rediscovery of our corporateness as *one* church might open the way for us to be able to affirm one another as persons, yet hold tightly to each other as integral parts of a uniquely mysterious "royal priesthood" and "holy nation," the temple and family of God (1 Pet. 2 and Eph. 3).[10] Such a corporate

10. One of the most profound and creative works on this matter was commissioned by the World Council of Churches, Paul Minear's *Images of the Church in the New Testament* (1960).

perspective would give us room to define evangelism as "primary initiation into the Kingdom of God" (Abraham 1989, 13).

Many years ago Donald McGavran made a case for "people-group" or "multi-individual" conversion. Although he met marked resistance at first, this more corporate and biblical viewpoint eventually won acceptance, primarily in Africa, Asia, and Latin America. However, we have yet to include this perspective in our theologizing in areas where modernity has reigned supreme. Could it be that postmodernity's challenge of modernity's penchant for individualism might stimulate us to discover anew what we have always known—that "there is one body and one Spirit . . . one Lord, one faith, one baptism; one God and Father of all, who is over all and through all and in all" (Eph. 4:4–5)?

We are not advocating here a visible unity of the kind suggested by an ecumenical movement that has lost its biblical moorings. Rather, we are speaking of an organic cohesion, a spiritual, covenantal, and relational corporateness that creates a congregation where the Pauline image of the body is given concrete, public reality. Such a congregation becomes the "central locus of the Kingdom of God" (Van Engen 1981, 283; 1991b, 59–71).[11] The concept of "congregation" must be a *corporate* reality, for the whole is to be larger than the sum of the individuals who constitute it.

To learn again how to be this kind of church, we may need non-Western perspectives and non-Western modes of being, of organic corporateness. In the West we need to rekindle a vibrant, joyful, corporate congregational life. We need a recovery in actual, visible life of what it means to live out the *koinōnia, kērygma, diakonia,* and *martyria* of the gospel together as the body of Christ (Van Engen 1981, 167; 1991b, 87–100). "By this all [people] will know that you are my disciples, if you have love for one another" (John 13:35 RSV). The result will be a dynamic, energized, transformed and transforming fellowship. For "fellowship, by definition, involves interpersonal relationships. It happens when Christian believers get to know one another, to enjoy one another, and to care for one another" (Wagner 1979c, 78). Further, "Jesus Christ's new presence in the loving fellowship (*koinonia*) of the disciples constitutes the Church. Without this presence of Christ, there is no Church. How do we so easily forget that it is only in the context of the love of disciple for Lord and disciple for disciple that the Church has life at all?" (Van Engen 1991b, 91).[12]

---

11. For glimpses of renewal of the corporate nature of the church see Newbigin 1989a, 222–33 ("The Congregation as Hermeneutic of the Gospel").

12. George Hunsberger (1990, 4) of the Gospel and Our Culture Network (GOCN) in North America recognized the importance of this matter: "The church's loss of 'place' in American life and its consequent experience of stress and dis-ease means that our missiological agenda must at its base be an ecclesiological one. There is a need for the church to 'find' itself, to re-image itself, to refocus its inner life for its missionary vocation. . . . The agenda, in other

Rationalism

Modernity

The myth of the autonomous individual goes hand in hand with a particular methodology of thought that modernity also fostered. From René Descartes and Francis Bacon to Immanuel Kant and Georg Hegel, modernity has carefully, intentionally, and pervasively fostered individualistic rationality (Smart 1990, 17):

> Although the term "modern" has a rather more ancient history, what Habermas (1983, 9) calls the *project* of modernity came into focus during the eigh teenth century. The idea was to use the accumulation of knowledge generated by many individuals working freely and creatively for the pursuit of human emancipation and the enrichment of daily life. . . . The development of rational forms of social organization and rational modes of thought promised liberation from the irrationalities of myth, religion, superstition, release from the arbitrary use of power as well as from the dark side of our human natures. Only through such a project could the universal, eternal, and the immutable qualities of all of humanity be revealed. [Harvey 1989, 12]

Even today, one of the most pervasive foundations for modernity's value system continues to be a faith in deductive logic, as Hunter Lewis has shown (1990, 43–44).

---

words, has to do with the church's identity. That means matching our concern to voice the gospel to those of the culture who are outside with the humbling task of allowing ourselves to engage in the internal dialogue with the culture within ourselves."

It is unfortunate that a report of a GOCN meeting two years later stated: "The third theme developed was the *church* in mission. The model of Fuller Seminary's Church Growth Movement was almost universally rejected by the members of the consultation, even though some present had earlier been attracted to it. [Rather], the task before the network is to continue the ecumenical work of exploring missionary structures of the church at the local level and relating them to an understanding of the church universal in mission" (West 1992, 2). This perspective is unfortunate for two reasons. First, to resurrect the "missionary structures of the congregation" movement of the 1960s is a dead end. This movement, associated with the World Council of Churches and the National Council of Churches of Christ in the United States, was heavily influenced by Johannes Hoekendijk's deep pessimism about the church. This pessimism in fact divorced the whole movement from the very congregations of which it had so much to say (Van Engen 1993; 1981, 309–23; and Scherer 1993a). Secondly, the only significant North American missiological movement of the last thirty years that has in fact taken both the context and the local congregation seriously has been the Church Growth movement. To dismiss so easily the only missiological movement that has wrestled with how to plant, develop, and grow viable local congregations in the West seems rather unwarranted and unwise. Though one might have reservations about aspects of the movement, its track record—the unprecedented amount of experimentation, the creation of new successful models of vibrant congregations, and the degree to which the movement has wrestled to present the gospel in a meaningful way to North American culture—calls into question the advisability of rejecting the Church Growth movement out of hand.

The Postmodern Critique of Rationalism

None of the foregoing should surprise us, for most of us have been well trained to think in these terms. However, it is one of postmodernity's strongest projects to call the entire framework along with its presuppositional foundations into question. Although postmodernism has emerged in a number of disciplines, its critique of rationality was particularly stimulated by Karl Popper, Michael Polanyi, and Thomas Kuhn. Polanyi's work in philosophy of knowledge, coupled with that of the University of Chicago philosophers of science and sociologists of knowledge, calls for a complete reconsideration of the concepts of objectivity and rationality, thus questioning the most basic assumptions that sustain modernity's concept of rationality (and therefore of truth).[13]

But the postmodern option has predominantly moved us toward nihilism and meaninglessness. As Adam Seligman (1990, 117–19) summarizes, "The debate between modernity and postmodernity is essentially a debate between reason and nihilism. . . . The very fundamental premises of modernity, based on the universality of reason and autonomy of the individual ego, led to a collapse of the distinction or difference between the universal and particular, and to the inability to represent the universal and particular as distinct and separate categories."[14]

Evangelical Rationalism

We need not belabor the point that during the twentieth century evangelical theology has depended heavily on Enlightenment-style rationality, principles of logic, and reason to gain acceptance and respectability in theological, philosophical, and social-science circles. We need only mention names like B. B. Warfield, Louis Berkhof, Edward John Carnell, Cornelius Van Til, Harold Lindsell, and Carl Henry to recognize that we are dealing with individual thinkers steeped in the Enlightenment's tenets of rationality. They represent what John Woodbridge, Mark Noll, and Nathan Hatch have called "the life of the mind" (1979, 18–134).

If we were to examine our evangelical theology of mission during the last fifty years, our strong dependence on Enlightenment-type reason to articulate and defend our positions would stand out (Van Engen 1990). We have depended heavily on particular individuals doing careful work in deductive logic in order to support our evangelical perspectives of the gospel. This could be viewed as essentially an evangelical version of the way al-

13. On the role played by philosophy of science see Fetzer 1992a and 1992b.
14. See, e.g., Flax 1990, 188, 192; Wyschogrod 1990; Jeffrey Kane 1984; and Polanyi 1958a; 1969.

most all modern theology, Protestant and Roman Catholic, has done its work.[15]

Of course the thoughts we think, the truths we hold, and the affirmations we make are crucial—and in many cases nonnegotiable. And they are always to be checked against Scripture. But that is exactly the point. When we look into Scripture we find that holiness and faith involve rationality and proposition, but offer a perspective of truth that is broader and deeper. It is covenantal, relational, and corporate. We have brought into the church the Greek assumption that ignorance is evil, and the antidote is knowledge. Yet we have always had difficulty being able to explain how to get from knowledge (how to think right) to commitment (how to live in a way that honors Jesus Christ).[16]

The Church as a *Holy* Community of Faith

Postmodernity's strong critique of the bankruptcy of modernity's myth of the rational could stimulate us to self-examination in terms of the holiness of the church. Modernity's dependence on human rationality ignores the fact of sin, and assumes that the fall did not impact our ability to reason. Scripture tells us otherwise. Now if we recognize that we cannot rely on rationality to give us indubitable, unquestionable truths about God, where do we find our certainty?

The biblical answer (though at the outset it may appear simplistic) is profound. The biblical answer is that we find our certainty in an encounter with the God who created the universe and created us. This encounter is through God's Son Jesus Christ, who is truth personified, and through the work of the Holy Spirit, who comes to us as the presence, love, and wisdom of God (Newbigin 1991, ch. 1). And this biblical certainty emanating from an intimate faith relationship with Jesus Christ is closely connected with being part of the body of Christ, where we are called to experience the presence of the holy. In the Book of Acts the Holy Spirit always comes when the disciples are gathered together (Acts 2:1–4; 4:31; 8:14–17; 10:44–48; 19:1–7). The experience is corporate; and, though it affects their minds, it transforms their whole person—not only their rationality. The corporate experience creates a broad range of ways by which a new kind of knowing occurs.

Are we willing to consider ways of experiencing and knowing the truth about God other than and complementary with rational propositions?

15. John Thiel 1991, ix, has made a case that there is a close connection between this century's theological enterprise as the exercise of individual and rational creativity and the assumptions of modernity.

16. Charles Kraft in a conversation with the author in 1993 regarding this chapter when it was first presented as a paper to the faculty of Fuller's School of World Mission. See also Kraft 1989, 26–35.

Maybe we could learn more from the traditional Pentecostal movement and the more recent charismatic movement in terms of images, stories, praise, music, metaphor—right-brain reflection as well as left-brain logical propositions. Maybe we need to be called back to a sense of holiness that is relational, covenantal, and celebrative. Maybe we need to create more space for a "hermeneutical spiral" that offers us ways of knowing Jesus Christ, the way, the truth, and the life, through narrative, poetry, wisdom literature, prophecy, and parable—as Grant Osborne has pointed out (1991, 153–251).

Biblical faith is based on more than logical affirmations; it consists of more than giving assent to a set of propositions. Biblical faith profoundly involves a personal relationship with Jesus Christ by the work of the Holy Spirit. This is a covenantal holiness that involves a knowing, a grasping of the love of Christ in the deeply intimate biblical sense—far broader, deeper, higher, and wider than the acknowledgment of a set of propositions (Eph. 3:14–19). We are called to "love the Lord [our] God with all [our] heart and with all [our] soul and with all [our] mind and with all [our] strength . . . [and] love [our] neighbor as [ourselves]" (Mark 12:29–31). The Old Testament background of this concept is clearly wholistic and relational, a love that is total, involving one's whole being (Lev. 19:18; Deut. 4:29–31; 6:5; Josh. 22:5; cf. 1 John 4:19–21).

Thus the Bible calls for us to understand that Enlightenment rationality is not enough. Solomon discovered that "the fear of the LORD is the beginning of wisdom" (Prov. 1:7). Paul asked, "Has not God made foolish the wisdom of the world?" (1 Cor. 1:20), and shortly thereafter affirmed, "My message and my preaching were not with wise and persuasive words, but with a demonstration of the Spirit's power, so that your faith might not rest on men's wisdom, but on God's power" (1 Cor. 2:4–5).

Maybe this is an ecclesiological variation akin to what Donald Bloesch is suggesting concerning revelation and knowledge in his *Theology of Word and Spirit* (1992, 21–22):

> I would call my position a *fideistic revelationalism*, in which the decision of faith is as important as the fact of revelation in giving us certainty of the truth of faith. The revelation is not simply assented to but is existentially embraced as the truth or power of salvation. Certainty of its truth becomes ours only in the act of decision and obedience by which the external truth becomes internalized in faith and life. This is not fideism in the narrow or reductionist sense because our faith has a sure anchor and basis in an objective revelation in history. It is not a positivism of revelation because we do not claim a rationally demonstrable or apodictic certainty nor even an intuitive or axiomatic certainty; instead, we have a practical or moral certainty that is ever more fully realized in a life of repentance and obedience.

I would suggest that a fideistic revelationalism is not possible except in the midst of the believing community. *Extra ecclesiam nulla salus.* It is only in the midst of the community of faith that we may experience the full breadth and depth of the presence of the holy God.

So instead of purely philosophical justifications of faith, maybe we need to point more intentionally to relationship with Jesus in the midst of the community of faith whose very public existence is itself part of the data of faith, a bridge between the individual and the social, between the private and the public (Moberg 1962; Newbigin 1989a). Rather than depend on purely rational propositions to justify the truth of what we affirm, maybe we need to emphasize the word-deed praxis, the lived-out holiness of a community of faith that publicly displays in word and deed the fruits of its relationship with Jesus Christ (Costas 1976; 1982; 1989). This kind of proclamation will not be purely propositional or verbal, not purely emotional, not only existential, not predominantly liturgical, nor mostly futurist. It will be all of these combined—not in logical argumentation, but in a life of faith as the people of God demonstrate in word and deed that Jesus Christ is Lord. Thus both the message and the essential being of the messenger community of faith will be used by the Holy Spirit to bring new holiness, new encounter with God, new transformation, and a new call to participate in God's mission (Isa. 6).

Scientific Positivism

Modernity

As we now recognize, at the heart of modernity's project lies a perspective of reality that reduces the real and the true to what is verifiable through scientific method. "The *project* of modernity [that] came into focus during the eighteenth century . . . amounted to an extraordinary intellectual effort on the part of the Enlightenment thinkers 'to develop objective science, universal morality and law, and autonomous art according to their inner logic'" (Harvey 1989, 12, quoting Habermas 1983, 9). Thus the rationality of the autonomous individual went hand in hand—supporting and supported by— the reduction of reality and truth to that which could be seen, tested, and verified through the inductive method of scientific materialism. Only that which could be seen, or hypotheses that could be tested and yield visible and controllable results, were accepted as objectively knowable and thus true. So our world was defined by modernity, a viewpoint whose values have tended increasingly to be based upon, and thoroughly permeated by, the perspectives and values of Enlightenment scientific positivism (Lewis 1990, 131).[17]

17. At the turn of the twentieth century, Charles Peirce, one of the most notable theoreticians of philosophy of science, propounded a pragmatist theory of truth "according to which

The Postmodern Critique of Scientific Positivism

Postmodernity has begun to ask soul-searching questions about the assumptions of scientific positivism. Michael Polanyi has had probably the most influence in this regard. Polanyi's concept of tacit knowledge is a telling critique of science's epistemological framework.[18] And it seems the postmodern critique has struck a chord in the hearts of many in the West because the Enlightenment project could not live up to the extravagant optimism of its claims:

> The twentieth century—with its death camps and death squads, its militarism and two world wars, its threat of nuclear annihilation and its experience of Hiroshima and Nagasaki—has certainly shattered [the earlier] optimism [in scientific progress, so strong during the first decades of this century]. Worse still, suspicion lurks that the Enlightenment project was doomed to turn against itself and transform the quest for human emancipation into a system of universal oppression in the name of human liberation. . . . There are those—and this is . . . the core of postmodernist philosophical thought—who insist that we should, in the name of human emancipation, abandon the Enlightenment project entirely. [Harvey 1989, 13–14][19]

The optimism of modernity pervaded liberal Protestantism in the United States at the beginning of the twentieth century, when the concepts of Manifest Destiny, progress, technology, and rationality were expected to bring

---

the true is the opinion that is destined to be agreed upon by the community of inquirers over the long run" (Fetzer 1992b, 477). Nicholas Rescher writes in his study of *Peirce's Philosophy of Science* (1978, ix, 1, 20): "I have come to regard Peirce as a more fertile and stimulating thinker than most in that somewhat scholastic tradition of the philosophy of science that has sprung up since his day. More than any student of the nature of science, he pries into the things we always wanted to know but were afraid to ask. . . . For Peirce, the inductive method used in the sciences leads inevitably to truth; its justification lies in being self-corrective. . . . Specifically, Peirce's theory was predicated on two contentions: (1) *Ultimate Correctness*—whatever science will come to maintain over the theoretical long run is indeed *true* . . . (2) *Ultimate Completeness*—all truth regarding the world will be realized by science in the theoretical long run. . . . The first of these stipulates the accuracy of theoretical-long-run science, its ability to get at the actual truth of things. The second stipulates its comprehensiveness (nay, potential omniscience), that no general truths about the world are in principle beyond its ken, that nature contains no ultimately occult compartments of inaccessible truth."

18. See Grene 1969; Polanyi 1958a; Polanyi and Prosch 1975. Drawing heavily from Polanyi's critique are Bosch 1991, 349–62; and Newbigin 1986, 65–80; 1991, 19–34, 51–60.

19. At the 1986 annual meeting of the Council on Theological Education of the Presbyterian Church (U.S.A.), Benton Johnson (1986, 15) called attention to the incredible optimism of turn-of-the-century liberal Protestantism: "What made classical liberalism so appealing to so many," he pointed out, "was the triumphalist vision adopted by many of its leaders. The whole project of Christianity was now defined as the upward march of humanity toward a culminating era of peace and justice, happiness and abundance. Moreover, it was not simply a march toward a perfect social order, it was also a march toward the perfection of the human personality." Clearly the world of postmodernity, the world of the 1990s and beyond, is radically different: there is no such simplistic optimism.

about all that any human could want. Postmodernism has rightly, and I believe convincingly, shown the fallacy of modernity's optimism.

But in reaction, postmodernity seems to be retreating into meaningless pluralism and mindless tolerance. In its rejection of any foundations upon which to build a worldview, it seems to be thrusting us into a world of almost idyllic subjectivism, where meaning is ascribed only by the knower, where ultimately there can be no judgment, no ethics, no values—only subjectivism and relativism that lead to atomization, and ultimately such meaninglessness that conversation no longer has a place. It is imperative that evangelicals take seriously the critique of modernity—but it is equally imperative that we offer our postmodern world a more excellent way.

Evangelical Valuation of the Scientific and Visible

As evangelicals we need to give ourselves a self-examination. We need to look again at how science has affected our values. For do we not seem just as enamored of highly visible scientific and pragmatic approaches as is the larger society around us in the West? During the last fifty years we evangelicals in North America have worked hard to create large denominations, highly visible institutions, and economically powerful organizations. Our penchant for largeness and visibility has moved us to use the benefits of science with little questioning of its presuppositions. We have been able to create evangelical television channels and programs, we have multiplied televangelists, and we have created large visible institutions. During the late 1970s and 1980s our growing political clout in the United States brought out a yearning for a new kind of Christendom: society would be governed by our principles—principles that were to be acknowledged as public truths. All this fostered the rise of very visible personalities—pastors, preachers, and singers—who figured large in the institutions they built and who too easily accepted all of the presuppositions of science's materialistic and naturalistic worldview.

In mission we have found it quite easy to use anthropology, statistical analysis, and sociology—along with agronomy, development economics, and mass media—as pragmatic means that are justified by our goals of world evangelization. We have also tended to emphasize visible proofs of the social validity of our churches and organizations along with their mission enterprises. But in accepting and using the modern advantages of science, we have too often tacitly accepted for ourselves the plausibility structures of modern scientific positivism. Further, to achieve our ends in our churches and mission organizations, we may have too easily used secular management principles whose bottom line was measurable production, not faith. We like results, we like to count our results, and we like to count what we can see. Thus, whether it be in church growth and evangelism or in relief and development, have we not tended to accept the scientific reduction of life to the material and visible, and then to justify our mission endeavors on the basis of visible results?

The Church as a *Catholic* Fellowship of Followers of Christ

In relation to the scientific worldview of the Enlightenment, we in the evangelical movement need to listen again to Jesus' conversations with Nicodemus and the woman of Sychar: "I tell you the truth, unless a man is born of water and the Spirit, he cannot enter the kingdom of God"; "True worshipers will worship the Father in spirit and truth. . . . God is spirit, and his worshipers must worship in spirit and in truth" (John 3:5; 4:23–24).[20] Here is the mystery of the catholicity of the church. By its very nature the catholic church of Jesus Christ is *invisibly visible*. As the body of Christ, what is seen (that is, the institution and organization) of the church is only partially what the church is. Its ligaments and relationships, its head, the Spirit that creates and sustains it, the mind of Christ (Phil. 2) that unites it—all these are of the essential nature of that body, and they are invisible. They have real existence, yet cannot be verified, not essentially, through empirical, material, visible, scientific processes. Clearly the church exists as it is embodied, shaped, and mobilized in organizational, institutional, and visible forms. However, the inordinate stress in the twentieth century on the organizational and visible (including notions of visible unity) calls us to reexamine the invisible, spiritual, organic, and communion-based reality of the church (Van Engen 1981, 48–61).

Here we find the Lausanne movement at its best. From its beginnings at the Wheaton and Berlin conferences of 1966 (and their antecedents), Lausanne has been an amorphous movement that is mostly organismic and invisible, a loose fellowship of associations of those who believe in Jesus Christ and affirm the church's calling for the evangelization of the whole world (i.e., catholicity).

Today's world church consists of one-and-a-half billion who, amid an incredible diversity of geography, culture, language, and worldviews, call themselves Christian. The catholicity of this church is something we accept on faith, because we are incapable of seeing—much less verifying—it on empirical, scientific terms (Van Engen 1991b, 54–57). In fact, it is the mystery hidden for ages of which Paul spoke: "Now, through the church, the manifold wisdom of God [is] made known to the rulers and authorities in the heavenly realms, according to his eternal purpose which he accomplished in Christ Jesus our Lord" (Eph. 3:10–11).

If we were to recapture this organic understanding of the church, we would begin to think of it as a global relational and spiritual network that is

20. See Roxburgh 1993, 61–62.

mostly invisible; unseen relationships, friendships, mutual support, and prayer are primary. We would begin to understand that ultimately the church is a fellowship of followers of Jesus. By keeping in view that the members are primary we would rediscover the Reformation's deep wisdom of the priesthood of all believers. We would also be much more concerned about renewal, revival, and reformation than about restructuring. Further, we would devote at least as much effort to the communion of relationships within our organizations as to the achievement of our stated goals in terms of visible and measurable results. Thus our corporate culture, our organizational dynamics, our missional administration, and our forms of evaluation might change substantially. Finally, we would celebrate the fact that the fellowship of missionary followers is invisible because it has been dispersed as salt and light throughout society. But we would also be mindful that its presence in the world is transformational only to the degree that it is different from the world (Matt. 5).

This is the direction in which Lesslie Newbigin (1989a, 222–33) pointed when he referred to the congregation as the hermeneutic of the gospel—a church that is essentially a "community of praise," a "community of truth," a community that "is deeply involved in the concerns of the neighborhood," a community that actively exercises a "priesthood in the world," a "community of mutual responsibility," and "a community of hope." This community is neither purely objective, nor purely subjective, but is at once both objective and subjective.[21] It lives in what Miroslav Volf (1992b, 15–16) has called "provisional absoluteness":

> I believe that "provisional absoluteness" not only transcends the false alternatives "indubitable—unreliable," but is also an authentically Christian way of talking about the ultimate reality rooted in the very nature of Christian existence. To be a Christian means to experience God and live in the world through the power of the [Holy] Spirit of the new creation. Yet this very real experience of God and this concrete new life are provisional: They are what the apostle Paul calls "a first installment" (2 Cor. 1:22) given under the conditions of the old world that is passing away. Within that old world there is no "sacred space" in which Christians can have an absolutely pure encounter with God or live absolutely true lives. The only "sacred space" is the future new creation of

21. Moltmann 1977, 154, points to the differentiation that the dialectical theologians (Karl Barth, Emil Brunner, Friedrich Gogarten, and Rudolf Bultmann) made between faith and religion. I do not intend here to drive the kind of wedge that they (and especially Brunner) did between faith and religion, between organism and organization, between fellowship and institution. Clearly the church is both and all of these at once. However, with scientific positivism being so prevalent in the West, we can afford a slight overemphasis on the organic side, the fellowship, communion, and faith of the church. See also Dulles 1974, 31–70; 1982, 41–52; and Van Engen 1981, 51–59. The stress on the church as organism was one of the most dynamic and transformational elements of the *aggiornamento* that occurred at Vatican II (Flannery 1975).

God toward which they, the pilgrim people of God, are traveling. The pere-
grine nature of Christian existence implies the provisional nature of Christian
knowledge. Because Christians are a people on the way to their final destiny,
their knowledge cannot be a knowledge of those who have already arrived. . . .
Until we come to see the triune God face to face, we will have to carry our religious treasure in earthen vessels—in provisional beliefs no less than in transient
bodies (cf. 2 Cor. 4:7). Our certitude is not that of seeing but of hoping; "in
hope we are saved" (Rom. 8:24) and it is therefore in hope that we know. Our
unsuppressible urge for the final truth must be tempered with the same patience
as our eager longing for the final liberation (Rom. 8:25)—patience to accept
the provisional nature of our own knowledge and patience to be open to the
truth claims of others.[22]

The church we have in view is deeply concerned with becoming a vibrant,
energized, transformed organism of the life of the Spirit (Allen 1962b). This
happens when the followers of Jesus live out a koinonia fellowship of love
in Christ's name (Van Engen 1991b, 87–100).[23] An emphasis on the organismic life of the communion of saints calls us to reevaluate the health of our
churches, our denominations, our organizations, our mission agencies, and
our ecclesiastical structures—not so much in terms of what they do or do
not produce, but rather on the basis of their proximity to or distance from
the Lord.[24]

Technology

Modernity

Clearly one of the most amazing and almost self-justifying aspects of modernity is the technological revolution it has produced. All of us depend on
modernity's technology, are facilitated by it in our work, and profit from it.
Technology is central to any discussion of modernity. Indeed, "social scien-
tists and historians have defined modernity in different ways, and they have
differed in their interpretations and prognoses regarding this phenomenon.
There is well-nigh universal agreement, however, on one proposition: a central feature of the modern world is technological production" (Berger et al.
1973, 23).

22. See also Newbigin 1991, 33–36.
23. Newbigin 1978 expands on this close relationship between the church's purpose and the
trinitarian mission of God.
24. Kraft 1992 refers to this reevaluation in terms of "allegiance encounter" and "truth encounter." Thus he affirms that "power encounters are not adequate by themselves." In his reflection on the relationship of power encounters with the two other types of encounters, Kraft
critiques some of the most basic tenets of modernity, and offers an option other than the one
postmodernity presents.

Now although the fact of technology as a product of modernity is accepted by most of us, few have reflected on the impact of technology on matters of value and belief. Newbigin (1991, 24) takes note of this deficiency: "No one can deny the brilliance of our technology. The problem is rather what our technology is used for. We display astounding brilliance in devising means for any end we desire, but we have no rational way of choosing what ends are worth desiring. We develop the technical wizardry of satellite television to bring a cataract of trash into our living rooms." Robert Wuthnow (1988, 282–83, 289) fears that technology itself may be determining our values and beliefs:

> If many of the traditional legitimating myths have begun to show some signs of erosion, either from a declining infrastructure or from subtle shifts in their meaning, there is, nevertheless, a new myth to which many give unquestioned allegiance—technology. Though scarcely a religion, it presents itself with religious force, combining seemingly inevitable developments in the social infrastructure with belief in the unassailable sanctity of these developments.
>
> Technology is particularly well qualified to serve as a basis for legitimating myths. . . . Technology becomes legitimate—something so much a part of the nature of things that we do not question it. To extend this legitimacy to the nation, or to its political and economic system, all that has to be done is show that the nation does a decent job of fostering technology. Like legitimating a regime as "defender of the faith," America gains legitimacy from technology by proving itself a worthy supporter of what must by all indications be sacred.
>
> The mythologization of technology, therefore, comes at the point when a full range of public values cannot be seriously debated because technical considerations have already ruled some of them out. . . . Technology becomes increasingly prominent as a legitimating myth because the expansion of the technological infrastructure makes it more difficult for public discourse to remain truly open to a full range of intrinsic values.

The Postmodern Critique of Technology

Until recently, at least in the United States, the general public's assumption was very strong that technology (and especially the inauguration of the computer era) would in the long run be able to solve most of Western society's, and perhaps the world's, problems. This attitude has been particularly characteristic of the yuppie generation of the 1980s. But the reality of the world in which we live has called this entire legitimating myth into question. We need mention only a few of the factors that have brought a deep pessimism to the West—a pessimism that, at least in reference to technology, is a new phenomenon in this century:

The incurability of the AIDS epidemic

The role of technology in waging wars and its capability for inhuman annihilation of people all over the globe

The inaccessibility of the newly available technology because of its cost

The destruction of the earth by the very technologies that were created to
save it

A deep fear of the cities that technology has produced[25]

The most pervasive, reactionary, and complex mark of postmodernity is
its rejection of the myth of technology. In relation to architecture Philip
Cooke (1988, 480) lists as the features of postmodernism "a new depthless-
ness based on the culture of the TV image; a weakening of historicity in the
face of new, speeded-up forms of private temporality; a reverence towards
'new technology' as a key emblem of the new world economic system; and
a change in the lived experience of the built space itself, domination and dis-
orientation being major intended effects." Cooke goes on to reflect on Los
Angeles as "a version of this overconsuming, socially polarized global-local
postmodern urbanity of which I have been trying to write" (p. 486). The
residents of Los Angeles—the Los Angeles of fires, earthquakes, and
floods—have been deeply affected by pessimism regarding technology.
How unfortunate that postmodernity, as Cooke has pointed out, has in reaction offered us little more than increased pessimism, deeper anomie, more
pervasive nihilism, and more fragmented atomization. After all is said and
done, are we going to be left with nothing more than Nietzschean struggles
for power?

Evangelical Use of Technology

We do not have space here to document what should be rather obvious.
During the last thirty years or so, we evangelicals have not been reticent
about using technology to achieve our own particular ends. We have, in fact,
been quite intentional about using mass media, global communications, and
the social sciences for world evangelization. Although a very strong advocate
of using any and all means possible for presenting the gospel to all those who
have not yet heard, nevertheless I wonder how much attention we have given
to the effect that this heavy use of technology may have had on our own
faithfulness to the gospel.

We need only mention the myriad ways in which we in the evangelical
movement have sought to use technology in doing our mission. Whether at
Lausanne (1974), Pattaya (1980), or Manila (1989), we have been anxious

---

25. Among major threats to human existence Messer 1992, 46–52, highlights the spectre of
nuclear annihilation, global warming caused by worldwide industrial expansion, the world crisis in food production, deforestation, disease, population growth, and genetic engineering.

to use the best in technology for the furthering of the gospel. Our love of strategy, our strong focus in the last thirty years on the how-to of mission, and our emphasis on producing results have, I fear, too seldom asked about the impact of that technology upon ourselves, our churches, and our mission agencies. We have not stopped often enough to inquire as to the assumptions behind the technology itself. We have wanted to know how to grow churches, for example, but too seldom asked what we were growing, or whether how we were doing it was theologically and biblically appropriate.

The Church as an *Apostolic* Agent of Reconciliation

Maybe we need to rethink our apostolicity and associate it closer with the Lord who sends us. If we are to develop a new understanding of ourselves as Christ's apostolic agents of reconciliation, 2 Corinthians 5 is a good place to start. We could begin by understanding that our nature as Christ's church does not derive from our traditions, our history, or our cultures. "Christ's love compels us" (5:14). Thus our nature and calling derive from the head of the church, the one who has sent us as his ambassadors in the world.

Secondly, we must recognize that our primary role is to be involved in the transformation of our world by working for *reconciliation*. Our reconciliation in Christ is of one piece with our apostolic nature, and our "sentness" entails in turn a "ministry of reconciliation" (5:18). Thus we see that our mission involves direct participation in God's mission, for it is "God [who is] reconciling the world to himself in Christ" (5:19). Thus our nature as Christ's church involves our imploring the world on Christ's behalf, "Be reconciled to God" (5:20).

Thirdly, we should begin to understand that this reconciliation is wholistic, involving such a radical transformation of reality that anyone who is in Christ "is a new creation; the old has gone, the new has come!" (5:17). This is a total transformation of each person-in-community, as together people are reconciled to themselves, to each other, to their world, and to God. For even "creation waits in eager expectation for the sons of God to be revealed . . . in hope that the creation itself will be liberated from its bondage to decay and brought into the glorious freedom of the children of God" (Rom. 8:19–21).

As Christ's apostolic agents of reconciliation, we must begin to rethink the way we evaluate and use technology. Our being (who we are as Christ's apostles) and our doing (the methods we employ in Christ's mission) should reflect our Lord as much as the ends we pursue. We must eschew whatever violates our mission of reconciliation. We must not unquestioningly use technology as if it were a value-free tool—rather, we must subject it to the scrutiny of the Scripture, to the operation of the Spirit, and to our apostolic call to be ambassadors of Jesus Christ.

Further, we might begin to understand our mission as mission-on-the-way, an ambassadorial, apostolic pilgrimage that is at once profoundly personal, private, and relational; and communal, public, and transformational.[26] The apostolic congregation bridges the personal faith of the disciple of Jesus Christ with the public values our world so desperately needs (Moberg 1962). Here is an apostolicity of sentness into the world, a world for whom, and in which, Christ died—a world that is called to total and wholistic reconciliation. The church is to understand that its essential life and task involve not strategy or the management of technological power, but faithfulness to the commission received from Jesus Christ the Lord. And empowered by the Holy Spirit (not technological expertise per se), the church becomes a *public* agent of transformation, an apostolic community that offers a return of the purpose for which God has created humankind.

Clearly this mandate would involve the church in the preservation of human life (the Noahic covenant), in a growing relationship with God (the Abrahamic covenant), in a call to governments to stand for the welfare of the people (the Mosaic covenant), and in a reminder to the world that there is only one Lord and Savior, one King of kings (the Davidic covenant) before whom one day every knee will bow and every tongue confess that Jesus Christ is Lord (the new covenant) (Phil. 2).

We are concerned about a non-Christian (and post-Christian) world that needs to know Jesus Christ as the only way, the truth, and the life. We are deeply troubled as to how to respond to the nihilism, relativism, pluralism, and the loss of the concept of truth that mark the foundationless character of postmodern society. We are concerned about the malaise, the breakup, the atomization of Western society; and the loss of a sense of direction, purpose, and value with its accompanying deep pessimism. We want to present an apology of the gospel as a public truth and to do so in ways that a postmodern culture will be able to accept (Newbigin 1986). And we accept our responsibility and role to be Christ's prophets who extend a word of hope in the midst of hopelessness.

All of these concerns are legitimate, urgent, and necessary. But all of them need to flow from a prior concern that deals with ourselves. Together as the body of Christ we need to re-examine ourselves. As the church-in-mission we need to ask again how the Lord of the harvest wants to renew and reshape us so that we may more faithfully embody a new missiological ecclesiology that is appropriate for a postmodern era.

If we are concerned about modernity, and are not satisfied with the options offered by postmodernity, then we need to reexamine our churches,

26. The full scope of our apostolic mission would involve what Bosch 1991, 369–510, has called "elements of an emerging ecumenical missionary paradigm."

mission agencies, and Christian organizations to see how the Holy Spirit may transform and renew us. This renewed understanding calls us to be the whole church (the one, holy, catholic, and apostolic congregation) taking the whole gospel (neither modernity nor postmodernity) to the whole world. Is it possible that we could offer our postmodern world a new plausibility structure, a renewed hermeneutic of the gospel (Newbigin 1989a, 222–33) that can provide a degree of provisional absoluteness (Volf 1992b) through a reshaped pilgrimage of faith in the hope of the coming of Christ's kingdom?

This chapter began with the thesis that a Christian critique of modernity would include an examination of ourselves as Christ's church to see how we may become authentic, contextually appropriate hermeneutical communities of the gospel in a postmodern world. Our reexamination has called us to become:

> *One* Global Communion of Disciples of Jesus:
>   more than individualist;
> A *Holy* Community of Faith:
>   more than rationalist;
> A *Catholic* Fellowship of Followers of Christ:
>   more than materialist;
> An *Apostolic* Agent of Reconciliation:
>   more than technologist.

May our Lord Jesus enable us to become who we are.

Part 7

Mission Theology and Ministry Formation

13

Portraits of the Pastor as Missionary Leader

"Don Daniel" was my pastor. Dramatically converted as a young man and trained in the National Presbyterian Church of Mexico's best seminary, Don Daniel was one of the most gifted, intelligent, compassionate, organized, and forward-looking pastors I have ever met. Having grown up in his church, listened to his preaching, and made profession of faith under his pastoral care, I regard him to this day my most significant model of a pastor as missionary leader. And yet I also learned from Don Daniel's experience that gifted, committed, and visionary leaders are not necessarily successful in leading. But that is jumping ahead of the story.

The person of the leader is a very significant part of the complex set of factors which move a local group of God's people toward participating in God's mission in the world. The leader is a catalyst to stimulate the people to follow in a mutually agreed direction in the midst of a particular spiritual, social, economic, political, and cultural context. The Holy Spirit, who establishes and mobilizes the church, uses the entire mix of complex factors to move God's people to be and do something new in the world. God-given leaders are in the center of it all, and yet they are only a part of the story. Because of the multiplicity of factors involved, there seems to be no assurance that a leader will in fact be successful in leading the church. This dynamic tension created by the interplay of numerous factors seems to be what the apostle Paul had in mind when he spoke of the upbuilding of the body of Christ in the midst of ministry until we all attain the stature of the fullness of Christ:

And he gave
  tous men apostolous (some to be apostles),
  tous de prophētas (some to be prophets),

tous de euangelistas (some to be evangelists),
   tous de poimenas kai didaskalous (some to be pastors and teachers),
for the equipping of the saints
   eis ergon diakonias (for the work of ministry),
   eis oikodomēn tou sōmatos tou Xristou
   (so that the body of Christ may be built up)
until we all attain
   eis tēn enotēta tēs pisteōs (the unity of the faith)
   kai tēs epignōseōs tou huiou tou theou
   (and the knowledge of the Son of God),
   eis andra teleion (toward complete manhood),
   eis metron hēlikias tou plērōmatos tou Xristou
   (to the measure of the fullness of Christ). [Eph. 4:11–13]

A detailed analysis of the dynamic relationship between leader and led, pastor and flock, servant and people of God in the process of building the church will make it clear that the pastoral role is difficult, multifaceted, and absolutely essential. We often consider the how-tos of an equipping ministry in the church. But having understood that the whole people of God are to be involved in ministry in the world, we must carefully analyze the implications of that for pastoral leadership. Here we are not speaking so much of what the pastor-builder does, but of who the leader is vis-à-vis the people of God on the one hand, and those outside the church on the other. Far deeper than the tasks of facilitating, training, and organizing are other aspects of the leader's incarnational call that involve a radical transformation of one's selfhood to become the stimulus for moving the people of God forward in mission and ministry in the world.

Don Daniel was just such a person. Often on horseback, and sometimes on foot, Don Daniel traveled the muddy trails of Chiapas, Mexico, itinerating all over the state, seeking a family here or there who were being gathered by the Spirit to become part of the church of Jesus Christ. While pastoring a local church and teaching in a Bible institute, Don Daniel was instrumental in evangelism and church planting among four Mayan language groups, working with missionaries and local Christians to establish the church in the midst of people who spoke languages other than his native Spanish.

Don Daniel exemplified for me the model which Paul has left us in Ephesians 4:11–13. There we are led to understand that the reason apostles, prophets, evangelists, pastors, and teachers are given is the ultimate upbuilding of the body of Christ by means of equipping local congregations for mission and ministry. Here lies the very special and crucial role which Paul himself fulfilled—the pastoral servant-leader who lived, dreamt, breathed, and labored for the building of the church as it was shaped through the work of the Holy Spirit in the midst of the people of God in mission in the world.

Sample

During my childhood I saw in the life and ministry of Don Daniel at least five portraits of the pastor as a leader of missionary churches in the world. First, he was an example.

In his work of building the church Paul often exhorted his new converts to imitate him (1 Cor. 4:9–16; 11:1; Phil. 3:1–17; 2 Thess. 3:7–9). Was this arrogant pride? I think not. It is as if Paul set himself before the new Christians as the first sample of the product, the firstfruits, the earliest demonstration of what the gospel can and should do in the life of the believer. In 2 Thessalonians 3:7 he says, "For you yourselves know how you ought to follow our example, because we did not act in an undisciplined manner among you" (NASB). His readers knew how to act because they saw it exemplified, typified, modeled, demonstrated by the first sample product, the prototype of the new creation in the gospel—Paul himself. J. Robert Clinton's massive data (1988) concerning the faith-pilgrimages of various leaders give us all the examples we need to be able to picture the kind of leaders God has used in the past to mobilize the church in mission in the world.

This component of the pastoral servant-leader speaks about who we are, not professionally, not intellectually, not in task, not in strategy—but personally. It speaks of how we order our priorities, how we handle our workload, how much time we have for people, how we shape our family life, what attitudes we express toward others, what openness and authenticity we show with others, how we resolve conflicts, what we choose as our standard of living, how we exercise self-discipline, and so on. No wonder Paul writes to one of the early builders of the church, "An overseer, then, must be above reproach . . ." (1 Tim. 3:1–15 NASB). Profoundly, our lifestyle, our spirituality, our personality formation, our interpersonal relationships, and our selfhood as the foundation for building trust are all significant factors impacting our effectiveness as we struggle to build the church.

Leon Draayer (1989) made a study of long-term pastorates in the Reformed Church in America. Although his primary objective was to examine the role of preaching in long-term pastorates, the factor he found to be overwhelmingly crucial to the health of long-term pastorates was the minister's ongoing development in personal spirituality. Preaching remains vibrant primarily as it expresses the living and constantly developing spirituality of the pastor.

Sage

We are just beginning to discover the tremendous resources available to the Christian church in the area of wisdom—the wisdom literature of the Old and

New Testaments, the wisdom of ancient and modern peoples, the wisdom of an understanding of life, humanity, and the forces of nature, and insight into the interdependence of human beings. This aspect of leadership is very ancient—and very modern. Be it the Hindu guru, the Islamic imam, the Mayan shaman, or the Jewish rabbi, the role of the sage is extremely important. There was a time when this aspect of leadership was very strong in the Christian church as well, particularly in the lives and teaching of the monks and religious. Augustine and Bernard of Clairvaux have their modern counterparts in people like Mother Teresa. Francis of Assisi speaks through the ages, inspiring the Christian church. Paul highlights this aspect of leadership in the church (1 Cor. 3:16–23; 2 Cor. 1:12; Col. 3:8–17; 4:5–6; 2 Tim. 3:14–15).

It is the role of wisdom to inquire of us whether we are truly men and women of God. The sage exhibits great wisdom about life, nature, personhood, and interpersonal relationships. The sage is healer, counselor, upbuilder, encourager, reconciler. Among essential characteristics are immersion in the wisdom of the Holy Scriptures and demonstration of a genuine personal piety which shines forth in conversation and action. The sage knows how to pray—and does so in the understanding of God's grace for his people. As missionary the sage, along with those others who join in the pilgrimage of faith toward the building up of the church, demonstrates loving concern in teaching the deep truths of spiritual maturity.

Seer

If we turn to the Book of Acts to look for the components which gave rise to the building of the church, we see a certain aspect emerging which was important then and is necessary now. In Acts 2, 13, 16, and in 1 Corinthians 16 we see that the church needs individuals who can look down the road into the future, and who will challenge, exhort, and urge new Christians to walk in a specific direction, seeking certain goals, objectives, and dreams. We immediately think of missionary strategists like William Carey, Samuel Zwemer, James Cantine, and John Scudder. Part of our servant-leader role in building missionary churches is to allow the Holy Spirit to so grip us that we in fact "see visions" and "dream dreams" (Acts 2). The seer is the organizer, the idea person, the provider of perspective as to where we are going. The seer seeks to involve God's people in long-range planning and goal setting, and is often asking disturbing and difficult questions which deal with the consequences of present practices. The seer is called to provide a certain unity of purpose and vision for a church's goals and strategies.

Clearly these goals and strategies need to be owned by everyone, and the group dreams must also be intimately related to the individual and personal goals of the members of the group. And yet there is always that special person who provides the initial dream or vision, the possibility thinker who devotes time and attention to what could be, and then shares these dreams with the people of God. They in turn will invariably reflect on, consider, judge, and probably modify those dreams as the Holy Spirit directs in moving God's people forward in mission in the world. We have underestimated the power of vision in the relationship of leaders with followers and in the creation of followership. Without vision, there is little reason for the membership to follow the leaders. And without the membership being willing to follow, there will be no leadership.

Here we should take note that one of the primary arenas where a pastoral leader may be able to articulate vision and stimulate followership is in preaching. Good preaching galvanizes the congregation and creates the urgency which motivates the members to want to follow the leader's vision. Unless such vision is articulated, leadership will not happen. On the other hand, if the pastoral leader uses preaching to articulate a vision which is not shared by, or is in opposition to the goals of, the membership, resistance and rebellion may replace followership.

Student

As we observe Paul in his never-ceasing work of building the churches of his time, we see a very strong cultural component as well. Study Romans 1–3, Galatians 3, and Colossians 3. Here we seem to glimpse the student of culture allowing the gospel to take root in humanity in such a way that it calls into question both Paul's own cultural milieu and that of his hearers. It is this very important role which Paul exemplifies in Acts 17:16–34. His is the genius that picks up the point of contact in Athenian philosophy, and utilizes it to open a door for the presentation of the gospel of Jesus Christ.

We must realize that this is the same Paul who was formerly Saul of Tarsus, the one who, until he came to grips with the total depravity of every human being before God and the failure of the law as a means of achieving grace, would not allow any modification of his perspective of the Old Testament law. We are called to just as radical a transformation. We are called to question the very foundations of our culture, our background, the great American way, our assumptions, methodologies, priorities, North Americanisms, and Western biases.

However, at the same time we are also called to be students of the cultural milieu in which we minister. Thus we will be specially equipped—more than anyone else—to show the way in which that new culture, as it incorporates the gospel, must also be profoundly and ultimately changed. For in the gospel of the kingdom of God there is neither Jew nor Greek, bond nor free, male nor female.

As servant-leaders involved in building the church, then, we find part of our challenge in the anthropological realm. It is part of our calling to ask questions of our own as well as other cultures and to understand new cultural forms of gospel incarnation. Pastoral leaders as students must be involved in examining cultural assumptions and discovering new ways in which the church may best witness to Jesus in the particular cultural contexts in which it is called to minister.

Sacrifice

"Greater love has no one than this," Jesus said to his disciples, the future leaders of his church, "that one lay down his life for his friends" (John 15:13). There seems to be an element of sacrifice inherent in leading the church forward in mission in the world. It is a giving of oneself for the sake of the body, an act of the will which places priority on the welfare, growth, development, and new direction of the church over and above one's own. The good shepherds of the flock lay down their lives for the sheep (John 10). But it is not for the sheep to make the shepherds suffer. It is for the shepherds to voluntarily choose to give their lives for the sake of the upbuilding of the body.

This seems to have been the role of Epaphroditus, whom Paul holds up as an example of the mind of Christ as described in Philippians 2:1–11 (cf. vv. 25–30). Numerous biblical examples may be given to demonstrate that sacrifice is an integral part of being leaders of the people of God. Moses, Samuel, Jeremiah, and Jesus are but a few of those who demonstrated the willingness to suffer that must also be included in our portraits of pastoral leaders in the church.

Although Don Daniel was a model leader, and although he beautifully and forcefully exemplified the qualities described above, yet in our local congregation he achieved very little leadership. In our congregation there was a critical absence of followership. Two-thirds of the congregation at one time or another refused to follow Don Daniel in almost every aspect of the church's life. Although Don Daniel was an exemplary leader, there was no leadership. And Don Daniel refused to move to another church where he would have found the kind of followership he needed. Subsequently the congregation split four ways; only a handful of the original church stayed with the pastor. Do I love my pastor any less because of the sad outcome of this story? No. Do I blame him for it, or do I exonerate him of all blame? Neither one nor the other. Rather, I recognize that the nature of leadership is incredibly mysterious and complex, and that the situation was not conducive to the kind of leadership which he and many of us so deeply wanted to see. Given our fallen humanity, leadership is not assured, even when exceptionally fine leaders are available. YHWH and Moses had quite a time with the rebellious Israelites on their way through the desert. And Paul struggled with those in Corinth who would not accept his apostleship nor exhibit the followership that would allow him to achieve leadership.

Does this mean that the wonderful portraits of Don Daniel given earlier were not true? Not at all. He remains for me a model of all five characteristics of the missionary leader. Does it mean we will turn pessimistic and cynical about being able to mobilize this strange voluntary association known as the church? I hope not. What it does mean is that we need to take much more seriously the complexity of the interplay of the numerous factors contributing to leadership, of which the person of the leader is only one. At the same time, an awareness of such complexity does not minimize the importance of the qualities of the leader as leader, nor excuse our seeming lack of concern with regard to the development of such qualities in our own lives if we want to be leaders of Christ's church.

Let us all humbly admit that none of us matches these portraits very well. They are touched-up pictures which show us in a better light than we see ourselves. We feel very much like square pegs in a round hole when this aspect of our pastoral call is highlighted. And yet we must allow the Holy Spirit to continually wear at the rough edges. We must allow him to develop within us those qualities which will make us worthy examples of the spiritual wisdom of the sage, the foresight of the seer, the humility of the student, and the self-giving of sacrifice in building the church toward mission in the world. One of my dreams over a lifetime has been that God by the Spirit would make me at least a little like Don Daniel in my own qualities as a missionary leader. By God's grace may I be as deeply spiritual, as wise, as visionary, as dedicated to learning, and as committed to the growth of the church as is Don Daniel. On the other hand, maybe I need to become more like Christ than like Don Daniel.

Paul said it this way:

> Speaking the truth in love, we are to grow up in all aspects into Him, who is the head, even Christ, from whom the whole body, being fitted and held together by that which every joint supplies, according to the proper working of each individual part, causes the growth of the body for the building up of itself in love.
>
> . . . Put on the new self, which in the likeness of God has been created in righteousness and holiness of the truth. [Eph. 4:15–16, 24 NASB]

14

Shifting Paradigms in Ministry Formation

The thesis of this chapter is that ministry formation for the twenty-first century must build on the best of past paradigms, integrating them in a new paradigm that involves a multilevel process of shaping the *being, knowing,* and *doing* of the members of the church for multifaceted ministries in the church and mission in the world.

I can still hear my father say, "Well, Dr. Blocker used to say. . . ." And how often have I caught myself quoting George Ladd, Geoffrey Bromiley, Paul Jewett, James Daane, Lewis Smedes, or David Allan Hubbard, those who taught me at Fuller Seminary in the early 1970s? Over the past twenty years, I have noticed that whenever pastors, missionaries, and seminary professors the world over begin to talk about seminaries and ministry, we invariably flash back to our own seminary or Bible college education. And the basis on which we evaluate the issue at hand is usually colored (or almost determined) by our own experience of seminary. But to think about ministry formation today on the basis of one's previous seminary training is inappropriate and unacceptable, for at least four reasons.

First, to project the form of our own theological education onto the present invariably blinds us to the wonderful richness of forms that came before our time and that may help us into the future. Second, to project onto the present the way we experienced seminary training is to ignore to our peril that the contexts of today's ministries have changed, both in North America and around the world. Third, sticking to our own ways renders us incapable of the freewheeling creativity that is needed for the next century. During the years I was involved in ministry formation in Mexico, I learned that for such programs to be successful, only the students are indispensable. Fourth, to project our past seminary training onto the present and future is to ignore the profound paradigm shift in which the world (and particularly the West) finds itself at this time. In all aspects and at all levels of society, we are in the midst of profound changes like nothing seen since the Industrial Revolution.[1] Given the paradigm shift that the church and the world are undergoing, we must free ourselves to reconceptualize the foundations, the forms, and the goals of ministry formation in the future. Ministry formation must likewise undergo a radical paradigm shift, so that it can appropriately serve the church in the world of tomorrow.[2]

Five Past Paradigms

Throughout their history the people of God (Israel and the church) have held a number of different perspectives concerning the selection, formation, and recognition of their leaders. These viewpoints can be summarized in five basic paradigms that competed with each other up until the late 1960s. During the last thirty years or so, a new postmodern situation has given rise to a sixth paradigm spearheaded especially by the churches in Asia, Africa, and Latin America. This new paradigm borrows aspects from the other five and reshapes them in a radically new configuration of in-ministry formation. At the risk of oversimplification and possible historical inaccuracies, we will survey the development of the five earlier paradigms of ministry formation, and then focus on the sixth.

Apprenticeships

Possibly the oldest paradigm of ministry formation involves a personal relationship between a teacher and one or more apprentices. In this paradigm someone very significant in the community because of recognized wisdom, experience, and skills usually selects those to whom the mantle will be passed on. In Scripture this paradigm can be seen, for example, in the relationship of Moses with Joshua, of Eli with Samuel, of Elijah with Elisha and the school of the prophets. By New Testament times apprenticeship had become a common mentoring and teaching form in the Jewish synagogues. This approach was followed by John the Baptist and Jesus with their disciples, by Gamaliel with Saul (Paul), and by Paul with his missionary band. For several

---

1. Tom Peters 1992 and Barker 1992 are among those who are pointing to the radical nature of the paradigm shift taking place in modern society.

2. In the last chapter of *Reflections of a Contrarian* (1989, 171–92), Lyle Schaller asks some very significant questions about theological education, questions that point to the urgent need to reconceptualize the paradigm that governs our expectations of seminaries and programs in ministry formation. See also Schaller 1987, 198–212; 1992, 94–114; Bennis 1989; Gerald Anderson 1993; De Pree 1989; 1992; Bosch 1991; Callahan 1983; and Elliston 1992.

hundred years after Christ, the church formed its leaders predominantly through apprenticing relationships.

This paradigm is still very much with us. Robert Coleman's *Master Plan of Evangelism* (1963) and the enormously significant program of the Navigators are two of the best-known models that build on this paradigm. The recent explosion of discipleship literature gives witness to the importance that this paradigm still holds in the church. John Nevius's discipling method in Korea has recently been adapted in the metachurch model of Carl George, for example, with its primary perspectives drawn from a mentoring paradigm. Paul Stanley and J. Robert Clinton (1992, 159) go so far as to affirm that mentoring is essential for leadership: "A growing leader needs a relational network that embraces mentors, peers, and emerging leaders in order to ensure development and a healthy perspective on his or her life and ministry." One of the common characteristics of the megachurches (congregations with tens of thousands of members) is their careful and intentional programs of apprenticing relationships that provide the framework to form their leaders for ministry.

The apprenticing paradigm has its strengths: the formation of the being of the disciple over an extended period of time, the accountability of apprentice to teacher, and the high degree of contextualization to a particular organization or culture. But it has at least three weaknesses. First, it can sometimes be ideological, manipulative, and oppressive if the mentor does not allow the disciple the freedom of self-expression and self-discovery. Second, this paradigm is limited to the wisdom, skills, and creativity of the mentor; and, third, it may not be transferable to new contexts ("universalizable").[3]

Monastic Discipline

After Constantine officially sanctioned Christianity, a new form of institutionalized ministry formation arose. Taking quite different forms over the centuries, this paradigm involved people living together in community for extended periods of time, if not for a lifetime. Usually associated with vows of loyalty, chastity, and poverty, the monastic movement exercised a tremendous influence on the church in the West. What had once been a rather individual affair of discipling now became an institutionalized corporate matter within the womb of the church.

The monastic movement was the cradle where popes and prelates were nurtured for the Roman church. The history of Christianity would be radically different and deeply impoverished without it. Roman Catholics and Protestants alike owe a great spiritual, ecclesiological, organizational, and

---

3. Of course, ministry formation within denominational seminaries shares a similar limitation.

missionary debt to the monastic movements (both male and female), including present-day orders like the Society of Holy Fathers, Mother Teresa's Missionaries of Charity, and the Maryknollers.

The monastic paradigm is not one that the Protestant traditions know how to deal with very well. The vows of obedience and separation are radical. The disciplined life of people in community is a formalized and institutionalized manner of mentoring in isolation over an extended period of time. The search for spirituality is profound. The degree of personal accountability to the faith community is astounding. This paradigm has its strengths: the spiritual formation of the disciple (being), prescribed habits of study and learning (knowing), and missionary expansion throughout the centuries (doing). However, because of its general tendency toward isolation, this paradigm has sometimes tended to be institutionally encapsulated by the powers of the church, and restrictive in the scope of the leaders it has formed, since conformity to the community has been so strong. And yet many of the church's most influential theologians and reformers were formed in the womb of the monastic movement.

Knowledge-Based Formation (the University)

The scientific revolution changed many things, not least being the way leaders were to be formed for ministry in church and world. The explosion of curiosity and learning of the Renaissance gave rise to the universities—and an integral part of the university structure was theological education. Although it eventually became only one department in the university, still the intimate tie of theological reflection with the university structures of the West is a phenomenon that influences our views of theological education more profoundly than we might guess.

As this paradigm developed over the centuries, it shaped theological education in a number of ways. First, ministry formation became predominantly knowledge-based. Learning to read, recite, and interact with the Greek and Latin thinkers became an early test of formation in ministry. Second, the structure of theological education became subdivided into all the smaller parts that are maintained to this day: history of thought, languages, biblical studies, theology, ethics, homiletics. Third, this paradigm began the breach between so-called theological education and the church; learning was to occur in the classroom, not in the sanctuary. Fourth, this paradigm gave rise to the search for academic excellence by individuals in theological education; in some ways this development was in opposition to the indoctrination, obedience, and corporate participation of the monastic movement. Fifth, this paradigm strongly affirmed all the winds of cultural change blowing through Europe and North America—the impact of which would be a story in itself.

The university-based paradigm is strong in the area of knowing, especially knowledge of past thought, traditions, theologians, perspectives—and strong in cultivating creativity for developing new thought. It has shown itself to be rather weak, however, in terms of doing, which relates to ministry skills in the church. It is weakest in the area of being. The university environment has simply not proven itself to be very conducive to the long-term formation of personal spirituality and piety. Some of the weaknesses of the university paradigm seem to have hastened the move toward seminaries.

Seminaries

As denominations took shape in North America, a new paradigm of ministry formation emerged: the seminaries. Predominantly connected to denominations, the seminaries separated from the universities and began to take on an identity of their own, incorporating a number of elements from earlier paradigms. They borrowed from the apprenticeship paradigm by building close relationships between faculty and students. As seminaries created their own subcultures, they borrowed from the monastic paradigm in the way the community of faculty, staff, and students sought communion, fellowship, and formation together. At the same time, in order to be academically acceptable, the seminaries borrowed from the university paradigm in structuring themselves predominantly in terms of knowledge-based and classroom-dependent instruction.

The seminaries fashioned the features they had borrowed into something new. They modified the apprenticeship paradigm by placing it in the classroom, and sometimes in the church through supervised ministry. They changed the ecclesiastical and institutional qualities of the monastic paradigm through their link to denominations. They became training centers for those who would become faithful transmitters of the theological tradition to which they belonged. Because the seminaries wanted to be more closely connected with the churches than the universities had been, they began internship programs that would involve their students in short-term forays into the life of congregations. Although seminaries wanted to be academically respectable, they modified their classroom and academic instruction and added a number of skill-based experiences that would help their graduates be more proficient in the exercise of ministry in the church. Mainline seminaries in particular shared the university's desire for relevant conversation with the surrounding culture, but modified it to include the congregation in that culture.

Professional Preparation

After the beginning of the twentieth century, denominations became less and less networks of congregations and more like corporations, with the congregations functioning as branch offices, so to speak. By midcentury, the seminaries had become predominantly centers for denominational induction, training stations in skills for particular programs in the church (e.g., liturgical renewal and counseling), and professional finishing schools that were gateways to jobs in the churches. After the mid-1960s the trend toward the professionalization of the clergy radically shifted the expectations under which seminaries labored, as Lyle Schaller has so aptly summarized in *Reflections of a Contrarian* (1989).[4]

Although the motivations behind the creation of the professional paradigm of the seminaries were laudable, the end product of this trend demonstrated significant weaknesses. The most glaring of these was the lack of personal spirituality and authenticity on the part of the professionals prepared in seminaries. The being of the person was almost totally ignored, since the person's professional function was stressed so heavily. The well-documented moral and personal failure of clergy today in North America may have been hastened by the professionalization of the clergy. Professionalization meant that congregations began hiring employees who had degrees rather than women and men who were called and formed for ministry in their midst; congregational expectations became nearly unbearable, and clergy-congregation relations quite unhealthy. Professionalization was also coupled with the model of leaders as enablers. That ended up fostering passivity, nonproductivity, and low-level direction in the clergy. Congregations were left floundering for direction at a time when they were most needful of strong leadership.

Lastly, because the seminaries were still somewhat separate from the congregations (and sometimes seemed to think they knew better than the people in the pew what the church should be about), the emphasis on certain professional skills ignored others that were highly valued by the people of the congregations. So loving relationships, motivating leadership, Bible teaching, expository preaching, knowing how to lead people to Christ in evangelism, participation in mission, and a host of other skills seemed to be missing— abilities that people in the pews expected from their seminary graduates. In fact, it seemed to some people in the congregations that the professional paradigm majored in the minors, ignoring some major aspects of ministry formation.[5]

The professional paradigm has now run its course, and its strengths and weaknesses can be assessed. What is most apparent is that the church and the

4. For example, Charles Fuller's purpose in starting Fuller Seminary had been to establish a training center for evangelists who would preach the gospel to North America. Instead, it has moved further and further toward a modified combination of the knowledge-based university paradigm (people study on their way to doctoral degrees) and a professional school for persons preparing for congregational ministries.

5. For some penetrating questions about the shift "from vocation to profession" see Schaller 1987, 198–212; see also George Hunter 1992, 112–13.

world have changed so dramatically (and the needs of ministry formation with them) that the professional paradigm needs to undergo radical reformation. I believe Kennon Callahan (1990, 4) has accurately described the results of this paradigm:

> Professional ministers are at their best (and they do excellent work) in a churched culture. But put them in an unchurched culture, and they are lost. In an unchurched culture, they do a reasonably decent job of presiding over stable and declining and dying churches. They maintain a sense of presence, dignity, decorum, and decency—with a quietly sad regret—much like the thoughtful undertaker who sees to keeping things in good order throughout the funeral.
>
> New understandings of being a minister are created for each new era. The professional-minister understanding, which was developed in the late forties and early fifties, served well its purpose for nearly forty years. . . . Each new generation must carve out an understanding of ministry that matches with its time.
>
> The day of the professional minister is over. The day of the missionary pastor has come.

Similar sentiments are echoed by Donald Messer (1992, 17, 21–22):

> In general, contemporary theological education has been oriented primarily toward the pastoral care of congregations, not the church's mission to the world. . . .
>
> In order to recover apostolic ministry, we must identify and discard dysfunctional theologies. Those theologies, more concerned about the inner life and system of a bureaucratic church than mission, develop a dysfunctional community of faith unresponsive to caring for the future of God's creation. Ministry detached from God's mission in the world is heretical.
>
> Instead of mission shaping the church and its ministry, management and maintenance predominate. Sociologists speak of this phenomenon as "professional deformation." . . . The dysfunctional church, oriented to its own perpetuation and support, neglects its responsibility for being the people of God serving the world.

Those who want to use the seminaries only as stepping-stones to certification and the opportunity to impose their own agendas on the church represent the wrong kind of leaders and the wrong direction for the church. They will lead the church toward death rather than toward new life. The church can no longer afford to support professional religionists who make a living off the church while accelerating the death of congregations. We need an alternative paradigm.

One of the very early forces in North America to offer an alternative to the university and the seminary styles of theological education was the Bible College (Institute) movement. We should not underestimate the significance of the Bible College movement as a check on some of the directions in which the two other paradigms led (Mulholland 1993). Moody Bible Institute, Columbia Bible College, and Reformed Bible College, to name but a few, have provided a style of ministry formation that has had tremendous impact on church and mission during the last 150 years. And although the Bible College movement has at times been considered (especially by the universities) somewhat nonacademic, yet its graduates often seem to be able to lead the churches effectively. This is due in part to the skill-based orientation of the Bible colleges, coupled with a strong emphasis on spiritual formation. The Bible College movement adapted elements from the apprenticeship and the monastic paradigms, yet to some extent defined itself against the university and professional paradigms. There is a sense, then, in which one might say that the Bible College movement was a precursor of, and provided some of the basic theoretical foundations for, the new paradigm we will examine shortly.

Meanwhile, the churches in Asia, Africa, and Latin America were less affected by the paradigms we have described. Because the university and professional paradigms did not fit the needs there, the churches in those contexts were compelled to lead the way in seeking a new paradigm. Maybe it is time we allow ourselves in North America the freedom to learn from Christians in other parts of the world, to step into a new future and consider the shape we might give to a new paradigm of ministry formation.

The New Paradigm: In-Ministry Formation

In the 1960s theological education in Africa, Asia, and Latin America underwent a phenomenal paradigm shift through the emergence of a movement called Theological Education by Extension (TEE). The cause necessitating the new movement was the lack of funds and personnel to train leaders quickly enough for the growing churches in those contexts. This need propelled a dramatic rethinking of the nature of ministry formation, a rethinking that has yet to dissipate. Beginning in a Presbyterian seminary in Guatemala and spearheaded by, among others, Ralph Winter, Ross Kinsler, and James Emory, TEE has spread all over the globe, transforming the way the churches conceive of preparing their leaders. A great deal has been written on its development in various parts of the world.[6] We will focus on its theological and theoretical characteristics.

The TEE movement began from scratch. All shibboleths of theological education were negotiable. In constructing their new paradigm the leaders of the movement consciously borrowed from earlier ones, yet with a creativity of adaptation and reconstruction not seen for centuries. The heart of this par-

6. Two of the best overviews are Winter 1969 and Kinsler 1983.

adigm is the search for a way to integrate the individual's being, knowing, and doing for ministry in the church and world.

Why?

The purpose of the in-ministry paradigm is to form leaders who can lead the church. The focus is on leadership, not ordination, function, profession, legitimation, or any other of a host of issues that sometimes cloud our perspectives of theological education. This would seem obvious, but it is actually quite radical. For we have assumed for over a century now that a person who has graduated from a university school of divinity or from a seminary is a leader—and especially if that person holds a paid staff position in a congregation or denomination. Nothing could be further from the truth. In fact, we are in a deep leadership crisis in North America, and position or function can no longer be equated with leadership. Warren Bennis (1989, 142) calls our attention to this crisis:

> The conspicuous absence of real leadership in the world reminds me of the Frenchman who was bowled over and nearly trampled by a noisy, unruly mob. As he stood up, he saw a small, meek man who was frantically chasing the mob, and called out, "Don't follow those people." The little man yelled back, "I have to follow them. I'm their leader."
>
> People without leadership, leaders who follow. The more we lack leadership, the more we hunger for it. Bewildered, we wander through the world that seems to have become morally dead, where everything, including the government, seems up for sale, and where, looking for the real villains, we confront ourselves everywhere.

So the new paradigm makes the radical shift from preparing professionals to forming leaders. Leadership can be defined in various ways. For example:

> Leadership is a corporate event. The people of God move forward in mission in the world as they live out their vision of God's call and will for them, stimulated by a number of leader-catalysts, and mobilized by the Holy Spirit in response to what God is doing in their midst and in their context of mission in the world. . . . Leadership happens as a corporate event when the believing community allows certain members to act as its leader-catalysts, inspiring it toward greater exercise of a whole range of spiritual gifts distributed throughout the members. Leaders, then, become the creative, motivational, visionary, enthusiastic, positive, and forward-looking catalysts to mobilize the people of God in mission in the world. [Van Engen 1991b, 165]

Aubrey Malphurs (1992, 20) has described leadership very simply: "A Christian leader [is] a godly person (character) who knows where he or she is going (vision) and has followers (influence)." Max De Pree (1989; 1992) has described leadership as an art that looks a lot like a jazz band. Joel Barker (1992, 163) says, "A leader is a person you will follow to a place you wouldn't go by yourself." All over the world, in church and mission as well as in society in general, people seem to agree: leadership is the key to a new future.[7]

Who?

To identify leaders, the in-ministry paradigm turns to the local congregation. Who are the natural leaders already recognized by the church for their giftedness in ministry, and in what kinds of ministries are they already participating? In some ways this question harks back to the first paradigm. There the people of God recognize the giftedness of natural leaders. The being (the character and influence) of these women and men is affirmed by the community of believers and legitimized by the recognition of those who may become their mentors. If seminaries used this as their criterion, no one would be accepted for training who had not already demonstrated a track record as a youth leader, Sunday School teacher, preacher, spiritual director, church and ministry organizer, evangelist, or missionary. Programs in ministry formation would be restricted to people who had already carried responsibility and demonstrated leadership capabilities in the church.[8] If this were the case, the motivation, character, style, orientation, and processing of those who study in our seminaries would be profoundly affected. I remember hearing David Allan Hubbard say in the early 1970s, "A seminary is only as good as its incoming students." It has taken me years to understand the depth of wisdom found in that affirmation.

Where?

The in-ministry paradigm recognizes that the place of leadership is the local congregation in mission to God's world. It holds as one of its deepest values the priesthood of all believers not only in regard to the reading and interpretation of Scripture, but equally profoundly in regard to ministry and mission. The new paradigm recognizes that the church is the body of Christ, and that the members are to exercise their gifts in the midst of the people of God. This perspective affirms the corporate nature of ministry formation, but locates it in the congregation rather than the monastery. The stress therefore is on ministry formation as a process, not a product. Programs of formation do not prepare people for ministry; rather, ministry can be enhanced by programs of formation. Thus ministry formation must take place among the people of God, not in the classroom. And ordination, rather than serving

7. See, e.g., Towns 1990, 212; Schaller 1992, ch. 4; Morris 1993, ch. 20.
8. In fact, this was precisely our requirement in the TEE program I administered in Chiapas, Mexico—and it brought us a wonderful group of persons.

as a prerequisite doorway to a position or function in the church, involves a corporate recognition by the church of giftedness in ministry.

In sum, the in-ministry paradigm views leadership as an organic and organismic event in the midst of the people of God rather than as something institutional and heavily organizational. The impact of this paradigm has been felt by the hierarchies of churches and denominations. In fact, around the world this paradigm (including TEE) has had a quite controversial relationship with the institutional structures of the churches. Many wonder if that controversy itself is a signal that this paradigm is pointing in the right direction (Van Engen 1989b).

How?

Borrowing from the apprenticeship paradigm, the in-ministry paradigm seeks to develop close personal, emotional, and spiritual relationships between those who are in the initial stages of the process of ministry formation and those who are further down the road in ministry. These mentoring relationships may involve other ordained pastors—but they may just as well involve other members of the congregation whose wisdom, character, track record in ministry in the church, and Spirit-led lives can make a contribution to those in the formation process. We might see much less clergy burnout and clergy moral failure in the future if these kinds of relationships were intentionally built into our perspectives of ministry.

Note that the in-ministry paradigm entails a redefinition of the concept of "academic" preparation. Whereas the university paradigm by and large defines "academic" in terms of knowledge of facts, the new paradigm defines academic excellence more in terms of character, wisdom, understanding of church and people, and influence in ministry and mission. (Here the latter paradigm shows similarities to the Bible College movement.)

The implications for the recognition of ministry are obvious. Clearly, congregational leaders and church structures on the local level become the primary players in recognizing those who are exercising leadership in ministry. Church leaders would also make in-ministry formation of each other and others to be one of their top priorities. This has implications for denominational polity as related to ordination as well as for the function of denominational seminaries. It seems appropriate to ask the people of God in the congregations to point out those whom they would be willing to follow, and what qualities need to be formed in these persons so that they will be accepted as leaders.

Wherefore?

Finally, the in-ministry paradigm has radically shifted the emphasis in terms of the goal of ministry. The monastic paradigm predominantly formed people to be obedient and productive members of the monastic community. The university paradigm formed people to be acceptable members of the educated upper classes, including the academy. The professional model mostly formed people for maintenance of the institutional church, servants to be likened to doctors, lawyers, and engineers. The in-ministry paradigm, on the other hand, harks back most closely to the objective of the apprentice paradigm—to shape the being of those who can lead the people of God forward in God's mission in the world. This last paradigm, then, would evaluate its effectiveness in terms of how well the leaders whom it has shaped catalyze the church for its own transformation in order to participate in God's mission in the world.

In an article entitled "Evangelicals, Liberals, and the Perils of Individualism," Robert Wuthnow (1991, 12) suggests that "privatizing one's religious views . . . has a dampening effect on the value people ascribe to caring for others. . . . [Studies have found that] people who said they feel it is important to develop their own religious beliefs independently of any church were also less likely to value caring for the needy than people who took issue with this popular form of religious individualism." These comments are echoed somewhat by Dean Hoge, Benton Johnson, and Donald Luidens in their study of the baby boomers (1994, 209). When discussing possible ways in which churches might minister to baby boomers, they suggest that

> moral authority might provide a basis for church involvement. . . . We know of some local congregations who have moved in this direction. They give foremost attention to questions about spirituality and how to live authentically in this society. In these groups, issues of social responsibility, life-style, and even political affiliation arise very soon, and they must be dealt with through participatory processes so that congregational unity and identity can be preserved. When this is successful, personal life and church life take on new meaning and vitality.[9]

If these observations are correct, then in-ministry formation must be based in the congregation, not in the classroom, and must be oriented toward mission rather than maintenance of present structures. Congregations would become the primary training centers for the ministry of God's people in church and world. And ministry in the church would be viewed as a dynamic process whereby the whole people of God will grow into the maturity of Jesus Christ, the head of the church (Eph. 4).

Now although all this may sound radical, it should not surprise us in the least. In addition to the worldwide explosion of Theological Education by Extension, a host of programs have followed the in-ministry paradigm. All

---

9. Roxburgh 1993 voices some of the same observations.

over the world, megachurches are now involved in forming their own leadership. Also showing us the way are programs like the Stephen Ministries, Bethel Bible, Greater Los Angeles Sunday School, Women's Bible Study Fellowship, Young Life, and InterVarsity. Each of these is shaped a little differently, varying somewhat from the others in structure and purpose. Yet they all share broadly the assumptions of the in-ministry paradigm.

So where does this leave us? Should my father quote Dr. Blocker, with whom he studied theology in the early 1940s? Should I keep quoting my former seminary professors? I think so—but we need to do so selectively, carefully, and with an eye to the big picture and the future. We need to draw selectively from all the paradigms of the past, for not one of them alone has prepared us for what lies ahead. Our paradigms of ministry formation must be fluid and creative, seeking to remain faithful to the basics of being God's people in God's world, yet searching for radically new ways to form new leaders for Christ's church. It is time for us to create new paradigms of in-ministry formation that will facilitate the emerging of a new cadre of leaders for the churches in the West—and we may need to learn from churches in other parts of the world in order to do so.

Conclusion

Faith, Love, and Hope:
A Theology of Mission-on-the-Way

In this time-between-the-times we live in the stressful dialectic of the kingdom of God, a kingdom that has already come in Jesus Christ, yet is still coming (Cullmann 1951). This realization becomes even more poignant when we focus on the last decade of the last century of a millennium. The already-and-not-yet character of God's rule means that the church and its mission constitute an interim sign. In the power of the Spirit the church points all humanity backward to its origins in God's creation and forward to the present and coming kingdom in Jesus Christ.[1]

Looking into the next millennium, we are filled with awe and no little fear. In *Transforming Mission* David Bosch lays out the broad features of our agenda for doing theology of mission into the foreseeable future. In the process he describes for us some of the most important "Elements of an Emerging Ecumenical Missionary Paradigm" (1991, 368–510).[2] It will take a num-

---

1. See Verkuyl 1978, 203; Glasser 1985, 12; Glasser and McGavran 1983, 30–46. The kingdom of God (and a biblical perspective of the *missio Dei* within it) has become a major point of consensus in global missiology. See, e.g., Arias and Arias 1980; Arias 1984; Van Engen 1981, 277–307; 1991b, 101–18; William Dyrness 1983; Linthicum 1991a; Blauw 1962; Küng 1968, 47–54; Ladd 1974; Bright 1953, 216, 231–38; Barth 1936–69, 4.2:655–60; Ridderbos 1962; Vicedom 1965; Pannenberg 1969; Padilla 1975; 1985; Costas 1979, 5–8; 1989; Senior and Stuhlmueller 1983, 141–60; Dempster, Klaus, and Petersen 1991, 1–58; Castro 1985, 38–88; World Council of Churches 1980; George Peters 1981, 37–47; Pentecost 1982; Pomerville 1985; Gnanakan 1989; Wagner 1987, 35–55, 96–112; Van Rheenen 1983, 1–20; and Abraham 1989.

David Bosch (1980, 75–83, 239–48; 1991, 368–93) has provided an excellent overview and critique of the *missio Dei* concept, especially as it was misused and unbiblically reshaped in the missiology of the World Council of Churches from 1965 to 1980. See, among others, Goodall 1953, 195–97; Scherer 1987, 126–34; Newbigin 1977, 63–68; 1978, chs. 4, 8, and 9; Andersen 1961; Bassham 1979, 33–40, 67–71, 168–69; and Verkuyl 1978, 2–4, 197–204.

2. These elements include the church-with-others, *missio Dei*, mediating salvation, the quest for justice, evangelism, contextualization, liberation, inculturation, common witness, ministry by the whole people of God, witness to people of other living faiths, theology, and action in hope.

ber of years and a host of conversations to find a way to deal with, and cohesively integrate, the many diverse elements Bosch presents. Although we reason like children and "see through a glass, darkly" (1 Cor. 13:11–12 KJV), we can at least look toward the horizon, and search for a road map of what may lie ahead. At the risk of being simplistic, partial, and too general, I would offer the following thesis: Going into the next millennium we need a trinitarian theology of mission that

> emanates from a deeply personal, biblical, and corporate *faith* in Jesus Christ (the King);
>
> is lived out in the body of Christ as an ecumenical fellowship of *love* (the central locus of Christ's reign);
>
> and offers *hope* for the total transformation of God's world (as a sign of the present inbreaking of the coming kingdom of God).

In offering this thesis, I have borrowed an organizing framework from the apostle Paul. As if it were a kind of signature, Paul salted his letters with references to a significant triad of missiological ideas: faith, hope, and love. Mixing their order, and interweaving them with other contextual agendas, Paul gives us a glimpse of what might be called the *habitus*[3] or integrating idea of his mission theology.[4] In what follows, the order of faith, love, and hope gives a sense of movement on the road to God's future.

Faith: The Holy Spirit Motivates the Church's Participation in God's Mission

Roland Allen (1962b) and Harry Boer (1961), among others, emphasize that the coming of the Holy Spirit at Pentecost brought a radically new and deeply personal relationship with Jesus Christ that is essential to mission. The traditional Pentecostal movement since the beginning of the twentieth century (and the Wesleyans before that), the charismatic movement of the last thirty years, and the Orthodox in their participation in the World Council of Churches have continually emphasized the role of the Holy Spirit, personal faith, and deep spirituality as foundational for Christian mission. In this vein, there is substantial agreement between, say, Section I of the *San Antonio Report* (World Council of Churches 1990), the *Manila Manifesto* (1989), and *Evangelii nuntiandi* and *Redemptoris missio*. This being the case, we will

---

3. See Van Engen 1987, 524–25; Bosch 1991, 489.
4. See, e.g., Rom. 5:1–5; 12:9–13; 1 Cor. 13:13; Gal. 5:5–6; Eph. 1:15; Col. 1:3–6; 1 Thess. 1:3; 5:8; 2 Thess. 1:3; 2:13–17; 1 Tim. 4:9–12; 2 Tim. 1:5, 13–14; Philem. 5–6; and—contingent on how we regard its authorship—Heb. 6:9–12. David Bosch ended his *Witness to the World* with a hint of this triad: "The church owes the world faith. . . . The church owes the world hope. . . . The church owes the world love" (1980, 245–47).

make six observations that center on faith as we look toward the horizon of a new millennium.

First, in certain circles faith, defined as trust in God's revelation in Jesus Christ enscripturated in the Bible and witnessed to by the Holy Spirit, is sometimes questioned, and even at times rejected. But mission that is not based on biblical revelation, the text that declares the uniqueness of Jesus Christ and offers a new birth through the Holy Spirit, may be church expansion or colonialist extension or sectarian proselytism—but it is not God's mission (Gnanakan 1992, 195–96).

God's mission emanates from the power of the resurrection (Eph. 1) "in the power of the Spirit" (Moltmann 1977). This also means that God's mission should be tested and tried. For, as John declared, "every spirit [and every enterprise of mission] that acknowledges that Jesus Christ has come in the flesh is from God, but every spirit that does not acknowledge Jesus is not from God" (1 John 4:2–3). A theocentric pluralist perspective that disavows the uniqueness of Jesus Christ may engage in polite conversation or even compassionate cooperation—but it is not the apostolate of God's mission. For when we are involved in God's mission, then we are participating in Jesus' mission: "As the Father has sent me, I am sending you" (John 20:21) (Glasser 1976, 3). Jesus calls us to be ambassadors entreating the world to be reconciled to God; such reconciliation is impossible apart from personal and corporate faith in Jesus Christ (2 Cor. 5).

Secondly, mission that derives from faith will take seriously the centuries of reflection by the people of God concerning what has been revealed by God in the Scriptures and how it has been understood by the community of faith since Abraham. This means that systematic and historical theology need to be given their appropriate place in filling out the meaning, scope, and implications of mission. But it also means that there can be no truly biblical development of systematic and historical theology unless they are thoroughly saturated with missional questions, intentions, and dimensions (Ray Anderson 1991).

Thirdly, mission from faith means that conversation with people of other faiths will occur at the deepest levels of shared convictions. This entails a radical differentiation between religion and culture, faith and worldview. To confuse religion and faith on the one hand with culture and worldview on the other too often means that once one affirms cultural relativity, one must immediately take the next step and accept religious pluralism. Such a confusion is quite evident in the writings of Wilfred Cantwell Smith, Karl Rahner, John Hick, John Cobb, Paul Knitter, and Wesley Ariarajah. One of the future tasks of theology of mission will be to distinguish these two aspects of human experience more clearly (Van Engen 1991a, 189–90).

Further, it will also be important to distinguish between the Holy Spirit (as a unique part of the Triune God) and the spirits (be these pantheistic, animistic, spiritist, New Age, or materialist). The lack of such a distinction was part of the issue that arose at the Seventh Assembly of the World Council of Churches (Canberra, 1991). Making the distinction would also help us differentiate the Holy Spirit from human spirituality—a crucial issue related to the difference between God's mission and our own expansionist agendas.

Fourthly, mission from faith will mean a continued search for ways in which our faith can become a public faith based on the facts of revelation. Especially in the West, this will involve wrestling with the straitjacket of the Enlightenment, which has forced the concept of faith into a privatist mold of individual taste, as Lesslie Newbigin (1986, 1989a) has so aptly demonstrated.[5] Missionary faith inevitably, rightly, and powerfully must be a public faith interested in the inner spiritual conversion of the person as part of a larger social, economic, political, and global reality. Each person's conversion on the microscale has implications for the transformation of society on the macroscale, and vice versa. No longer can we maintain a dichotomy between the two. Mission theology into the next millennium must find a way to speak to both as part of the same reality. This means that missiology must find a way to integrate spirituality, psychology, anthropology, and sociology in a wholistic understanding that more closely approximates reality.

Fifthly, mission from faith will mean we are deeply concerned about 4.5 billion people and thousands of unreached people groups who have not yet experienced the transformation of the Spirit through faith in Jesus Christ. Our hearts will ache for them (Rom. 9:1–3), we will consider ourselves their debtors (Rom. 1:14), and we will yearn deeply to see them touched by the Holy Spirit and converted to Jesus Christ (Van Engen 1981). This is a mission theology that cannot stop short of committed plans and action, a mission theology that understands that it exists for the sake of those who have not yet become part of the people of God. "Missiology may never become a substitute for action and participation. . . . If study does not lead to participation, whether at home or abroad, missiology has lost her humble calling" (Verkuyl 1978, 6).[6]

Lastly, not only will mission from faith through the Holy Spirit use the gifts of the Spirit for ministry in the world, it will occur when the fruits of the Spirit emanate through the lives of the people of God (Gal. 5:22–26). One

5. The October 1991 issue of *Missiology* (19.4) is an excellent introduction to some of these issues.

6. Some people seem to be using the year 2000 as an instrument of promoting urgency, making rather frantic claims that the world must be converted by 2000. I wonder if this perspective allows one to trust in faith that the God of history may have plans for the human race beyond the year 2000. To affirm that all people must be converted by 2000 goes far beyond the limits of the watchword of Edinburgh 1910—"the evangelization of the world in this generation." John R. Mott and J. H. Oldham never intended the phrase to mean that all people would become Christians in their generation. Christ wills that none should perish. But Scripture also takes account of the fall and recognizes that "all we like sheep have gone astray" (Isa. 53:6 KJV). Many will choose not to respond to God's invitation.

would wish that down through the history of mission the motivations, means, and goals of mission had been more thoroughly washed with love, joy, peace, patience, kindness, goodness, faithfulness, gentleness, and self-control. For the church to be believable, it will need to be conscious of Christ's lordship in the midst of God's people and to conduct its mission as an expression of the fruit of the Spirit.

Love: Jesus Christ Activates His Body's Participation in God's Mission

"All [people] will know that you are my disciples if you love one another" (John 13:35). Jesus calls for *agapē* love as the supreme quality of the fellowship of missionary disciples. As never before, the church of Jesus Christ must discover what it means to be a fellowship of love—especially now that the church circles the globe, and its center of gravity has shifted from North and West to South and East. Never before in the history of humanity has the Christian faith been adhered to by people of so many cultures. Today we can empirically observe what we implicitly knew: the gospel is infinitely "translatable" into all human cultures (Sanneh 1989). The theological implications of this fact are staggering. We will highlight a few.

In the first place, a multicultural world church calls for a new paradigm that more closely relates church, unity, and mission. When we say "church," for example, we need to carefully balance the local and the universal, as the Orthodox tradition so often reminds us. No longer can we mean only the older denominations with roots in Western Europe, nor even their daughter churches in Africa, Asia, and Latin America, as in the phrase "World Council of Churches." New religious movements in Asia, indigenous independent churches in Africa, new ecclesial groups in Latin America, new denominations all over the world, metachurches of hundreds of thousands that are denominations in their own right—all these have developed since the 1960s, and they have given a whole new meaning to the word *church* (Walls 1976).

We need a new paradigm of ecumenicity.[7] Mission in love means first that we learn to love, listen to, understand, and be corrected by one another in the Christian church (Van Engen 1990).[8] This involves more than tolerance as the highest value, and more than the celebration of total diversity with little commonality. Mission in love is also deeper than *Learning about Theology from the Third World* (William Dyrness 1990), although it clearly begins with such learning. René Padilla (1992, 381–82) has said it well:

7. For an excellent starting point for discussion see *International Review of Mission* 81, no. 323 (July 1992); see also Saayman 1990; Bosch 1991, 457–67.
8. See also *Mission and Evangelism* 1983, 9.

From the perspective of wholistic mission, there is no place for the polarization between an ecumenical outlook and an evangelical one. To be an ecumenical Christian is to be a Christian who conceives of the whole oikoumene [the inhabited world] as the place of God's transforming action. . . . To be an evangelical Christian is to be a Christian who conceives of the gospel as good news of the love of God in Jesus Christ, the living Word witnessed to by the Bible, the written Word of God. It is to confess and to live out the gospel of Jesus Christ as Lord of the whole of life in the power of the Holy Spirit. It is to work together in the proclamation of the gospel to all the peoples of the earth . . . and in the formation of local Christian congregations that nurture and share the faith.

Mission in love will hold tightly to the truth of the gospel as revealed in the Scriptures, and hold loosely to the provincial agendas of one's own particular Christian tradition, be that evangelical, ecumenical, Roman Catholic, Orthodox, Pentecostal, or charismatic (Bryant Myers 1992).

Secondly, mission in love will affect the way we do theology on a global, multi-worldview scale into the next millennium. The basis on which we do theology of mission, the data we incorporate, the methodologies we use, the people we listen to, and the issues we address will probably undergo considerable change. World conferences, their pronouncements, and the studies and papers emanating from such conferences will probably become less important for theology of mission. Instead, we will need to listen carefully to the people of God in local contexts, and then strive to find ways in which local theologizing may impact the world church, and vice versa.

If the church is the loving body of Christ, a community of faith and love that exists for and in mission to the world, then neither local theologies nor a monolithic supercultural theology is viable for a theology of mission that goes "Beyond Anti-Colonialism to Globalism" (Hiebert 1991, 263). Rather, we must find ways to affirm *both* the local and the universal (Hendrikus Berkhof 1985, 71–73). Following Augustine (as well as the Vincentian canon), we must consider truth to lie in "what has everywhere, always, by all been believed" (Van Engen 1981, 200–211). As William Dyrness (1990, 13) rightly observes:

If it is true that theology that matters will be a theology of the majority of Christians, then "theology in the Third World is now the only theology worth caring about" [Walls 1976, 182]. If theology is to be rooted in the actual lives of Christians today, increasingly it will have to be from the poor to the poor, in Africa, Latin America, and Asia. And theology done in the West, if it is not to become increasingly provincial, [Walls] notes, will have to be done in dialogue with the theological leaders in the Third World.

If this way of theologizing were given its place in the world church, more weight might need to be ascribed to the theological principle articulated, for example, by Gamaliel in Acts 5:33–39. This principle calls for all new theological ideas to be tested by the people of God. Over time (sometimes centuries) they will determine whether an idea should ultimately be accepted or rejected by the church.

A third implication of mission in love has to do with nuancing our theology of the kingdom of God to include the strong covenantal perspectives found in Scripture. Kingdom thinking tends to support concepts of hierarchy and order. Covenant, on the other hand, tends to empower the weak and strengthen them through new relationships. The biblical idea of covenant is impossible without the broader concept of the reign of God in Jesus Christ. But we may discover that our perspective of the kingdom of God is best worked out through covenantal relationships that pick up the feminine images of God's care: giving birth, embracing, loving, self-giving, providing, and protecting.

Thus in developing a biblical hermeneutic of the church's participation in God's mission a covenant/kingdom mission theology would take seriously the situation of refugees, women, the poor, the marginalized, the weak, and the foolish. What is needed is a missiological theology that arises from and speaks to the entire community (Hauerwas and Willimon 1991; Motte 1991). This is the mission wisdom conveyed in the stories of Hagar, Ruth, Esther, Daniel, the widow of Zarephath (Luke 4:25–26), and the Canaanite woman (Matt. 15:21–28). This is mission from weakness and foolishness (1 Cor. 1:18–31). The third millennium may bring us back to a situation reminiscent of the early church, a mission necessarily from weakness, foolishness, and poverty. This would entail a radical paradigm shift in mission theology. This shift may not be optional. The drastic ecological, economic, political, social, religious, and demographic changes happening on our small globe are presenting us with a new reality that may well call for a new paradigm of theology of mission.

Hope: God's Mission Is to Create a New Heaven and a New Earth

First Peter places our evangelistic confession in the context of a missional encounter of church and world, and hope is the central motif: "But in your hearts set apart Christ as Lord. Always be prepared to give an answer to everyone who asks you to give the reason for the hope that you have. But do this with gentleness and respect" (3:15). Hope is possibly the most explosive concept that missiology has to offer today, a fact Oscar Cullmann recognized already in 1961: "The genuine primitive Christian hope does not paralyze Christian action in the world. On the contrary, the proclamation of the Christian Gospel in the missionary enterprise is a characteristic form of such action, since it expresses the belief that 'missions' are an essential element in the eschatological divine plan of salvation. The missionary work of the Church is the eschatological foretaste of the Kingdom of God, and the Biblical hope of the 'end' constitutes the keenest incentive to action" (pp. 42–43).

Today we are a long way from the inordinate optimism of a hundred years ago regarding Western civilization, technology, and cultural Protestantism. These high hopes proved themselves to be empty and misguided, precisely because they were centered on faith in technology and civilization rather than on Jesus Christ. But such a recognition should not blind us to the influence that hope and hopelessness can have on the way people participate in God's mission. For example, during the exile the Israelites seem to have wavered between hopelessness and hope—and the difference entailed radically distinct hermeneutics of God's mission and their part in it. On the one hand, some were prone to moan, "How can we sing the songs of the LORD while in a foreign land?" (Ps. 137:4). But others followed the lead of Daniel and Esther. Even the weeping prophet Jeremiah advocated a hope-filled approach: "Build houses and live in them; plant gardens and eat their produce. Take wives and have sons and daughters; . . . multiply there, and do not decrease. But seek the welfare of the city where I have sent you into exile, and pray to the LORD on its behalf, for in its welfare you will find your welfare" (Jer. 29:5-7 RSV). Here is a perspective that offers, precisely in its hopefulness, the possibility of reconciliation in a deeply biblical sense (Schreiter 1992). It represents a mission paradigm that Sunday Aigbe (1991) of Nigeria has called the "prophetic mandate."

The last couple of years have convinced me that hope is probably the most important single concept that the church of Jesus Christ has to offer the world of the next millennium. There was a particular period of about twenty-six days when for the first time in my life I thought we might actually live in a world of peace. The Berlin Wall was coming down, Eastern Europe was changing, negotiations were going on in the Middle East, Latin America was beginning to find its way politically and economically, South Africa was beginning its tortuous process of change, other African nations were beginning to find new paths, Asia was exploding economically and technologically, and China was on the move to new things. But the hiatus was short-lived.

Today as I sit and write these lines I am reminded of cities in which I have experienced the most terrible tragedy of all: the nearly total loss of hope. Be it São Paulo, Sarajevo, or Mexico City, Kuwait City after the war, Los Angeles after the riots, or Miami after the hurricane—what I keep hearing is an almost complete loss of hope. Especially in Latin America, the demise of Marxism as a viable approach, along with the failure of democratization to offer anything new for the welfare of the poor masses, has brought a spirit of hopeless resignation that deeply concerns me. When I was a child growing up in southern Mexico, there was always a degree of optimism. Tomorrow, next week, the next governor, the next president, more education, and better organization would eventually change things. That hope seems to have died.

A missiology of hope[9] is central to Paul's missiological praxis.[10] This hope is neither breezy escapism, nor empty optimism, nor blind conformism, nor unrealistic utopianism, all of which can be found in the missiologies of this century. Rather, Paul's missiology of hope is based on at least three substantive components.

First, a missiology of hope means that Christians care, and care so deeply that they will risk hoping for the new. They dare hope because they know that in Christ's kingdom God's grace through faith brings about a radical and total transformation. "Therefore, if anyone is in Christ, he is a new creation; the old has gone, the new has come!" (2 Cor. 5:17).

Secondly, a missiology of hope means that Christians dare to believe that together they can change the world (David Barrett 1983, 151). This is at the heart of mission. But we must remember that God's kingdom is "not yet" as well as "already." We in the United States believed we could change the world on our own. We followed Johannes Hoekendijk in his pessimism about the church, and thought we could achieve anything through Lyndon Johnson's Great Society, through the Peace Corps, and through computer technology. As a result, many of us today are indelibly marked with pessimism and cynicism. We discovered that we could not change even the cities in which we created Christian communes, much less the world. We missed the mark by failing to realize our own sinfulness and the true extent of the fall, by failing to grasp that we can neither bring in the kingdom, nor create the utopias envisioned by the ideologues. Rather, as we participate in God's mission, God's reign comes when people accept Jesus as Lord and in obedience begin to see God's will being done "on earth as it is in heaven" (Matt. 6:10). This involves structural and societal change as well as personal. It involves the whole person, not only the spiritual aspects. It involves all of life, not only the ecclesiastical facet.[11]

Thirdly, a missiology of hope means that Christians profess certainty of that which they do not see (Heb. 11:1). It means participating with Jesus in being a "light to the Gentiles" (Acts 13:47–49; Luke 2:32; 4:18–21). Living in the time between the ascension and the parousia, we recognize the pres-

9. Although Jürgen Moltmann and others developed a theology of hope in the 1960s, the concept did not result in new missiological directions. A missiology of hope is at once individual, social, and structural; and it derives from a deep sense of identity, purpose, and the *missio Dei*. For further exploration see Bosch 1980, 234–38.

10. See, e.g., Eph. 1:18; 2:12; Col. 1.5, 23, 27; 1 Thess. 1:3; 2:19; 4:13; 2 Thess. 2:16; cf. Prov. 13:12; 19:18; Heb. 6:18; 10:23; 1 Pet. 1:3; 3:15.

11. The papers and declaration of the Consultation on the Church in Response to Human Need (Wheaton, 1983) are a good place to begin one's reflection on these issues (Samuel and Sugden 1987).

ence of God's kingdom, live out its ethics (Matt. 5–7), and call people and structures to be reconciled with creation, with themselves, with each other, and with God (2 Cor. 5:18–21). This missiology of hope is deeply and creatively transformational, for it seeks to be a sign of the present and coming kingdom of God. Through it we recognize our profound commitment to radical transformation when we pray, "Your kingdom come" (Matt. 6:10).

Yet at the same time we will remember that the kingdom is present and coming only as the King comes. Our mission does not hasten Christ's coming, nor does it create the kingdom. Rather, the kingdom of God defines our mission (Costas 1979, 8–9), for only Jesus the King can bring the kingdom. Our mission, like that of Jesus, is to "preach the good news of the kingdom of God to the other towns also, because that is why [we have been] sent" (Luke 4:43; Acts 13:46–49). "Even so, come, Lord Jesus" (Rev. 22:20 KJV).

In this time-between-the-times, our participation in God's mission into the next millennium awaits us like an adventure, a journey in the midst of, and moving toward, the present and coming reign of God, a running forward to discover what we already know—Jesus Christ is King!

Works Cited

Aagaard, Johannes. 1974. "Mission after Uppsala 1968." In *Mission Trends No. 1,* edited by Gerald H. Anderson and Thomas F. Stransky, 13–21. Grand Rapids: Eerdmans and New York: Paulist.

Abraham, William. 1989. *The Logic of Evangelism.* Grand Rapids: Eerdmans.

Accornero, Christine, and Juanita Evans Leonard. 1995. "Narrative Theology: Missiological Reflection from the Perspective of Women's Stories and Organizational Culture." Doctoral tutorial paper, Fuller Theological Seminary School of World Mission, Pasadena.

Aigbe, Sunday. 1991. "Cultural Mandate, Evangelistic Mandate, Prophetic Mandate: Of These Three the Greatest Is. . . ." *Missiology* 19.1 (January): 31–43.

Aldrich, Joseph C. 1981. *Life-Style Evangelism: Crossing Traditional Boundaries to Reach the Unbelieving World.* Portland, Oreg.: Multnomah.

Aldwinckle, Russell. 1982. *Jesus: A Savior or the Savior?* Macon, Ga.: Mercer University Press.

Allen, Roland. 1962a. *Missionary Methods: St. Paul's or Ours?* Grand Rapids: Eerdmans.

———. 1962b. *The Spontaneous Expansion of the Church.* Grand Rapids: Eerdmans.

Allison, Norman. 1985. "AEPM News and Views: A Report on the National Meeting." *Evangelical Missions Quarterly* 21.1 (January): 66–68.

Alter, Robert. 1981. *The Art of Biblical Narrative.* New York: Basic Books.

Anastasios of Androussa. 1989. "Orthodox Mission—Past, Present, Future." In *Your Will Be Done—Orthodoxy in Mission,* edited by George Lemopoulos, 79–81, 89. Geneva: World Council of Churches.

Andersen, Wilhelm. 1961. "Further toward a Theology of Mission." In *The Theology of the Christian Mission,* edited by Gerald H. Anderson, 300–313. New York: McGraw-Hill.

Anderson, Elijah. 1990. *Streetwise: Race, Class, and Change in an Urban Community.* Chicago: University of Chicago Press.

Anderson, Gerald H. 1988. "American Protestants in Pursuit of Mission: 1886–1986." *International Bulletin of Missionary Research* 12.3 (July): 98–118.

———. 1989. "The Truth of Christian Uniqueness." *International Bulletin of Missionary Research* 13.2 (April): 49.

———. 1990. "Christian Mission and Religious Pluralism: A Selected Bibliography of 175 Books in English, 1970–1990." *International Bulletin of Missionary Research* 14.4 (October): 172–76.

———. 1993. "Theology of Religions and Missiology: A Time of Testing." In *The Good News of the Kingdom,* edited by Charles Van Engen et al., 200–208. Maryknoll, N.Y.: Orbis.

Anderson, Gerald H., ed. 1961. *The Theology of the Christian Mission.* New York: McGraw-Hill.

———. 1967. *Christian Mission in Theological Perspective.* Nashville: Abingdon.

Anderson, Gerald H., and Thomas F. Stransky, eds. 1974. *Mission Trends No. 1: Crucial Issues in Mission Today.* Grand Rapids: Eerdmans and New York: Paulist.

———. 1975. *Mission Trends No. 2: Evangelization*. Grand Rapids: Eerdmans and New York: Paulist.

———. 1976. *Mission Trends No. 3: Third World Theologies*. Grand Rapids: Eerdmans and New York: Paulist.

———. 1981a. *Mission Trends No. 5: Faith Meets Faith*. Grand Rapids: Eerdmans and New York: Paulist.

———. 1981b. *Christ's Lordship and Religious Pluralism*. Maryknoll, N.Y.: Orbis.

Anderson, Norman, ed. 1950. *The World Religions*. Grand Rapids: Eerdmans.

Anderson, Ray S. 1991. *The Praxis of Pentecost: Revisioning the Church's Life and Mission*. Pasadena: Fuller Theological Seminary. (Republished in 1993 as *Ministry on the Fireline*. Downers Grove, Ill.: InterVarsity.)

Apel, Karl-Otto. 1989. "Perspectives for a General Hermeneutic Theory." In *The Hermeneutics Reader*, edited by Kurt Mueller-Vollmer, 320–45. New York: Continuum.

Archer, Gleason. 1979. "Contextualization: Some Implications from Life and Witness in the Old Testament." In *New Horizons in World Mission: Evangelicals and the Christian Mission in the 1980s*, edited by David J. Hesselgrave, 199–216. Grand Rapids: Baker.

Ariarajah, S. Wesley. 1990. "Religious Pluralism and Its Challenge to Christian Theology." *Perspectives* 5.2 (February): 6–9.

Arias, Esther, and Mortimer Arias. 1980. *The Cry of My People: Out of Captivity in Latin America*. New York: Friendship.

Arias, Mortimer. 1984. *Announcing the Reign of God: Evangelization and the Subversive Memory of Jesus*. Philadelphia: Fortress.

Armerding, Carl, ed. 1977. *Evangelicals and Liberation*. Nutley, N.J.: Presbyterian and Reformed.

Armstrong, Richard S. 1984. *The Pastor as Evangelist*. Philadelphia: Westminster.

Athyal, Saphir. 1976. "The Uniqueness and Universality of Christ." In *The New Face of Evangelicalism*, edited by C. René Padilla, 51–66. Downers Grove, Ill.: InterVarsity.

Attalah, Ramez. 1975. "Some Trends in the Roman Catholic Church Today." In *Let the Earth Hear His Voice*, edited by J. D. Douglas, 872–82. Minneapolis: World Wide.

Augsburger, David W. 1972. *Communicating Good News*. Scottdale, Pa.: Herald.

Bakke, Raymond. 1987. *The Urban Christian: Effective Ministry in Today's Urban World*. Downers Grove, Ill.: InterVarsity.

Bakker, R., R. Fernhout, J. D. Gort, and A. Wessels, eds. 1985. *Religies in nieuw perspectief*. Kampen: J. H. Kok.

Banks, Robert, and Julia Banks. 1989. *The Church Comes Home: A New Base for Community and Mission*. Claremont, Calif.: Albatross.

Barbour, Ian. 1974. *Myths, Models, and Paradigms*. New York: Harper and Row.

———. 1990. *Religion in an Age of Science*. San Francisco: Harper.

Barker, Joel Arthur. 1992. *Future Edge: Discovering the New Rules of Success*. New York: William Morrow.

Barna, George. 1991. *What Americans Believe*. Ventura, Calif.: Regal.

Barr, James. 1961. *The Semantics of Biblical Language*. New York: Oxford University Press.

———. 1966. *Old and New in Interpretation: A Study of the Two Testaments*. New York: Harper and Row.

Barrett, C. K. 1955. *The Gospel according to St. John*. Philadelphia: Westminster.

Barrett, David. 1983. "Silver and Gold Have I None: Church of the Poor or Church of the Rich?" *International Bulletin of Missionary Research* 7.4 (October): 146–51.

Barrett, David, ed. 1982. *The World Christian Encyclopedia*. New York: Oxford University Press.

Barrett, Lois. 1986. *Building the House Church*. Scottdale, Pa.: Herald.

Barth, Karl. 1933. *The Epistle to the Romans*. London: Oxford University Press.

———. 1936. *The Church and the Churches*. Grand Rapids: Eerdmans.

———. 1936–69. *Church Dogmatics*. 13 vols. Edinburgh: T. and T. Clark.

————. 1961. "An Exegetical Study of Matthew 28:16–20." In *The Theology of the Christian Mission*, edited by Gerald H. Anderson, 55–71. New York: McGraw-Hill.

————. 1962. *Theology and Church: Shorter Writings, 1920–1928*. New York: Harper and Row.

————. 1980. "The Revelation of God as the Abolition of Religion." In *Christianity and Other Religions*, edited by John Hick and Brian Hebblethwaite, 32–51. Philadelphia: Fortress.

Bassham, Rodger. 1968. "Seeking a Deeper Theological Basis for Mission." *International Review of Mission* 67, no. 267 (July): 329–34.

————. 1979. *Mission Theology, 1948–1975: Years of Worldwide Creative Tension—Ecumenical, Evangelical and Roman Catholic*. South Pasadena, Calif.: William Carey Library.

Bast, Robert. 1987. "Good News" newsletter (August). New York: Reformed Church in America, General Program Council.

————. 1991a. "Evangelism Ideas and Resources" (letter).

————. 1991b. "Where a Generation Hungers." *Church Herald* 48.4 (April): 11–14.

Bauckham, Richard. 1979. "Universalism—A Historical Survey." *Themelios* 4.2 (January): 48–53.

Bausch, William J. 1984. *Storytelling, Imagination and Faith*. Mystic, Conn.: Twenty-Third.

Bavinck, Herman. 1956. *Our Reasonable Faith*. Grand Rapids: Eerdmans.

————. 1967. *Gereformeerde dogmatiek*. Vol. 4. Kampen: J. H. Kok.

Bavinck, J. H. 1977. *An Introduction to the Science of Missions*. Nutley, N.J.: Presbyterian and Reformed.

Beardsley, Frank. 1912. *A History of American Revivals*. New York: American Tract Society.

Beaver, R. Pierce, ed. 1976. *Emerging Models of Christian Mission*. Ventnor, N.J.: Overseas Ministries Study Center.

————. 1977. *American Missions in Bicentennial Perspective*. Pasadena: William Carey Library.

Bellah, Robert N., et al. 1985. *Habits of the Heart: Individualism and Commitment in American Life*. New York: Harper and Row.

Bennis, Warren. 1989. *Why Leaders Can't Lead: The Unconscious Conspiracy Continues*. San Francisco: Jossey-Bass.

Berger, Peter. 1980. *The Heretical Imperative: Contemporary Possibilities of Religious Affirmation*. Garden City, N.Y.: Doubleday.

Berger, Peter, et al. 1973. *The Homeless Mind: Modernization and Consciousness*. New York: Random House.

Berkhof, Hendrikus. 1979. *Christian Faith: An Introduction to the Study of the Faith*. Grand Rapids: Eerdmans.

————. 1985. *Introduction to the Study of Dogmatics*. Grand Rapids: Eerdmans.

————. 1988. "The Double Image of the Future." *Perspectives* 3.1 (January): 8–9.

Berkhof, Hendrikus, and Philip Potter. 1964. *Key Words of the Gospel*. London: SCM.

Berkhof, Louis. 1932. *Reformed Dogmatics*. Grand Rapids: Eerdmans.

Berkouwer, G. C. 1955. *General Revelation*. Grand Rapids: Eerdmans.

————. 1965. *The Second Vatican Council and the New Catholicism*. Grand Rapids: Eerdmans.

————. 1976. *Studies in Dogmatics*. Vol. 14, *The Church*. Grand Rapids: Eerdmans.

Berney, James E., ed. 1979. *You Can Tell the World*. Downers Grove, Ill.: InterVarsity.

Bettenson, Henry, ed. and trans. 1970. *The Later Christian Fathers*. London: Oxford University Press.

Bevans, Stephen. 1985. "Models of Contextual Theology." *Missiology* 13.2 (April): 185–202.

————. 1992. *Models of Contextual Theology*. Maryknoll, N.Y.: Orbis.

————. 1993. "The Biblical Basis of the Mission of the Church in *Redemptoris Missio*." In *The Good News of the Kingdom*, edited by Charles Van Engen et al., 37–44. Maryknoll, N.Y.: Orbis.

Beyerhaus, Peter. 1971. *Missions: Which Way? Humanization or Redemption*. Grand Rapids: Zondervan.

————. 1972. *Shaken Foundations*. Grand Rapids: Zondervan.

————. 1975a. In *Reich Gottes oder Weltgemeinschaft?* edited by W. Künneth and Peter Beyerhaus, 307–8. Bad Liebenzell.

————. 1975b. "World Evangelization and the Kingdom of God." In *Let the Earth Hear His Voice,* edited by J. D. Douglas, 283–302. Minneapolis: World Wide.

Birkey, Del. 1988. *The House Church: A Model for Renewing the Church.* Scottdale, Pa.: Herald.

Blauw, Johannes. 1962. *The Missionary Nature of the Church.* Grand Rapids: Eerdmans.

Bloesch, Donald. 1973. *The Evangelical Renaissance.* Grand Rapids: Eerdmans.

————. 1992. *A Theology of Word and Spirit: Authority and Method in Theology.* Downers Grove, Ill.: InterVarsity.

Blum, E. A. 1979. "Shall You Not Surely Die?" *Themelios* 4.2 (January): 58–61.

Bockmuhl, Klaus. 1977. "Pre-Suppositions in Contemporary Theological Debate." In *The Conciliar-Evangelical Debate: The Crucial Documents, 1964–1976,* edited by Donald McGavran, 351–59. South Pasadena, Calif.: William Carey Library.

————. 1979. *Evangelicals and Social Ethics.* Downers Grove, Ill.: InterVarsity.

Boer, Harry. 1961. *Pentecost and Missions.* Grand Rapids: Eerdmans.

Boff, Clodovis. 1987. *Theology and Praxis: Epistemological Foundations.* Maryknoll, N.Y.: Orbis.

Boff, Leonardo. 1978. *Jesus Christ Liberator: A Critical Christology for Our Time.* Maryknoll, N.Y.: Orbis.

————. 1979. *Liberating Grace.* Maryknoll, N.Y.: Orbis.

————. 1986a. *Church: Charism and Power.* New York: Crossroad.

————. 1986b. *Ecclesiogenesis: The Base Communities Reinvent the Church.* Maryknoll, N.Y.: Orbis.

Boff, Leonardo, and Clodovis Boff. 1987. *Introducing Liberation Theology.* Maryknoll, N.Y.: Orbis.

Bohr, David. 1977. *Evangelization in America.* New York: Paulist.

Bonhoeffer, Dietrich. 1963. *The Communion of Saints.* New York: Harper.

Bortnowska, Halina. 1974. "The Hermeneutical Process in Evangelism." *International Review of Mission* 63, no. 249 (January): 64–76.

Bosch, David J. 1978. "The Why and How of a True Biblical Foundation for Mission." In *Zending op weg naar de toekomst: Essays aangeboden aan Prof. Dr. J. Verkuyl,* edited by Jerald D. Gort, 33–45. Kampen: J. H. Kok.

————. 1980. *Witness to the World: The Christian Mission in Theological Perspective.* Atlanta: John Knox.

————. 1983. "An Emerging Paradigm for Mission." *Missiology* 11.4 (October): 485–510.

————. 1987. "Evangelism: Theological Currents and Cross-currents Today." *International Bulletin of Missionary Research* 11.3 (July): 98–103.

————. 1988a. "The Church in Dialogue: From Self-Delusion to Vulnerability." *Missiology* 16.2 (April): 131–47.

————. 1988b. "'Ecumenicals' and 'Evangelicals': A Growing Relationship." *Ecumenical Review* 40.3–4 (July–October): 458–72.

————. 1991. *Transforming Mission: Paradigm Shifts in Theology of Mission.* Maryknoll, N.Y.: Orbis.

————. 1993. "Reflections on Biblical Models of Mission." In *Toward the 21st Century in Christian Mission,* edited by James M. Phillips and Robert T. Coote, 175–92. Grand Rapids: Eerdmans.

Braaten, Carl. 1981. "The Uniqueness and Universality of Jesus Christ." In *Mission Trends No. 5,* edited by Gerald H. Anderson and Thomas F. Stransky, 69–92. Grand Rapids: Eerdmans and New York: Paulist.

————. 1987. "Christocentric Trinitarianism vs. Unitarian Theocentrism: A Response to Mark Heim." *Journal of Ecumenical Studies* 24.1 (Winter): 17–21.

———. 1987–88. "The Meaning of Evangelism in the Context of God's Universal Grace." *Journal of the Academy for Evangelism in Theological Education* 3:9–19.

———. 1988. Review of *The Myth of Christian Uniqueness,* edited by John Hick and Paul Knitter. *International Bulletin of Missionary Research* 12.3 (July): 136.

———. 1990. "The Triune God: The Source and Model of Christian Unity and Mission." *Missiology* 18.4 (October): 415–28.

Bradley, James E. 1993. "*Logos* Christology and Religious Pluralism: A New Evangelical Proposal." Unpublished paper, Fuller Theological Seminary, Pasadena.

Branson, Mark, and C. René Padilla, eds. 1986. *Conflict and Context: Hermeneutics in the Americas.* Grand Rapids: Eerdmans.

Breech, James. 1989. *Jesus and Postmodernism.* Minneapolis: Augsburg Fortress.

Bria, Ion. 1991. *The Sense of Ecumenical Tradition: The Ecumenical Witness and Vision of the Orthodox.* Geneva: World Council of Churches.

Bria, Ion, ed. 1980. *Martyria/Mission: The Witness of the Orthodox Churches Today.* Geneva: World Council of Churches.

Briggs, Kenneth. 1991. "Shopping for God." *Church Herald* 48.4 (April): 8–10.

Bright, John. 1953. *The Kingdom of God.* Nashville: Abingdon.

———. 1959. *A History of Israel.* Philadelphia: Westminster.

Brouwer, Arie. 1977. *Reformed Church Roots.* New York: Reformed Church in America.

Brown, Harold. 1987. "Will Everyone Be Saved?" *Pastoral Renewal* 11.11 (June): 11–16.

Brown, Robert McAfee. 1978. *Theology in a New Key: Responding to Liberation Themes.* Philadelphia: Westminster.

———. 1984. *Unexpected News: Reading the Bible with Third World Eyes.* Philadelphia: Westminster.

Brownson, William. 1988. "Hope for All." *Perspectives* 3.8 (October): 13–15.

Brueggemann, Walter. 1991. *Abiding Astonishment: Psalms, Modernity, and the Making of History.* Louisville: Westminster/John Knox.

———. 1992. *Old Testament Theology: Essays on Structure, Theme, and Text.* Minneapolis: Augsburg Fortress.

Brunner, Emil. 1949. *The Christian Doctrine of God.* Philadelphia: Westminster.

Bunting, Ian. 1992. "Training for Urban Mission in the United Kingdom." *Urban Mission* 10.2 (December): 16–27.

Bush, Frederic. 1992. "Images of Israel: The People of God in the Torah." In *Studies in Old Testament Theology,* edited by Robert L. Hubbard, Jr., et al., 99–115. Waco: Word.

Buswell, James O. 1978. "Contextualization: Theory, Tradition and Method." In *Theology and Mission,* edited by David J. Hesselgrave, 87–111. Grand Rapids: Baker.

Cairns, Earle E. 1986. *An Endless Line of Splendor: Revivals and Their Leaders from the Great Awakening to the Present.* Wheaton, Ill.: Tyndale.

Callahan, Kennon L. 1983. *Twelve Keys to an Effective Church.* New York: Harper and Row.

———. 1990. *Effective Church Leadership: Building on the Twelve Keys.* San Francisco: Harper.

Calver, Clive, et al., eds. 1984. *A Guide to Evangelism.* London: Marshalls.

Calvin, John. 1960. *Institutes of the Christian Religion.* Translated by F. L. Battles. Philadelphia: Westminster.

Carpenter, Joel A. 1984. "The Fundamentalist Leaven and the Rise of an Evangelical United Front." In *The Evangelical Tradition in America,* edited by Leonard I. Sweet, ch. 9. Macon, Ga.: Mercer University Press.

Carpenter, Joel A., and Wilbert R. Shenk, eds. 1990. *Earthen Vessels: American Evangelicals and Foreign Missions, 1880–1980.* Grand Rapids: Eerdmans.

Carroll, Jackson W., et al. 1978. *Religion in America.* San Francisco: Harper and Row.

Carson, D. A. 1984a. "A Sketch of the Factors Determining Current Hermeneutical Debate in Cross-Cultural Contexts." In *Biblical Interpretation and the Church,* edited by D. A. Carson, 11–29. Nashville: Thomas Nelson.

Carson, D. A., ed. 1984b. *Biblical Interpretation and the Church: The Problem of Contextualization.* Nashville: Thomas Nelson.

Castro, Emilio. 1967. "Conversion and Social Transformation." In *The Church amid Revolution,* edited by Harvey Cox, 90–108. New York: Association.

———. 1985. *Freedom in Mission—The Perspective of the Kingdom of God: An Ecumenical Inquiry.* Geneva: World Council of Churches.

Centore, F. F. 1991. *Being and Becoming: A Critique of Post-Modernism.* New York: Greenwood.

Cerfaux, Lucien. 1959. *The Church in the Theology of St. Paul.* New York: Herder and Herder.

Chafin, Kenneth. 1978. "Evangelism and the Local Church." In *Evangelism: The Next Ten Years,* edited by Sherwood E. Wirt, 115–23. Waco: Word.

Chapman, Colin. 1990. "The Riddle of Religions." *Christianity Today* 34.8 (May 14): 16–22.

Childs, Brevard. 1970. *Biblical Theology in Crisis.* Philadelphia: Westminster.

———. 1985. *Old Testament Theology in a Canonical Context.* Philadelphia: Fortress.

Chopp, Rebecca. 1986. *The Praxis of Suffering: An Interpretation of Liberation and Political Theologies.* Maryknoll, N.Y.: Orbis.

Claerbaut, David. 1983. *Urban Ministry.* Grand Rapids: Zondervan.

Clements, R. E. 1978. *Old Testament Theology: A Fresh Approach.* Atlanta: John Knox.

Clinton, J. Robert. 1988. *The Making of a Leader.* Colorado Springs: NavPress.

Cloete, G. D., and D. J. Smit, eds. 1984. *A Moment of Truth.* Grand Rapids: Eerdmans.

Clooney, Francis. 1989. "Christianity and World Religions." *Religious Studies Review* 15.3 (July): 198–204.

Cobb, John. 1975. *Christ in a Pluralistic Age.* Philadelphia: Westminster.

Cocoris, G. Michael. 1984. *Evangelism: A Biblical Approach.* Chicago: Moody.

Coe, Shoki. 1976. "Contextualizing Theology." In *Mission Trends No. 3,* edited by Gerald H. Anderson and Thomas F. Stransky, 19–24. Grand Rapids: Eerdmans and New York: Paulist.

Coggins, Wade T. 1980. "COWE: An Assessment of Progress and Work Left Undone." *Evangelical Missions Quarterly* 16.4 (October): 225–32.

Coleman, Robert E. 1963. *The Master Plan of Evangelism.* Westwood, N.J.: Revell.

———. 1986. "The Great Commission Life-style." In *Evangelism on the Cutting Edge,* edited by Robert E. Coleman, 127–42. Old Tappan, N.J.: Revell.

Comstock, Gary L. 1987. "Two Types of Narrative Theology." *Journal of the American Academy of Religion* 55.4 (Winter): 687–717.

Cone, James H. 1991. *Martin and Malcolm and America: A Dream or a Nightmare.* Maryknoll, N.Y.: Orbis.

Congar, Yves. 1960. *The Mystery of the Church.* Baltimore: Helicon.

Congregation for the Evangelization of Peoples and the Pontifical Council for Interreligious Dialogue. 1992. "Dialogue and Proclamation (Excerpts)." *International Bulletin of Missionary Research* 16.2 (April): 82–86.

Conn, Harvie. 1977. "Contextualization: Where Do We Begin?" In *Evangelicals and Liberation,* edited by Carl Armerding, 90–119. Nutley, N.J.: Presbyterian and Reformed.

———. 1978. "Contextualization: A New Dimension for Cross-Cultural Hermeneutic." *Evangelical Missions Quarterly* 14.1 (January): 39–46.

———. 1982. *Evangelism: Doing Justice and Preaching Grace.* Grand Rapids: Zondervan.

———. 1984. *Eternal Word and Changing Worlds: Theology, Anthropology, and Mission in Trialogue.* Grand Rapids: Zondervan.

———. 1987. *A Clarified Vision for Urban Mission.* Grand Rapids: Zondervan.

———. 1993a. "A Contextual Theology of Mission for the City." In *The Good News of the Kingdom,* edited by Charles Van Engen et al., 96–106. Maryknoll, N.Y.: Orbis.

———. 1993b. "Urban Mission." In *Toward the 21st Century in Christian Mission,* edited by James M. Phillips and Robert T. Coote, 318–37. Grand Rapids: Eerdmans.

Conn, Harvie, ed. 1990. *Practical Theology and the Ministry of the Church, 1952–1984: Essays in Honor of Edmund P. Clowney.* Phillipsburg, N.J.: Presbyterian and Reformed.

Cook, Guillermo. 1984. "The Protestant Predicament: From Base Ecclesial Community to Establishment Church—A Brazilian Case Study." *International Bulletin of Missionary Research* 8.3 (July): 98–102.

———. 1985. *The Expectation of the Poor: Latin American Base Ecclesial Communities in Protestant Perspective.* Maryknoll, N.Y.: Orbis.

———. 1987. "Grassroots Churches and Reformation in Central America." *Latin America Pastoral Issues* 14.1 (June): 5–23.

Cook, Guillermo, ed. 1994. *New Face of the Church in Latin America.* Maryknoll, N.Y.: Orbis.

Cooke, Philip. 1988. "Modernity, Postmodernity and the City." *Theory, Culture and Society* 5.2–3 (June): 475–92.

Coote, Robert T. 1982. "The Uneven Growth of Conservative Evangelical Missions." *International Bulletin of Missionary Research* 6.3 (July): 118–23.

———. 1990. "Lausanne II and World Evangelization." *International Bulletin of Missionary Research* 14.1 (January): 10–17.

Coote, Robert T., and John Stott, eds. 1980. *Down to Earth: Studies in Christianity and Culture.* Grand Rapids: Eerdmans.

Cosby, Mary. 1985. "Called and Committed: The Spirituality of Mission." *Today's Ministry* 2.3 (Spring/Summer): 1, 4.

Costas, Orlando. 1974a. *The Church and Its Mission: A Shattering Critique from the Third World.* Wheaton, Ill.: Tyndale.

———. 1974b. "Evangelism and the Gospel of Salvation." *International Review of Mission* 63, no. 249 (January): 24–37.

———. 1976. *Theology of the Crossroads in Contemporary Latin America: Missiology in Mainline Protestantism, 1969–1974.* Amsterdam: Rodopi.

———. 1979. *The Integrity of Mission: The Inner Life and Outreach of the Church.* San Francisco: Harper and Row.

———. 1982. *Christ outside the Gate: Mission beyond Christendom.* Maryknoll, N.Y.: Orbis.

———. 1985. "Dean's Column: Leadership for Holistic Church Growth." *Today's Ministry* 2.3 (Spring/Summer): 5, 8.

———. 1989. *Liberating News: A Theology of Contextual Evangelization.* Grand Rapids: Eerdmans.

Cottrell, Jack, and Stephen Burris. 1993. "The Fate of the Unreached: Implications for Frontier Missions." *International Journal of Frontier Missions* 10.2 (April): 1–6.

Covell, Ralph. 1993. "Jesus Christ and World Religions: Current Evangelical Viewpoints." In *The Good News of the Kingdom,* edited by Charles Van Engen et al., 162–80. Maryknoll, N.Y.: Orbis.

Coward, Harold. 1985. *Pluralism: Challenge to World Religions.* Maryknoll, N.Y.: Orbis.

"COWE: 200,000 by the Year 2000" (Editorial). 1980. *Christianity Today* 24.14 (August 8): 10–11.

Cox, Harvey. 1965. *The Secular City.* New York: Macmillan.

———. 1984. *Religion in the Secular City.* New York: Simon and Schuster.

Cox, Harvey, ed. 1967. *The Church amid Revolution.* New York: Association.

Cragg, Kenneth. 1986. *The Christ and the Faiths.* Philadelphia: Westminster.

Crites, Stephen. 1968. "Myth, Story, History." In *Parable, Myth and Language,* edited by Tony Stoneburner, 65–88. Cambridge: Church Society for College Work.

———. 1971. "The Narrative Quality of Experience." *Journal of the American Academy of Religion* 39.3 (September): 291–311.

Crockett, William V., and James G. Sigountos, eds. 1991. *Through No Fault of Their Own? The Fate of Those Who Have Never Heard.* Grand Rapids: Baker.

Cullmann, Oscar. 1951. *Christ and Time.* London: SCM and Philadelphia: Westminster.

———. 1961. "Eschatology and Missions in the New Testament." In *The Theology of the Christian Mission,* edited by Gerald H. Anderson, 42–54. New York: McGraw-Hill.

Culver, Robert D. 1984. *A Greater Commission: A Theology for World Missions.* Chicago: Moody.

Cupitt, Don. 1990. *Creation out of Nothing.* London: SCM and Philadelphia: Trinity Press International.

Curry, Dean, ed. 1984. *Evangelicals and the Bishops' Pastoral Letter.* Grand Rapids: Eerdmans.

Dale, Robert D., and Delos Miles. 1986. *Evangelizing the Hard-to-Reach.* Nashville: Broadman.

Daniels, Wilbur. 1987. "Equipping the People of God for Ministry." D.Min. thesis, California Graduate School of Theology, Glendale.

Danker, William, and W. J. Kang, eds. 1971. *The Future of the Christian World Mission.* Grand Rapids: Eerdmans.

Dawe, Donald, and John Carman, eds. 1978. *Christian Faith in a Religiously Plural World.* Maryknoll, N.Y.: Orbis.

Dayton, Donald W. 1976. *Discovering an Evangelical Heritage.* New York: Harper and Row.

Dayton, Edward R. 1981. "Evangelism as Development." In *Perspectives on the World Christian Movement,* edited by Ralph D. Winter and Steven C. Hawthorne, 732–34. Pasadena: William Carey Library.

Dayton, Edward R., and David Fraser. 1980. *Planning Strategies for World Evangelization.* Grand Rapids: Eerdmans.

De Groot, A. 1966. *The Bible on the Salvation of Nations.* De Pere, Wis.: St. Norbert Abbey.

De Gruchy, John W. 1978. "The Great Evangelical Reversal: South Africa Reflections." *Journal of Theology for Southern Africa* 24 (September): 45–57.

De Jong, Gerald F. 1978. *The Dutch Reformed Church in the American Colonies.* Grand Rapids: Eerdmans.

Dekker, James. 1985. "The 8th Reformed Missions Consultation: Covenant in Search of Mission." *RES Mission Bulletin* 5.1 (March): 1–12.

Dempster, Murray, Byron Klaus, and Douglas Petersen. 1991. *Called and Empowered: Global Mission in Pentecostal Perspective.* Peabody, Mass.: Hendrickson.

De Pree, Max. 1989. *Leadership Is an Art.* New York: Dell.

———. 1992. *Leadership Jazz.* New York: Doubleday.

De Ridder, Richard. 1975. *Discipling the Nations.* Grand Rapids: Baker.

Dodd, C. H. 1953. *The Interpretation of the Fourth Gospel.* Cambridge: Cambridge University Press.

Douglas, J. D. 1980. "Lausanne's Extended Shadow Gauges Evangelism Progress." *Christianity Today* 24.14 (August 8): 43–44.

Douglas, J. D., ed. 1975. *Let the Earth Hear His Voice: International Congress on World Evangelization, Lausanne, Switzerland. Official Reference Volume.* Minneapolis: World Wide.

———. 1990. *Proclaim Christ Until He Comes: Calling the Whole Church to Take the Whole Gospel to the Whole World.* Minneapolis: World Wide.

Draayer, Leon. 1989. "Preaching: An Essential Component in a Long Pastorate." D.Min. diss., Western Theological Seminary, Holland, Mich.

Drucker, Peter F. 1993. *Post-Capitalist Society.* New York: HarperCollins.

DuBose, Francis. 1978. *How Churches Grow in an Urban World.* Nashville: Broadman.

Dudley, Carl S. 1979. *Where Have All Our People Gone?* New York: Pilgrim.

Duke, David Nelson. 1986. "Theology and Biography: Simple Suggestions for a Promising Field." *Perspectives in Religious Studies* 13.2 (Summer): 137–49.

Dulles, Avery. 1974. *Models of the Church.* Garden City, N.Y.: Doubleday.

———. 1982. *A Church to Believe In: Discipleship and the Dynamics of Freedom.* New York: Crossroad.

———. 1992. *The Craft of Theology: From Symbol to System.* New York: Crossroad.

Dunn, Edmond J. 1980. *Missionary Theology: Foundations in Development*. Lanham, Md.: University Press of America.

Dunn, James D. G. 1980. *Christology in the Making: A New Testament Inquiry into the Origins of the Doctrine of the Incarnation*. Philadelphia: Westminster.

Du Plessis, J. G. 1990. "For Reasons of the Heart: A Critical Appraisal of David J. Bosch's Use of Scripture in the Foundation of Christian Mission." *Missionalia* 18.1 (April): 75–85.

Dyrness, Grace. 1992. "Urban Anthropology." Unpublished syllabus and reader, Fuller Theological Seminary, Pasadena.

Dyrness, William A. 1983. *Let the Earth Rejoice: A Biblical Theology of Holistic Mission*. Pasadena: Fuller Seminary Press.

———. 1990. *Learning about Theology from the Third World*. Grand Rapids: Zondervan.

Eichrodt, Walther. 1961, 1967. *Theology of the Old Testament*. 2 vols. Philadelphia: Westminster.

Ellis, E. Earle. 1978. *Prophecy and Hermeneutic in Early Christianity*. Grand Rapids: Eerdmans.

Ellison, Craig, ed. 1974. *The Urban Mission*. Grand Rapids: Eerdmans.

Elliston, Edgar J. 1992. *Home Grown Leaders*. Pasadena: William Carey Library.

Elliston, Edgar J., and J. Timothy Kauffman. 1993. *Developing Leaders for Urban Ministries*. New York: Peter Lang.

Ellul, Jacques. 1970a. *The Meaning of the City*. Grand Rapids: Eerdmans.

———. 1970b. *Prayer and Modern Man*. New York: Seabury.

Engel, James F. 1979. *Contemporary Christian Communications: Its Theory and Practice*. Nashville: Thomas Nelson.

Engel, James F., and Wilbert Norton. 1975. *What's Gone Wrong with the Harvest?* Grand Rapids: Zondervan.

Erickson, Millard. 1991. "The State of the Question." In *Through No Fault of Their Own?* edited by William V. Crockett and James G. Sigountos, 23–34. Grand Rapids: Baker.

Escobar, Samuel. 1970. "The Social Responsibility of the Church in Latin America." *Evangelical Missions Quarterly* (Spring): 129–52.

———. 1971. "Social Concern and World Evangelism." In John Stott et al., *Christ the Liberator*, 189–209. Downers Grove, Ill.: InterVarsity.

———. 1982. "Beyond Liberation Theology: Evangelical Missiology in Latin America." *International Bulletin of Missionary Research* 6.3 (July): 108–14.

———. 1987. *La fe evangélica y las teologías de la liberación*. El Paso: Casa Bautista.

———. 1991. "Evangelical Theology in Latin America: The Development of a Missiological Christology." *Missiology* 19.3 (July): 315–32.

Espinoza, Hector. 1975. "The Biblical Mission of the Church in Worship, Witness, and Service." In *Let the Earth Hear His Voice*, edited by J. D. Douglas, 1093–1100. Minneapolis: World Wide.

"*Evangelii nuntiandi.*" 1976. *The Pope Speaks* 21.1 (Spring): 4–51.

Evangelism in Reformed Perspective: An Evangelism Manifesto. 1977. Grand Rapids: Church Herald/Banner.

Fackre, Gabriel. 1973. *Do and Tell: Engagement Evangelism in the '70s*. Grand Rapids: Eerdmans.

———. 1975. *Word in Deed: Theological Themes in Evangelism*. Grand Rapids: Eerdmans.

———. 1983. "Narrative Theology: An Overview." *Interpretation* 37.4 (October): 340–53.

———. 1984. *The Christian Story*. Rev. ed. Grand Rapids: Eerdmans.

Featherstone, Mike. 1988. "In Pursuit of the Postmodern: An Introduction." *Theory, Culture and Society* 5:2–3 (June): 195–216.

Feinberg, John S., ed. 1988. *Continuity and Discontinuity: Perspectives on the Relationship between the Old and New Testaments*. Westchester, Ill.: Crossway.

Felder, Cain H. 1989. *Troubling Biblical Waters: Race, Class, and Family*. Maryknoll, N.Y.: Orbis.

Ferm, Deane William. 1986. *Third World Liberation Theologies: An Introductory Survey.* Maryknoll, N.Y.: Orbis.

Fernando, Ajith. 1987. *The Christian's Attitude toward World Religions.* Wheaton, Ill.: Tyndale.

Fetzer, James H. 1992a. *Philosophy of Science.* New York: Paragon House.

Fetzer, James H., ed. 1992b. *Foundations of the Philosophy of Science: Recent Developments.* New York: Paragon House.

Fife, Eric, and Arthur Glasser. 1961. *Missions in Crisis.* Chicago: InterVarsity.

Finger, Thomas N. 1987. *Christian Theology: An Eschatological Approach.* Vol. 1. Nashville: Nelson.

Fish, Roy J., and J. E. Conant. 1976. *Every Member Evangelism for Today.* New York: Harper and Row.

Flannery, A. P., ed. 1975. *Documents of Vatican II.* Grand Rapids: Eerdmans.

Flax, Jane. 1990. *Thinking Fragments: Psychoanalysis, Feminism, and Postmodernism in the Contemporary West.* Berkeley: University of California Press.

Fleming, Bruce. 1980. *The Contextualization of Theology.* Pasadena: William Carey Library.

Ford, Leighton. 1966. *The Christian Persuader.* New York: Harper.

——. 1970. *One Way to Change the World.* New York: Harper.

Forman, Charles. 1964. *The Nation and the Kingdom: Christian Mission in the New Nations.* New York: Friendship.

——. 1977. "A History of Foreign Mission Theology in America." In *American Missions in Bicentennial Perspective,* edited by R. Pierce Beaver, 69–145. Pasadena: William Carey Library.

——. 1993. "Christian Dialogues with Other Faiths." In *Toward the 21st Century in Christian Mission,* edited by James M. Phillips and Robert T. Coote, 338–47. Grand Rapids: Eerdmans.

Foster, Hal, ed. 1983. *The Anti-Aesthetic: Essays on Postmodern Culture.* Port Townsend, Wash.: Bay.

Fowler, James. 1974. *To See the Kingdom: The Theological Vision of H. Richard Niebuhr.* Nashville: Abingdon.

——. 1981. *Stages of Faith.* San Francisco: Harper and Row.

Fowler, James, and Sam Keen. 1978. *Life Maps: Conversations on the Journey of Faith.* Waco: Word.

Fowler, James, Robin Lovin, et al. 1980. *Trajectories in Faith: Five Life Stories.* Nashville: Abingdon.

Fowler, Robert Booth. 1982. *A New Engagement: Evangelical Political Thought, 1966–1976.* Grand Rapids: Eerdmans.

Frank, Douglas W. 1986. *Less than Conquerors: How Evangelicals Entered the Twentieth Century.* Grand Rapids: Eerdmans.

Frei, Hans W. 1974. *The Eclipse of Biblical Narrative: A Study in Eighteenth and Nineteenth Century Hermeneutics.* New Haven: Yale University Press.

——. 1975. *The Identity of Jesus Christ: The Hermeneutical Bases of Dogmatic Theology.* Philadelphia: Fortress.

——. 1986. "The 'Literal Reading' of Biblical Narrative in the Christian Tradition: Does It Stretch or Will It Break?" In *The Bible and the Narrative Tradition,* edited by Frank McConnell, 36–77. New York: Oxford University Press.

Frenchak, David, and Sharrel Keyes, eds. 1979. *Metro-Ministry: Ways and Means for the Urban Church.* Elgin, Ill.: David C. Cook.

Frenchak, David, and Clinton Stockwell, compilers. 1984. *Signs of the Kingdom in the Secular City.* Chicago: Covenant.

Gallup, George, Jr., and George O'Connell. 1986. *Who Do Americans Say That I Am?* Philadelphia: Westminster.

Garreau, Joel. 1991. *Edge City.* New York: Doubleday.

Gellner, Ernest. 1992. *Postmodernism, Reason and Religion*. New York: Routledge.

Getz, Gene. 1979. *The Measure of a Church*. Glendale, Calif.: Gospel Light/Regal.

Gibellini, Rosino, ed. 1979. *Frontiers of Theology in Latin America*. Maryknoll, N.Y.: Orbis.

Gilliland, Dean S. 1983. *Pauline Theology and Mission Practice*. Grand Rapids: Baker.

———. 1989a. "New Testament Contextualization: Continuity and Particularity in Paul's Theology." In *The Word among Us: Contextualizing Theology for Mission Today*, edited by Dean S. Gilliland, 52–73. Waco: Word.

Gilliland, Dean S., ed. 1989b. *The Word among Us: Contextualizing Theology for Mission Today*. Waco: Word.

Gilliland, Dean S., and Evertt W. Huffard. N.d. "The Word Became Flesh: A Reader in Contextualization." Unpublished reader, Fuller Theological Seminary, Pasadena.

Glasser, Arthur F. 1971. "The Evangelicals: World Outreach." In *The Future of the Christian World Mission*, edited by William Danker and W. J. Kang, 98–113. Grand Rapids: Eerdmans.

———. 1976. "The Missionary Task: An Introduction." In *Crucial Dimensions in World Evangelization*, edited by Arthur F. Glasser et al., 3–10. Pasadena: William Carey Library.

———. 1977. "Bangkok: An Evangelical Evaluation." In *The Conciliar-Evangelical Debate: The Crucial Documents, 1964–1976*, edited by Donald A. McGavran, 297–305. South Pasadena, Calif.: William Carey Library.

———. 1979a. "Missiological Events." *Missiology* 7.2 (April): 233–45.

———. 1979b. "Help from an Unexpected Quarter or, the Old Testament and Contextualization." *Missiology* 7.4 (October): 401–10.

———. 1980. "Liberation Is In, the Unreached Out in Melbourne's View of the Kingdom." *Christianity Today* 24.12 (June 27): 48–50.

———. 1985. "The Evolution of Evangelical Mission Theology since World War II." *International Bulletin of Missionary Research* 9.1 (January): 9–13.

———. 1989. "Mission in the 1990s: Two Views." *International Bulletin of Missionary Research* 13.1 (January): 2–8.

———. 1992. "Kingdom and Mission: A Biblical Study of the Kingdom of God and the World Mission of His People." Unpublished syllabus, Fuller Theological Seminary, Pasadena.

Glasser, Arthur F., and Donald A. McGavran. 1983. *Contemporary Theologies of Mission*. Grand Rapids: Baker.

Glover, Robert. 1946. *The Bible Basis of Missions*. Los Angeles: Bible House of Los Angeles.

Gmelch, George, and Walter P. Zenner. 1988. *Urban Life: Readings in Urban Anthropology*. Prospect Heights, Ill.: Waveland.

Gnanakan, Ken R. 1989. *Kingdom Concerns: A Biblical Exploration towards a Theology of Mission*. Bangalore: Theological Book Trust.

———. 1992. *The Pluralist Predicament*. Bangalore: Theological Book Trust.

Goldberg, Michael. 1981. *Theology and Narrative: A Critical Introduction*. Nashville: Abingdon.

Goodall, Norman, ed. 1953. *Missions under the Cross*. London: Edinburgh House and New York: Friendship.

Good News People Training Manual. 1976. New York: Reformed Church in America, General Program Council.

Gort, Jerald D. 1979. "The Contours of the Reformed Understanding of Christian Mission." *Mission Focus* 7.3 (September): 37–41.

Gort, Jerald D., ed. 1978. *Zending op weg naar de toekomst: Essays aangeboden aan Prof. Dr. J. Verkuyl*. Kampen: J. H. Kok.

Gort, Jerald D., et al., eds. 1992. *On Sharing Religious Experience: Possibilities of Interfaith Mutuality*. Grand Rapids: Eerdmans.

Gottwald, Norman. 1959. *A Light to the Nations: An Introduction to the Old Testament*. New York: Harper and Row.

———. 1979. *The Tribes of Yahweh: A Sociology of the Religion of Liberated Israel, 1250–1050 B.C.* Maryknoll, N.Y.: Orbis.

———. 1987. "Social Matrix and Canonical Shape." In *The Best in Theology,* edited by J. I. Packer, 1:59–73. Carol Stream, Ill.: Christianity Today.

Grabowski, Stanislaus. 1957. *The Church: An Introduction to the Theology of St. Augustine.* St. Louis: Herder.

Graham, Billy. 1980. "An Agenda for the 1980s." *Christianity Today* 24.1 (January 4): 23–27.

Graham Center, Billy. 1979. *An Evangelical Agenda: 1984 and Beyond.* Pasadena: William Carey Library.

Graham, W. Fred. 1980. "Declining Church Membership: Can Anything Be Done?" *Reformed Journal* 30.1 (January): 7–13.

Gration, John. 1985. "Key Issues in Missiology Today." *Evangelical Review of Theology* 9.3 (July): 244–50.

Grau, José. 1975. "The Kingdom of God among the Kingdoms of Earth." In *Let the Earth Hear His Voice,* edited by J. D. Douglas, 1083–90. Minneapolis: World Wide.

Green, Bryan. 1951. *The Practice of Evangelism.* New York: Scribner.

Green, Michael. 1970. *Evangelism in the Early Church.* Grand Rapids: Eerdmans.

———. 1977a. "Jesus in the New Testament." In *The Truth of God Incarnate,* edited by Michael Green, 18–50. Grand Rapids: Eerdmans.

Green, Michael, ed. 1977b. *The Truth of God Incarnate.* Grand Rapids: Eerdmans.

Greenway, Roger S. 1973. *Calling Our Cities to Christ.* Nutley, N.J.: Presbyterian and Reformed.

———. 1978. *Apostles to the City.* Grand Rapids: Baker.

———. 1992. "Biblical Perspectives on the City." *Reformed Ecumenical Council Mission Bulletin* 12.3:3–13.

Greenway, Roger S., ed. 1976. *Guidelines for Urban Church Planting.* Grand Rapids: Baker.

———. 1979. *Discipling the City.* Grand Rapids: Baker.

Greenway, Roger S., and Timothy M. Monsma. 1989. *Cities: Missions' New Frontier.* Grand Rapids: Baker.

Grene, Marjorie, ed. 1969. *Knowing and Being: Essays by Michael Polanyi.* Chicago: University of Chicago Press.

Grenz, Stanley J. 1993. *Revisioning Evangelical Theology: A Fresh Agenda for the 21st Century.* Downers Grove, Ill.: InterVarsity.

———. 1994. *Theology for the Community of God.* Nashville: Broadman and Holman.

Griffiths, Michael. 1975. *God's Forgetful Pilgrims: Recalling the Church to Its Reason for Being.* Grand Rapids: Eerdmans.

———. 1980. *The Confusion of the Church and the World.* Chicago: InterVarsity.

Grigg, Viv. 1984. *Companion to the Poor.* Sutherland, Australia: Albatross.

———. 1992. *Cry of the Urban Poor.* Monrovia, Calif.: MARC.

Grimes, Ronald L. 1986. "Of Words the Speakers, of Deeds the Doers." *Journal of Religion* 66.1 (January): 1–17.

Groome, Thomas. 1991. *Sharing Faith: A Comprehensive Approach to Religious Education and Pastoral Ministry.* San Francisco: Harper.

Grounds, Vernon C. 1969. *Evangelicalism and Social Responsibility.* Scottdale, Pa.: Herald.

Guder, Darrell L. 1985. *Be My Witnesses.* Grand Rapids: Eerdmans.

Guelich, Robert A. 1989. "What Is the Gospel?" Inaugural lecture as professor of New Testament, Fuller Theological Seminary, Pasadena.

Gulick, John. 1989. *The Humanity of Cities: An Introduction to Urban Societies.* Granby, Mo.: Bergin and Garvey.

Gundry, Robert H. 1994. "Diversity and Multiculturalism in New Testament Christology." Unpublished paper, Westmont College, Santa Barbara.

Gunn, David M. 1987. "New Directions in the Study of Biblical Hebrew Narrative." *Journal for the Study of the Old Testament* 39 (October): 65–75.

Gustafson, James M. 1988. *Varieties of Moral Discourse: Prophetic, Narrative, Ethical, and Policy.* Grand Rapids: Calvin College and Seminary.

Gutiérrez, Gustavo. 1974. *A Theology of Liberation.* Maryknoll, N.Y.: Orbis.

———. 1984a. *The Power of the Poor in History.* Maryknoll, N.Y.: Orbis.

———. 1984b. *We Drink from Our Own Wells.* Maryknoll, N.Y.: Orbis.

Habermas, Jürgen. 1983. "Modernity: An Incomplete Project." In *The Anti-Aesthetic,* edited by Hal Foster, 3–15. Port Townsend, Wash.: Bay.

———. 1987. *The Philosophical Discourse of Modernity.* Cambridge, Mass.: MIT Press.

Hadaway, C. Kirk, et al. 1987. *Home Cell Groups and House Churches.* Nashville: Broadman.

Haight, Roger. 1985. *An Alternative Vision: An Interpretation of Liberation Theology.* New York: Paulist.

Hale, J. Russell. 1977. *Who Are the Unchurched? An Exploratory Study.* Washington, D.C.: Glenmary.

Haleblian, Krikor. 1982. "Evaluation of Existing Models of Contextualization." In Krikor Haleblian, "Contextualization and French Structuralism: A Method to Delineate the Deep Structure of the Gospel," 34–50. Ph.D. diss., Fuller Theological Seminary School of World Mission, Pasadena.

———. 1983. "The Problem of Contextualization." *Missiology* 11.1 (January): 95–111.

Hallencreutz, Carl. 1969. *New Approaches to Men of Other Faiths.* Geneva: World Council of Churches.

———. 1988. "Tambaram Revisited." *International Review of Mission* 77, no. 307 (July): 354.

Handy, Robert T. 1984. *A Christian America: Protestant Hopes and Historical Realities.* New York: Oxford University Press.

Hanson, P. D. 1986. *The People Called: The Growth of Community in the Bible.* New York: Harper and Row.

Hao, Yap Kim. 1974. "Evangelism Today." *International Review of Mission* 63, no. 249 (January): 49–56.

Harder, Ben. 1980. "The Student Volunteer Movement for Foreign Missions and Its Contribution to 20th Century Missions." *Missiology* 8.2 (April): 141–54.

Haring, Bernard. 1974. *Evangelization Today.* Notre Dame: Fides.

Harr, Wilber C., ed. 1962. *Frontiers of the Christian World Mission since 1938: Essays in Honor of Kenneth Scott Latourette.* New York: Harper.

Harrell, David E., Jr., ed. 1981. *Varieties of Southern Evangelicalism.* Macon, Ga.: Mercer University Press.

Harvey, David. 1989. *The Condition of Postmodernity: An Enquiry into the Origins of Cultural Change.* Cambridge, Mass.: Basil Blackwell.

Hauerwas, Stanley. 1974. *Vision and Virtue.* Notre Dame: Fides.

———. 1977. *Truthfulness and Tragedy.* Notre Dame: University of Notre Dame Press.

———. 1981. *A Community of Character: Toward a Constructive Christian Social Ethic.* Notre Dame: University of Notre Dame Press.

Hauerwas, Stanley, and L. Gregory Jones, eds. 1989. *Why Narrative?* Grand Rapids: Eerdmans.

Hauerwas, Stanley, and William Willimon. 1989. *Resident Aliens: Life in the Christian Colony.* Nashville: Abingdon.

———. 1991. "Why *Resident Aliens* Struck a Chord." *Missiology* 19.4 (October): 419–29.

Hayes, John H. 1979. *An Introduction to Old Testament Study.* Nashville: Abingdon.

Hayes, John H., and Frederick Prussner. 1985. *Old Testament Theology: Its History and Development.* Atlanta: John Knox.

Hedlund, Roger E. 1985. *The Mission of the Church in the World: A Biblical Theology.* Grand Rapids: Baker.

Hedlund, Roger E., ed. 1981. *Roots of the Great Debate in Mission.* Madras: Evangelical Literature Service.

Heim, Mark. 1985. *Is Christ the Only Way? Christian Faith in a Pluralistic World.* Valley Forge, Pa.: Judson.

———. 1987. "Thinking about Theocentric Christology." *Journal of Ecumenical Studies* 24.1 (Winter): 1–16.

Hempel, Carl G. 1965. *Aspects of Scientific Explanation.* New York: Free.

———. 1966. *Philosophy of Natural Science.* Englewood Cliffs, N.J.: Prentice-Hall.

Henderson, Robert T. 1980. *Joy to the World: An Introduction to Kingdom Evangelism.* Atlanta: John Knox.

Hendrick, John R. 1977. *Opening the Door of Faith: The Why, When, and Where of Evangelism.* Atlanta: John Knox.

Hendriksen, William. 1954. *The Gospel of John.* 2 vols. Grand Rapids: Baker.

Henry, Carl. 1947. *The Uneasy Conscience of Modern Fundamentalism.* Grand Rapids: Eerdmans.

———. 1957. *Evangelical Responsibility in Contemporary Theology.* Grand Rapids: Eerdmans.

———. 1967. *Evangelicals at the Brink of Crisis.* Waco: Word.

———. 1974. "Editorial." *Christianity Today* 18.24 (September 13): 67.

———. 1976. *Evangelicals in Search of Identity.* Waco: Word.

———. 1980. "Evangelicals: Out of the Closet but Going Nowhere?" *Christianity Today* 24.1 (January 4): 16–22.

———. 1987. "Narrative Theology: An Evangelical Appraisal." *Trinity Journal* 8.1 (Spring): 3–19.

———. 1991. "Is It Fair?" In *Through No Fault of Their Own?* edited by William V. Crockett and James G. Sigountos, 245–56. Grand Rapids: Baker.

Henry, Carl, and Stanley Mooneyham, eds. 1967. *One Race, One Gospel, One Task: World Congress on Evangelism, Berlin, 1966. Official Reference Volumes.* Minneapolis: World Wide.

Henson, Les. 1992a. "The Momina Theme of Life: Developed Biblically, Theologically and Contextually." Master's thesis, Fuller Theological Seminary, Pasadena.

———. 1992b. "Narrative Theology: How It Links the Bible and Worldview and Enables the Development of a More Deeply Biblical Theology of Mission." Unpublished paper, Fuller Theological Seminary School of World Mission, Pasadena.

Herion, Gary A. 1988. "The Impact of Modern and Social Science Assumptions on the Reconstruction of Israelite History." In *The Best in Theology,* edited by J. I. Packer, 2:45–70. Carol Stream, Ill.: Christianity Today.

Hesselgrave, David J. 1980. "Tomorrow's Missionaries: To What Drumbeat Will They March?" *Christianity Today* 24.13 (July 18): 24–27.

———. 1981. "Evangelicals and Interreligious Dialogue." In *Mission Trends No. 5,* edited by Gerald H. Anderson and Thomas F. Stransky, 123–27. Grand Rapids: Eerdmans and New York: Paulist.

———. 1984. "Contextualization and Revelational Epistemology." In *Hermeneutics, Inerrancy, and the Bible,* edited by Earl D. Radmacher and Robert D. Preus, 693–738. Grand Rapids: Zondervan.

———. 1988. *Today's Choices for Tomorrow's Mission: An Evangelical Perspective on Trends and Issues in Missions.* Grand Rapids: Zondervan.

———. 1990. "Christian Communication and Religious Pluralism: Capitalizing on Differences." *Missiology* 18.2 (April): 131–38.

Hesselgrave, David, ed. 1978. *Theology and Mission.* Grand Rapids: Baker.

———. 1979. *New Horizons in World Mission.* Grand Rapids: Baker.

Hesselgrave, David, and Edward Rommen. 1989. *Contextualization: Meanings, Methods, and Models.* Grand Rapids: Baker.

Hian, Chua Wee. 1991. "Evangelism of Whole Families." In *Perspectives on the World Christian Movement,* edited by Ralph D. Winter and Steven C. Hawthorne, 617–21. Pasadena: William Carey Library.

Hick, John. 1982. *God Has Many Names*. Philadelphia: Westminster.

Hick, John, and Brian Hebblethwaite, eds. 1980. *Christianity and Other Religions: Selected Readings*. Philadelphia: Fortress.

Hick, John, and Paul Knitter, eds. 1988. *The Myth of Christian Uniqueness: Toward a Pluralistic Theology of Religions*. Maryknoll, N.Y.: Orbis.

Hiebert, Paul G. 1978. "Conversion, Culture and Cognitive Categories." *Gospel in Context* 1.3 (July): 24–29.

———. 1979a. "The Gospel and Culture." In *The Gospel and Islam: A 1978 Compendium*, edited by Don McCurry, 58–70. Monrovia, Calif.: MARC.

———. 1979b. "Sets and Structures: A Study of Church Patterns." In *New Horizons in World Mission*, edited by David J. Hesselgrave, 217–27. Grand Rapids: Baker.

———. 1982. "The Flaw of the Excluded Middle." *Missiology* 10.1 (January): 35–47.

———. 1983. "The Category 'Christian' in the Mission Task." *International Review of Mission* 72, no. 287 (July): 421–27.

———. 1985. *Anthropological Insights for Missionaries*. Grand Rapids: Baker.

———. 1987. "Critical Contextualization." *International Bulletin of Missionary Research* 11.3 (July): 104–11.

———. 1989. "Form and Meaning in Contextualization of the Gospel." In *The Word among Us*, edited by Dean S. Gilliland, 101–20. Waco: Word.

———. 1991. "Beyond Anti-Colonialism to Globalism." *Missiology* 19.3 (July): 263–82.

———. 1993. "Evangelism, Church, and Kingdom." In *The Good News of the Kingdom*, edited by Charles Van Engen et al., 153–61. Maryknoll, N.Y.: Orbis.

———. 1994. *Anthropological Reflections on Missiological Issues*. Grand Rapids: Baker.

Higgins, Edward. 1992. "Narrative and Values in the Quaker Journals of Thomas Chalkley, Elizabeth Ashbridge and John Woolman." Ph.D. diss., Graduate School of the Union Institute, Cincinnati.

Hillman, Eugene. 1968. *The Wider Ecumenism: Anonymous Christianity and the Church*. New York: Herder and Herder.

Hinson, William. 1987. *A Place to Dig In: Doing Evangelism in the Local Church*. Nashville: Abingdon.

Hocking, William. 1932. *Re-Thinking Missions: A Layman's Inquiry after One Hundred Years*. New York: Harper.

Hodges, Melvin L. 1953. *The Indigenous Church*. Springfield, Mo.: Gospel.

———. 1972. "Are Indigenous Principles Outdated?" *Evangelical Missions Quarterly* 9.1 (Fall): 43–46.

———. 1977. *A Theology of the Church and Its Mission: A Pentecostal Perspective*. Springfield, Mo.: Gospel.

———. 1978. *The Indigenous Church and the Missionary*. South Pasadena, Calif.: William Carey Library.

Hoekendijk, Johannes. 1950. "The Call to Evangelism." *International Review of Missions* 39, no. 154 (April): 162–75.

———. 1952. "The Church in Missionary Thinking." *International Review of Missions* 41, no. 163 (April): 324–36.

———. 1961. "Christ and the World in the Modern Age." *Student World* 54.1–2:75–82.

———. 1964. *De kerk binnenste buiten*. Amsterdam: ten Have.

———. 1966a. *The Church Inside Out*. Philadelphia: Westminster.

———. 1966b. "Notes on the Meaning of Mission(ary)." In *Planning for Mission: Working Papers on the New Quest for Missionary Communities*, edited by Thomas Wieser, 37–48. New York: U.S. Conference for the World Council of Churches.

Hoekstra, Harvey. 1979. *The World Council of Churches and the Demise of Evangelism*. Wheaton, Ill.: Tyndale.

Hoff, Marvin. 1965. *Structures for Mission*. Grand Rapids: Eerdmans.

Hoge, Dean R. 1976. *Division in the Protestant House: The Basic Reasons behind Intra-Church Conflicts*. Philadelphia: Westminster.

Hoge, Dean R., Benton Johnson, and Donald A. Luidens. 1994. *Vanishing Boundaries: The Religion of Mainline Protestant Baby Boomers*. Louisville: Westminster/John Knox.

Hoge, Dean R., and David A. Roozen, eds. 1979. *Understanding Church Growth and Decline*. New York: Pilgrim.

Hogg, William Richey. 1952. *Ecumenical Foundations: A History of the International Missionary Council and Its Nineteenth-Century Background*. New York: Harper.

Hohensee, Donald. 1980. "Rundi World View and Contextualization of the Gospel." D.Miss. diss., Fuller Theological Seminary, Pasadena.

Hoke, Donald, ed. 1978. *Evangelicals Face the Future*. Pasadena: William Carey Library. (Part II was edited by the Billy Graham Center and published in 1979 as *An Evangelical Agenda*.)

Holmes, Urban T. 1981. *Turning to Christ: A Theology of Renewal and Evangelism*. New York: Seabury.

Horner, Norman, ed. 1968. *Protestant Crosscurrents in Mission*. New York: Abingdon.

Hubbard, Robert L., Jr. 1992. "Doing Old Testament Theology Today." In *Studies in Old Testament Theology*, edited by Robert L. Hubbard, Jr., et al., 31–46. Dallas: Word.

Hubbard, Robert L., Jr., et al., eds. 1992. *Studies in Old Testament Theology: Historical and Contemporary Images of God and God's People*. Dallas: Word.

Hunsberger, George. 1990. "Network News." *The Gospel and Our Culture* 2.4 (December): 4.

Hunter, George G., III. 1979. *The Contagious Congregation: Frontiers in Evangelism and Church Growth*. Nashville: Abingdon.

———. 1987. *To Spread the Power: Church Growth in the Wesleyan Spirit*. Nashville: Abingdon.

———. 1992. *How to Reach Secular People*. Nashville: Abingdon.

Hunter, James D. 1983. *American Evangelicalism: Conservative Religion and the Quandary of Modernity*. New Brunswick, N.J.: Rutgers University Press.

———. 1987. "The Evangelical Worldview since 1890." In *Piety and Politics*, edited by Richard J. Neuhaus and Michael Cromartie, 19–53. Washington, D.C.: Ethics and Public Policy Center.

Hutcheson, Richard. 1981a. "Crisis in Overseas Mission: Shall We Leave It to the Independents?" *Christian Century* 98.9 (March 18): 290–96.

———. 1981b. *Mainline Churches and the Evangelicals*. Atlanta: John Knox.

Inch, Morris A. 1978. *The Evangelical Challenge*. Philadelphia: Westminster.

———. 1982. *Doing Theology across Cultures*. Grand Rapids: Baker.

International Missionary Council. 1938. *The World Mission of the Church*. London: International Missionary Council.

———. 1952. *The Missionary Obligation of the Church*. London: Edinburgh House.

Jacobs, Donald R. 1993. "Contextualization in Mission." In *Toward the 21st Century in Christian Mission*, edited by James M. Phillips and Robert T. Coote, 235–44. Grand Rapids: Eerdmans.

Jewett, Paul K. 1991. *God, Creation, and Revelation: A Neo-Evangelical Theology*. Grand Rapids: Eerdmans.

Jocz, Jakob. 1968. *The Covenant*. Grand Rapids: Eerdmans.

Johnson, Ben. 1983. *An Evangelism Primer: Practical Principles for Congregations*. Atlanta: John Knox.

———. 1984. *Friend-Maker Resources*. Atlanta: John Knox.

Johnson, Benton. 1986. "Is There Hope for Liberal Protestantism?" In *Mainstream Protestantism in the Twentieth Century: Its Problems and Prospects*, edited by Dorothy Bass et al., 13–26. Louisville: Committee on Theological Education, Presbyterian Church in the USA.

Johnson, David. 1961. "What Does God Expect from Us?" In *Facing the Unfinished Task*, compiled by J. O. Percy, 152–54. Grand Rapids: Zondervan.

Johnson, Douglas W. 1974. *Managing Change in the Church*. New York: Friendship.

Johnson, F. I. 1948. *Leadership and Evangelism*. Louisville: Pentecostal.

Johnston, Arthur P. 1974. *World Evangelism and the Word of God*. Minneapolis: Bethany Fellowship.

———. 1978. *The Battle for World Evangelism*. Wheaton, Ill.: Tyndale.

Jones, E. Stanley. 1959. *Conversion*. Nashville: Abingdon.

Jongeneel, Jan A. B., ed. 1992. *Pentecost, Mission and Ecumenism's Essays on Intercultural Theology: Festschrift in Honor of Professor Walter J. Hollenweger*. New York: Peter Lang.

Jorstad, Erling. 1981. *Evangelicals in the White House: The Cultural Maturation of Born Again Christianity*. New York: Edwin Mellen.

Kane, Herbert. 1981. "The Work of Evangelism." In *Perspectives on the World Christian Movement*, edited by Ralph D. Winter and Steven C. Hawthorne, 564–68. Pasadena: William Carey Library.

Kane, Jeffrey. 1984. *Beyond Empiricism: Michael Polanyi Reconsidered*. New York: Peter Lang.

Kantzer, Kenneth. 1991. "Preface." In *Through No Fault of Their Own?* edited by William V. Crockett and James G. Sigountos, 11–15. Grand Rapids: Baker.

Kelley, Arleon. 1982. *Your Church: A Dynamic Community*. Philadelphia: Westminster.

Kelley, Dean. 1972. *Why Conservative Churches Are Growing*. New York: Harper and Row.

Kelly, J. N. D. 1960. *Early Christian Doctrines*. New York: Harper.

Kerr, Hugh T., and John M. Mulder. 1983. *Conversions*. Grand Rapids: Eerdmans.

Keyes, Lawrence. 1983. *The Last Age of Missions: A Study of Third World Mission Societies*. Pasadena: William Carey Library.

Kik, J. Marcellus. 1958. *Ecumenism and the Evangelical*. Philadelphia: Presbyterian and Reformed.

King, Robert. 1985. "A Design for Witnessing." *Church Herald* 42.7 (April 5): 12–13.

Kinsler, F. Ross, ed. 1983. *Ministry by the People: Theological Education by Extension*. Geneva: World Council of Churches.

Kirk, J. Andrew. 1975. "The Kingdom of God and the Church in Contemporary Protestantism and Catholicism." In *Let the Earth Hear His Voice*, edited by J. D. Douglas, 1071–82. Minneapolis: World Wide.

———. 1992. *Loosing the Chains: Religion as Opium and Liberation*. London: Hodder and Stoughton.

Kittel, Gerhard, and Gerhard Friedrich, eds. 1964–76. *Theological Dictionary of the New Testament*. 10 vols. Grand Rapids: Eerdmans.

Klooster, Fred. 1988. "The Biblical Method of Salvation: A Case for Continuity." In *Continuity and Discontinuity: Perspectives on the Relationship between the Old and New Testaments*, edited by John S. Feinberg, 131–60. Westchester, Ill.: Crossway.

Knapp, Stephen. 1976. "Contextualization and Its Implications for U.S. Evangelical Churches and Missions." Unpublished paper, Partnership in Mission, Abington, Pa.

———. 1977. "Mission and Modernization: A Preliminary Critical Analysis of Contemporary Understanding of Mission from a 'Radical Evangelical' Perspective." In *American Missions in Bicentennial Perspective*, edited by R. Pierce Beaver, 146–209. Pasadena: William Carey Library.

Knight, George A. F. 1976. *Theology as Narration: A Commentary on the Book of Exodus*. Grand Rapids: Eerdmans.

Knitter, Paul. 1974. *Towards a Protestant Theology of Religions: A Case Study of Paul Althaus and Contemporary Attitudes*. Marburg: Etwert.

———. 1985. *No Other Name? A Critical Survey of Christian Attitudes toward the World Religions*. Maryknoll, N.Y.: Orbis.

———. 1989. "Making Sense of the Many." *Religious Studies Review* 15.3 (July): 204–7.

Kolb, Robert. 1984. *Speaking the Gospel Today: A Theology for Evangelism*. St. Louis: Concordia.

Kort, Wesley A. 1975. *Narrative Elements and Religious Meanings*. Philadelphia: Fortress.

Kraemer, Hendrik. 1938. *The Christian Message in a Non-Christian World.* London: Edinburgh House.

Kraft, Charles H. 1979. *Christianity in Culture: A Study in Dynamic Biblical Theologizing in Cross-Cultural Perspective.* Maryknoll, N.Y.: Orbis.

———. 1983. *Communication Theory for Christian Witness.* Nashville: Abingdon.

———. 1989. *Christianity with Power: Your Worldview and Your Experience of the Supernatural.* Ann Arbor: Servant.

———. 1991. "Allegiance, Truth and Power Encounter in Christian Witness." *Evangelical Missions Quarterly* 27.3 (July): 258–65.

———. 1992. "Allegiance, Truth and Power Encounter in Christian Witness." In *Pentecost, Mission and Ecumenism's Essays on Intercultural Theology,* edited by Jan A. B. Jongeneel, 215–30. New York: Peter Lang.

Kraft, Charles H., and Tom Wisley, eds. 1979. *Readings in Dynamic Indigeneity.* Pasadena: William Carey Library.

Krass, Alfred. 1978. *Five Lanterns at Sundown: Evangelism in a Chastened Mood.* Grand Rapids: Eerdmans.

———. 1980. "Mission as Inter-Cultural Encounter: A Sociological Perspective." In *Down to Earth,* edited by Robert T. Coote and John Stott, 231–58. Grand Rapids: Eerdmans.

———. 1982. *Evangelizing Neopagan North America.* Scottdale, Pa.: Herald.

Kraus, C. Norman. 1993. *The Community of the Spirit: How the Church Is in the World.* Scottdale, Pa.: Herald.

Kuhn, Thomas S. 1962. *The Structure of Scientific Revolutions.* Chicago: University of Chicago Press.

———. 1977. *The Essential Tension: Selected Studies in Scientific Tradition and Change.* Chicago: University of Chicago Press.

Küng, Hans. 1968. *The Church.* New York: Sheed and Ward.

———. 1987. *The Incarnation of God.* New York: Crossroad.

Küng, Hans, and David Tracy, eds. 1989. *Paradigm Change in Theology: A Symposium for the Future.* New York: Crossroad.

Kuyper, Abraham. 1883. *Tractaat van de reformatie der kerken.* Amsterdam: Hoveker.

Ladd, George E. 1974. *The Presence of the Future: The Eschatology of Biblical Realism.* Grand Rapids: Eerdmans.

Lakatos, Imre. 1978. "Falsification and the Methodology of Scientific Research Programmes." In *The Methodology of Scientific Research Programmes,* edited by John Worrall and Gregory Currie, 1:8–101. Cambridge: Cambridge University Press.

Lakatos, Imre, and Alan Musgrave, eds. 1970. *Criticism and the Growth of Knowledge.* Cambridge: Cambridge University Press.

Lankheet, James. 1991. "Opening Doors." *Church Herald* 48.4 (April): 15–17.

Larson, Bruce. 1965. *Dare to Live Now.* Grand Rapids: Zondervan.

Latourette, Kenneth Scott. 1953. *A History of Christianity.* New York: Harper.

———. 1970. *A History of the Expansion of Christianity.* Vol. 1. Grand Rapids: Zondervan.

Lauritzen, Paul. 1987. "Is 'Narrative' Really a Panacea? The Use of 'Narrative' in the Work of Metz and Hauerwas." *Journal of Religion* 67.3 (July): 322–39.

Lausanne Committee for World Evangelization. 1989. *The Manila Manifesto: An Elaboration of the Lausanne Covenant Fifteen Years Later.* Pasadena: Lausanne Committee for World Evangelization.

"The Lausanne Covenant." 1974. *International Review of Mission* 63, no. 252 (October): 570–76.

Lausanne Occasional Papers No. 21: Evangelism and Social Responsibility—An Evangelical Commitment. 1982. Grand Rapids: Lausanne Committee for World Evangelization/World Evangelical Fellowship.

Lee, Bernard J., and Michael A. Cowan. 1986. *Dangerous Memories: House Churches and Our American Story.* Kansas City, Mo.: Sheed and Ward.

Lemopoulos, George, ed. 1989. *Your Will Be Done: Orthodoxy in Mission.* Geneva: World Council of Churches.

Levison, John R., and Priscilla Pope-Levison. 1994. "Toward an Ecumenical Christology for Asia." *Missiology* 22.1 (January): 3–18.

Lewis, Hunter. 1990. *A Question of Values: Six Ways We Make the Personal Choices That Shape Our Lives.* San Francisco: Harper and Row.

Lind, Millard. 1982. "Refocusing Theological Education to Mission: The Old Testament and Contextualization." *Missiology* 10.2 (April): 141–60.

Lindsell, Harold. 1949. *A Christian Philosophy of Missions.* Wheaton, Ill.: Van Kampen.

———. 1955. *Missionary Principles and Practice.* Westwood, N.J.: Revell.

———. 1961. "Fundamentals for a Philosophy of the Christian Mission." In *The Theology of the Christian Mission,* edited by Gerald H. Anderson, 239–49. Nashville: Abingdon.

———. 1962. "Faith Missions since 1938." In *Frontiers of the Christian World Mission since 1938,* edited by Wilbur C. Harr, 189–230. New York: Harper.

———. 1971. "The Evangelical Missions: The Home Base." In *The Future of the Christian World Mission,* edited by William Danker and W. J. Kang, 88–97. Grand Rapids: Eerdmans.

———. 1979. "Evangelicals and the 1980s." In *New Horizons in World Mission,* edited by David J. Hesselgrave, 33–47. Grand Rapids: Baker.

Lindsell, Harold, ed. 1966. *The Church's Worldwide Mission.* Waco: Word.

Linthicum, Robert C. 1991a. *City of God, City of Satan: A Biblical Theology for the Urban Church.* Grand Rapids: Zondervan.

———. 1991b. *Empowering the Poor: Community Organizing among the City's "Rag, Tag and Bobtail."* Monrovia, Calif.: MARC.

Little, Paul E. 1966. *How to Give Away Your Faith.* Chicago: InterVarsity.

Loder, James. 1981. *The Transforming Moment: Understanding Convictional Experiences.* San Francisco: Harper and Row.

Loewen, Jacob. 1976. "Evangelism and Culture." In *The New Face of Evangelicalism,* edited by C. René Padilla, 177–89. Downers Grove, Ill.: InterVarsity.

———. 1986. "Which God Do Missionaries Preach?" *Missiology* 14.1 (January): 3–19.

Loffler, Paul. 1977. "The Confessing Community: Evangelism in Ecumenical Perspective." *International Review of Mission* 66, no. 264 (October): 339–48.

Long, V. Philips. 1987. "Toward a Better Theory and Understanding of Old Testament Narrative." *Presbyterion* 13.2 (Fall): 102–9.

Longman, Tremper, III. 1988. "The Literary Approach to the Study of the Old Testament: Promise and Pitfalls." In *The Best in Theology,* edited by J. I. Packer, 2:31–44. Carol Stream, Ill.: Christianity Today.

Lovelace, Richard. 1979. *The American Pietism of Cotton Mather.* Grand Rapids: Eerdmans.

———. 1981. "Completing an Awakening." *Christian Century* 98.9 (March 18): 296–300.

Luidens, Don, and Roger Nemeth. 1987. "The RCA Today." *Church Herald* 44.3 (February 6): 5–7; 44.4 (February 20): 12–14; and 44.6 (March 20): 11–14.

Luther, Martin. 1955. *Luther's Works.* Vol. 39. Philadelphia: Fortress.

Lutheran World Federation. N.d. *Together in God's Mission: A Lutheran World Federation Contribution to the Understanding of Mission.* LWF Documentation, no. 26. Geneva: Lutheran World Federation.

Luzbetak, Louis. 1981. "Signs of Progress in Contextual Methodology." *Verbum* 22:39–57. Reproduced also in "The Word Became Flesh," edited by Dean S. Gilliland and Evertt W. Huffard, 39–57. Unpublished reader, Fuller Theological Seminary, Pasadena.

———. 1988. *The Church and Cultures.* Maryknoll, N.Y.: Orbis.

McClendon, James William, Jr. 1974. *Biography as Theology: How Life Stories Can Remake Today's Theology.* Nashville: Abingdon.

McConnell, Frank, ed. 1986. *The Bible and the Narrative Tradition.* New York: Oxford University Press.

McCurry, Don. 1976. "Cross-Cultural Models of Muslim Evangelism." *Missiology* 4.3 (July): 268–69.

McCurry, Don, ed. 1979. *The Gospel and Islam: A 1978 Compendium.* Monrovia, Calif.: MARC.

McFague, Sallie. 1975. *Speaking in Parables: A Study in Metaphor and Theology.* Philadelphia: Fortress.

McGavran, Donald A. 1968. "Will Uppsala Betray the Two Billion?" *Church Growth Bulletin* 4.5 (May): 1–6.

———. 1984. *Momentous Decisions in Missions Today.* Grand Rapids: Baker.

———. 1990. *Understanding Church Growth.* Grand Rapids: Eerdmans.

McGavran, Donald A., ed. 1972a. *Crucial Issues in Missions Tomorrow.* Chicago: Moody.

———. 1972b. *Eye of the Storm: The Great Debate in Mission.* Waco: Word.

———. 1977. *The Conciliar-Evangelical Debate: The Crucial Documents, 1964–1976.* South Pasadena, Calif.: William Carey Library.

McGee, Gary B. 1986a. "Assemblies of God Mission Theology: A Historical Perspective." *International Bulletin of Missionary Research* 10.4 (October): 166–70.

———. 1986b, 1989. *This Gospel—Shall Be Preached: A History and Theology of Assemblies of God Foreign Missions.* 2 vols. Springfield, Mo.: Gospel.

———. 1993. "Pentecostal and Charismatic Missions." In *Toward the 21st Century in Christian Mission,* edited by James M. Phillips and Robert T. Coote, 41–56. Grand Rapids: Eerdmans.

McGrath, Alister. 1991. "The Biography of God: Narrative Theologians Point to the Divine Stories That Shape Our Lives." *Christianity Today* 35.8 (July 22): 22–24.

———. 1994. *Christian Theology: An Introduction.* Cambridge, Mass.: Blackwell.

MacIntyre, Alasdair. 1989a. "Epistemological Crises, Dramatic Narrative, and the Philosophy of Science." In *Why Narrative?* edited by Stanley Hauerwas and L. Gregory Jones, 138–57. Grand Rapids: Eerdmans.

———. 1989b. "The Virtues, the Unity of a Human Life, and the Concept of a Tradition." In *Why Narrative?* edited by Stanley Hauerwas and L. Gregory Jones, 89–112. Grand Rapids: Eerdmans.

Mackay, John A. 1933. *The Other Spanish Christ: A Study in the Spiritual History of Spain and South America.* New York: Macmillan.

———. 1935. *That Other America.* New York: Friendship.

———. 1963. *The Latin American Church and the Ecumenical Movement.* New York: National Council of Churches.

McKnight, Edgar V. 1988. *Postmodern Use of the Bible: The Emergence of Reader-Oriented Criticism.* Nashville: Abingdon.

McKnight, John. 1989. "Why 'Servanthood' Is Bad." *The Other Side* 25.1 (January–February): 38–40.

McLoughlin, William G. 1978. *Revivals, Awakenings, and Reform: An Essay on Religion and Social Change in America, 1607–1977.* Chicago: University of Chicago Press.

MacNulty, W. Kirk. 1989. "The Paradigm Perspective." *Futures Research Quarterly* 5.3 (Fall): 35–53.

Mains, David. 1971. *Full Circle: The Creative Church for Today's Society.* Waco: Word.

———. 1978. "Can My Church Be Changed?" *Eternity* 29.8 (August): 12–16.

Makunike, Ezekiel C. 1974. "Evangelism in the Cultural Context of Africa." *International Review of Mission* 63, no. 249 (January): 56–63.

Malphurs, Aubrey. 1992. *Developing a Vision for Ministry in the 21st Century: Six Steps to Building Vision.* Grand Rapids: Baker.

The Manila Manifesto. 1989. Pasadena: Lausanne Committee for World Evangelization.

Mann, John. 1991. "(Shhhh . . .) Narrative Theology (Explodes!)" *Modern Churchman* 32.4:42–46.

Margull, Hans J. 1971. "Mission '70—More a Venture than Ever!" *International Review of Mission* 60, no. 277 (January): 50–59.

Marsden, George. 1975. "From Fundamentalism to Evangelicalism: A Historical Analysis." In *The Evangelicals,* edited by David F. Wells and John D. Woodbridge, 122–42. Nashville: Abingdon.

———. 1980. *Fundamentalism and American Culture: The Shaping of Twentieth-Century Evangelicalism 1870–1925.* New York: Oxford University Press.

Marsden, George, ed. 1984. *Evangelicalism and Modern America.* Grand Rapids: Eerdmans.

Marshall, I. Howard. 1970. *Luke: Historian and Theologian.* Grand Rapids: Zondervan.

Martin, Ralph P. 1972. *Mark: Evangelist and Theologian.* Grand Rapids: Zondervan.

Martinson, Paul V. 1987. *A Theology of World Religions.* Minneapolis: Augsburg.

Marty, Martin. 1970. *Righteous Empire: The Protestant Experience in America.* New York: Dial.

———. 1981. "The Revival of Evangelicalism and Southern Religion." In *Varieties of Southern Evangelicalism,* edited by David E. Harrell, Jr., 7–21. Macon, Ga.: Mercer University Press.

———. 1984. *Pilgrims in Their Own Land: Five Hundred Years of Religion in America.* Boston: Little, Brown.

Mayers, Marvin. 1974. *Christianity Confronts Culture: A Strategy for Cross-Cultural Evangelism.* Grand Rapids: Zondervan.

"Message from Melbourne." 1981. *International Bulletin of Missionary Research* 5.1 (January): 29.

Messer, Donald E. 1992. *A Conspiracy of Goodness: Contemporary Images of Christian Mission.* Nashville: Abingdon.

Metz, Donald L. 1967. *New Congregations: Security and Mission in Conflict.* Philadelphia: Westminster.

Metz, Johann Baptist. 1980. *Faith in History and Society.* New York: Seabury.

———. 1989. "A Short Apology of Narrative." In *Why Narrative?* edited by Stanley Hauerwas and L. Gregory Jones, 251–62. Grand Rapids: Eerdmans.

Meyendorff, John. 1962. *The Orthodox Church: Its Past and Its Role in the World Today.* New York: Pantheon.

———. 1974. "The Orthodox Church and Mission: Past and Present Perspectives." In *Mission Trends No. 1,* edited by Gerald H. Anderson and Thomas F. Stransky, 59–71. Grand Rapids: Eerdmans and New York: Paulist.

Meyers, Eleanor Scott, ed. 1992. *Envisioning the New City: A Reader on Urban Ministry.* Louisville: John Knox.

Míguez-Bonino, José. 1975. *Doing Theology in a Revolutionary Situation.* Philadelphia: Fortress.

———. 1981. "Fundamental Questions in Ecclesiology." In *The Challenge of Basic Christian Communities,* edited by Sergio Torres and John Eagleson, 145–49. Maryknoll, N.Y.: Orbis.

Miles, Delos. 1983. *Introduction to Evangelism.* Nashville: Broadman.

Minear, Paul. 1960. *Images of the Church in the New Testament.* Philadelphia: Westminster.

Mission and Evangelism, An Ecumenical Affirmation: A Study Guide. 1983. New York: National Council of Churches.

Mitchell, W. J. T., ed. 1981. *On Narrative.* Chicago: University of Chicago Press.

Moberg, David. 1962. *The Church as a Social Institution: The Sociology of American Religion.* Englewood Cliffs, N.J.: Prentice-Hall.

———. 1972. *The Great Reversal: Evangelism and Social Concern.* Philadelphia: Lippincott.

———. 1975. "Fundamentalists and Evangelicals in Society." In *The Evangelicals,* edited by David F. Wells and John D. Woodbridge, 122–42. Nashville: Abingdon.

Moberly, R. W. L. 1986. "Story in the Old Testament." *Themelios* 11.3 (April): 77–82.

Moffett, Samuel. 1981. "Evangelism: The Leading Partner." In *Perspectives on the World Christian Movement,* edited by Ralph D. Winter and Steven C. Hawthorne, 729–31. Pasadena: William Carey Library.

Moltmann, Jürgen. 1977. *The Church in the Power of the Spirit: A Contribution to Messianic Ecclesiology.* New York: Harper and Row.

———. 1990. *The Way of Jesus Christ: Christology in Messianic Dimensions.* San Francisco: Harper.

Morgan, Donn F. 1988. "Canon and Criticism: Method or Madness?" In *The Best in Theology,* edited by J. I. Packer, 2:71–81. Carol Stream, Ill.: Christianity Today.

Morris, Linus J. 1993. *The High Impact Church: A Fresh Approach to Reaching the Unchurched.* Houston: Touch.

Motte, Mary. 1991. "The Poor: Starting Point for Mission." In *Mission in the 1990s,* edited by Gerald H. Anderson et al., 50–54. Grand Rapids: Eerdmans.

Mouw, Richard J. 1980. *Called to Holy Worldliness.* Philadelphia: Fortress.

Mouw, Richard J., and Sander Griffioen. 1993. *Pluralisms and Horizons: An Essay in Christian Public Philosophy.* Grand Rapids: Eerdmans.

Mueller-Vollmer, Kurt, ed. 1989. *The Hermeneutics Reader.* New York: Continuum.

Mulder, Dirk C. 1985. "Alle geloven op éen kussen?" In *Religies in nieuw perspectief,* edited by R. R. Bakker et al., 137–51. Kampen: J. H. Kok.

Mulholland, Kenneth B. 1993. "Missiological Education in the Bible College Tradition." Paper presented at the Missiological Education for the 21st Century Conference, Pasadena.

Muller, Richard A. 1991. *The Study of Theology: From Biblical Interpretation to Contemporary Formulation.* Grand Rapids: Zondervan.

Murch, James DeForest. 1956. *Cooperation without Compromise: A History of the National Association of Evangelicals.* Grand Rapids: Eerdmans.

Murphy, Nancey. 1990. *Theology in the Age of Scientific Reasoning.* Ithaca, N.Y.: Cornell University Press.

Murphy, Nancey, and James William McClendon, Jr. 1989. "Distinguishing Modern and Postmodern Theologies." *Modern Theology* 5.3 (April): 191–214.

Myers, Bryant. 1992. "A Funny Thing Happened on the Way to Evangelical-Ecumenical Cooperation." *International Review of Mission* 81, no. 323 (July): 397–407.

Myers, David. 1980. "Faith and Action: A Seamless Tapestry." *Christianity Today* 24.20 (November 21): 16–19.

Nash, Ronald H. 1963. *The New Evangelicalism.* Grand Rapids: Zondervan.

———. 1987. *Evangelicals in America.* Nashville: Abingdon.

Neighbour, Ralph W., Jr. 1990. *Where Do We Go from Here? A Guidebook for Cell Group Churches.* Houston: Touch.

Neill, Stephen. 1950. "Conversion." *Scottish Journal of Theology* 3.4 (December): 352–62.

———. 1957. *The Unfinished Task.* London: Edinburgh House.

———. 1959. *Creative Tension.* London: Edinburgh.

———. 1964. *A History of Christian Missions.* New York: Penguin.

———. 1970. *Christian Faith and Other Faiths.* New York: Oxford University Press.

———. 1984. "How My Mind Has Changed about Mission." Videotaped lecture at the Overseas Ministries Study Center, Ventnor, N.J.

Neill, Stephen, Gerald H. Anderson, and John Goodwin, eds. 1971. *Concise Dictionary of the Christian World Mission.* Nashville: Abingdon.

Nelson, J. Robert. 1967. "Christian Theology and the Living Faiths of Men." In *Christian Mission in Theological Perspective,* edited by Gerald H. Anderson, 109–24. Nashville: Abingdon.

Nelson, Marlin, ed. 1976. *Readings in Third World Missions.* South Pasadena, Calif.: William Carey Library.

Netland, Harold. 1988. "Toward Contextualized Apologetics." *Missiology* 16.3 (July): 289–303.

———. 1991. *Dissonant Voices: Religious Pluralism and the Question of Truth.* Grand Rapids: Eerdmans.

———. 1994. "Response to 'The Uniqueness of Christ: Shaping Faith and Mission' by Charles Van Engen." Unpublished paper, Evangelical Theological Society/Evangelical Missiological Society Midwestern Conference, Chicago, March 17–19.

Neuhaus, Richard J., and Michael Cromartie, eds. 1987. *Piety and Politics: Evangelicals and Fundamentalists Confront the World.* Washington, D.C.: Ethics and Public Policy Center.

Newbigin, Lesslie. 1954. *The Household of God: Lectures on the Nature of the Church.* New York: Friendship.

———. 1958. *One Body, One Gospel, One World.* London: International Missionary Council.

———. 1963. *The Relevance of the Trinitarian Doctrine for Today's Mission.* London: Edinburgh House.

———. 1969. *The Finality of Christ.* Richmond: John Knox.

———. 1977. *The Good Shepherd: Meditations on Christian Ministry in Today's World.* Grand Rapids: Eerdmans.

———. 1978. *The Open Secret.* Grand Rapids: Eerdmans.

———. 1979. "Context and Conversion." *International Review of Mission* 68, no. 271 (July): 301–12.

———. 1981a. "The Gospel among the Religions." In *Mission Trends No. 5,* edited by Gerald H. Anderson and Thomas F. Stransky, 3–19. Grand Rapids: Eerdmans and New York: Paulist.

———. 1981b. "Integration—Some Personal Reflections 1981." *International Review of Mission* 70, no. 280 (October): 247–55.

———. 1986. *Foolishness to the Greeks: The Gospel and Western Culture.* Grand Rapids: Eerdmans.

———. 1987. "Can the West Be Converted?" *International Bulletin of Missionary Research* 11.1 (January): 2–7.

———. 1989a. *The Gospel in a Pluralist Society.* Grand Rapids: Eerdmans.

———. 1989b. "Religious Pluralism and the Uniqueness of Jesus Christ." *International Bulletin of Missionary Research* 13.2 (April): 50–54.

———. 1990. "Religious Pluralism and the Uniqueness of Jesus Christ." In *The Best in Theology,* edited by J. I. Packer, 4:267–74. Carol Stream, Ill.: Christianity Today.

———. 1991. *Truth to Tell: The Gospel as Public Truth.* Grand Rapids: Eerdmans.

———. 1992. "The Legacy of W. A. Visser 't Hooft." *International Bulletin of Missionary Research* 16.2 (April): 78–82.

———. 1994. "Ecumenical Amnesia." *International Bulletin of Missionary Research* 18.1 (January): 2–5.

New Delhi Report. 1962. New York: Association.

Newsome, James D., Jr. 1984. *The Hebrew Prophets.* Atlanta: John Knox.

Nicholls, Bruce J. 1975. "Theological Education and Evangelization." In *Let the Earth Hear His Voice,* edited by J. D. Douglas, 634–45. Minneapolis: World Wide.

———. 1979. "The Exclusiveness and Inclusiveness of the Gospel." *Themelios* 4.2 (January): 62–69.

———. 1980. "Towards a Theology of Gospel and Culture." In *Down to Earth,* edited by Robert T. Coote and John Stott, 49–62. Grand Rapids: Eerdmans.

———. 1984. "A Living Theology for Asian Churches." In *The Bible and Theology in Asian Contexts,* edited by Bong Rin Ro and Ruth Eshenaur, 119–38. Taichung: Asia Theological Association.

———. 1990. "The Church and Authentic Dialogue." In *Practical Theology and the Ministry of the Church, 1952–1984: Essays in Honor of Edmund P. Clowney,* edited by Harvie Conn, 255–72. Phillipsburg, N.J.: Presbyterian and Reformed.

Nicholls, Bruce J., ed. 1985. *In Word and Deed: Evangelism and Social Responsibility.* Grand Rapids: Eerdmans.

Nida, Eugene A. 1960. *Message and Mission.* New York: Harper.

Niebuhr, H. Richard. 1937. *The Kingdom of God in America.* New York: Willett, Clark.

———. 1941. *The Meaning of Revelation.* New York: Macmillan.

———. 1951. *Christ and Culture.* New York: Harper.

Niles, D. T. 1959. *The Preacher's Calling to Be Servant.* London: Lutterworth.

———. 1962. *Upon the Earth: The Mission of God and the Missionary Enterprise of the Churches.* New York: McGraw-Hill.

Nissen, Karsten. 1974. "Mission and Unity." *International Review of Mission* 63, no. 252 (October): 539–50.

Noble, John. 1988. *House Churches: Will They Survive?* Eastbourne, Eng.: Kingsway.

Noble, Lowell. 1987. *Sociotheology.* Jackson, Mich.: Lowell Noble.

Noll, Mark, et al. 1983. *The Search for Christian America.* Westchester, Ill.: Crossway.

Noth, Martin. 1963. "The 'Re-Presentation' of the Old Testament Proclamation." In *Essays on Old Testament Hermeneutics,* edited by Claus Westermann, 76–88. Richmond: John Knox.

Ockenga, Harold. 1960. "Resurgent Evangelical Leadership." *Christianity Today* 5.1 (October 10): 11–15.

Olley, John W. 1990. "God's Agenda for the City: Some Biblical Perspectives." *Urban Mission* 8.1 (September): 14–23.

Orchard, Ronald K., ed. 1964. *Witness in Six Continents.* London: Edinburgh.

Ortlund, Raymond C. 1983. *Let the Church Be the Church.* Waco: Word.

Osborne, Grant R. 1991. *The Hermeneutical Spiral: A Comprehensive Introduction to Biblical Interpretation.* Downers Grove, Ill.: InterVarsity.

Packer, J. I. 1961. *Evangelism and the Sovereignty of God.* Downers Grove, Ill.: InterVarsity.

———. 1986. "'Good Pagans' and God's Kingdom." *Christianity Today* 30.1 (January 17): 22–25.

Packer, J. I., ed. 1987, 1988, 1989, 1990. *The Best in Theology.* Vols. 1, 2, 3, 4. Carol Stream, Ill.: Christianity Today.

Padilla, C. René. 1980. "Hermeneutics and Culture: A Theological Perspective." In *Down to Earth,* edited by Robert T. Coote and John Stott, 63–78. Grand Rapids: Eerdmans.

———. 1985. *Mission between the Times: Essays on the Kingdom.* Grand Rapids: Eerdmans.

———. 1986. "Toward a Contextual Christology from Latin America." In *Conflict and Context,* edited by Mark Branson and C. René Padilla, 81–91. Grand Rapids: Eerdmans.

———. 1987. "A New Ecclesiology in Latin America." *International Bulletin of Missionary Research* 11.4 (October): 156–64.

———. 1992. "Wholistic Mission: Evangelical and Ecumenical." *International Review of Mission* 81, no. 323 (July): 381–82.

Padilla, C. René, et al. 1975. *El Reino de Dios y América Latina.* El Paso: Casa Bautista.

Padilla, C. René, ed. 1976. *The New Face of Evangelicalism: An International Symposium on the Lausanne Covenant.* Downers Grove, Ill.: InterVarsity.

Panikkar, Raimundo. 1978. *Intrareligious Dialogue.* New York: Paulist.

Pannell, William. 1992. *Evangelism from the Bottom Up.* Grand Rapids: Zondervan.

Pannenberg, Wolfhart. 1969. *Theology and the Kingdom of God.* Philadelphia: Westminster.

Parvin, Earl. 1985. *Missions U.S.A.* Chicago: Moody.

Patelos, Constantine. 1978. *The Orthodox Church in the Ecumenical Movement: Documents and Statements, 1902–1975.* Geneva: World Council of Churches.

Patrick, Dale. 1987. "The Kingdom of God in the Old Testament." In *The Kingdom of God in 20th-Century Interpretation,* edited by Wendell Willis, 67–79. Peabody, Mass.: Hendrickson.

Patterson, George. 1981. "The Spontaneous Multiplication of the Church." In *Perspectives on the World Christian Movement,* edited by Ralph D. Winter and Steven C. Hawthorne, 601–16. Pasadena: William Carey Library.

Pelikan, Jaroslav. 1971. *The Christian Tradition.* Chicago: University of Chicago Press.

Pentecost, Edward C. 1974. *Reaching the Unreached.* South Pasadena, Calif.: William Carey Library.

———. 1982. *Issues in Missiology: An Introduction.* Grand Rapids: Baker.

Percy, J. O., comp. 1961. *Facing the Unfinished Task: Messages Delivered at the Congress on World Missions.* Grand Rapids: Zondervan.

Pervo, Richard I. 1987. *Profit with Delight: The Literary Genre of the Acts of the Apostles.* Philadelphia: Fortress.

Peters, George W. 1970. *Saturation Evangelism.* Grand Rapids: Zondervan.

———. 1972. *A Biblical Theology of Missions.* Chicago: Moody.

———. 1981. *A Theology of Church Growth.* Grand Rapids: Zondervan.

Peters, Tom. 1992. *Liberation Management: Necessary Disorganization for the Nanosecond Nineties.* New York: Alfred Knopf.

Petersen, J. Randall. 1981. "Church Growth." *Christianity Today* 25.6 (March 27): 18–23.

Phillips, James M., and Robert T. Coote, eds. 1993. *Toward the 21st Century in Christian Mission.* Grand Rapids: Eerdmans.

Pickard, William M. 1991. "A Universal Theology of Religion?" *Missiology* 19.2 (April): 143–51.

Pierard, Richard V. 1970. *The Unequal Yoke: Evangelicalism and Political Conservatism.* Philadelphia: Lippincott.

Piet, John. 1970. *The Road Ahead: A Theology for the Church in Mission.* Grand Rapids: Eerdmans.

Pinnock, Clark H. 1991. "Acts 4:12—No Other Name under Heaven." In *Through No Fault of Their Own?* edited by William V. Crockett and James G. Sigountos, 107–16. Grand Rapids: Baker.

———. 1992. *A Wideness in God's Mercy: The Finality of Jesus Christ in a World of Religions.* Grand Rapids: Zondervan.

Pippert, Rebecca Manley. 1979. *Out of the Saltshaker and into the World.* Downers Grove, Ill.: InterVarsity.

Polanyi, Michael. 1958a. *Personal Knowledge: Towards a Post-Critical Philosophy.* London: Routledge and Kegan Paul.

———. 1958b. *The Study of Man.* Chicago: University of Chicago Press.

———. 1969. *Knowing and Being: Essays.* Chicago: University of Chicago Press.

Polanyi, Michael, and Harry Prosch. 1975. *Meaning.* Chicago: University of Chicago Press.

Pomerville, Paul. 1985. *The Third Force in Missions: A Pentecostal Contribution to Contemporary Mission Theology.* Peabody, Mass.: Hendrickson.

Popper, Karl. 1965. *The Logic of Scientific Discovery.* New York: Harper and Row.

———. 1972. *Objective Knowledge: An Evolutionary Approach.* New York: Oxford University Press.

Punt, Neal. 1987. "All Are Saved Except." *Christianity Today* 31.5 (March 20): 43–44.

Quebedeaux, Richard. 1974. *The Young Evangelicals: Revolution in Orthodoxy.* New York: Harper and Row.

———. 1978. *The Worldly Evangelicals.* San Francisco: Harper and Row.

Radmacher, Earl D., and Robert D. Preus, eds. 1984. *Hermeneutics, Inerrancy, and the Bible.* Grand Rapids: Zondervan.

Rahner, Karl. 1980. "Christianity and the Non-Christian Religions." In *Christianity and Other Religions,* edited by John Hick and Brian Hebblethwaite, 52–79. Philadelphia: Fortress.

Ramm, Bernard L. 1973. *The Evangelical Heritage.* Waco: Word.

Ramseyer, Robert L., ed. 1979. *Mission and the Peace Witness: The Gospel and Christian Discipleship.* Scottdale, Pa.: Herald.

Rauschenbusch, Walter. 1917. *A Theology for the Social Gospel.* New York: Macmillan.

Read, David H. C. 1978. *Go and Make Disciples.* Nashville: Abingdon.

Recinos, Harold J. 1989. *Hear the Cry! A Latino Pastor Challenges the Church.* Louisville: Westminster/John Knox.

Reepsome, James. 1980. "A Smaller, More Studious Lausanne—in Thailand." *Christianity Today* 24.10 (May 23): 47–49.

Reisinger, Ernest C. 1982. *Today's Evangelism.* Phillipsburg, N.J.: Craig.

Rescher, Nicholas. 1978. *Peirce's Philosophy of Science.* Notre Dame: University of Notre Dame Press.

Rhem, Richard A. 1988. "The Habit of God's Heart." *Perspectives* 3.7 (September): 8–11.

Rice, Phyllis Mather. 1984. "Interview with Ben Johnson." *Your Church* 30.2 (March/April): 8–10.

Richards, Larry. 1980. "The Great American Congregation: An Illusive Ideal." *Christianity Today* 24.20 (November 21): 20–23.

Richardson, William J. 1977. *Social Action vs. Evangelism: An Essay on the Contemporary Crisis.* South Pasadena, Calif.: William Carey Library.

Ricoeur, Paul. 1981. "Narrative Time." In *On Narrative,* edited by W. J. T. Mitchell, 165–86. Chicago: University of Chicago Press.

Ridderbos, Herman. 1962. *The Coming of the Kingdom.* Philadelphia: Presbyterian and Reformed.

———. 1975. *Paul: An Outline of His Theology.* Grand Rapids: Eerdmans.

Rin Ro, Bong. 1984. "Contextualization: Asian Theology." In *The Bible and Theology in Asian Contexts,* edited by Bong Rin Ro and Ruth Eshenaur, 63–77. Taichung: Asia Theological Association.

Rin Ro, Bong, and Ruth Eshenaur, eds. 1984. *The Bible and Theology in Asian Contexts: An Evangelical Perspective on Asian Theology.* Taichung: Asia Theological Association.

Robinson, P. J. 1984. "The 1982 Belhar Confession in Missionary Perspective." In *A Moment of Truth,* edited by G. D. Cloete and D. J. Smit, 42–52. Grand Rapids: Eerdmans.

Roof, Wade Clark, and William McKinney. 1987. *American Mainline Religion: Its Changing Shape and Future.* New Brunswick, N.J.: Rutgers University Press.

Roozen, David, William McKinney, and Jackson W. Carroll. 1984. *Varieties of Religious Presence: Mission in Public Life.* New York: Pilgrim.

Rose, Larry, and C. Kirk Hadaway, eds. 1984. *An Urban World: Churches Face the Future.* Nashville: Broadman.

Rosell, Garth M. 1986. "Billy Graham and Worldwide Evangelization." In *American Christianity: A Case Approach,* edited by Ronald White et al., 179–83. Grand Rapids: Eerdmans.

Rosin, H. H. 1972. *Missio Dei: An Examination of the Origin, Contents and Function of the Term in Protestant Missiological Discussion.* Leiden: Inter-University Institute for Missiological and Ecumenical Research.

Roth, Robert Paul. 1985. *The Theater of God: Story in Christian Doctrines.* Philadelphia: Fortress.

Roth, Wolfgang, and Rosemary Ruether. 1978. *The Liberating Bond.* New York: Friendship.

Roukanen, Miikka. 1990. "Catholic Teaching on Non-Christian Religions at the Second Vatican Council." *International Bulletin of Missionary Research* 14.2 (April): 56–61.

Rouner, Leroy S., ed. 1983. *Foundations of Ethics.* Notre Dame: University of Notre Dame Press.

Rowley, H. H. 1955. *The Missionary Message of the Old Testament.* London: Carey Kingsgate.

Roxburgh, Alan J. 1993. *Reaching a New Generation: Strategies for Tomorrow's Church.* Downers Grove, Ill.: InterVarsity.

Runia, Klaas. 1975. "The Trinitarian Nature of God as Creator and Man's Authentic Relationship with Him." In *Let the Earth Hear His Voice,* edited by J. D. Douglas, 1008–20. Minneapolis: World Wide.

———. 1984. *The Present-Day Christological Debate.* Downers Grove, Ill.: InterVarsity.

Saayman, Willem. 1990. "Bridging the Gulf: David Bosch and the Ecumenical/Evangelical Polarisation." *Missionalia* 18.1 (April): 99–108.

Samartha, Stanley. 1981. "The Lordship of Jesus Christ and Religious Pluralism." In *Christ's Lordship and Religious Pluralism,* edited by Gerald H. Anderson and Thomas F. Stransky, 19–36. Maryknoll, N.Y.: Orbis.

Samartha, Stanley, ed. 1977. *Faith in the Midst of Faiths: Reflections on Dialogue in Community.* Geneva: World Council of Churches.

Sample, Tex. 1984. *Blue-Collar Ministry.* Valley Forge, Pa.: Judson.

———. 1990. *U.S. Lifestyles and Mainline Churches: A Key to Reaching People in the 90's.* Louisville: Westminster/John Knox.

Sampson, Philip. 1993. "The Rise of Postmodernity." Preconference paper for the Lausanne Consultation on Modernity, June 10–15, Uppsala.

Samuel, Vinay, and Chris Sugden, eds. 1984. *Sharing Jesus in the Two-Thirds World.* Grand Rapids: Eerdmans.

———. 1987. *The Church in Response to Human Need.* Grand Rapids: Eerdmans.

The San Antonio Report. 1990. Geneva: World Council of Churches.

Sandeen, Ernest R. 1970. *The Roots of Fundamentalism: British and American Millenarianism 1800–1930.* Chicago: University of Chicago Press.

Sanders, James A. 1984. *Canon and Community: A Guide to Canonical Criticism.* Philadelphia: Fortress.

———. 1987. *From Sacred Story to Sacred Text: Canon as Paradigm.* Philadelphia: Fortress.

Sanders, John. 1992. *No Other Name: An Investigation into the Destiny of the Unevangelized.* Grand Rapids: Eerdmans.

Sanneh, Lamin. 1989. *Translating the Message: The Missionary Impact on Culture.* Maryknoll, N.Y.: Orbis.

Savage, Peter. 1976. "The Church and Evangelism." In *The New Face of Evangelicalism,* edited by C. René Padilla, 103–25. Downers Grove, Ill.: InterVarsity.

Schaff, Philip, ed. 1974. *Nicene and Post-Nicene Fathers.* Vol. 1. Grand Rapids: Eerdmans.

Schaller, Lyle E. 1978. *Assimilating New Members.* Nashville: Abingdon.

———. 1979. "How Do You Initiate New Members in the Tribe?" *Church Growth America* 5.5 (November–December): 8–9.

———. 1983. *Growing Plans.* Nashville: Abingdon.

———. 1987. *It's a Different World! The Challenge for Today's Pastor.* Nashville: Abingdon.

———. 1989. *Reflections of a Contrarian: Second Thoughts on the Parish Ministry.* Nashville: Abingdon.

———. 1992. *The Seven-Day-a-Week Church.* Nashville: Abingdon.

Scharpff, Paulus. 1966. *History of Evangelism: Three Hundred Years of Evangelism in Germany, Great Britain, and the United States of America.* Grand Rapids: Eerdmans.

Scherer, James A. 1987. *Gospel, Church and Kingdom: Comparative Studies in World Mission Theology.* Minneapolis: Augsburg.

———. 1993a. "Church, Kingdom, and Missio Dei: Lutheran and Orthodox Correctives to Recent Ecumenical Mission Theology." In *The Good News of the Kingdom,* edited by Charles Van Engen et al., 82–88. Maryknoll, N.Y.: Orbis.

———. 1993b. "Mission Theology." In *Toward the 21st Century in Christian Mission,* edited by James M. Phillips and Robert T. Coote, 193–202. Grand Rapids: Eerdmans.

Scherer, James A., and Stephen B. Bevans, eds. 1992. *New Directions in Mission and Evangelization: Basic Statements 1974–1991.* Maryknoll, N.Y.: Orbis.

Schillebeeckx, Edward. 1987. *The Schillebeeckx Reader.* Edited by Robert Schreiter. New York: Crossroad.

Schlink, Edmund. 1968. *The Coming Christ and the Coming Church.* Philadelphia: Fortress.

Schmemann, Alexander. 1961. "The Missionary Imperative in the Orthodox Tradition." In *The Theology of the Christian Mission,* edited by Gerald H. Anderson, 250–57. New York: McGraw-Hill.

———. 1979. *Church, World, Mission: Reflections on Orthodoxy in the West.* Crestwood, N.Y.: St. Vladimir's Seminary Press.

Schreiter, Robert. 1985. *Constructing Local Theologies.* Maryknoll, N.Y.: Orbis.

———. 1990. "Jesus Christ and Mission: The Cruciality of Christology." *Missiology* 18.4 (October): 429–38.

———. 1992. "Reconciliation as a Missionary Task." *Missiology* 20.1 (January): 3–10.

Schuller, Robert. 1974. *Your Church Has Real Possibilities.* Glendale, Calif.: Regal.

Scott, Waldron. 1979. "The Evangelical World Mission and the World Evangelical Fellowship." In *New Horizons in World Mission*, edited by David J. Hesselgrave, 49–53. Grand Rapids: Baker.

———. 1980. *Bring Forth Justice: A Contemporary Perspective on Mission*. Grand Rapids: Eerdmans.

———. 1981a. "'No Other Name'—An Evangelical Conviction." In *Christ's Lordship and Religious Pluralism*, edited by Gerald H. Anderson and Thomas F. Stransky, 58–74. Maryknoll, N.Y.: Orbis.

———. 1981b. "The Significance of Pattaya." *Missiology* 9.1 (January): 57–75.

Segundo, Juan Luís. 1973. *The Community Called Church*. Maryknoll, N.Y.: Orbis.

———. 1976. *The Liberation of Theology*. Maryknoll, N.Y.: Orbis.

———. 1985. *Theology and the Church*. London: Winston.

Seligman, Adam B. 1990. "Towards a Reinterpretation of Modernity in an Age of Postmodernity." In *Theories of Modernity and Postmodernity*, edited by Bryan S. Turner, 117–35. London: Sage.

Senior, Donald, and Carroll Stuhlmueller. 1983. *The Biblical Foundations for Mission*. Maryknoll, N.Y.: Orbis.

Sexton, Virgil. 1971. *Listening to the Church: A Realistic Profile of Grass Roots Opinion*. Nashville: Abingdon.

Shaw, R. Daniel. 1988. *Transculturation: The Cultural Factor in Translation and Other Communication Tasks*. Pasadena: William Carey Library.

Shelley, Bruce L. 1967. *Evangelicalism in America*. Grand Rapids: Eerdmans.

Shenk, Wilbert R. 1978. "Missionary Congregations." *Mission Focus* 6.4 (March): 13–14.

———. 1993a. "The Culture of Modernity as a Missionary Challenge." In *The Good News of the Kingdom*, edited by Charles Van Engen et al., 192–99. Maryknoll, N.Y.: Orbis.

———. 1993b. "Mission Strategies." In *Toward the 21st Century in Christian Mission*, edited by James M. Phillips and Robert T. Coote, 218–34. Grand Rapids: Eerdmans.

Shenk, Wilbert, ed. 1984. *Anabaptism and Mission*. Scottdale, Pa.: Herald.

Shepherd, Jack F. N.d. "Understanding Other Religions from an Evangelical Point of View." Unpublished lecture notes, Fuller Theological Seminary School of World Mission, Pasadena.

Sheppard, David. 1974. *Built as a City: God and the Urban World Today*. London: Hodder and Stoughton.

Shriver, Donald W., Jr., and Karl A. Ostrom. 1977. *Is There Hope for the City?* Philadelphia: Westminster.

Sider, Ronald. 1977. *Rich Christians in an Age of Hunger*. Downers Grove, Ill.: InterVarsity.

Sider, Ronald, ed. 1980. *Cry Justice!* New York: Paulist.

———. 1981. *Evangelicals and Development: Toward a Theology of Social Change*. Philadelphia: Westminster.

———. 1982. *Lifestyle in the Eighties*. Philadelphia: Westminster.

Smalley, Stephen S. 1978. *John: Evangelist and Interpreter*. Exeter, Eng.: Paternoster.

Smalley, William, ed. 1978. *Readings in Missionary Anthropology II*. Pasadena: William Carey Library.

Smart, Barry. 1990. "Modernity, Postmodernity and the Present." In *Theories of Modernity and Postmodernity*, edited by Bryan S. Turner, 14–30. London: Sage.

Smith, Barbara Herrnstein. 1981. "Narrative Version, Narrative Theories." In *On Narrative*, edited by W. J. T. Mitchell, 209–32. Chicago: University of Chicago Press.

Smith, Michael Peter, ed. 1988. *Power, Community, and the City*. New Brunswick, N.J.: Transaction.

Smith, Timothy. 1962. *Called unto Holiness: The Story of the Nazarenes*. Kansas City, Mo.: Nazarene.

Smith, Wilfred Cantwell. 1980. "The Christian in a Religiously Plural World." In *Christianity and Other Religions*, edited by John Hick and Brian Hebblethwaite, 87–107. Philadelphia: Fortress.

Snyder, Howard. 1975. "The Church as God's Agent in Evangelism." In *Let the Earth Hear His Voice*, edited by J. D. Douglas, 327–60. Minneapolis: World Wide.

———. 1976. "Co-operation in Evangelism." In *The New Face of Evangelicalism*, edited by C. René Padilla, 113–34. Downers Grove, Ill.: InterVarsity.

———. 1977. *The Community of the King*. Downers Grove, Ill.: InterVarsity.

———. 1983. *Liberating the Church*. Downers Grove, Ill.: InterVarsity.

Sobrino, Jon. 1981. *Resurrección de la verdadera iglesia: Los pobres, lugar teológico de la eclesiología*. Santader, Spain: Editorial Sal Terrae.

———. 1984. *The True Church and the Poor*. Maryknoll, N.Y.: Orbis.

Song, C.-S. 1975. *Christian Mission in Reconstruction—An Asian Analysis*. Maryknoll, N.Y.: Orbis.

———. 1987. "God's Grace in the World of Religions." *Perspectives* 2.1 (January): 4–7.

Spindler, Marc R. 1988. "Bijbelse fundering en oriëntatie van zending." In *Oecumenische inleiding in de missiologie*, edited by F. J. Verstraelen, 132–54. Kampen: J. H. Kok.

Spykman, Gordon, et al. 1988. *Let My People Live: Faith and Struggle in Central America*. Grand Rapids: Eerdmans.

Stadler, Anton P. 1977. "Dialogue: Does It Complement, Modify or Replace Mission?" *Occasional Bulletin of Missionary Research* 1.3 (July): 2–9.

Stamoolis, James. 1987. *Eastern Orthodox Mission Theology Today*. Maryknoll, N.Y.: Orbis.

Stanley, Paul D., and J. Robert Clinton. 1992. *Connecting: The Mentoring Relationships You Need to Succeed in Life*. Colorado Springs: NavPress.

Starling, Allan, ed. 1981. *Seeds of Promise: World Consultation on Frontier Missions, Edinburgh, '80*. Pasadena: William Carey Library.

Steele, Shelby. 1990. *The Content of Our Character*. New York: HarperCollins.

Steffan, Thomas. 1993. *Passing the Baton: Church Planting That Empowers*. La Habra, Calif.: Center for Organization and Development.

Stevick, Daniel. 1964. *Beyond Fundamentalism*. Richmond: John Knox.

Stoeffler, F. E., ed. 1976. *Continental Pietism and Early American Christianity*. Grand Rapids: Eerdmans.

Stoneburner, Tony, ed. 1968. *Parable, Myth and Language*. Cambridge: Church Society for College Work.

Stott, John. 1967. *Our Guilty Silence*. Grand Rapids: Eerdmans.

———. 1970. *Christ the Controversialist*. Downers Grove, Ill.: InterVarsity.

———. 1971. *Christ the Liberator*. Downers Grove, Ill.: InterVarsity.

———. 1975a. "The Biblical Basis of Evangelism." In *Mission Trends No. 2,* edited by Gerald H. Anderson and Thomas F. Stransky, 4–23. Grand Rapids: Eerdmans and New York: Paulist.

———. 1975b. *Christian Mission in the Modern World*. Downers Grove, Ill.: InterVarsity.

———. 1979. "The Living God Is a Missionary God." In *You Can Tell the World*, edited by James E. Berney, 20–32. Downers Grove, Ill.: InterVarsity.

———. 1980. "Saving Souls and Serving Bread." *Christianity Today* 24.19 (November 7). 50–51.

———. 1981. "Dialogue, Encounter, Even Confrontation." In *Mission Trends No. 5*, edited by Gerald H. Anderson and Thomas F. Stransky, 156–72. Grand Rapids: Eerdmans and New York: Paulist.

———. 1985. "Salt and Light: The Christian Contribution to Nation-Building." *Evangelical Review of Theology* 9.3 (July): 267–76.

———. 1989. "John Stott on Hell: Taking a Closer Look at Eternal Torture." *World Christian* 8.5 (May): 31–37.

Stott, John, and Robert T. Coote, eds. 1979. *Gospel and Culture*. Pasadena: William Carey Library.

Stott, John, and Basil Meeking, eds. 1986. *The Evangelical–Roman Catholic Dialogue on Mission, 1977–1984*. Grand Rapids: Eerdmans.

Stowe, David. 1981. "What Did Melbourne Say?" *Missiology* 9.1 (January): 23–35.

Stransky, Thomas F. 1981. "A Roman Catholic Reflection." *Missiology* 9.1 (January): 41–51.

Stroup, George W. 1981. *The Promise of Narrative Theology: Recovering the Gospel in the Church.* Atlanta: John Knox.

Sundkler, Bengt. 1965. *The World of Mission.* Grand Rapids: Eerdmans.

Sweazey, George E. 1953. *Effective Evangelism.* New York: Harper.

———. 1958. *Evangelism in the United States.* London: Lutterworth.

———. 1976. *Preaching the Good News.* Englewood Cliffs, N.J.: Prentice-Hall.

Sweet, Leonard I., ed. 1984. *The Evangelical Tradition in America.* Macon, Ga.: Mercer University Press.

Syrdal, Rolf A. 1977. *Go, Make Disciples.* Minneapolis: Augsburg.

Taber, Charles R. 1979a. "Contextualization: Indigenization and/or Transformation." In *The Gospel and Islam,* edited by Don McCurry, 143–54. Monrovia, Calif.: MARC.

———. 1979b. "The Limits of Indigenization in Theology." In *Readings in Dynamic Indigeneity,* edited by Charles H. Kraft and Tom Wisley, 388–97. Pasadena: William Carey Library.

Taber, Charles R., and Betty J. Taber. 1992. "A Christian Understanding of 'Religion' and 'Religions.'" *Missiology* 20.1 (January): 69–78.

Tannehill, Robert C. 1986, 1990. *The Narrative Unity of Luke-Acts: A Literary Interpretation.* 2 vols. Philadelphia: Fortress.

Taylor, John V. 1963. *The Primal Vision: Christian Presence amid African Religion.* London: Student Christian Movement.

———. 1973. *The Go-Between God: The Holy Spirit and the Christian Mission.* London: Student Christian Movement.

———. 1981. "The Theological Basis of Interfaith Dialogue." In *Mission Trends No. 5,* edited by Gerald H. Anderson and Thomas F. Stransky, 93–110. Grand Rapids: Eerdmans and New York: Paulist.

Terry, John Mark. 1994. *Evangelism: A Concise History.* Nashville: Broadman and Holman.

"The Thailand Statement." 1981. *International Bulletin of Missionary Research* 5.1 (January): 29–31.

Thiel, John. 1991. *Imagination and Authority: Theological Authorship in the Modern Tradition.* Minneapolis: Fortress.

Thiemann, Ronald F. 1985. *Revelation and Theology: The Gospel as Narrated Promise.* Notre Dame: University of Notre Dame Press.

———. 1987. "Radiance and Obscurity in Biblical Narrative." In *Scriptural Authority and Narrative Interpretation,* edited by Garrett Green, 21–41. Philadelphia: Fortress.

Thiselton, Anthony C. 1980. *The Two Horizons: New Testament Hermeneutics and Philosophical Description with Special Reference to Heidegger, Bultmann, Gadamer, and Wittgenstein.* Grand Rapids: Eerdmans.

Thomas, Nancy. 1994. "Cleofilas and Elizabeth: Two Immigrant Stories as Examples of Narrative Theology through Fiction and Spiritual Autobiography." Unpublished paper, Fuller Theological Seminary School of World Mission, Pasadena.

Thomas, Owen C. 1969. *Attitudes toward Other Religions.* New York: Harper and Row.

Thomsen, Mark. 1990. "Confessing Jesus Christ within the World of Religious Pluralism." *International Bulletin of Missionary Research* 14.3 (July): 115–18.

Thomson, D. P. 1968. *Aspects of Evangelism.* Crieff, Scotland: Research Unit.

Thorogood, Bernard. 1994. *Gales of Change: The Story of the London Missionary Society, 1945–1977.* Geneva: World Council of Churches.

Tilley, Terrence W. 1985. *Story Theology.* Wilmington, Del.: Michael Glazier.

Tillich, Paul. 1980. "Christianity Judging Itself in the Light of Its Encounter with the World of Religions." In *Christianity and Other Religions,* edited by John Hick and Brian Hebblethwaite, 108–21. Philadelphia: Fortress.

Tink, Fletcher L. 1989. "Downtown Los Angeles as Urban Jungle: An Alternative Model to the Homogeneous Unit Principle Understanding of the City." Unpublished presentation, Lausanne II, Manila.

Tippett, Alan R. 1987. *Introduction to Missiology*. Pasadena: William Carey Library.

Tonna, Benjamin. 1985. *A Gospel for the Cities: A Socio-Theology of Urban Ministry*. Maryknoll, N.Y.: Orbis.

Torres, Sergio, and John Eagleson, eds. 1981. *The Challenge of Basic Christian Communities*. Maryknoll, N.Y.: Orbis.

Toulmin, Stephen. 1961. *Foresight and Understanding*. New York: Harper.

———. 1972. *Human Understanding*. Vol. 1, *The Collective Use and Evolution of Concepts*. Princeton, N.J.: Princeton University Press.

Towns, Elmer L. 1990. *Ten of Today's Most Innovative Churches: What They're Doing, How They're Doing It and How You Can Apply Their Ideas in Your Church*. Ventura, Calif.: Regal.

Toy, Dottie. 1985. "Planning as Teachers." *Alert* (May): 10–13.

Tracy, David. 1981. *The Analogical Imagination: Christian Theology and the Culture of Pluralism*. New York: Crossroad.

———. 1988. *Blessed Rage for Order: The New Pluralism in Theology*. San Francisco: Harper and Row.

Trible, Phyllis. 1984. *Texts of Terror*. Philadelphia: Fortress.

Troeltsch, Ernst. 1971. *The Absoluteness of Christianity*. Richmond: John Knox.

———. 1980. "The Place of Christianity among the World Religions." In *Christianity and Other Religions*, edited by John Hick and Brian Hebblethwaite, 11–31. Philadelphia: Fortress.

Turner, Bryan S. 1990a. "Periodization and Politics in the Postmodern." In *Theories of Modernity and Postmodernity*, edited by Bryan S. Turner, 1–13. London: Sage.

Turner, Bryan S., ed. 1990b. *Theories of Modernity and Postmodernity*. London: Sage.

Utuk, Efiong S. 1986. "From Wheaton to Lausanne: The Road to Modification of Contemporary Evangelical Mission Theology." *Missiology* 14.2 (April): 205–18.

Van Dusen, Henry P. 1961. *One Great Ground of Hope: Christian Missions and Christian Unity*. Philadelphia: Westminster.

Van Engen, Charles. 1977. "Church Growth, Yes! But Which Kind?" *Church Herald* 34.16 (August 5): 12, 13, 28.

———. 1978a. "Let's Contextualize Kingdom Growth." *Church Herald* 35.22 (November 3): 10–12.

———. 1978b. "Your Church Cannot Grow—without the Holy Spirit." *Church Herald* 35.8 (April 21): 6–8.

———. 1981. *The Growth of the True Church*. Amsterdam: Rodopi.

———. 1984. "The Holy Catholic Church—On the Road through Ephesians." *Reformed Review* 37.3 (Spring): 187–201.

———. 1985. *Hijos del pacto: Perdón, conversión y misión en el bautismo*. Grand Rapids: T.E.L.L.

———. 1987. "Responses to James Scherer's Paper from Different Disciplinary Perspectives: Systematic Theology." *Missiology* 15.4 (October): 523–25.

———. 1989a. "The New Covenant: Knowing God in Context." In *The Word among Us*, edited by Dean S. Gilliland, 74–100. Waco: Word.

———. 1989b. "Pastors as Missionary Leaders in the Church." *Theology, News and Notes* 36.2:15–18.

———. 1990. "A Broadening Vision: Forty Years of Evangelical Theology of Mission, 1946–1986." In *Earthen Vessels*, edited by Joel A. Carpenter and Wilbert R. Shenk, 203–32. Grand Rapids: Eerdmans.

———. 1991a. "The Effect of Universalism on Mission Effort." In *Through No Fault of Their Own?* edited by William V. Crockett and James G. Sigountos, 183–94. Grand Rapids: Baker.

———. 1991b. *God's Missionary People: Rethinking the Purpose of the Local Church.* Grand Rapids: Baker.

———. 1992a. "Biblical Foundations of Mission." Unpublished syllabus, Fuller Theological Seminary, Pasadena.

———. 1992b. "Theologizing in Mission." Unpublished course syllabus, Fuller Theological Seminary, Pasadena.

———. 1992c. *You Are My Witnesses: Drawing from Your Spiritual Journey to Evangelize Your Neighbors.* New York: Reformed Church.

———. 1993. "The Relation of Bible and Mission in Mission Theology." In *The Good News of the Kingdom,* edited by Charles Van Engen et al., 27–36. Maryknoll, N.Y.: Orbis.

———. 1994. "Constructing a Theology of Mission for the City." In *Jerusalem! Jerusalem! In Search of a Theology of Mission for the City,* edited by Charles Van Engen and Jude Tiersma, 241–85. Monrovia, Calif.: MARC.

Van Engen, Charles, et al., eds. 1993. *The Good News of the Kingdom: Mission Theology for the Third Millennium.* Maryknoll, N.Y.: Orbis.

Van Engen, Charles, and Jude Tiersma, eds. 1994. *God So Loves the City: Seeking a Theology for Urban Mission.* Monrovia, Calif.: MARC.

Van Huyssteen, Wentzel. 1989. *Theology and the Justification of Faith: Constructing Theories in Systematic Theology.* Grand Rapids: Eerdmans.

Van Rheenen, Gailyn. 1983. *Biblical Anchored Mission: Perspectives on Church Growth.* Austin: Firm Foundation.

Van Ruler, A. A. 1971. *The Christian Church and the Old Testament.* Grand Rapids: Eerdmans.

Veenhof, Jan. 1977. *Kuyper en de Kerk: Leestukken bij het Doctoraalkollege Dogmatiek, Kursus 1977–1978.* Amsterdam: Free University.

Verkuyl, Johannes. 1978. *Contemporary Missiology: An Introduction.* Grand Rapids: Eerdmans.

———. 1986. "Contra de twee kernthesen van Knitter's theologia religionum." *Wereld en Zending* 2:113–20.

———. 1989. "Mission in the 1990s." *International Bulletin of Missionary Research* 13.2 (April): 55–58.

———. 1993. "The Biblical Notion of Kingdom: Test of Validity for Theology of Religion." In *The Good News of the Kingdom,* edited by Charles Van Engen et al., 71–81. Maryknoll, N.Y.: Orbis.

Verstraelen, F. J., ed. 1988. *Oecumenische inleiding in de missiologie: Teksten en konteksten van het wereldchristendom.* Kampen: J. H. Kok.

Vicedom, Georg. 1965. *The Mission of God: An Introduction to a Theology of Mission.* St. Louis: Concordia.

Vidales, Raul. 1979. "Methodological Issues in Liberation Theology." In *Frontiers of Theology in Latin America,* edited by Rosino Gibellini, 34–57. Maryknoll, N.Y.: Orbis.

Vischer, Lukas. 1963. *A Documentary History of the Faith and Order Movement.* St. Louis: Bethany.

Visser 't Hooft, W. A. 1959. *The Pressure of Our Common Calling.* Garden City, N.Y.: Doubleday.

———. 1963. *No Other Name: The Choice between Syncretism and Christian Universalism.* Philadelphia: Westminster.

———. 1974. "Evangelism in the Neo-Pagan Situation." *International Review of Mission* 63, no. 249 (January): 81–86.

———. 1977. "Evangelism among Europe's Neo-Pagans." *International Review of Mission* 66, no. 264 (October): 349–60.

Volf, Miroslav. 1992a. "De uitdaging van het protestants fundamentalisme." *Fundamentalisme* 92.3:82–90.

———. 1992b. "Provisional Absoluteness: The Unique Christ and the Challenge of Modernity." Unpublished paper presented to the Manila Conference of the World Evangelical Fellowship Theological Commission and Asia Theological Association, July.

von Allmen, Daniel. 1979. "The Birth of Theology." In *Readings in Dynamic Indigeneity*, edited by Charles H. Kraft and Tom Wisley, 325–48. Pasadena: William Carey Library.

von Rad, Gerhard. 1962. *Old Testament Theology*. New York: Harper.

Vos, Geerhardus. 1979. *The Teaching of Jesus concerning the Kingdom of God and the Church*. Phillipsburg, N.J.: Presbyterian and Reformed.

Vroom, Hendrik M. 1989. *Religions and the Truth: Philosophical Reflections and Perspectives*. Grand Rapids: Eerdmans.

Wagner, C. Peter. 1973. *Look Out! The Pentecostals Are Coming*. Carol Stream, Ill.: Creation House.

———. 1974a. "Concepts of Evangelism Have Changed over the Years." *Evangelical Missions Quarterly* 10.1 (January): 41–42.

———. 1974b. *Your Spiritual Gifts Can Help Your Church Grow*. Glendale, Calif.: Regal.

———. 1976. *Your Church Can Grow*. Glendale, Calif.: Regal.

———. 1979a. "The Cost of Church Growth." *Church Growth America* 5.5 (November–December): 4–7, 10, 13–14.

———. 1979b. *Our Kind of People*. Atlanta: John Knox.

———. 1979c. *Your Church Can Be Healthy*. Nashville: Abingdon.

———. 1980. "Aiming at Church Growth in the Eighties." *Christianity Today* 24.20 (November 21): 24–27.

———. 1981. *Church Growth and the Whole Gospel*. San Francisco: Harper and Row.

———. 1984. *Leading Your Church to Growth*. Ventura, Calif.: Regal.

———. 1986. "A Vision for Evangelizing the Real America." *International Bulletin of Missionary Research* 10.2 (April): 59–64.

———. 1987. *Strategies for Church Growth: Tools for Effective Mission and Evangelism*. Ventura, Calif.: Regal.

Walker, Alan. 1957. *The Whole Gospel for the Whole World*. New York: Abingdon.

———. 1975. *The New Evangelism*. Nashville: Abingdon.

Wallace, Mark I. 1989. "The New Yale Theology." In *The Best in Theology*, edited by J. I. Packer, 3:169–86. Carol Stream, Ill.: Christianity Today.

Wallis, Jim. 1976. *An Agenda for Biblical People*. New York: Harper and Row.

Walls, Andrew. 1976. "Toward an Understanding of Africa's Place in Christian History." In *Religion in a Pluralist Society*, edited by J. S. Pobee, 180–89. Leiden: Brill.

———. 1981. "The Gospel as the Prisoner and Liberator of Culture." *Faith and Thought* 108.1–2 (October): 39–52.

Walrath, Douglas A. 1984. *Planning for Your Church*. Philadelphia: Westminster.

Walsh, David. 1990. *After Ideology: Recovering the Spiritual Foundations of Freedom*. San Francisco: Harper.

Walvoord, John. 1961. "Foreign Mission in Relation to the Second Coming of Christ." In *Facing the Unfinished Task*, compiled by J. O. Percy, 251–56. Grand Rapids: Zondervan.

Ward, Ted. 1979. "The Future of Missions: Hangovers, Fallout, and Hope." In *New Horizons in World Mission*, edited by David J. Hesselgrave, 17–32. Grand Rapids: Baker.

Warren, Max. 1974. *Crowded Canvas*. London: Hodder and Stoughton.

———. 1976. *I Believe in the Great Commission*. Grand Rapids: Eerdmans.

———. 1978. "The Fusion of the IMC and the WCC at New Delhi: Retrospective Thoughts after a Decade and a Half." In *Zending op weg naar de toekomst*, edited by Jerald D. Gort, 190–202. Kampen: J. H. Kok.

Wasdell, David. 1977. "The Evolution of Missionary Congregations." *International Review of Mission* 66, no. 264 (October): 366–72.

Watson, David. 1976. *I Believe in Evangelism.* Grand Rapids: Eerdmans.

———. 1979. *I Believe in the Church.* Grand Rapids: Eerdmans.

———. 1982. *Called and Committed: World-Changing Discipleship.* Wheaton, Ill.: Harold Shaw.

———. 1986. "Salt to the World: An Ecclesiology of Liberation." In *Conflict and Context,* edited by Mark Branson and C. René Padilla, 114–38. Grand Rapids: Eerdmans.

———. 1990. *God Does Not Foreclose: The Universal Promise of Salvation.* Nashville: Abingdon.

Webber, Robert E. 1978. *Common Roots: A Call to Evangelical Maturity.* Grand Rapids: Zondervan.

Weber, Otto. 1981. *Foundations of Dogmatics.* Grand Rapids: Eerdmans.

Webster, Douglas. 1958. "The Missionary Appeal Today." *International Review of Missions* 47.3, no. 187 (July): 279–88.

———. 1964. *What Is Evangelism?* London: Highway.

———. 1980. "Social Concern Begins in the Local Church." *Christianity Today* 24.17 (October 10): 28–31.

Weiss, G. Christian. 1961. "An Inquiry into the Obligation of Christians." In *Facing the Unfinished Task,* compiled by J. O. Percy, 259–61. Grand Rapids: Zondervan.

Wells, David F., and John D. Woodbridge. 1975. *The Evangelicals.* Nashville: Abingdon.

Welsh, John R. 1986. "Comunidades Eclesiais de Base: A New Way to Be Church." *America* 154.5 (February 8): 85–88.

Wessels, Anton. 1992. "The Experience of the Prophet Mohammed." In *On Sharing Religious Experience,* edited by Jerald D. Gort et al., 228–44. Grand Rapids: Eerdmans.

West, Charles C. 1992. "Notes to Colleagues on the GOCN Consultation." *The Gospel and Our Culture* 4.2 (June): 1–3.

West, Charles C., and David Paton, eds. 1959. *The Missionary Church in East and West.* London: SCM.

Westermann, Claus, ed. 1963. *Essays on Old Testament Hermeneutics.* Richmond: John Knox.

"What the *Christianity Today*–Gallup Poll Found Out about Attitudes toward Winning the World for Christ." 1980. *Christianity Today* 24.13 (July 18): 28.

White, Hayden. 1981. "The Value of Narrativity in the Representation of Reality." In *On Narrative,* edited by W. J. T. Mitchell, 1–24. Chicago: University of Chicago Press.

White, Ronald, et al., eds. 1986. *American Christianity: A Case Approach.* Grand Rapids: Eerdmans.

Whyte, William. 1989. *City: Rediscovering the Center.* New York: Doubleday.

Wielenga, B. 1992. "Hermeneutics and Mission." *Missionalia* 20.1 (April): 28–37.

Wieser, Thomas, ed. 1966. *Planning for Mission: Working Papers on the New Quest for Missionary Communities.* New York: U.S. Conference for the World Council of Churches.

Wiggins, James B., ed. 1975. *Religion as Story.* New York: Harper and Row.

Wilcox, Clyde. 1986. "Evangelicals and Fundamentalists in the New Christian Right: Religious Differences in the Ohio Moral Majority." *Journal for the Scientific Study of Religion* 25.3 (September): 355–63.

Williams, Colin. 1963. *Where in the World?* New York: National Council of Churches.

———. 1964. *What in the World?* New York: National Council of Churches.

———. 1966. *For the World.* New York: National Council of Churches.

———. 1968. *The Church.* Philadelphia: Westminster.

Willimon, William H. 1978. *The Gospel for the Person Who Has Everything.* Valley Forge, Pa.: Judson.

Willis, Wendell, ed. 1987. *The Kingdom of God in 20th-Century Interpretation.* Peabody, Mass.: Hendrickson.

Wilson, Robert L. 1983. "How the Church Takes Shape." *Church Growth Bulletin* 20.6 (November–December): 325–27.

Wilson, Ron. 1980. "Parachurch: Becoming Part of the Body." *Christianity Today* 24.16 (September 19): 18–20.

Winter, Ralph D. 1978. "Ghana: Preparation for Marriage." *International Review of Mission* 67, no. 267 (July): 338–53.

———. 1979. "The Future of the Church: The Essential Components of World Evangelization." In *An Evangelical Agenda: 1984 and Beyond*, 135–63. Pasadena: William Carey Library.

———. 1980. "1980: Year of Three Missions Congresses." *Evangelical Missions Quarterly* 16.2 (April): 79–85.

Winter, Ralph D., ed. 1969. *Theological Education by Extension*. Pasadena: William Carey Library.

Winter, Ralph D., and Steven C. Hawthorne, eds. 1981. *Perspectives on the World Christian Movement: A Reader*. Pasadena: William Carey Library.

Wirt, Sherwood Eliot, ed. 1978. *Evangelism: The Next Ten Years*. Waco: Word.

Witherington, Ben, III. 1994. *Paul's Narrative Thought World: The Tapestry of Tragedy and Triumph*. Louisville: Westminster/John Knox.

Wolff, Hans Walter. 1963. "The Hermeneutics of the Old Testament." In *Essays on Old Testament Hermeneutics*, edited by Claus Westermann, 160–99. Richmond: John Knox.

Wong, James, et al. 1973. *Mission from the Third World*. Singapore: Church Growth Study Center.

Woodbridge, John D., Mark A. Noll, and Nathan O. Hatch. 1979. *The Gospel in America: Themes in the Story of America's Evangelicals*. Grand Rapids: Zondervan.

World Christian Encyclopedia. 1982. Edited by David Barrett. New York: Oxford University Press.

World Council of Churches. 1962. *The New Delhi Report*. New York: Association.

———. 1968. *The Church for Others and the Church for the World: A Quest for Structures for Missionary Congregations*. Geneva: World Council of Churches.

———. 1980. *Your Kingdom Come: Mission Perspectives*. Geneva: World Council of Churches.

———. 1983. *Mission and Evangelism, An Ecumenical Affirmation: A Study Guide*. New York: National Council of Churches.

———. 1987. "Statement of the Stuttgart Consultation on Evangelism." March 23–27.

———. 1990. *The San Antonio Report*. Geneva: World Council of Churches.

World Council of Churches/Commission on World Mission and Evangelism. 1989. *Mission from Three Perspectives*. Geneva: WCC/CWME.

Wright, G. Ernest. 1950. *The Old Testament against Its Environment*. Chicago: Allenson.

———. 1952. *God Who Acts: Biblical Theology as Recital*. Chicago: H. Regnery.

Wright, N. T. 1975. "Universalism and the World-Wide Community." *Churchman* 89.3 (July–September): 197–212.

———. 1979. "Towards a Biblical View of Universalism." *Themelios* 4.2 (January): 54–58.

Wuthnow, Robert. 1988. *The Restructuring of American Religion*. Princeton, N.J.: Princeton University Press.

———. 1991. "Evangelicals, Liberals, and the Perils of Individualism." *Perspectives: A Journal of Reformed Thought* 6.5 (May): 10–13.

Wyschogrod, Edith. 1990. *Saints and Postmodernism: Revisioning Moral Philosophy*. Chicago: University of Chicago Press.

Yoder, John Howard. 1972. *The Politics of Jesus—Vicit Agnus Noster*. Grand Rapids: Eerdmans.

———. 1983. "'But We Do See Jesus': The Particularity of Incarnation and the Universality of Truth." In *Foundations of Ethics*, edited by Leroy S. Rouner, 57–75. Notre Dame: Notre Dame University Press.

Ziegenhals, Walter E. 1978. *Urban Churches in Transition*. New York: Pilgrim.

Index